Words of Life

John D. Caputo, *series editor*

PERSPECTIVES IN
CONTINENTAL
PHILOSOPHY

Edited by BRUCE ELLIS BENSON
and NORMAN WIRZBA

Words of Life

New Theological Turns
in French Phenomenology

FORDHAM UNIVERSITY PRESS
New York ■ 2010

BL
51
.W763
2010

Library of Congress Cataloging-in-Publication Data

Words of life : new theological turns in French phenomenology / edited by Bruce Ellis Benson and Norman Wirzba.—1st ed.
    p.   cm.— (Perspectives in Continental philosophy)
    Includes bibliographical references and index.
    ISBN 978-0-8232-3072-3 (cloth : alk. paper)
    SBN 978-0-8232-3073-0 (pbk. : alk. paper)
    1. Phenomenological theology.   2. Philosophy, French.   I. Benson, Bruce Ellis,
1960–   II. Wirzba, Norman.
BL51.W763   2010
230.01—dc22   2009020983

Printed in the United States of America
12 11 10   5 4 3 2 1
First edition

Contents

Acknowledgments

Kevin Hart's chapter, "it / is true," first appeared in *Studia Phaenomeno-logica* VIII (2008): 219–39. Jean-Luc Marion's chapter, "The Phenome-nality of the Sacrament—Being and Givenness," first appeared in *Communio* XXVI:5 (2001): 59–75. Norman Wirzba's chapter, "The Witness of Humility," first appeared in *Modern Theology* XXIV:2 (2008): 225–44. Anthony J. Steinbock's chapter, "The Poor Phenomenon: Mar-ion and the Problem of Givenness," first appeared in *Alter: revue de phe-nomenology* 15 (2007): 357–72.

The editors would like to thank Christopher Manzer for compiling the index.

Words of Life

Introduction

BRUCE ELLIS BENSON

Many who read this introduction will immediately know that the phrase
on which the subtitle of this collection of essays is based—the so-called
theological turn in French phenomenology—comes from a text of Dominique Janicaud.[1] Indeed, one can read this volume as a companion to *Phenomenology and the "Theological Turn": The French Debate*, which appears
in this same series. In his official report to the French government that
details the contours of the development of philosophy in France from
1975 to 1990, Janicaud claims that philosophy (in particular phenomenology, the dominant mode of philosophy in France today) has taken on
a decidedly theological tone and agenda. The principal figures that Janicaud cites are Emmanuel Levinas, Jean-Luc Marion, Michel Henry, and
Jean-Louis Chrétien. Since much secondary research has been done on
the work of Marion, and considerably more on Levinas, the conference at
which many of these essays were first presented focused particularly on
the work of Henry and Chrétien.[2] Those essays are here augmented by
chapters on and by Marion, as well as chapters that relate to but build
upon the work of these various figures.

In the same way that Janicaud begins his report by considering the
phenomenological project as laid out by Edmund Husserl, so we briefly
need to consider the contours of Husserlian phenomenology as a back-
drop against which this supposed theological turn takes place. For Husserl, the motto of phenomenology is "to the things themselves" (*zu den*

Sachen selbst). Thus, the concern in phenomenology is—as much as possible—to arrive at an *"adaequatio intellectus et rei"* (literally, adequation of the intellect and the thing) or as close a correlation between consciousness and the object of consciousness. Husserl works this out in terms of intentionality, intuition, and immanence. We "intend" an object by way of consciousness and it is thus "intuited." While there are degrees to which an object can be fully intended (or made present to consciousness), the ultimate goal would be a kind of "adequation," in which the intended object is as fully immanent to consciousness as possible and so "itself there," "immediately intuited."[3] Put in phenomenological terms, the act of thinking (*noesis*) becomes the exact equivalent to its object (*noema*). But the goal of phenomenology is also that the *logos* of the phenomenon should arrive from the phenomenon itself. Husserl explains this by way of what he calls "the principle of all principles" in which *"everything originarily . . . offered* to us *in 'intuition' is to be accepted simply as what it is presented as being, but also only within the limits in which it is presented there."*[4] Such a principle would seem to call for a kind of phenomenological neutrality, in which the object—and the object *alone*—sets the conditions for its appearance. Ostensibly, then, Husserl offers a methodology that is "objective" and "scientific." Indeed, an essential feature of phenomenology is the "bracketing" of all prejudices or assumptions about the "reality" of the object perceived: Husserl calls for a *"phenomenological reduction"* that serves to *"exclude all that is posited as transcendent."*[5] We would seem to be left with an orientation in which the object is immanently given to a neutral consciousness.

Yet, if (as the traditional formula of intentionality would have it) "all consciousness is conscious of something," does either that consciousness or the "something" intended have priority in this relationship? While such a question might seem simple or easy to answer, how one responds to the question determines whether one counts as an "orthodox" phenomenologist. According to the assumed Husserlian orthodoxy, consciousness—more specifically, the horizon that frames intuition—maintains the upper hand. Or, to quote the second part of the "principle of principles," an object is presented to us *only within the limits in which it is presented.* The "limits" to which the object is subjected are set by the horizon of consciousness. Put in other terms, the object appears "as such," intended in a particular way. Thus, I perceive a tree *as* a tree. Husserl himself claims: "I can simply look at that which is *meant as such* and grasp it absolutely."[6] Once again, Husserl puts forward a seemingly incoherent idea of intentionality: he supposes that we can perceive something "absolutely"—which would appear to imply a neutrality or objectivity—

but Husserl qualifies that perception by saying that we perceive something "as such." However, one can argue that—despite any claims to being the true phenomenological orthodoxy—such an insistence is fundamentally unphenomenological. For, if the object *"is to be accepted simply as what it is presented as being"* (to quote the first part of the "principle of principles"), then the *object* should have the upper hand. Instead of being limited by the horizon, the object sets its own limits. To make this move, of course, is to diverge from the presumed phenomenological orthodoxy. In a heated exchange with Marion, Jacques Derrida accuses him of committing "the first heresy in phenomenology" for giving up the "as such." Yet, even after quoting Levinas as maintaining that "without horizon there is no phenomenology," Marion goes on to say: "I boldly assume he was wrong."[7] And so we come to a showdown of sorts in which the very structure of phenomenology is put into question.

Let us consider exactly what is at stake. Instead of the constituting ego being at the center of the phenomenological act, suddenly the object itself takes the stage. No longer are the limits of the object to be dictated by the subject; instead, the *object* determines its limits. Yet this move "subjects" the subject to the object, so that the subject is called into being by the object's appearing. Marion speaks of certain kinds of objects as "saturated phenomena," phenomena so rich that they exceed the limits of any horizon or "as such." In effect, intuition outstrips any categories of the horizon or "as such." In turn, the immanence of intentionality that had bracketed transcendence would—at the very least—be subject to further examination. Can there be a kind of transcendence within immanence or does the theological turn simply introduce transcendence in its fullest form? On Janicaud's read, with Levinas we find "nothing less than the God of the biblical tradition."[8] Of course, Janicaud's critique presupposes that phenomenology should be either agnostic or even atheistic. The writers of the essays in this collection are unwilling to concede that such a starting point is either obvious or necessarily desirable.

Yet, contrary to Janicaud's contention that phenomenology has been taken hostage by theology, might it not be more accurate to say that the very conception of phenomenology has been radically reformulated? Or perhaps better put: might we now say that phenomenology has finally been allowed to be true to itself—finally true to the "things themselves"? While some would no doubt dismiss this "reversed phenomenology" as something like "post-phenomenology" or "anti-phenomenology," the writers in this collection generally see themselves as following the basic principles of phenomenology (and, in many cases, being more *rigorously phenomenological*), even if that means interpreting those principles somewhat differently.

However, as will quickly become evident, at stake here is much more than simply phenomenological principles or theoretical questions. Instead, these papers quickly move from abstract issues to deeply practical ones that concern the nature of the human self and its relation to both the human and the divine other. Themes such as faith, hope, love, grace, the gift, suffering, joy, life, the call, listening, wounding, and humility are woven throughout the various meditations in this volume.

Reflections on the Theological Turn

The first of these essays, "Continuing to Look for *God in France*" by J. Aaron Simmons, surveys the general terrain of philosophy in France that has—in one way or another—been connected to religion, theology, or God. *God in France* includes the philosophers already mentioned (with the strange absence of Chrétien) but likewise extends to Paul Ricoeur, René Girard, Derrida, Jean-François Lyotard, and Jean-Yves Lacoste (one of the authors in this collection).[9] What links the authors of the essays in *God in France* is their insistence that there has not been so much a true "theological turn" in French phenomenology—or even a "turn" or "return to religion"[10]—but a deepening and reinvigorating of phenomenology. Yet Simmons contends that this particular reformulation of phenomenology—as welcome to some as it might be—does not really bring phenomenology and theology any closer; instead, it deepens their division. In contrast, Simmons argues for a post-ontotheological phenomenology in which God is "not contaminated by Being" (since, not being part of the structure of onto-theology, God is not simply the greatest being) but also not kept outside of phenomenology.

Jeffrey Bloechl turns this idea around, speaking not of "God without Being"[11] but "Being without God." If one begins with the Heideggerian starting point of distinguishing Being from beings (the so-called ontological difference), then one is left without any explicit reference to God. So how might we approach God without God becoming either a being or even "Being"? Turning to Augustine, Bloechl suggests that God "precedes our relation with the world." Further, since all knowledge is a kind of implicit knowledge of God, then we can say that God is the foundation of knowledge. However, such a claim must be carefully qualified. Since God cannot be contained within the present and even can only be past in the sense of being "immemorial" (that is, having never been truly "possessed"), the state of being receptive for God is always one of faith and hope in which neither contact nor possession is possible and God's coming "remains forever a matter of faith."

In his chapter, "The Appearing and the Irreducible," Jean-Yves Lacoste notes not merely that Husserl's concept of the *epochê* comes relatively late in his philosophy but also that the "natural attitude" (our normal way of looking at the world in which we believe in its "reality"—precisely what the *epochê* is designed to suspend) already contains within it a kind of "reduction." Normal, everyday experience is simply such that we experience objects and others without concentrating on their being. Thus, the phenomenological reduction is unnecessary as an aid to concentrating on the phenomenon itself. Yet Lacoste takes this point further by arguing that, when the reduction is applied to the human other, it actually serves to reduce the other's humanity. Instead, when we meet a "Thou," we encounter an "irreducible alterity" (something that cannot be "reduced" to something other). Certainly God's existence must be such that it is irreducible in an essential way, so that it *cannot* be reduced merely to the content of one's experience. In other words, such experience is always ontologically different from the transcendent object of that experience. Like Bloechl, Lacoste concludes that God is known in the mode of faith and that the intrusion of any reduction risks disfiguring of the divine even more than the human.

Starting with the basic idea that phenomenology is "a response to what is given," Kevin Hart turns to the question of how literature—particularly poetry—provides ways of understanding phenomenology in his essay "it / is true." For instance, we learn much about the phenomenological reduction from Franz Kafka, precisely because we see how consciousness is constituted. But it is the poem "September Song" by Geoffrey Hill that is the primary focus of Hart's attention. As Derrida notes, literature is a kind of "philosophy" and poems perform the *epochê* even if their authors are unaware that they are suspending the natural attitude and yet showing consciousness as embedded in its horizons. Hill's poem, about a child killed in the Shoah, raises for Hart the question whether the poem *fully* performs the reduction. As Levinas and Marion agree, the face can say to us "Thou shalt not kill" only because the reduction is *not* complete. Further, what would it mean for this elegy to "be" true? In what *way* does it speak the truth? Hart concludes that the aesthetic may be in service of phenomenology and ethics—in short, the truth—but it is always in the danger of occluding them.

Jean-Luc Marion

Marion's own chapter, "The Phenomenality of the Sacrament—Being and Givenness," concerns the question of how the symbol of something sacred can be a "visible form" of "invisible grace." While this is certainly a theological question, and indeed first arises in theology, it has to do not merely with the symbolic but even with the nature of manifestation itself. How does the thing itself appear? But, even more, how does the *invisible* appear in the form of something as mundane as bread or wine? For, in effect, the visible thing "doubles" as the visibility for two different phenomena. To be sure, such a question cannot be "answered," since it presents us with an insurmountable aporia. Marion considers three models as explanations of this gap. The first, that of substance and its accidents, immediately raises the questions of both how the substance and accidents themselves relate and how (more specifically) the body of Christ relates to a substance that is quite distinct from its incarnation. The second, then, is the model of an invisible cause bringing about a visible effect, though even if this can be appropriately applied to the sacrament how the two could relate is unclear. A final model is that of semiotics, utilizing the duality of the sign. Yet there is no "sign" of grace per se, only a sensible being (bread, wine). Further, what sort of authority would it require to connect the invisible with the visible? Marion traces these difficulties to the very concept of a phenomenon in Kant. A phenomenon is related to an object by the transcendental *I*. Perhaps this is sufficient for certain phenomena, but it is highly problematic for the phenomenon of the other. But, even then, does not the phenomenon require something like a "self," if as Heidegger would put it, it shows itself from itself? Ultimately, the basis for the sacrament is God giving *Himself* as the Son and "icon of the invisible God." Of course, this ability to show itself beyond itself—to bring to sight an invisibility—is *already* present in the material things of the world: for instance, water's ability to alleviate thirst or bread to alleviate hunger goes beyond pure "materiality." To see them "as such" requires more than mere perception. Marion concludes that, by way of analogy, it is possible to envision a phenomenon that gives itself radically. Indeed, it is Christ who gives *Himself* with such radicality that even the Father is thereby shown to us.

In "The Human in Question," Jeffrey L. Kosky reminds us that, although the "new" French phenomenology first reached English-speaking readers via Marion's *God Without Being* (1991), with its concern for proper theological thinking of God, the question of human finitude has been an almost equally important question for these phenomenologists.

Since Marion himself moves from a Dionysian to a more Augustinian-inspired model, Kosky proposes reading Marion's later work in terms of human finitude. In Augustine, one finds a conception of the human subject that is always more than can be understood. Thus, it is not just God who is incomprehensible—it is also we ourselves. In question is not just possession or mastery of the other but likewise the self. But this very impossibility—as surprising as it might at first sound—is what keeps human beings from sinking to the level of an object, poor and unsouled. Self-knowledge, then, is more dangerous than lack of it. Following Augustine and Heidegger, Marion asserts that we do not appear to ourselves as knowledge but instead as a question. Yet this structure of exceeding oneself is all the more pronounced as one emphasizes one's origin in God. One becomes a witness to a calling that exceeds one and to which one can never properly respond. We witness more than we could ever bear and so being authentically human means admitting our weakness. Loving the truth requires that we acknowledge that it overcomes us and humiliates us, leaving us as its receivers rather than makers.

Anthony J. Steinbock, in his chapter "The Poor Phenomenon," turns to what would be the opposite of Marion's saturated phenomenon. What exactly is the "poor" phenomenon, to which Marion devotes relatively little attention, and how does it differ from the saturated phenomenon? Whereas the sheer power of the saturated phenomenon undoes the "giver" of sense (the consciousness) and makes it into the receiver, the poor phenomenon is impoverished. Lacking in content, it is purely formal or eidetic in nature. Like its relative, the "common phenomenon," the possibility of its mastery exists. Yet Steinbock considers a variety of "poor" phenomena to show that there may be more here than Marion admits. Even in the case of passive synthesis, the sense of an object occurs before the activity of the subject, producing what Husserl terms a "constitutive duet." The result is that there is always *more* than one intends, a point that even Husserl concedes is "an essential contradiction." Although it is the saturated phenomena that Marion claims call to us, Husserl actually speaks of a call coming from the poor phenomenon. What Steinbock terms "humble phenomena" are those common objects—like pots and pans—that have their own surplus and even in their humbleness are more than what they seem. Here one cannot help but think of Marion's own examples of bread and wine. "Denigrated phenomenon" is the term Steinbock uses for phenomena that are not allowed to be in their fullest sense. Such a phenomenon, suggests Steinbock, might be termed "secularized," for its poverty is because it is denied its full presence. As such, it is not "neutral" but arbitrarily limited. It is a phenomenon that is rightly "saturated" but wrongly eviscerated. The violence of this limitation is particularly illustrated by the face of the Other, which is simply seen as an object. Finally, Steinbock considers how pride might lead to the poverty of the gift. Marion speaks of the "responsal" of "wanting" to receive the gift. Yet this requires that the gifted be willing to give itself to the gift. Should one be unwilling due to pride, then such "given-over-ness" remains impossible. Considering these examples of poor phenomena not only helps illuminate their difference from saturated phenomena but also shows ways in which they are similar.

Michel Henry

In "Michel Henry's Theory of Disclosive Moods," Jeffrey Hanson considers tonalities that Henry thinks are privileged in their ability to reveal truth. Suffering and joy (which Henry sees as fundamentally the same) have this important status because they emerge from the phenomenalization of Being's essence. Henry sees himself—as he sees Kierkegaard—as a philosopher of immanence. In addition to suffering and joy, despair and (in his later philosophy) anxiety reveal the impossibility of the self breaking from itself (that is, its non-freedom) and thus its status of being radically immanent to itself. So despair in effect allows the self to see its connection to life itself. In Henry's later thought, however, despair becomes less a source of disclosure than a problem itself, for it actually blocks access to our selves. Anxiety, then, is what helps us overcome our forgetfulness of ourselves and reveals who we truly are. Yet Henry's read of anxiety differs from that of Heidegger in that Henry sees the revelation to self that anxiety brings as coming from our immanence (rather than transcendence). Still, even from this immanence comes a call that Henry terms the "second founding intuition of Christianity," a call that Henry insists needs no hermeneutics since it comes directly and unmediatedly.

In her chapter, Christina Gschwandtner takes up this last aspect—immanence and hermeneutics—when she asks, "Can We Hear the Voice of God?" She begins with examples of Moses, Abraham, Gideon, and Mary—all of whom were either spoken to by God and else received an indirect communication (as in Gideon's case). Henry's final book, *Paroles du Christ*, considers this question. Not only can we hear the voice of God, claims Henry, but we can also clearly distinguish it from any human voice. Further, he contends that Christ's words come to us without any phenomenological horizon or need of hermeneutics: they are direct and immediate (and thus *immanent*). It is this difference of immediacy that separates divine from human speech: the former comes without delay and in full presence. Since there is no distance between the said and the one who speaks divinely, there is no need of assurance that it is truly the voice of God that speaks. Such speech is self-justifying and needs nothing further than itself for legitimacy. In contrast, hermeneutics is necessary for the words that come from the world. Yet, not surprisingly, Gschwandtner asks whether this distinction is truly tenable. Can there be divine words that have no need of hermeneutics? It would seem that hermeneutics would be the necessary condition for both correct interpretation and appropriate response to the divine words. It is also hermeneutics that makes communication of the divine message to others possible. Without hermeneutics, Gschwandtner argues, we cannot meaningfully hear the voice of God.

This immediate sort of experience of God is likewise the focus of Ronald L. Mercer Jr.'s chapter "Radical Phenomenology Reveals a Measure of Faith and a Need for a Levinasian Other in Henry's Life." Yet Mercer argues that there must be a kind of transcendence in God's appearance, precisely because it is not reducible to the *I*. What Henry needs, then, is the "correction" of a Levinasian Other that would "haunt" Henry's conception of "Life" that ends up seeming to be all too much like Levinas's "same." Thus, despite what Henry would say, his conception of "Life" must be taken as transcendent rather than immanent, and it must in turn be connected to God. To be sure, making God transcendent in this way means that Henry's "grasp" of God is shown to be problematic. Yet this transcendence is modified by what Saint Paul terms "a measure of faith," which allows the self to be oriented toward the transcendent. It is faith that makes the connection between the self and the transcendent God possible.

The relation of transcendence and immanence in Henry is likewise taken up by Clayton Crockett in his chapter "The Truth of Life." On Crockett's read, the danger of Henry's "rhetorical excessiveness" is that it verges on Gnosticism and thus actually serves to remove human beings from the world. Throughout Henry's writings, there is a focus on life and its immanence. Yet what does "life" mean for human beings? To answer that question, Crockett turns to Henry's work on Marx. What Henry finds remarkable in Marx is the way his notion of praxis brings together theory and practice and thus reverses the priority in their relationship. Yet Crockett argues that Henry overemphasizes the distance of theory from life and then, in *I Am the Truth*, disconnects life from the world. The result is a quasi-Gnosticism in which life is a strange sort of "immanent transcendence" that is ultimately otherworldly.

Jean-Louis Chrétien

In "The Call of Grace," Joshua Davis advances the claim that "Christian radical phenomenology" invokes both grace and the supernatural in a way that distorts phenomenology precisely because they are a priori categories that in turn regulate phenomenological experience. While his critique focuses on Chrétien, it can be read as equally against Lacoste, Marion, and Stanislas Breton. What unites their thought is an indebtedness to, on the one hand, Maurice Blondel and Henri Bergson, and, on the other hand, Husserl and Heidegger. Although these radical phenomenologists assume the Heideggerian priority of revealability over revelation, their deployment of religious categories—revelation for Marion, prayer/liturgy for Lacoste, election/the call for Chrétien—puts that assumption into question. Yet Davis argues that radical phenomenology is, nonetheless, not characterized by a move to theology from phenomenology. At stake, then, are what we mean by "phenomenological intelligibility" and "theological coherence." With these issues in mind, Davis turns to the influence of Henri de Lubac upon Chrétien. Central to Lubac's thought is that all humanity receives a divine call that is only heard in response. Thus, the call is already an answer, one that can never adequately correspond to the invitation, and the one who responds is in effect a dispossessed subject. This paradoxical situation is fundamental to both Lubac's and Chrétien's thought, and in Chrétien it takes the form of reversing revealability and revelation. Ultimately, Chrétien's theological categories are simply phenomenologically unintelligible.

What is a "call"? Such is the question that Joseph Ballan attempts to unpack in his chapter "Between Call and Voice." It is the interlacing of sight and hearing with touch that is both Chrétien's and Ballan's focus. For Chrétien, the "modality" of the call need not be auditory but it is always present in one dimension or another. Utilizing a surprisingly diverse collection of mystics, poets, Platonists, and biblical writers, Chrétien weaves a narrative of the call that Ballan takes to be a kind of "hermeneutical phenomenology," precisely because it draws upon such a maze of historical traditions. Chrétien emphasizes the transitivity of the senses, the opening of the senses both to themselves and to the other. He is concerned with how they are provoked by wonder and result in gratitude and praise. Whether the "silence in painting" or the silence found in music, the beautiful that charms and calls is an event in which we encounter the beautiful and are opened up to it and wounded by it in a way even more radical than Kant's sublime. The encounter is marked by excess that both insists on our response and yet somehow inhibits it. It is this gap between the call's insistence and our inability to respond adequately that results in a proper sense of humility.

Bruce Ellis Benson turns to this aspect of wounding in "Chrétien on the Call That Wounds." It is prayer that Chrétien calls "the wounded word," for it both tears open the lips and unveils the one who prays. Indeed, one might suggest that this very structure of wounding—the opening of the self to the call of the other—is central not just to Chrétien's thought but the theological turn in general. We have already noted that the call always precedes us, leaving us "entangled in speech" before we ever speak. Benson suggests that this call could be traced back to the Trinity itself, a kind of *perichôreis* in which the divine dance is supplemented with a divine discourse of ceaseless calls. In any case, by the time it reaches us, our response can never be our own, for it always contains the traces of others. Thus, the *I* is a polyphony of voices rather than any self-constituted and delimited *I*. Yet, just as prayer is wounding, this polyphony is likewise a kind of wounding in which our encounters with the other reshape us. To be opened to the other is to "suffer" in the sense of submitting to the other. This happens in speech, but it particularly takes place in our encounters with the divine. Yet, rather than conclude that such suffering is simply gratuitous and thus to be avoided, Chrétien brings together the French *blesser* (wound) and the English "bless" by arguing that the "wound can bless." To illustrate that connection, Chrétien turns to the strange story of Jacob wrestling with the angel of God. While Jacob's hip is put out of joint, he likewise receives a blessing and thereafter becomes Israel. "Who is the victor? Who is the vanquished?" asks Chrétien. Given that no "philosophical parousia" exists, for Chrétien we are left in the phenomenological middle in which blessing and wounding are strangely mixed.

In "Embodied Ears: Being in the World and Hearing the Other," Brian Treanor considers the relation of the senses in Chrétien. Philosophy has long been dominated by visual metaphors and has likewise used the visual gaze to dominate others and otherness in its quest for the adequation between *noesis* and *noema*. In contrast, aural metaphors lack this sense of dominance. Yet, as we have seen, Chrétien suggests that the sense of touch is actually more fundamental than either. Touch is universal in that it is always at work; as tactile, embodied beings, touch imbues all that we encounter and our very being. Nor is it localized: it belongs not merely to our fingertips but to all of our body. Further, in the same way that aural metaphors forgo a grasping dominance, so touch emphasizes contact with the infinite that cannot be grasped. Unlike seeing or hearing, touching always results in *being touched*, so it goes in both directions. Although visual or aural metaphors still have their place, adding tactile metaphors gives us a deeper and fuller phenomenological account of our encounter of the other.

To be honest about our "creaturely condition," suggests Norman Wirzba in his chapter "The Witness of Humility," is truly a challenge. Such folly is difficult to shake, for the pride of seeing ourselves as independent comes so naturally. When we lack humility, we are literally gripped by a lunacy, a "delusional belief" that thinks only the *I* exists. In contrast, humility is a way of being that helps us to see ourselves aright. Yet that requires a complete reorientation in which we come to realize that we are dependent on both others and God. Moreover, simply defining and understanding humility is itself a task when our very way of thinking is so firmly fixed with the self at the center. We can easily be seduced by false humility that turns out to be even worse than blatant arrogance. But Chrétien insists that we can have a revelatory experience of "excess," of that which exceeds us beyond all that we could possibly comprehend. Thus, we come to realize that no amount of saying "Thank You" or "I am sorry" could possibly be enough. When we recognize that we are simply because God wills us into existence and delights in our being, humility comes more naturally. If we understand our creatureliness, we will admit our fundamental dependence upon God and others, resulting in a right understanding of ourselves and the possibility of true friendship with God.

In one way or another, all of these essays contend with the limits and expectations of phenomenology. As such, they are all concerned with what counts as "proper" phenomenology and even the very structure of phenomenology. What should be clear, however, is that none of them are *limited* to such questions. Indeed, the rich tapestry that they weave tells us much about human experience. In short, the authors of this volume use striking examples to illuminate the structure and limits of phenomenology and, in turn, phenomenology serves to clarify those very examples. Thus, practice clarifies theory and theory clarifies practice.

PART $\boxed{\text{I}}$

Reflections on the Theological Turn

Continuing to Look for *God in France*

On the Relationship Between Phenomenology and Theology

J. AARON SIMMONS

The relationship between phenomenology and theology is as complex and troubled as is the relationship between faith and reason. Following the publication of a collection of essays entitled *God in France* in 2005,[1] the debate concerning the "theological turn" that was primarily inaugurated by Dominique Janicaud in 1991 might itself be viewed as having taken a new "turn."[2] What connects the nine essays in this important collection is the supposition that, despite Janicaud's contention, there has not been a theological turn in recent French phenomenology. Instead, in various ways, all of the authors argue that within "new phenomenology" there has merely been a deepening of the phenomenological impulse itself. This may indeed push phenomenology beyond the limits that were laid out by Husserl in *Logical Investigations* and *Ideas I.* Nonetheless, the work being done by Marion, Henry, Levinas, Derrida, Girard, and Lacoste[3] is still properly described and correctly regarded as "phenomenology."

It would be wrong to conclude, however, that the text edited by Peter Jonkers and Ruud Welten has finally decided the issue on the relationship between phenomenology and theology. Quite the opposite is the case. The result of the contestation of Janicaud's reading of recent French philosophy is not a renewed suggestion for theo-phenomenology or phenomenological theology but rather an extension of Janicaud's deeper position regarding the fact that "phenomenology and theology make two."[4] *God in France* does not open a new space for thinking a new relationship between phenomenology and theology, but merely a new reading of phenomenology itself. Of course, the authors recognize that this will have implications for theology. Yet, like Janicaud, they all stop short of actually articulating exactly what these implications are and how a contestation of the theological turn might provide a new conversation across these boundaries that continue to be too rigid.

Writing in the wake of this important collection, I do three things in this essay. First, I detail the way in which *God in France* contests Janicaud's estimation of the theological turn. Second, I demonstrate the way in which this reevaluation simply serves to further instantiate the division between phenomenology and theology. Finally, I offer suggestions as to how we can rethink the relationship between theology and phenomenology by arguing that while Janicaud's *separatist* strategy occludes the historical situatedness of reason and the contextuality of all human thought, the strategy of *God in France* comes close to merely *reconstructing* theology on phenomenological grounds and thereby replacing the particularity of a specific religion with the abstraction of the postmodern "religious." In response, I advocate a notion of *reconstructive separatism* that maintains the distinctiveness of each discourse while avoiding the dangers of worldlessness and abstraction that accompany the first two strategies respectively. In conclusion, I briefly outline the way in which reconstructive separatism opens the space for a postmodern apologetic enterprise.

Phenomenologists After All?

In his very informative and provocative introduction to *God in France*, Peter Jonkers argues that "it seems . . . incorrect to interpret the attention of contemporary (French) philosophy for God and religion as a turn to religion or theology, as some do."[5] As examples of the "some" to whom he refers, Jonkers mentions Hent de Vries and Dominique Janicaud. The position of Janicaud is aptly summarized by Bernard Prusak as follows:

> The "new phenomenology" . . . [that Levinas, Marion, Chrétien and Henry] practice is no longer phenomenological. Put dramatically, Janicaud inverts the scenario of Plato's *Apology*: he indicts Levinas et al. for corrupting the future of French philosophy by introducing into phenomenology a god—the biblical God—who does not belong there.[6]

This God does not "belong" in phenomenology because of the Husserlian contention that phenomenology is concerned only with that which *appears*. Since God does not appear as an object for intentional consciousness, God is not properly within the domain of phenomenological inquiry. This should be sufficient to exclude all God-talk, but in particular it would place the God of a particular historical religious tradition out of bounds. A "phenomenology of the inapparent," as Heidegger referred to it in 1973,[7] would be simply nonphenomenological as such.

Janicaud's position contains three major interrelated assertions: (1) phenomenology must be about appearances; (2) thus, phenomenology is intrinsically about immanence and, as such, stays true to Husserl's "principle of all principles";[8] and (3) ultimately, then, any discussion of "absolute" and "transcendent" being "shall remain excluded from the new field of research which is to be provided" by phenomenology.[9] "Between the unconditional affirmation of Transcendence and the patient interrogation of the visible," Janicaud asserts, "the incompatibility cries out; we must choose. But are we going to do so with the head or with the heart—arbitrarily or not? The task, insofar as it remains philosophical and phenomenological, is to follow the sole guide that does not buy itself off with fine words: interrogation of method."[10]

Differentiating between Merleau-Ponty's method of "intertwining" and Emmanuel Levinas's method of "aplomb," Janicaud concludes that the only method that emerges as truly phenomenological is that which is neutral with respect to questions about transcendence. Phenomenology, on Janicaud's reading, is essentially agnostic (if not atheistic) and only as such can it continue to be properly philosophical as opposed to theological. The distinction between the two is clearly articulated during Janicaud's engagement with Levinas. According to Janicaud, the non-phenomenology of Levinas

> supposes a metaphysico-theological montage, prior to philosophical writing. The dice are loaded and choices made; faith rises majestically in the background. The reader, confronted by the blade of the absolute, finds him- or herself in the position of a catechumen who has no other choice than to penetrate the holy words and lofty dogmas. . . . All is acquired and imposed from the outset, and this all is no little thing: nothing less than the God of the biblical tradition. Strict treason of the reduction that handed over the transcendental I to its nudity, here theology is restored with its parade of capital letters. But this theology, which dispenses with giving itself the least title, installs itself at the most intimate dwelling of consciousness, as if that were as natural as could be. Must philosophy let itself be thus intimidated? Is this not but incantation, initiation?[11]

Reminiscent of John Rawls's idea that public reason should be void of "comprehensive doctrines,"[12] Janicaud suggests that for a method to be philosophical instead of theological it must start from a position of pre-suppositionlessness. Only then can philosophy continue to strive to be a "rigorous science" and not simply a creedal expression of one's prior commitments. The question of the theological intimidation of philosophy is not simply an innocuous quandary. It is a positive assertion regarding the status of philosophy as neutral both methodologically and, far more problematically, in regard to its content as well. Notice that, for Janicaud, the phenomenological method is not simply about *how* to proceed in philosophical investigation; it is also about *what* is available for the investigation in the first place. It is here that the apparent neutrality of phenomenology breaks down on Janicaud's model and simultaneously invites the replies offered to Janicaud by the authors of *God in France*.

To delimit the domain of phenomenological inquiry from the outset is to already resist the supposed neutrality of the phenomenological method. To say that phenomenology is a method of studying that which appears in its very way of appearing, and describing it as a movement "to the things themselves," is not to determine prima facie how appearance functions, but instead should be understood as a stance of openness and receptivity to all possible modes of appearance. Indeed, as Guido Vanheeswijck says of Girard: it would also include the very possibility of appearance itself;[13] Johan Goud writes of Levinas: it would also be to investigate the way in which alterity "appears" (or doesn't appear) as a trace;[14] Ruud Welten says of Henry: Life is the very conditionality of appearance and is coordinate with all that appears;[15] and of Marion: unless we interrogate the possibility of "givenness" (*donation*) then we are starting our inquiry too late.[16] On the interpretation offered by all of these authors, Husserl's phenomenology cannot and should not be limited to a mundane conception of appearance in the way that Janicaud's interpretation of it seems to require. If phenomenology, as phenomenological, is willing to give an account of the "appearance" of the underside of the table and the backside of the computer screen, why should there be an automatic, prima facie exclusion of the "appearance" of Marion's givenness, Henry's Life, Girard's mimetic desire, and Lacoste's liturgy? Surely a "phenomenology of the inapparent" is already involved in every phenomenological approach to the readily apparent.

Now, it might seem that this is a bad analogy because the (non)appearance of the underside of a table cannot be compared to the transcendence of God. Although I certainly do not want to suggest that there is some sort of equivocation going on here, I do find this analogy to be appropriate on two fronts. First, the weight of Husserl's point is not that the underside of the table *could* appear if we were to just change our position in relation to the table—that is, look underneath it. Rather, he rightly notes the way in which appearance is always only a particular adumbration and not a complete picture. As such, the "underside" is a structural claim and not merely an empirical one. That is, no matter what perspective I occupy in relation to the table, there is always a side that does not "appear." It is this inapparent that subtends every adumbrated appearance that is relevant to my argument here. Second, the side that I do see always points to, or indicates, the side that must be filled in, as it were. Hence, phenomenological inquiry always involves a directed pointing-to. In the same essay in which he refers to the "phenomenology of the inapparent," Heidegger admits of this directed pointing-to when he notes that "phenomenology is a path that leads away to come before . . . and it lets that before which it is led show itself."[17]

Of course, to be fair to Janicaud, it is important to note that he does allow Merleau-Ponty's discussions of the "invisible" to be phenomenologically viable because they avoid any reference to transcendence and instead refer everything back to the domain of the immanent experiential world. Hence, it might be more accurate to say that the "invisible" is all right as long as it remains of this world, and, hence, definitively not referred to as "God." So, Janicaud might allow for the "appearance" of the back side of an angel's wing if we could actually experience the front side. On this account, the inapparent is not denied as such, but is simply restricted to the inapparent that could become apparent given different sorts of existential locations. Yet, this just begs the question as to what criterion Janicaud uses in his decision to understand the notion of "appearance" as being localized and limited in this way. The point here is that the burden of proof is on Janicaud's shoulders as to exactly how the above examples are disanalogous with the inapparent that Husserl already recognized in the notion of apperception that subtends the reality of infinite perceptual adumbrations, and even more explicitly in the concept of the "horizon." For these reasons, I take *God in France* to demonstrate successfully the way in which the apparent and the inapparent are not as radically separable as Janicaud's reading of phenomenology would suggest.[18]

Yet, would not this simply confirm the reality of a theological turn within phenomenology? That is, does this not demonstrate the way in which phenomenology has taken a decisive move toward the biblical God as the proper name for the transcendence that underlies and accompanies the immanent phenomena? Undoubtedly, there is a reason to believe that this is the case. Levinas does not refer simply to the Heideggerian-Hölderlinian "gods," but also to the God of Abraham, Isaac, and Jacob. He does not offer "Quasi-religious Writings," but *Talmudic Writings.* Similarly, although Marion uses examples from aesthetics to illuminate his notion of the "saturated phenomenon,"[19] he also goes as far as suggesting that the example par excellence is Christian incarnation. In *God Without Being,* Marion does not merely talk about the possibility of various iconic rituals; he speaks of the importance of the Eucharist (in its specifically Catholic conception).[20] This liturgical framework can also be found in Lacoste's discussions of presenting oneself before God[21] and Chrétien's focus on the phenomenon of prayer.[22] Further examples could no doubt be offered to support the idea of a theological turn, but, according to Jonkers, all of these examples sidestep important realities about the way in which these thinkers relate to the examples that they offer.

What we find in these texts, Jonkers contends, is not an apologetic enterprise, but a heuristic one. These thinkers "consider the way in which the Bible and Christian mystics speak about God as showing a sensitivity to a radical mystery, which, time and again, eludes notice of traditional metaphysics in spite or just because of its thinking force."[23] It is this sentiment that gives me pause as to how far apart Jonkers actually is from de Vries. Although de Vries is coupled with Janicaud as affirming the theological turn, or, as de Vries terms it, "the turn to religion," it is important to note that, unlike Janicaud, he goes to great lengths to demonstrate the way in which contemporary French philosophy has merely tapped into an *archive* that it would do well to not quickly bypass.[24] De Vries seems to be in agreement with the idea that the continental interest in theology does not positively advocate the doctrinal positions and creedal commitments of a particular faith, but is rather a helpful source for how to think after, or beyond, metaphysics. As such, he affirms Jonkers's contention regarding the solidly heuristic aspect of such an appropriation.

The second aspect of Jonkers's rationale for rejecting the theological turn is the disregard for any "religious consequences" that characterizes the thought of Derrida and Lyotard.[25] It is here that we might rightly question the inclusion of Lyotard as one of the eight central figures of the volume and simultaneously resist the tie between him and Derrida rather than him and Levinas, for example. To my mind, it is as strange to include Lyotard as it is to omit Chrétien and I do not believe that this decision is accidental. That is, a similar reading of Chrétien could be given as is provided for Marion, Levinas, and Lacoste—namely, his focus is primarily with the possibilities of appearance rather than the specifics of a particular faith. Accordingly, I find that Chris Doude van Troostwijk's essay on Lyotard's "Hidden Philosophy of Religion" is the essay that stands out among the rest as having a different agenda from the others. The intention of the chapters on Ricoeur, Girard, Levinas, Henry, Derrida, Marion, and Lacoste is to demonstrate the way in which God-talk is not, by itself, a sufficient condition for doing theology. The chapter on Lyotard almost goes the opposite way and argues that despite the apparent irrelevance of "God" for Lyotard's philosophy, Lyotard is deeply concerned with the "question of God [as] primarily a question about how the absolute penetrates the discourse where it can only be present in a repressed way."[26]

Beginning the essay by referring to Derrida's essay "How Not to Speak?" (*Comment ne pas parler?*) allows van Troostwijk to emphasize the question of God as a linguistic difficulty rather than a religious problem. The decision to link Lyotard to Derrida does more than just highlight a point of grammatological convergence. It also serves to distance Derrida and Lyotard from the more problematic theological inclinations of Levinas, Marion, and others. Although the essay on Lyotard goes a long way toward supporting the argument of the book as a whole, it does so in a roundabout way. If it can be demonstrated that both the apparently theological writings of Levinas, Marion, Henry, Girard, and others are actually thoroughly phenomenological and also that the obviously nontheological work of Lyotard and the early Derrida is already engaged with the same sorts of questions being raised by the more theologically inclined, then what we are witnessing is a radicalization of phenomenology itself rather than a theological influx into it. For this reason, I find the essay on Lyotard to be the most intriguing of the volume—and ultimately the most important for the overarching argument of the book itself.

However, as a mere conjecture, one might wonder how far Lyotard is from Levinas's claim that the word "God" ruptures ordinary speech?[27] As Levinas writes, "The *word* 'God' is unique in that it is the only word that neither extinguishes nor smothers nor absorbs its Saying. It is only a word, but it overwhelms semantics."[28] If the connection between Lyotard and Derrida is supplemented by the resonance between them both and Levinas, we run into a bit of difficulty maintaining Jonkers's claim regarding Derrida's indifference to the "religious consequences" of his work alongside the original connection Jonkers draws between Lyotard and Derrida.

The difference between Levinasian discussions of the word "God" and Lyotard's *not-speaking* about "God" is clearly seen when we remember that, for Levinas, "hear[ing] a God not contaminated by Being is a human possibility no less important and no less precarious than to bring Being out of the oblivion in which it is said to have fallen in metaphysics and in onto-theology."[29] In the "reversal" and "referral" of the desirable to the nondesirable that attends the ethical relation to the other person, Levinas argues, "God is torn out of the objectivity of presence and out of being.

God is no longer an object or an interlocutor in a dialogue."[30] What these passages demonstrate is the way in which Levinas actively sets out to rethink God on the basis of ethics. For Lyotard, such an intention could hardly be philosophically viable and would actually come dangerously close to reentrenching a "metanarrative" about ethics that would be just as problematic as an ontological, or onto-theological, one. With this said, it is easy to believe Jonkers's contention as to the religious indifference in Lyotard. Yet, we should also consider Derrida's suggestion in *The Gift of Death*:

> We should stop thinking about God as someone, over there, way up there, transcendent, and, what is more . . . capable, more than any satellite orbiting in space, of seeing into the most secret of the most interior places. It is perhaps necessary, if we are to follow the traditional Judeo-Christiano-Islamic injunction, but also at the risk of turning it against that tradition, to think of God and of the name of God without such idolatrous stereotyping or representation. Then we might say: God is the name of the possibility I have of keeping a secret that is visible from the interior but not from the exterior.[31]

Certainly this passage can plausibly be read as a clear-cut example of Derrida's deep concern for the "religious consequences" of his deconstructive retrieval of the biblical traditions.[32] As in Levinas, we begin to see in Derrida's later work an active attempt to rethink "God" according to the insights of postmodernity's resistance to onto-theological speculations that presuppose a dangerously transhistorical and noncontextual vision of rationality and subjectivity. By uniting Lyotard and Derrida, this aspect of Derrida's thought is downplayed instead of being dealt with directly. I would argue that rather than appealing to the lack of religious consequences as support for resisting the idea of a theological turn, it would be a better strategy to actually say that a direct concern for thinking religion *otherwise* (that is, deconstructively, phenomenologically, postmodernly, non-onto-theologically, and so forth) would itself be a strong indication of the purely phenomenological direction of recent French philosophy.

Despite its significant contribution to the debate surrounding whether there has been a theological turn in French thought, *God in France* actually serves to concede to Janicaud the apparent obviousness that phenomenology is no longer phenomenological if it is *theo*-logical. That the two ought to be kept separate is never clearly asserted. As in Janicaud, there is a supposition that such a normative claim is beyond the scope of the more sociological description of the philosophical landscape. Again in harmony with Janicaud, there is an underlying ease with the way in which these thinkers are labeled philosophers and not theologians. Ruud Welten argues that although Henry's discussion of Life and transcendence might be drawing on Christianity, "Henry is not a theologian or a mystic."[33] In his essay on Marion, Welten claims that both Henry and Marion "approach theology phenomenologically, not dogmatically."[34] Marion resists simply doing theology because he does not "show us God; he just makes sure there is room for God to show *Himself!*"[35] Johan Goud is comfortable contesting the "one-sided moral and non-religious interpretations" of Levinas, and although he even goes as far as saying that Levinas's "philosophical thought hinges on philosophical theology,"[36] Goud solidly insists that Levinas does not "discuss God in theological terms."[37] "In short," Goud concludes, "Levinas' thought must be read, valued and perhaps criticized as a philosophy."[38]

I do not want to cover over the close readings that *God in France* gives to the decidedly biblical cast given to God by Girard, Levinas, Henry, and Lacoste. Nevertheless, I do want to illuminate the way in which even these readings are presented as attempts to restore the phenomenological (that is, philosophical) weight of these thinkers and as such distance them from a theological agenda. The unannounced premise that runs throughout Janicaud and *God in France* is that if something is theological it is *not* philosophical. Must this be the case? How should we view the relationship between theology and phenomenology? In the next section I will offer three possible strategies (separatism, reconstruction, and reconstructive separatism)[39] and argue that only the third offers a promising way forward for this important debate.

At What Cost? Rethinking the Relationship with Theology

1. The Strategy of Separatism and the Question of Neutrality

The first way in which theology and phenomenology can be wedged apart from each other is according to a separatist strategy in which philosophy is positioned as neutral in both method and content. I discussed this strategy briefly above in relation to Janicaud's distinction between Merleau-Ponty and Levinas. According to Janicaud, Merleau-Ponty's work remains "passionately" phenomenological "in that it seeks to think phenomenality intimately, the better to inhabit it." Thus, he "excludes nothing, but opens our regard to the depth of the world."[40] As we saw above, this stands in stark contrast from the "loaded dice" that Levinas throws upon the table of philosophical discourse.

This separatist strategy is *separatist* in that it intends to place theology over and against phenomenology due to (1) the object of the inquiry being inapparent and its being subsequently termed "God" (that is, a phenomenology of the invisible—albeit in a particular sense—is not a phenomenology at all), (2) the starting point being a presupposition of particular tradition or discourse (that is, the dice are not simply loaded with "gods" but with the biblical God), and (3) the nonscientific dogmatism of theology (that is, there is no possibility of a "rigorous science" because we are solidly in the domain of faith).

Janicaud's overriding worry is that contemporary French phenomenologists are simply postmodern versions of Francis Schaeffer.[41] That is, they are Schaefferian in their affirmation of specifically religious presuppositions and they are postmodern in their contestation of the absolute status of religious doctrines. For Janicaud, it is as if they have done philosophically what our parents do in preparation for an Easter egg hunt: hide in the morning that which we are to go find in the afternoon. But, again, it becomes clear that instead of offering an innocuous method of neutrality, what Janicaud does is to just as problematically place out of bounds that which he does not want to find later in the middle of the playing field. It is important to realize that presuppositionalism can take both positive and negative forms.

The problem with the "neutral" and "presuppositionless" approach to phenomenology in particular and philosophy in general is that it necessarily retains the modern worldless subject that it was meant to overcome. It is one thing to say that we must be already *in-a-world* in order to take account of the way in which things present themselves to consciousness, but it is quite another to say that this embeddedness is itself a neutral starting point. The first is a descriptive recognition of the way in which the subject/object dualism so present in philosophy following Descartes has been overcome in favor of the realization that consciousness is always a *consciousness-of.* The second goes beyond this recognition and actually sets up a criterion for why this recognition itself is the only legitimate origin for philosophical investigation.

It is an open question how Husserl's early thought would have been transformed if the notion of the "Lifeworld" (*Lebenswelt*) were already present therein. Regardless, it is problematic to simply assume a particular definition of what a "rigorous science" is and then claim that this definition is offered from a neutral position regarding the objects of investigation at issue. Moreover, to predetermine what "appearance" means and how it can be made manifest is already to delimit certain methodological aspects that will remain untouched by the phenomenological reduction.

All of the aspects that differentiate theology from phenomenology according to separatism require a decidedly non-neutral origin and require certain presuppositions. This might all be fine, but if so then how are we to continue to reject theology according to its doing precisely what phenomenology does in order to differentiate itself from it?

2. The Strategy of Reconstruction and the Question of Positive Content

Whereas separatism tries to isolate theology from phenomenology according to certain criteria, the reconstructivist strategy does not differentiate between theology and phenomenology by placing God-talk beyond the bounds of phenomenology or by presupposing a narrow definition of "appearance." Rather, it distinguishes between radical phenomenological talk of the "transcendent," "givenness," and "absolute alterity" on the one hand, and theological speech within a particular religious tradition on the other. If separatism eliminates the quasi-religious aspect from phenomenology, reconstructivism reconceives God as no longer residing within decidedly theological boundaries. What results is not a phenomenological inquiry into Christianity, Judaism, or Islam, but a postmodern conception of transcendence that, although it makes reference to specific religious traditions, lacks any strong connection to the content of a determinate religion. That is to say, it is related to a tradition without being a part of it.

Rico Sneller's essay on Derrida articulates this strategy nicely. "I think that Derrida aims at *renewing* traditional God talk (within the philosophical-religious traditions)," Sneller comments, "and not, as for example Sartre did, at abandoning it as if it were something obsolete."[42] The *renewed* discourse is not properly about God as an object, but about "God" as a linguistic, existential, and performative phenomena. For Derrida, "'God' means: relation, interplay, interaction-between-inside-and-outside, or even *correlation*."[43] Similarly, for Lyotard, "God cannot be a metaphysical 'object'" but instead "'God' in a certain genre of discourse, the name for the absolute singularity."[44] Additionally, for Marion (and we might say for Levinas as well), the subject is "no longer God, but the non-ontological way in which God appears."[45]

The appropriate questions to ask in response to this reconstructed "God" are not absent from *God in France*; but they appear as having not been asked. The questions are: "Does God feel at home in France?"[46] and, "[do] men and women [feel] at ease with this 'French' God?"[47] These questions are not asked inasmuch as they both appear at the end of essays as rhetorical methods of exposing areas that continue to be left open. I both applaud this openness and contest the ease with which it is repeatedly sidestepped. Regarding the first question, it is not unproblematic to reconstruct the biblical God into a deconstructive "God" or "gods." Although it maintains the distinctiveness of phenomenology while allowing for a more theological orientation, it does so at the cost of detaching transcendence from the particular historical narratives on God in which it has been embedded. If separatism resulted in a modern conception of the detached subject by forgetting sociohistorical embeddedness, reconstruction solidly affirms historicity while failing to engage the particularity and specificity of a determinate religious tradition (that is, doctrines, creeds, confessions, or rituals).

In no way do I mean to suggest that in order to remain true to the uniqueness of particular religious traditions that we must maintain the onto-theological frameworks and metaphysical schemes in which they have commonly been articulated. Exactly the opposite is the case. What decidedly unites the figures discussed in *God in France* is the way in which each attempts to think God non-onto-theologically. The importance of such a project cannot be overstated. However, such a rethinking need not entail a rejection of the doctrinal and creedal components of the Jewish or Christian religions; merely a rejection of the way in which such doctrines and creeds are appropriated and held. As Merold Westphal suggests in *Overcoming Onto-Theology*, abandoning the God's Eye View does not mean that we abandon Christian orthodoxy.[48] It simply means that the important aspects of orthodoxy might reside elsewhere than in our conception of God as the *Summum Bonum* or *Summum Ens*. The value of Marion and Levinas in particular is that they offer ways of understanding orthodoxy as a commitment to God's love as constitutive of human reality, which is expressed in the relation to the neighbor, instead of understanding it as a metaphysical conception of God's Being.

Regarding the second question about the comfort of religious believers with this "French God," I want to suggest that the potential danger of reconstruction is that it can actually end up patronizing committed religious believers. Rather than opening a new space for Christianity, Judaism, or Islam in a postmodern context, it can leave them behind in the name of a nondescript relation with alterity. Only by taking the particular narratives seriously can we actually tap the theological archive by being *invested* in it, rather than merely appropriate it for our own (intrinsically) political purposes.[49] While the first is a method of hospitality, the second comes dangerously close to being nothing but a power play under the guise of openness.[50]

3. Reconstructive Separatism and the Question of Authority

Rather than the restrictive negative dogmatism of separatism and the potentially patronizing emptiness of reconstruction, I want to suggest a third way of understanding the relation (and distinction) between phenomenology and theology. I term this strategy "Reconstructive Separatism" because it maintains the valuable aspects of each of the two former options while rejecting the worldlessness of the first and the problematic relationality of the second. On this view phenomenology and theology are separated, but only because of the variant sources of authority to which they appeal—and not because of the content of one or the other. Phenomenology should be distinguished from theology not because it is "neutral" as opposed to being biased, but according to the particular biases that shape its discourse. Theology begins from the authority of divine revelation, canonical scriptural texts, and ecclesial frameworks. Phenomenology begins from the openness to investigating appearance in whatever form, or lack thereof, appearance takes.

This strategy maintains the decidedly philosophical character of phenomenological inquiry by resisting an easy move from dialogical openness to creedal faith. It is *separatist* inasmuch as it says that phenomenology must not appeal to any authority other than its own method. Yet, this does not result in the worldless modern subject. Rather, this strategy begins from the recognition of the deep situatedness of rationality itself—and therefore of the phenomenological method as well. This method admits that there is no such thing as "neutral" reason. Reason is always internal to the play of human discourse. Hence, reconstructive separatism does not say that phenomenology is different from theology because of its rationality and theology's fideism. To do so would be to assume that reason could be a criterion outside of the specificities of the particular language games in which it operates. However, it does differentiate between the reason that is internal to a revelational context and the reason that starts out trying to discover the possibility of revelation in the first place. The difference is not that phenomenology is presuppositionless while theology is not; it is merely a difference in the content of the presuppositions themselves. It should go without saying that this admits of a bias at the heart of phenomenology. However, this is not as troubling as it might initially seem when we remember that this is a methodological bias that allows for critical engagement with whatever authoritative source to which our discourse appeals. Theology can be *critical*, that is, philosophical, theology inasmuch as it can weigh and consider the particular tenants of its own tradition and the various interpretations it has received in historically situated communities. To the extent that theology is philosophical, however, it is only such in relation to a revealed narrative that is itself the final criterion. What is at stake is how to understand the revelation, not whether the revelation is authoritative.

Although theology might indeed appropriate phenomenological methodology in order to investigate particular aspects of its own tradition—prayer, worship, forgiveness, the Eucharist, and so forth—it does so by still affirming the authority of its sacred texts and ecclesial structures. Alternatively, phenomenology is not prima facie cut off from theological concerns. Instead, if the investigation into phenomena (whether apparent or unapparent) leads toward the insights of a particular religious tradition, then that movement is perfectly valid according to Socrates' instruction that the "lover of inquiry must follow his beloved wherever it may lead."[51] Due to the inherent contextuality of reason, the beloved may indeed lead toward a God who is "otherwise than Being," but this is not to say that it will necessarily evacuate the specificities of determinate religion. To be *reconstructive* on this model is not to say that religious discourse is allowed *if* it has been reconceived according to phenomenological norms. Reconstructive separatism maintains the possibility of a postmodern *Christianity,* a postmodern *Judaism,* and a postmodern *Islam,* rather than merely a nondescript *religion without religion.* Granted, these postmodern versions may not be acceptable to many Christians, Jews, and Muslims, but this is not because the new alternative is really *new*; but merely because it is *newly presented.*

Conclusion: Toward a Postmodern Apologetics

The value of the reconstructed separatism that I have outlined is that it actually opens the space for more than a merely heuristic relation between phenomenology and theology. *It actually leaves room for the possibility of a postmodern apologetics.* That is, an apologetics offered on the hither side of onto-theology's deconstruction. It might be the case that phenomenology actually allows for a deep argument in favor of the uniqueness of the biblical God as already being "not contaminated by Being," as Levinas would say. To close this possibility off from the outset is to be narrow-mindedly atheistic rather than scientifically agnostic. As such, it is a preconception that should be resisted.

This does not mean that we should do phenomenology in order that we might convince our interlocutors of religious truth. It does mean that we remain as open to the possibility that our inquiry may indeed point toward the truth of a religious tradition as we are to the possibility that it would lead away from it. Postmodern apologetics is oxymoronic only if we assume that apologetics can operate only on the basis of neutral reason and natural theology.[52] This notion of apologetics hangs or falls with the fate of onto-theology. To overcome onto-theology is not to overcome apologetics, nor is it to overcome God, it is simply to move beyond the interpretations of God that ignore human existence and defenses of faith that operate outside history. Contemporary continental philosophy of religion continues to attest to the possibility of doing more than arguing *against* onto-theology by actually arguing *for* a non-onto-theological Christianity.[53] In no way does this reduce phenomenology to theology or philosophy to religion. The point is simply that keeping these distinct is not to keep them separate, but merely to keep open a conversation between different perspectives. Maintaining such a conversation is valuable not only for increasing rigor in theological thinking, but also for the expansion of philosophical horizons. I agree with Adriaan Peperzak when he claims that, "A post-postmodern renaissance of Christian spirituality in philosophy is necessary."[54] It is necessary in order that our phenomenology not become nearsighted and our theology not become stagnant.

By taking seriously the real differences between phenomenology and theology (and likewise, reason and faith) while leaving open the space for seeing their potential subsequent interplay (the situatedness of reason always already involves a certain amount of faith), we do not simply reject Janicaud, but recognize him as a critical interlocutor in the project of continuing to look for God in France (or wherever else God might be found).

Being Without God

JEFFREY BLOECHL

Être/Le premier venu.

René Char, "L'amour," in *Arsenal* (1929)

Whether or not we may now speak globally or even retrospectively about a distinctively "French" phenomenology—and both the meaning and the possibility of such an adjective have never been clear to me—we may nonetheless attend with interest to a few basic theses in the work of some contemporary French thinkers who have conduct their research in the wake of Husserl and, more so, Heidegger. *More so, Heidegger.* One may rightly wonder, what does it mean to grant Heideggerian thought all rights and privileges when speaking of phenomenology? And second, what does it mean to suppose that phenomenology as such is unavoidable, even if in many respects it is also unsatisfying? In France, a considerable number of thinkers have sought to determine the meaning and limits of philosophy strictly in terms of a study of the rigor specific to phenomenology. And, at virtually the same time, the reception of phenomenology has been determined, with few exceptions (one thinks immediately of Merleau-Ponty, but also of Didier Franck), by the reception specifically of Heidegger, whereupon the need of a "retrocession" to Husserl may or may not be felt.[1]

Among the consequences of this acceptance of Heidegger is the considerable disturbance it can bring to religious thought, at least insofar as established forms of such thought have suggested a confident passage from

Being to God. For the Philosopher in France, this is evidently no longer possible. Hence is born an inquiry that, if not unique to France (one should not forget Welte, and I will recall Rahner), does take a general direction that is distinctly French. The point of departure has long been so familiar as to call for only brief mention: When the approach to the question of the meaning of Being is clarified as a matter of respecting the ontological difference between Being and beings, there emerges a conception of our being in the world that makes no positive reference to a relation to the absolute God. If we accept the inner coherence of this position, there is no avoiding the question of whether religion is no longer thinkable or else is simply in need of rethinking.[2]

I. Errancy

It is well known that when phenomenology frees the concept of Being from definitions previously ventured from the perspective of beings, Being immediately becomes the primordial horizon for the meaning of engagement with the world and everything in it. The *logical expression* of this insight could not be simpler: If Being truly differs from beings without becoming a being in its own right, then Being transcends beings without standing wholly apart from them. The *existential implications*, however, are lasting and profound. In Heidegger's hermeneutics of facticity, the notion that Being transcends beings translates easily into the notion that our relation with beings is always and already a relation with Being. Can there be any surprise that the latter relation is to be concretized in an experience of the limits of the former, when one senses in the finitude of meaning the eventuality of death? To propose that we are constantly concerned with beings according to an underlying care for our own being, or more boldly to insist that that concern is generally cast in an oblivion of our own mortality, is at the same time to argue that meaning is subtended by an abyss of meaning that announces itself in the approach of death. The relation with Being as distinct from beings is fundamentally a relation with death as the essential end of life. Conversely, all that may intervene between me and my death, or between me and my relation with Being, is my relation with beings. Fundamental ontology assumes the death of God. The "ontological difference" is a name for an experience of abandonment to the world.

That the temporal movement of *Dasein*, as being toward death, functions as the center of all intelligibility throughout the first (and only published) part of *Sein und Zeit* has been remarked often enough. In the present context this unifying principle is worth recalling especially because it calls attention to the fact that the ontological difference signifies an intimacy between Being and beings that the very word "difference" might otherwise cause us to forget. Of course, our relations to Being and to beings are distinct, but still they can hardly be separate. In our encounter with beings we also comport ourselves toward Being, and Being is always and only comprehended as beings. It is in our comportment, then, or more generally in our human being that Being is comprehended as beings; it is in human being that Being is, as it were, revealed to itself. The fabric of this event, in all its concrete historicity, is what Heidegger understands as "world." Hence the more elongated proposal at the onset of *Vom Wesen der Wahrheit*: human being, in attending to its own care and concerns, is the irruption of Being as beings in the openness of a world.

I invoke Heidegger's essay on truth because it highlights an interest in the thought that we are able to properly judge about beings only, or perhaps ultimately, according to a comportment that is always already attuned to Being. After all, in order to formulate a true proposition one must measure a claim against the being that it holds in view, which itself must be received with an openness that lets it show itself as itself. And to the degree that we manage this openness, or even seek it, we reveal ourselves to be free of determinations pressed upon us by the ontical conditions of being in the world. To Heidegger, this suggests that our freedom is the substance of a relation not only with beings—since, after all, it transcends the ontical—but also with Being. Accordingly, that relation of freedom to Being must be the horizon within which beings have meaning and within which propositions about their meaning can be judged. At the same time, this also tells us that our freedom thus conducts itself without ulterior ground or authority. Freedom is the ceaseless engagement with beings in which its relation with Being is also played out. A converse statement of the position brings us closer to the heart of the matter: our free comportment toward Being opens immediately onto beings, without a revelation of Being as Being. There is, in short, no external vantage point on our relation with beings, even if there is nonetheless a more primordial relation with Being. Perhaps the diverse options of realism or pragmatism will suffice for our worldly affairs; what "seems to work" will be "good enough." But then those affairs will be conducted without any sense of the mysterious condition of their own possibility. What "seems to work" will prove superficial and ill defined. Yet greater depth and sharper definition are necessarily elusive. There is no access to what recedes from its own accessibility. Being destines us to an errancy that has nothing at all to do with simple error (errance: *die Irren*, not *der Irrtum*), for there is no question of an avoidable failure so long as Being as Being abides in the mystery of what is concealed by its own unconcealment. Heidegger's word "errancy" signifies the inevitability of forgetting the mystery that shrouds our existence. This inevitable forgetting of the mystery of Being is our abandonment to the world.[3]

Let us take stock. If from this notion of "errancy" we learn that beings always distract us from a proper understanding of the greater horizon in which we encounter them, a correct understanding of the special notion of "forgetting" that accompanies it helps us recognize that that distraction is not due to some shortcoming on our part. As finite *Dasein, one cannot not err.* If here one is tempted to recognize a close approximation of what Hegel sometimes calls "the rule of finitude,"[4] one must also bear in mind that Heidegger excludes the possibility of any recuperation into a higher unity: our ontological condition is such that our comportment always particularizes, always renders meaning within the network of relations that is our world.

At this point, it is necessary to admit a parenthetical concern. We may wonder whether the foregoing means that everything we encounter thus receives its meaning according to an externalization of some trait or attribute of our own. In fact, this is difficult to uphold in the face of Heidegger's careful insistence that the meaning of beings is determined in our world, a world that undoubtedly has its own history, a history that can hardly be without some bearing on each new particularization. Moreover, all of this occurs against the background of a relation with Being that is decidedly not an externalization of anything originating in us because it is anterior to the very possibility of externalization. In short, externalization, no more and no less than any other force at work in meaning-giving, is a possibility admitted by the transcendence of Being over our finite comprehension (*Verstehen*).

This returns us to the notion of an erring that is not mere mistakenness, and to a forgetting that does not result from some deficiency in us. More than that, the forgetting of the mystery of Being is a forgetting without previous possession of the forgotten, and therefore also without a future recovery—a forgetting that does not imply and cannot await an exercise of remembering its own principle. And this is evidently consistent with the notion of thrownness into the world in the absence, and indeed the impossibility of an authentic ground or reason—without chance of being at home there. For Heidegger, it is as homeless and shrouded in mystery that we interpret our world and everything in it, without ever grasping the primordial source of our condition in the Being that remains (un)concealed in beings.

II. Being Without God

It can hardly occasion much surprise that the philosophy that follows such a course has sometimes taken a lively interest in Christian theology, which opens itself to experiences of a ground for our existence beyond the ontological difference. Nor can it be surprising that some religious thinkers, theologians among them, have felt compelled to engage that philosophy. What would it mean to know the absolute God? How might such knowledge avoid reducing God to a being or indeed *mistaking God for Being*? Christian thought has addressed these questions in the form of a critique of the concupiscence by which we succumb to the appeal of worldly existence. How to banish concupiscence from the approach to God? One knows the experience of Augustine—indeed, Heidegger's own work is not without a certain echo of it—of a turn inward and away from the dark appeal of worldly things until being drawn powerfully upward and beyond them. For Augustine, God had been present in the depths of his soul already before any possibility of recognizing and turning toward him. And only upon understanding this relation with God who has always already come to him could he truly understand himself and the world in which he finds himself called. Perhaps, then, our relation with God precedes our relation with the world, and perhaps our knowledge of that God completes our knowledge of the world that remains open to God. Or better, perhaps all knowledge of the world and everything in it is already, for those who have eyes to see, knowledge of God.

Should this vision simply be kept clear of Heidegger's proposals? If it is a question only of strategy, this is no doubt possible, but not without rejecting out of hand the possibility of a coherent vision of being in the world that seems *not* to cry out for any completion by a positive notion of God. The urgency of this very discussion is dramatized in the early Rahner's philosophy of religion, where an attempt to appropriate much of Heidegger's existential analytic is tempered by an undisguised sympathy for Christian theology. One cannot follow the progress of *Hörer des Wortes* without observing a constant tension between the necessity of recognizing the specificity of the secular dimension of our being and a rival insistence on subverting that effort with analyses purporting to show that our secularity in fact only suppresses our deeper relation with God. Interestingly, in that work, as in *Geist in Welt* before it, the argument takes the form of an attempt to reinvigorate a Scholastic theory of knowledge: all knowledge, we are told, is implicitly knowledge of God, and however productive a godless theory of knowledge might be, final coherence still depends on explicitly recognizing God as its sole and proper foundation.

Needless to say, if God is to prove more than another being comprehended among beings, this argument can be verified only through a radical conversion of the sort that Augustine describes in his *Confessions*. The nature of the problem virtually defines its only possible solution: God must be known from before and beyond the reach of what Heidegger has defined, in the strict sense, as human comprehension.

There are, to be sure, a number of technical problems with the terminology appearing in Rahner's argument, if not also in his understanding of Heidegger—"Being" is a synonym for "God," though without using the former concept quite in a sense that Heidegger would have recognized, and so forth[5]—but these may be left aside in order to get at a more fundamental issue of immediate interest. Provoked especially by the portion of Heidegger's argument that the final horizon for our movement in the world is the relation with Being, Rahner sets aside his evident interest in the event of divine revelation, a revelation that must breach what Jean-Luc Marion calls the screen/filter of Being (*l'écran de l'Être*),[6] and turns first to the task of redefining the anterior structure of our very being in the world. Perhaps we can accept this as a reformulation of the Augustinian question in the wake of Heidegger: By what condition of our *Dasein* might we be related not only to the world and everything in it, and not only to the Being that transcends the beings we encounter there, but also—and first—to the absolute God?

Rahner's notion of a "supernatural transcendental" is a commonplace of contemporary Roman Catholic theology. The notion that our being contains within itself a ready anchor or opening to the absolute God is in any case indispensable to any positive thought of religious experience and faith. If God is meaningful as God, then our being must admit of a "*potentia oboedentialis*" for divine revelation. And yet, as Jean-Yves Lacoste has observed in an important remark, the indispensable notion is not therefore an unambiguous one.[7] The effort toward an "epistemological validation of theology" (Rahner's expression) moves inevitably through a claim for transcendental experience of God to propose an antecedent, prethematic encounter with God. From here, of course, the aforementioned subversion of a secular a priori detected in the philosophy of Heidegger is thought to be accomplished in a discovery that the true a priori is religious and, literally, anarchical. As Lacoste points out, at least two difficulties receive short shrift in all of this. To begin with, it is never made clear that what Rahner considers the implicit experience of God in our experience of the world and everything in it is not in fact experience only of the sacrality of the world.[8] Second, when, as was foreseeable, Rahner comes up against the fact that no amount of discipline, whether intellectual or spiritual, guarantees that a divine word will in fact be heard, he speaks only—no more than twice, and with evident uncertainty[9]—of the mysterious "silence of God," even though he himself has been at great pains elsewhere to emphasize that God's revelation, while free, is voiced from eternity. There is ample reason to withdraw from the specter of a God who, perversely, speaks only to some or only at some times. But this leaves us with only a single solution to this problem, and moreover one that lies outside the precincts of Rahner's perspective: Being can truly deafen us to the word of God.

III. From the a Priori to the Immemorial

Either God simply withholds divine revelation from some of those who aspire to holiness and fidelity, or Being is capable of muting that revelation. The former thesis shatters the traditional conception of a God who is absolute, therefore perfectly simple and, without lack, supremely Good. The latter thesis relinquishes any further temptation to argue for transcendental experience of God, whereupon the question of our possible relation with God no longer strictly coincides with the question of our relation to Being. One has a relation with beings and with Being. This much is certain and cannot be denied in the attempt to argue for a relation with God. It must be shown that the relation with God is free of determination by our relation with Being, and yet unopposed to it. Or, conversely, it must be shown that although our being in the world is without a priori openness to God, the relation with God remains an intelligible possibility.

Theologians, especially those still attentive to the stakes of the so-called modernist crisis in twentieth-century Roman Catholicism, will recognize in this latter position a somewhat radicalized version of the "extrinsicist" position, which is to say the position that considers properly religious experience of God to become possible only according to a divine initiative from beyond nature *in se*. On this point, the discussion with Rahner is especially instructive: though on one hand Rahner, too, subscribes to extrinsicism insofar as he strives to recognize the independent worth of a philosophy that makes no conceptual recourse to God, on the other hand this effort is repeatedly checked by his own concern to show that any such philosophy, no less than the way of life it embodies, is in fact necessarily incomplete. Having recognized the ambiguities inhabiting his position and now charted a course away from them, it seems necessary to concede the genuine viability of a way of life that professes itself to be godless,[10] and—with an eye specifically on Heidegger—the evident consistency of an account of our condition that takes root there. Still, this is far from ruling out the possibility of an equally viable way of life and an equally consistent account of our condition that does profess an experience of the absolute God. One anticipates the general perspective: whereas those who do not hear the word of God would live solely within the sphere of the relation with beings and Being, those who do hear such a word would recognize and respect that former, godless way of life from the perspective of a transcending relation with God. On the level of basic religious anthropology this suggests a dimension in us that exceeds our mortality without consuming it or erasing it—a dimension in which everything in us that is attached to this life and enjoys the things that it offers us is complemented and perhaps eventually sanctified by a spirit opened by the experience of God. But of course, it is precisely this experience that remains in need of verification if we are to accept it into any philosophical anthropology.

It falls doubly to phenomenology to investigate the conditions under which the experience of God can and/or cannot be verified under the foregoing conditions. First, and on the level of discourse, theology, as the thinking about faith unfolded from within faith, takes that experience as its unquestioned starting point and *Faktum*. Second, now on the level of abstract concepts, it must be observed that the religious relation itself, far from requiring this verification for its fulfillment, appears strictly indifferent to the question of whether or not it becomes discernible in the fabric of human experience. Crudely put, God may well and truly exist apart from any experience of God, as the Deists have perhaps understood. Bearing this in mind, let me try to render the problem as a question for phenomenology alone: Is it possible for us to find ourselves thrown into the world, and perhaps abandoned *entirely* to this world, and yet also become otherwise and more than in the world? Could it be shown that we, or at least those of us who have encountered the absolute God, are not wholly of this world, even while nonetheless being in it? To be sure, strict phenomenological evidence is precluded from any answer, since the absolute God by definition does not offer itself to us as a being in our world. Recognizing this, one might rather attempt, still partly inspired by Heidegger, to describe the religious way of life in its specificity, evoking possibilities unaccountable in ordinary existential-phenomenological terms (a fundamental attunement irreducible to anxiety at my death, a hope that shoots past mundane futurity, and so forth). Yet even these efforts are in need of mooring to be sought necessarily in a move, according to an especially apt expression of the French, upstream from (*en amont de*) our being in the world—sought only in the traces of an exposure to the absolute God that is not yet absorbed into our relation to world, beings, and Being. One would have to find a means to validate, or at least defend, the separate integrity of the claims of the faithful to find themselves called by a God whose intelligibility is not a function of our understanding but instead overflows that understanding, coming, as it were, with its own horizon. Such a God will never have been contained in the present because such a God will have antedated any possible present from a past deeper than the reach of either extrapolation or memory. Contemporary philosophy, when it has felt inclined to attend to these matters (for example, in different ways, by E. Levinas, J. Derrida, and J.-L. Chrétien), has sometimes spoken of a past that is properly "immemorial."

The first thing to notice about this strange concept is that it says more about the limits of memory than it does about the God who transcends it. As Husserl has shown, memory in its most elemental form deploys the past in the service of the present. Each new datum we encounter becomes meaningful only through a process of association with data already on hand from previous encounters. In this sense, memory is the inertia of the past exerting itself on the meaning of the present. It is a spontaneous, even passive form of possession. If this is so, then to say that God abides in the immemorial past is to recognize that God neither can nor ever could be associated with the finite data registered in memory because God has always already transcended the work of memory and the process of meaning-giving. The latter, so carefully analyzed by Husserl especially in his genetic phenomenology, would transpire as it were after the fact or in the wake of God—a God whose passing is well and good accomplished, but whose second coming remains forever a matter of faith. This is already enough for us to now recognize the work that the concept would be expected to accomplish: as the condition for the possibility of the experience of God but not for any transcendental knowledge of God (Rahner), the concept of the immemorial designates an openness in us where the absolute God *may or may not* be revealed.

IV. Phenomenology and Attention

Being is not God and we do not need the word of the master to be sure of this,[11] for we already know that the happiness sometimes given to the religious seeker, arriving from beyond anticipation or expectation, is withheld from the meditative thinker. There is, to be sure, an intriguing correspondence between the two figures, but still no denying that the (un)concealment of Being leaves *Dasein* to comprehend Being as beings in a forgetfulness that not even the most rigorous ascesis lifts so much as it ameliorates the desire for such a lifting. The thinker thus finds serenity, whereas the believer may be given joy.[12]

But the fact that a person may seem to experience a sudden revelation of God without having prepared for it cannot mean that the life of faith is therefore without need of its own discipline and effort. Lacoste has already reminded us of the silence of God in the lives even of those who commit themselves to the words and gestures of faith. If, as seems incontestable, it is impossible to think that I will reach intimacy with the absolute God solely according to my own efforts, still nothing prevents me from laboring to prepare myself for God to come to me. To the contrary, it belongs to one and the same thought—Augustinian, once again—to resist the notion that one can make one's way to God and to insist that one may nonetheless reduce one's distance from God by letting go of everything else that one is tempted to put first (and an attachment to one's own intellect counts among them). The practice of simplicity and the cultivation of humility belong necessarily to Christian life, as the labor of hope and the invocation of God. One empties oneself of all else in the hope of becoming filled with God at God's own initiative.

Perhaps it is difficult for the phenomenologist to judge the success of religious hope, but one might well inquire after its possibility. If hope truly exceeds mere optimism about worldly goods, it opens itself to a Good (the believer says "God") that would be always already there from before any question of having been present, then lost, and now recalled. By what condition could the hopeful person at one and the same time believe that God truly is and accept that God enters experience only according to a time that is entirely God's own? The thought virtually compels us to envision a movement toward a final state of stillness, no doubt turgid with a desire that, paradoxically enough, renders itself immobile. Phenomenology ignores at its own peril the dense passages that mystics have devoted to this experience, in which subjectivity arrests itself in a waiting that is neither lifeless and inert nor, however, certain of its prospects. In the terms of an economy of desire, every finite and accessible good is wagered for a Good that is infinite but therefore, *in sensu stricto*, inaccessible. One makes oneself ready by rendering oneself fully receptive, suspending every movement of possession—every movement of comprehension, of engagement with beings and Being—until arriving at, precisely, the nonmovement of readiness that Simone Weil has called "attention" (invoking, needless to say, an affinity with the French word *attente*: waiting). And for Weil, too, there is no guarantee that waiting for God necessarily passes over into an experience of God. It is a matter not of spiritual accomplishment so much as existential possibility. To wait for

God is to contest the ordinary conditions of our being in the world, in favor of conditions that are evidently rooted elsewhere, or perhaps otherwise.

All of this contributes to a theory of the subject that no longer privileges either the relation with beings and Being or the mortality in which their authentic meaning would announce itself to us. The very desire to exempt oneself from the conditions of our being in the world suggests possibilities and a structure that the hermeneutics of facticity appears to have overlooked, if not suppressed. Heidegger depicts a *Dasein* that fails in its care for itself so long as it persists in fleeing from its own death, when in fact care succeeds only in the form of a resolute acceptance that would mark the end of flight and its anxieties. Inauthentic *Dasein* dreams of a self-sufficiency that is impossible for finite beings; authentic *Dasein* reconciles itself to that impossibility. What they share is a conviction that the question of sufficiency—let us say: fulfillment, happiness—is to be decided as a matter of one's own capacity to achieve it. It is this that the religious attitude refuses, though of course without denying that "want" does belong to our condition as beings in the world. Is it certain that the authentic relation to that desire consists in conforming it to the limits of what I myself can do about it? It is not necessary to transform phenomenology into eschatology in order to entertain some doubt. A phenomenology that concentrates on beginnings rather than on ends—a protological phenomenology—suggests that it is the native tendency of our desire to aim beyond every horizon before succumbing to the qualifications inevitably demanded by our finitude.[13] If this is so, then the hope of the believer, reaching all the way to the stillness of religious waiting, may express a mode of being that rediscovers and insists on that more native tendency. Such a mode of being, moreover, is recuperable into fundamental ontology only according to the violence of explanation by ulterior causes, whether psychological, social, or cultural. And it has counted among the merits of the phenomenological method to deny itself precisely this.

This is not without important metaphysical implications. The phenomenon of religious hope is not possible unless Being admits at least a hint or trace of the absolute God. Let us therefore rephrase an earlier proposition: Being does not impede divine revelation all the way to rendering it completely inaudible in every case. What can become faith and hope develop in pursuit of a foretaste of the divine, which, however, is neither contact nor possession. The human drama of faith and faithlessness is grounded in the riddle of our uneven relation to Being, by which this foretaste is detected and indeed seized upon by some while others either take no notice of it or discover little interest there. Whereas the latter phenomenon is no doubt readily understood within the limits of our relation to Being, the former becomes intelligible only on the premise that that relation can be interrupted by a germ or seed of what it is not. Though the context certainly calls for the notion of a seed of non-Being, one hesitates to invoke it since the negation in question here cannot be one of absence or lack (and in any case this is not the meaning intended by the Neoplatonists, with whom that expression is most readily associated). The seed that contains the possibility of interrupting our relation to Being, opening us toward the coming of a God who transcends Being, may have this effect only if it is distinct from Being and yet in commerce with it—capable of soliciting the attention of a being that finds itself thrown into a primordial relation with Being.

These last few thoughts yield two simple indications for future reflection. Being, we are led to think, is not irreducibly plural, since it is possible to resist it in its entirety. But it does not therefore exhibit the unity of a plenum, since our relation to it admits of modes as diverse as resolute acceptance of the limits it prescribes and hopeful openness toward what would come from wholly beyond those limits. Between these two, one might speculate—here the thought can only be mentioned—that Being entails gravity, and displays gradations in our relation to it. And at this point, it may at last be conceded to Heidegger, this time after full consideration, that the relation with Being has priority over all other relations. I have not contested it: for us, openness to the very idea of transcending Being—of denying that Being is the ultimate horizon—necessarily arises within the relation to Being, both as an idea and as an aim. Yet I have nonetheless suggested that our humanity also contains the possibility of subverting that primacy. For the believer, our relation to Being appears in retrospect, as a point only of first arrival. Thrown into engagement with Being as beings, the believer already looks toward richer pastures.

The Appearing and the Irreducible

JEAN-YVES LACOSTE

I

The "reduction," or *epochê*, is officially a latecomer in the phenomenological landscape. Husserl's first published text to propose the concept is the first book of the *Ideas*, published in 1913.[1] It certainly would not be difficult to show that the reduction is already present in an inchoate fashion in the 1905–1906 lectures on the theory of consciousness,[2] and we can suspect that the reduction is present *in nuce* from the *Logical Investigations* onward. Yet let us stick with the official version and focus on the *Ideas*. To begin at the beginning, in the beginning was not phenomenology, that is, philosophy, but what Husserl calls a "natural attitude" in relation to the world, in relation to ourselves, and in relation to the other person. The natural attitude has a major characteristic: the "natural human" (a term authorized by Husserl) "believes" in reality or in the transcendent, extramental "existence" of all that sensation gives to us. What is known, is known independently of all theory, is believed to be real, *wirklich*; and whoever says "reality," here says exteriority in relation to consciousness. Born as "children of the world," *Weltkinder*,[3] we are persuaded by the reality of the world and of those who inhabit it. And it is this that phenomenology is supposed to go beyond in order to achieve the status of "science." How do I deal with what appears to me philosophically? Introducing a Husserlian key term as soon as its presence becomes vital, how do I describe phenomena philosophically? Response: by taking leave of any natural attitude. Why? Certainly not because I doubt the "existence" of the world and of its furnishings: Husserl is not Cartesian, and feels no need to reach "certainty" or an *inconcussum*. His reason and his ambitions are different; his goal is to enable the most exact ("scientific") description possible. One should admit easily that existence is nothing that we could describe however we might conceptualize it. We describe "what" things are, not the fact that they are ("things" here include objects, other people, values, mathematical entities, and so forth). And Husserl tells us that if we take the requirement of description seriously, we will have to place all "natural" belief in extramental (external to consciousness) reality of things within parentheses. Several paragraphs before the reduction appears, Husserl articulates his "principle of principles": "All originally giving intuition is by right a source of knowledge."[4] What appears to us *is* by full right inasmuch as it appears. Consciousness thus need not worry over the transcendent existence of things when it is occupied with knowing them (we are again quite far from Cartesian preoccupations). Description (and philosophy as rigorous science is a philosophy constituted as descriptive science) never encounters the need to be based on a judgment of existence.[5] Of course I exist and survive unruffled by what Husserl does not hesitate to call "annihilation" of the world in the act of reduction.[6] Later the master will say that in this I need not be rigidly human: it could be angelic.[7] Be that as it may on this point, one reality cannot (integrally) be placed within parentheses: that of philosophizing consciousness—admittedly a trivial remark, since no one ever believed that consciousness would be "real" in the same way as what is exterior to it is "real."

It is hence clear that the transition from the natural attitude to the phenomenological attitude is of an ascetic order. (Husserl, for his part, will speak of a "profession."[8]) According to Husserl, no one is born as a phenomenologist. Husserl is not interested in an interpretation of "facts" or of "facticity," for which the highest experiences would be "natural" experiences and in which no other me than a human I would be present. In order to become a philosopher, thus in order to let things appear as they are and describe them as they are, one must break with natural life, with natural perception, and so forth. The reason is not that the natural attitude deceives us: the short description of the natural world Husserl offers us[9] contains nothing dramatic. Moreover, once placed within parentheses, the world does not cease to be there: we simply find that we no longer need its transcendent reality when we determine to describe it correctly.[10] We want philosophical knowledge, and we are free to proceed by way of reduction—where we have spoken of asceticism, Husserl speaks of "complete freedom."[11] What the philosopher does not "need" is only useless—useless for the ends of philosophical work. Husserl's text does not lack clarity. And we do not finally reach knowledge through the aid of the work of reduction; rather we reach a new field of knowledge, which is quite a different matter.

II

Very well. But do we really require an act of perfect freedom to open the path toward adequate description? We can suspect that this is not the case when we read the paragraph devoted to the "world of the natural attitude."[12] It is quite certain that this is not a world that deceives us about what things really are, and it is also clear that its description is not completely different from the description licensed by the *epoché*. In the world of the natural attitude, things really are *wirklich* (real) and *vorhanden* (present, at-hand). We believe in their existence. (But, in fact, we will continue to believe that when we place them within parentheses.) The important point, however, is that the drapery is yellow, and not that the drapery "is" or that "there is" drapery. Maybe there are phenomena we can describe without acknowledging (beforehand or within the course of discussion) that they cannot be subjected to a work of reduction (we will see that there are such phenomena and that they probably are the most interesting ones). But are there also phenomena with which we deal spontaneously without the least interest in the "real" existence of the thing? The question is not pointless. Let us attempt to say that a certain form of reduction is already at work at the heart of the natural attitude.

(a) In order to open the discussion, let us ask whether the idea of a perception or intuition of existence is deprived of meaning. "Experience" must be understood in its most inclusive sense: sensorial perception, memory, imagination, sensing, allowing values to appear, mathematical intuition, and so forth. (Of course, a Martian's experience could be richer than ours.) What then becomes most familiar to us in any event of experience? To what do we pay attention? The question does not require a long response: experience is experience of "what" we perceive, sense, and so forth. And as the sum of saying that it is this or that which we experience, we do not say that "there is" (*il y a*) this or that, but that this or that is such or such and that it appears to us as such and such. Experience tells us what things are, not that they are. It certainly would not tell us what they are if there were no things, in the most general sense of the term. In any case, what they are interests us more than the fact that they are and more than the mode in which they are. There is no experience of a pure "there is" (*il y a*). Thus when we say that x is x (when we describe what we perceive, sense, imagine, and so on), the fact that there is x passes totally into the background—it would be a strange consciousness that would be primarily interested in existence or the mode of existence and not interested in what things are.

Some experiences are more complex than others and require a more complex account than many others. If one asks me to speak about what I have dreamed, I must first have mentioned that I dreamed, that is, that something has taken place in my consciousness and only in it, something of which now I can have only a memory, and of which I will attempt to furnish a description in supposing that this "has taken place" or "was." But if we restrict the analysis to sensory perception, then the priority of the content of experience over the existence of the object is properly undeniable. I do not see that there is a table: I see a table. I do not hear that one plays a prelude by Bach: I hear Bach's prelude. All questioning of "existence" (Is there existence outside of my consciousness or is there only pseudo-existence?) is placed between parentheses, we may say, when we see the table or hear the prelude. Being concerned with their ontic status amounts to being unconcerned with what they are. What appears to us "is": as much phenomenality, so much being. The modes of being, however, here present little weight in the logic of experience. We certainly do not "need" for the work of art to have a reality external to consciousness when we contemplate it: its miracle is to manifest its entire being in its being-for-us. When we hear Bach's prelude, nothing exceeds our perception—for once there is adequation between being and being-perceived. Consequently, a judgment of existence would be superfluous or supererogatory. Indisputably we are here dealing with being. Yet what fascinates us and what appears to us, is not the "fact" that something appears to us. And the mode of being in which something appears to us matters little. When a motif of Bach delights us, it matters little whether the prelude is heard or whether it is remembered.

(b) The case of dreams provides us with a pure example. After having dreamed, I know that what appeared to me last night appeared to my consciousness and nowhere else. What I dreamed was not outside of me, although in it I probably remembered or I desired things that were outside of me and generally remain so. But when I dream, two points attract my attention. The first is that I do not "believe" in the extramental existence of what I dream: I am content to dream, and not to examine the content of my dream or the mode of being of what appeared to my dreaming consciousness. The second is that the dream is an experience (we "live in" the dream) and that we can describe this experience (afterwards) as we can describe a perception (of course with greater difficulty). Having dreamed, one can trace a line of demarcation between what one perceives now and what appeared in the dream, between evidence proper to the perceived and evidence proper to the dream. But within the limits of the natural attitude, dream and sensorial perception are only two cases of the same ability: not that of making an impossible experience of existence but of what one could name the "essence" or quiddity, or the *eidos*.

(c) We are therefore constrained from giving the description its full status, hence from the well-known goal of phenomenology. If we attend to that most "natural" of all human acts, sensory perception, we notice right away that to perceive and to describe cannot be dissociated as soon as we are forced to say what we have perceived. If we follow Husserl's meticulous analyses of perception,[13] we are constrained to admit that perception is an eminently synthetic activity, for which we cannot give a discursive account without describing at the same time the conscious activity itself and the perceived thing itself. It matters little to the work of description whether the perceived thing has a "transcendent" existence or not. The perceiving "I" indisputably exists (even if it would be useless for this "I" to prove its own existence to itself or even if its mode of being were endowed with a first evidence). Yet does it matter in any way that the house or the cube or Bach's prelude exist independently of their present appearance? Probably not. Again, what perception undertakes to know, in its way, is the "essence" of the cube, and not the fact that there is a cube or a house here or there, in a situation of exteriority in relation to consciousness. "There is" (*Il y a*) a cube or a house. On the other hand, in the act of perception consciousness has no opinion about the nature of this "there is" (*il y a*) or the manner of being of what appears to it here and now. It cannot have an opinion, since it would form one only if it were to cease to perceive in order to attend to the how of its perception and the how of the perceived. "Essence" hence pushes "existence" into the background. It would not be to exaggerate too much to suggest that in the examples we have highlighted consciousness is not concerned with existence.

This "disinterest in regard to existence" is what we propose to name "spontaneous reduction." To give it this name suggests that the break Husserl established between natural attitude and phenomenological attitude is less radical than he believed. A short *retractio* is required. We have said that we are not born phenomenologists. This is not entirely certain. In fact, we live in a sphere of pre-predicative evidences. "To live" here precedes "to judge." We cannot deny that we believe that there is a world and that there are things outside of us. Yet does this belief or persuasion[14] interfere with our original contact with the cube, the house, or Bach's prelude? It is pretty much evident that they do not. No such belief is present when we listen to the prelude. We listen to the prelude and, in doing so, we cannot do anything else—listening while asking oneself whether the prelude "is" immanent or transcendent to consciousness would be part of a teratology of experience; pondering the mode of being of the prelude while listening to it would make us lose contact with it and in fact we would cease to listen to it. In short: *the attention the thing demands is not attention to its mode of being.* There are cases (and we will get to them) where existence, that is to say extramental reality, counts above all. In any case, the lesson to be learned here is clear enough: We need not take leave of the natural attitude in order to have to do with "essences" in an original fashion. After all, the "principle of principles" comes before the concept of reduction in the *Ideas.*[15] Barring error, the principle applies to any field of experience (the "natural" perception of a house or of a prelude is an "originally giving intuition"). It is hence not necessary to go further for concluding that spontaneous reduction is a "legitimate source of knowledge" and, even more, of phenomenological knowledge. And hence that phenomenology precedes itself in its spontaneous work of reduction.

The presence of an incognito phenomenology at work in our daily manner of dealing with what appears to us therefore must not pass unnoticed. This presence is not that of a project, even less that of a "scientific" project. But to examine the examples that have come to mind, one would search in vain for discontinuity between spontaneous reduction and reduction born of a method; and rather than of discontinuity, one should probably speak of radicalization. Let us say, therefore, that in these cases the phenomenological attitude radicalizes the natural attitude. I place all interest for the ontic status of the prelude between parentheses when I listen to it. Reduction is already present in this, more remarkable for not being the work of the will. And what is present here in the mode of spontaneity is present as methodical work when we start a phenomenological journey. But despite what Husserl believes, we do not discover a new continent when we place all transcendence between parentheses. We have actually "known" this continent as soon as we have begun to "know," as soon as we have begun to be concerned with what things are more than with the fact that they are. Consequently, we were the practitioners of an "anonymous phenomenology."

This conclusion is not without importance. After all, Husserl's true goal never was to add an extra theory on top of the collection of existing theories, but to clear the way for so-called original experiences, that is to say for the sphere of experience that merits this name while preceding all theory.[16] "Passive syntheses," "active syntheses," and so forth—the pre-predicative life of consciousness is complex. But regardless of the way one gives an account of it, our conclusion is valid. The naive look we cast on the majority of things is already a phenomenological gaze. (The case certainly would be different if we were to pass from gaze to description: This would cause our certainty that there are things "out there" to intervene.) Naive experience has to do with phenomena—without phenomena, no experience. And when the philosopher decides to deal exclusively with phenomenality, in agreeing on this term, thus dealing exclusively with what appears in the field of consciousness, phenomenology merely increases in quite a few respects what pre-philosophy spontaneously does in a thousand experiences, and what it has to do if these experiences are to be coherent.

We can also conclude from this that the common distinction between "realistic" phenomenology and "idealistic" phenomenology (the latter emerging in the *Ideas*) is perfectly useless and causes more confusion than it sheds light on the texts.[17] One must not hurry to take Husserl at his word when he tells us in a hyperbolic instant that reduction "annihilates" the world:[18] What the text says is that we no longer "need" the world (in its external reality) in order to describe what appears to us, and if the world finds itself rhetorically "annihilated," it is for the duration of phenomenological work. We could wonder what happens to entities such as numbers, values, or logical laws after the reduction has done its work—after all, the *Logical Investigations* have as their primary goal to forbid the confusion of logic and of psychology. The reply would be reasonably simple. To place the world in parentheses (and in its most general sense by including logical laws and values) does not mean to say that things cease to appear to us. And if we take their immanence to consciousness or their pseudo-existence into account, it is really only so we can turn them into products of conscious life. The law of the excluded middle appears to me "as" the table appears to me: certainly each has an original mode of phenomenality, but both appear and "appearing" must not be understood equivocally. We can decide whether a logical law is "real" and not a product of conscious life. We can make the same decision about the table. But once the work of reduction is accomplished, the two "realities" are still there. For all that, the table and the logical law have not become creatures of consciousness—they are described only as beneficiaries of the hospitality of consciousness, and that is something quite different. Even in his introductory courses on ethics, at a time one commonly supposed him to have succumbed entirely to "idealism," Husserl sticks to the "objectivity" of "values":[19] Values do not occupy a place outside of consciousness but for all that do not come from consciousness. Rather they appear to it as numbers or things do. One says of the "idealist" phenomenology that it worries (almost) exclusively about "what" things are and this is correct. The "essence," the *eidos*, appears only in the field of consciousness, which returns at the very most to defining "appearing." But it is enough, for example, to remember my activities from this morning in order to notice (a) that what I remember is not the product of my mental activity, and (b) that this "exists" only to the extent to which I am now conscious of it. One could have taken pictures of me while I ate breakfast, while I read my mail and worked on an article, but that possesses no pertinence at all—no more than we would contribute to the discussion by saying that the law of the excluded middle is found in any manual of logic. There are things of which no one is conscious, no one has ever dreamed, and so on. Phenomenology is content with dealing with things inasmuch as they appear. And in order to go back to the paradox of spontaneous reductions, one must say that the natural attitude is simultaneously that of a realist and of an idealist. That of a realist, because we believe here (tacitly) in the existence of the world. And that of an idealist, because we largely deal with essences, and because it is not certain that essence "implies existence," or, if one prefers, that a description constrains us to make a judgment about existence.

III

Phenomenality, of course, is not uniform. In the mode of the natural attitude, we are present as those who represent, judge, sense, will, pay attention. In this we deal with things inscribed in space and time, for animals and humans. We allow present, past, and future to appear. Our world arbitrates values, goods, and practices (for example, which glass is for drinking). One counts friends or enemies, the other person here is close or stranger.[20] And one suspects that the "simple thing" that merits no more than a distracted glance of an eye does not appear as tool, friend, or work of art would appear. There is more. The world of natural existence also offers hospitality to what Husserl names the "ideal" worlds. We maintain a "natural," pre-reductive relation with idealities. Theoretical attitudes (observing, explaining, introducing a concept, counting, and so forth) are part of the world of the natural attitude. The furnishings of this world then include ideal entities: numbers, for example. And by adopting an "arithmetic attitude," we do not therefore leave the natural attitude: It remains in the background of all other attitudes. The world populated with things and values, the world populated by other humans, the world populated with theoretical entities: One cannot accuse Husserl of having impoverished the world of the natural attitude and the worlds connected to it. Such a wealth therefore requires that we be concerned with the multiplicity of ways of appearing. Two examples will suffice, of which the first is no more than a remark.

(a) It is self-evident for Husserl that the other human is there with me in the world on which the reduction has not yet exercised its power. Yet we are there without speaking. The other human is simply present, *vorhanden*, in my world. We can speak of "our world." But the fifteen short lines of §29 of the *Ideas* do not tell us more. The problem of intersubjectivity does not exist for the "children of the world." (b) The case of mathematical objects is richer. The number π and table belong to the same set (the somewhat vague group of all phenomena); yet π and the table appear univocally (they are present to consciousness) but differently. There are modes of appearing, and it would not be wise to neglect them: to do so would lead us into a night where all phenomena are gray. We are immemorially familiar with the fact. It is not necessary to demonstrate that tables are not numbers. The case of π furnishes a perfect illustration. Do we believe, after all, that π "exists" in some way or other? The majority among us does not ask the question and follows Wittgenstein's recommendation: We do not wonder about what numbers are but use them for buying apples. Some will not understand the question and describe the symbol instead of "describing" the number it symbolizes. But even if we have only a confused idea of what this number is, we vaguely concede that "there are" numbers and that they are present to consciousness; and what is more, we certainly admit that we do not have to understand their mode of being exactly before trying to describe them. (We know entirely enough of the theory of sets in order to know that a number is a group of sets—but we can say this without being concerned with ontology, if there is one that underlies the theory of sets.) Do we believe in the "existence" of π? Must we agree about this "existence" before speaking of π (or before using it)? Obviously not. And the fact that the mode of being of mathematical objects matters so little to us (except if we practice philosophy of mathematics) proves sufficiently well that we are interested in what they are and not in their pure and simple "reality." Whatever their badly defined existence might be (and we would finish without a doubt by no longer speaking of existence in their regard—"subsistence" would be more prudent), we do not require the least effort to place this existence into parentheses. We do not treat numbers as we treat books placed on a desk or as we treat all that we believe instinctually to be located outside of our consciousness. On one hand, no one is familiar only with things or only with numbers, on the other hand, no one would attribute the same mode of being to things and to numbers. Let us insist in any case: In any "natural" situation (we will soon qualify this "any"), the real appears to us *such* as it is—hence in its quality—and not in a situation of radical exteriority in relation to consciousness. We can therefore describe without appealing to such an exteriority.

So far we have not done a whole lot, except in some way to "demythologize" the reduction. To turn the reduction into a philosophical phantom is something for which one could even believe Husserl himself responsible. On one hand, Husserlian phenomenology has as a goal to pave a way toward our more primitive experiences—*Experience and Judgment* says that better than any other text of the corpus. Yet on the other hand, primitive experiences put the human being into play as a being of consciousness, and a systematic inquiry into consciousness or into subjectivity (at issue here is only a part of our humanity) is the only mode of exploration Husserl knows. Being conscious is not being solitary, and Husserl knows the world and its existence, although his world is not the same as that of Heidegger. But the world is "here" for being known, and knowledge comes (axiomatically) in and by consciousness. And it is not necessary to travel far with Husserl to understand his concern about an accomplished cognitive situation: that is, his concern with a methodical reduction that avoids knowing consciousness only as simple consciousness and that confers on it the highest cognitive powers, those of knowing fully what things are while striking the fact that they are with indifference, wherever they might be. This comes with a precise reservation: that one admit that there is no rupture between natural attitude and phenomenological attitude, and that reducing is also something that we do by instinct in our daily interest for what things are . . . Phenomenology is not something we would have to learn by beginning from nothing. Phenomenological attitude and natural attitude are not separated by a gulf that only a method or a "profession" would permit to cross. The "myth," then, of reduction—of reduction as instituting a new mode of being human and a new mode of dealing with things—must be dispelled.[21]

Certainly not all problems have been resolved by a few well-founded assertions. No science of existence is possible, whether that be according to Husserl or according to common sense, and we can practice only a science of quiddities or of essences. Existence cannot be described and phenomenology is a science of rigorous description. And we can even suggest that existence (at least in Husserl) is no more than existence and that in whatever manner existence and pseudo-existence might well be different (which is not the same thing as being outside and of uniquely possessing an extramental existence), it matters little when the issue is that of deciding *what* things are. Phenomenology has to do with phenomena, phenomena are the real inasmuch as it is given to us, and what is present to us "in flesh and blood" is *what* things are and not the fact that they *are*. One can refuse to agree with this thesis. Putting the "fact of being" between parentheses can damage our description of the outlines, the content, and the meaning of appearance. And in order to make this disagreement altogether respectable, it is enough to raise a question and to respond to it. Are there, indeed, phenomena that resist the work of reduction (ones that lose their meaning if they are submitted to this work)? Is it possible that reduction might imperil the end assigned to it? Is there space in the field of experience for the "irreducible," for realities that elude all reduction? In order to respond to these questions, it would be useless to fall back on a "prejudice in favor of existence." In whatever manner we might interpret Meinong's impossible objects, they have an "essence" without having the least "existence," and the fact that they do not exist and cannot exist is totally devoid of importance: We could always describe the squared circle as being a circle and as being squared; there is then an essence (which one could always analyze as a being and a set of properties) without having an existence. It thus suggests the perfect example of an unbridgeable gap between essence and existence, but its nonexistence is perfectly devoid of interest. And hence we encounter nothing here that we could place between parentheses.

However we would decide in respect to such strange entities, in any case, the majority of things share one or another form of existence: and the question of the "real itself" hence cannot disappear for the only reason that there is also the radically unreal. It is perfectly clear (according to Husserl[22]) that all of what is real (more exactly all that is "world") can be submitted to a work of reduction. Phenomenology suggests that it can be useless to say and think that facts, things, propositions, and so on "exist"; what is philosophically useful is to know what they are; and regarding what they are, we do not learn anything by learning that they exist outside of the field of consciousness and not within the limits of that field. Things appear as they are and that seems to suffice. Yet is that really certain? Possibly this is the case: it seems true of our experience of the work of art. Yet there are always counterexamples. Intersubjectivity (in order to give its Husserlian name to the phenomenon) has a lesson to teach here.

IV

The foundation of intersubjectivity is a notoriously Husserlian problem, and from 1905 to 1935 Husserl engaged in magnificent but sterile efforts[23] to prove the "existence" of the other human, which we have seen is presupposed by the natural attitude. To say that these efforts were sterile amounts to answering a question before having asked it. It is not inadvertently, however, that we reach a verdict so quickly. Who could really doubt that another human appearing to us exists, thus that mere pseudo-existence interior to consciousness is not sufficient? And more precisely, who could describe this appearing by placing all existence between parentheses? We can only have a lateral or subsidiary perception of the other human, which authorizes us to describe it as we describe all we perceive at the same time. In this case, the other human appears as an object in the landscape: neither more nor less. And if that is the case—and in numerous situations it is incontestably the case—its phenomenality would be similar and often identical to any other. Implicitly comparing another person and, for example, a motorcycle, we can legitimately be interested in the style (*l'allure*) of the one and the speed (*l'allure*) of the other. The other human is a "this," the motorcycle is a "that," but the two have (roughly speaking) the same manner of appearing; and, one must hence admit that this same mode of phenomenality (the mode of phenomenality for which it suffices to notice that something appears in the horizon of the world) includes the possibility of putting between parentheses the existence of both—spontaneously, we do not "need" that the other person and the motorcycle exist. It is enough to perceive them. But, do we always perceive the other human in a lateral or subsidiary manner? Do people always appear to us as any being of the world appears to us? It is Levinas's phenomenological merit to have attempted to show that this is never the case, and to have demonstrated how it happens that this would not be the case. Let us look at the proof.

In Levinas's analysis, the other human does not appear on the phenomenological scene as a body regarding which I ask myself whether it is a flesh and hence another me, but as something regarding which I do not have the time to ask what it is. In appearing, the other human cannot become an object among all those with which phenomenology is occupied and that it describes (except as a perversion of the meaning of its appearing), hence an object of which we could ask what its exact status or its mode of being is, for we are "taken hostage" by it as soon as it is there: the other appears as the one to whom we are obligated, precisely, as an other than us (*un autre que nous*) to whom we owe a duty. This appearing, which is no more, is not to be treated as the condition of possibility of an intersubjective experience (the other person does not appear as a potential "you"), and here does not have anything to do with the solemn reality of an "epiphany" (with a presence or a phenomenality such that only the face of a human could possess it) that places into parentheses all reality other than it—the world disappears when the other human intervenes. There are certainly dreams and hallucinations (Levinas never takes their possibility into account). These dreams and hallucinations, however, do not possess the character of an epiphany. Rather, they lack a characteristic that is primordial: that of the event of speech (*parole*). The phenomenality of the other human is actually that of a saying (*un dire*), and of a prescriptive saying. As soon as it is there (as soon as I become conscious of its presence), we must hear it say, "you shall not kill." Could we then say that we only have to do with an "essence" or an *eidos*? The logic appropriate to such an appearing forbids us to respond affirmatively. We can certainly describe "what" we face here, as we can describe whatever it is that appears to us from the world. But for a phenomenology (like that of Levinas) that attempts to confer on ethics the status of first philosophy, we would commit a major error. What we describe in this manner would not be what *happens* when we see the face of a human in the way in which it has to be seen. The other human comes from beyond the field of consciousness (and that is certainly no less remarkable). More importantly, it would be (almost) devoid of meaning to be content with saying that the other "is." The other appears and "speaks." Even more, he does not appear to us as such if we do not hear what he wants to say to us. He certainly says little (however much Levinas has to say about him). But this little weighs with a great theoretical weight; and that constrains us to admit that there are things outside of consciousness that cannot be enlisted among the entities that we describe so much better when the reduction has done its work.

Hence, it requires little attention here to prove that reduction—the reduction of the other human to his existence in consciousness—would be a denial of humanity, and that Husserl's texts are aporetic because Husserl is perpetually tempted to deny humanity to the other person or to load constant doubts on its subject. Intersubjectivity—the word suffices to say it—is an issue of mutual transcendence. The other human certainly also has a noematic "existence," as do all intentional objects, and it would not be wise to be blind to that fact. The other human, however, is not just any other object. And if we cannot deny that it is indisputably true that "any object whatsoever can have noematic existence," in this case this truth is almost devoid of pertinence: it speaks to us of the other human inasmuch as she does not appear or is not received as being another me. What would remain of the *alter ego* if we were to decide to submit it to reduction? Would she *be able* to appear to us if her existence were only a pseudo-existence? One requires little philosophy and little common sense to give the right response: What would remain after reduction has done its work would no longer be the other human. The event of speech (*parole*) that reveals its presence (its "epiphany") would be quite simply prohibited.

We certainly have not dealt with every question. After all, numerous alterities, maybe the majority of them, survive reduction without problem, and we can find ourselves peacefully in their company once the phenomenological work of description is finished. We do not know them better in a natural, non-reduced attitude than we know them in the mode of reduction. Reduction can give us better access to what they are, but reduction does not become established (phenomenological work is not coextensive with life). Reduction does, however, permit us to concentrate on what is given to be known—that is to say on what presents itself to intuition and to it alone.[24] The encounter with the other human, if it takes place in conformity with Levinasian descriptions, hence constitutes an exception (note that we do not speak of *the* exception). We see the face of a human as ("as") we see a portrait, and in a certain way we look at this face as we look at the portrait. Yet we have underlined a fact of primary importance: To place the transcendent reality of the work of art within parentheses is the best manner of allowing it to appear as such; we need not be concerned with the ontic status of the portrait. Can we therefore say that we notice a human face as we notice a portrait? We cannot refuse to say that we "see" (*voyons*) and "look at" (*regardons*) the other, and it would be mere rhetoric if we were to suggest that we are seen and looked at, in this case, more than we see and look at. And nevertheless we stumble here on a vision where seeing encounters the irreducible—something that cannot fall under the blow of the reduction without losing all of its reality and signification. In this case the phenomenon exceeds and prohibits all reduction—or rather it condemns it, when we insist on practicing it, by no longer being concerned with the thing "itself." To say it differently, the evidence proper to the phenomenon in question is evidence of what refuses reduction. Such evidence is certainly precarious, and Husserl's prudent approach is still possible. It is a perpetual possibility to utilize the awkward concept of "empathy," *Einfühlung*, to forge access to intersubjectivity. The epiphany of which Levinas speaks is not essential (if it were essential, why would we need to have an ethics?). And it is hence a perpetual possibility not to notice that we deal here with a phenomenon that is an event of speech and that the one facing me here and now demands my solicitude much more than he needs to be perceived and described. But if we admit this possibility, we must be careful: our "intuition" will not be "originary" but crippled; we will not have the right to treat it as a source of knowledge.

V

One case of irreducibility leads to another, and we must now imagine a problem much vaster than Husserlian phenomenology, that of the possible reducibility of language. In the posthumous texts as well as in the fifth *Cartesian Meditation*, language is notoriously absent—the other body that one must prove to be a flesh faces us in silence. (Furthermore, we encounter such an absence of language again in Levinas: the described "epiphany" is an event of language, but one in which no word needs to be uttered.) The goal of the fifth *Cartesian Meditation* is to find a foundation for a "transcendental we," but neither I nor the other I is here required to speak. One ought to be surprised by this. We encounter (or rather we do not encounter) throngs of humans to whom or with whom we do not speak (or in regard to whom we do not manifest any "solicitude"[25]). But when we speak (albeit only for asking the time or exchanging rushed hellos), no sane spirit would deny that we, an empirical we that does not seem to require the least transcendental foundation, is there and certainly there. There are cases where we speak to very complex machines or where these machines speak to us. There is maybe even a certain form of linguistic interaction between us and these machines. But we do not *encounter* machines. We know that they are machines and this makes their situation rather different from that of the "speaking animals" in C. S. Lewis who indisputably hold the rank of persons. Humans, on the other hand, are present as so many possibilities of encounter. There are silent encounters. Linguistic (inter)action, however, is paradigmatic of humans' encounter with each other. (Of the encounter of one human with another human: We can certainly develop the concept of a divine-human encounter, but it will imply no linguistic interaction, or rather little and only in exceptional circumstances.) And when the other human speaks to me (whether for asking me the time or calling for help), she certainly possesses noematic existence (for the good reason that anything that appears to us acquires such a status); but, and it is on this point that one must insist, she exists no less in an "irreducible" mode. What I am told is not said in order to be described, but to be heard and to receive a response. Its mode of appearing therefore is such that if I did not believe that these words come from somewhere else and do not have my consciousness as their sole place, I would not really be able to describe what appears to me. We can certainly submit everything to a work of reduction, the words spoken to us just like everything else. Yet alterity is still there after this work has been accomplished: What exists in pseudo-fashion in my consciousness is distinct from consciousness itself, as the customer is distinct from the restaurant where she dines. There is more when we are concerned with the alterity of words—with the words the other addresses to us. The most antiphenomenological of all philosophers who has not read a single line of Husserl, Wittgenstein, was completely ignorant of the problem of intersubjectivity, first because he simply knew nothing of consciousness and subjectivity and then because the "we" is evident and native for him;[26] and even if he had heard someone speak of consciousness or would have wanted to speak in terms of consciousness, he would have indisputably held to the existence of an original and native "we." That is not to suggest that Wittgenstein was right. Consciousness is not a pseudo-entity, even if we can give it other names. And as soon as consciousness has the right to enter the scene, reduction is always possible, spontaneous or methodological. This is said, however, in order to signal that there are phenomena that lose all their phenomenal meaning if they are submitted to a work of reduction, in order to signal that the "empirical we," whose reality cannot be denied except in pathological cases, is primordially constructed in language and that its construction resists all reduction. (Heideggerian) "everydayness" would furnish ample ammunition to any consciousness practicing reduction. Those we pass on the way to the university have no "need," of some sort, to be more than "what" they are in consciousness. We need not "care" about the majority among them. Yet even everydayness hides semantic transactions, and these are phenomena that extend beyond their phenomenality, or whose phenomenality proves to be irreducible. We can place the "real" existence of a pure and simple piece of information between parentheses. If someone tells us in passing that snow is white, we have no need to believe in the existence of the passerby, or in believing that the words have arrived from outside of our consciousness, in order to understand what "snow is white" is supposed to mean. The meaning is the same, whether the words come from outside or inside our field of consciousness. Speech, however, such as it enters into the constitution of the "we," is not merely a simple given of information. It says that an other (*un autre*) is present who speaks to me. What he says to me can be insignificant, but the fact that he speaks to me, from himself, outside of me, is strictly original. And if the outside-me—transcendence—is original, the conclusion comes quickly: putting it into parentheses would be to act in ignorance.

A good way to prove this further would be to outline a comparison between what we could name "my words" and "your words," or "my speaking" and "your speaking." I hear the words I pronounce and the words you pronounce (certainly in quite a different manner). I am conscious of one and the other. Yet I am not content merely to hear (*entendre*) words, for words have a meaning and are formulated in order to be understood. I must say that I "understand" (*entends*) what I want to say and what you want to say, hence that I hear (*entends*) meanings. Yet do your words appear to me as mine appear to me? The response is "no" without qualification. I understand my words and I understand yours, although I am conscious of what I *want* to say and of what you *want* to say. We have a language in common. And what we cannot forget (what we would never forget in a life lived in the "natural attitude" except in a psychopathological case, and what we do not have the right to forget when we adopt a "phenomenological attitude") is that this "we" can in no case be abolished—and that reduction would amount to abolishing it. "Essence" in this case implies "existence," and more precisely, existence transcendent to consciousness. We can place the world between parentheses, Husserl tells us, but the words spoken to us are not a part of the world (they belong to the world only as sounds made by the words), any more than the face of the other (*autrui*) in Levinas is not a being of the world. And even if we concede a partial legitimacy to Husserl's work on intersubjectivity, we do so because "your words" and "your body" are part of two distinct groups of phenomena. I can wonder about your body, or rather about this body here—if it is a matter of *your* body the question of intersubjectivity is really already settled—and ask whether it is a flesh, not a three-dimensional solid among others but a body that is an I. In respect to your words, on the other hand, no such question can arise. What I am told here is intelligible only to the extent to which it comes from outside. I have an exclusive "opening" to what comes from exterior of my consciousness. (Just as I have an exclusive possibility of harboring everything coming from the outside in the interior of the field of consciousness.) This opening allows me to manifest an exclusive interest in "what" is said to me more than the "fact" that it is said. To forget one for the other, however, would be a major phenomenological error in the present case: It would be to neglect that it belongs to "the fundamental mode of objectivity" of the words said to me, that their "fundamental mode of existence" is one that cannot be described except as coming from outside of my consciousness. The faithfulness of phenomenology to its project requires that it would be capable of recognizing the irreducible.

Because reduction is often spontaneous, and because this spontaneity is a manner of knowing, a phenomenology that would be ignorant of the reduction at bottom would be pre-phenomenological, that is to say pre-philosophical. In the majority of experiences (*Erlebnisse*), the existence of what comes to experience is of no interest to us. We believe in the existence of the world, but this belief is not fit for knowledge or for rigorous knowledge. These affirmations, however, are not valid universally, and we have come up against their limits. The reduction had better be perpetually possible (the only exception would be that of our body, of which we do not believe that it exists, but of which we truly possess an immemorial knowing). We can, however, misjudge it and turn it into pseudo-experience. And for this reason, we would be wise not to say that we are content to "believe" in the existence of the other or her words, and not to posit that existence, in this case, cannot be put between parentheses. (Husserlian) phenomenology hence encounters one of its decisive proofs when it has to do with the irreducible. We are able not to know (or we are able to give ourselves the theoretical means not to know) that the irreducible exists, and we can describe the irreducible as we describe all of what lets itself be submitted to reduction without any loss of meaning. But our description will be false. And when coming up against the irreducible and certainly admitting that not everything is irreducible (the irreducible is rare), we can describe correctly when we recognize the radical exteriority of what we describe. I believe "naturally" that your words come from beyond my consciousness. But there is something more interesting: We can also not conceive a "phenomenological attitude" that would not maintain the same belief, would be founded on it, and would furnish it with all necessary credentials. We do not hear only words, that's all there is to it, but also words pronounced by another human. We encounter in the other (*autrui*) a phenomenon that forbids all constitution of our I as a transcendental I. And if this is the case, the empirical "we" no longer needs to be elevated to the dignity of a transcendental "we." The same "we" puts in a token appearance in daily ("natural") experience and in philosophical experience. (This fact confirms furthermore the native project of Husserlian phenomenology.)

Pre-philosophical experience is not ignorant of the reduction, philosophical experience is or should be familiar with the irreducible—and the two dimensions cannot be disjointed. Consciousness is consciousness of what can always be reduced to its "essence," consciousness is also consciousness of what would remain unintelligible if we did not agree that it is essential to it to come from the outside. We have no "need" that the painting exists outside my consciousness: it is given without remainder to our experience. But we would not be able to hear what the clear meaning of words "would mean," the words pronounced by the other (*autrui*), if we did not admit or intuitively believe that they come from outside of our consciousness and can only be described exactly as coming from this outside. For all that, we have not finished with the reality of the irreducible, and a final question must be asked. In his programmatic exposition of the reduction, Husserl posits firmly that even the existence of God must fall under the blow of reduction. The *epochê* is "universal,"[27] and this affirmation is to be taken in the strict sense. And if this is the case (if phenomenology does not deal with a region of experience but with all possible experience that it puts into play as "outside of me"), then divine "essence" would have to be described outside of all belief in the "existence" of God and, by believing it to be the goal which guides the process of reduction, this description would maybe be the best. Yet, can we really speak of God by placing his existence between parentheses?

VI

A first response would consist in saying that a certain form of reduction is theologically lawful and more than lawful. One commonly says that it was Calvin's merit to have raised the question "who is God" (*quis sit Deus*) before "is there a God" (*an sit Deus*). But having said this, it is as certain as it is possible that the second question remains lawful and, even more, that the first is only asked from within belief: the God of whom one asks who he is, is a god of whom one believes that he is. This is not an existence that would be that of an existent, which would treat God like a stone or like works of art. And when we wonder who God is, then the best terms of an inquiry are probably those of the theologian whose first lines are devoted to distinguishing between the "existence" of God, the "reality" of God and his "relation with us," in order to devote a first chapter to "God for me"; "¿Quién eres tú para mí? ¿Quién soy para tí?"[28] That is a good entry into theology. And if that is also good phenomenology, it can only be a phenomenology that recognizes the reality of the irreducible (here, that of the "you") and knows itself powerless to put aside the transcendent reality of what it describes. A reduction that wants to have universal ambitions could not realize them. These stumble over the experience of the irreducible, here that of a "you" or of a "Thou," of which we can certainly make a "he," but regarding which we certainly cannot abandon the belief that he exists outside the field of our consciousness, be it only because of concern for method and for faithfulness to the "profession" of philosopher. We cannot wonder whether anything exists out there if we do not know what that something is. The idea of a judgment of existence that would precede all description is an absurd idea.

And even if we believe vaguely or firmly in the "real" existence of a thousand beings who, according to all probability, are not content with pseudo-existing in our consciousness (I do not believe in the real existence of centaurs, but I believe in the real existence of the statue of a centaur as I believe in the real existence of my books), we are spontaneously interested in what they are and not in the fact that they are. Could one, however, add that the existence of God is of slender methodological importance, and that this existence matters only after we have agreed on "what" God is? It is a trivial fact that we can describe nonexisting gods. We are not interested in the existence of Epicurus' gods. But let us be careful: We certainly are not interested in them, but we also no longer foster belief concerning them, or rather we believe spontaneously that they do not exist—and when Husserl prescribes to put our beliefs in parentheses, the "belief-that-there-is-not" is not included in the ensemble of beliefs. Therefore, when we ask ourselves if there is a god, or if God exists, the question obviously cannot receive a response as long as we cannot furnish an elementary description of "God." If we pass from such a rudimentary interrogation to theological work, however, we do not have far to go in order to discover that the theologian does not wonder whether God exists. Theology is thoroughly descriptive (or narrative, the two largely intersect here). But it is descriptive at the interior of this act of belief. In his *Confessions*, Augustine speaks of God in speaking to God. Anselm inserts a philosophical-theological argument within a prayer. If one must first ask who God is, it is by presupposing tacitly that he is. We are situated there outside reduction.

The fate of God and that of the other human hence are partially linked, at least for an elementary analysis. An objection that we have met with in the space of a parenthesis now demands to receive a response. Whoever says "Thou" or "He" says irreducible alterity. But, the cases are not lacking—dreams, hallucinations—where the "Thou" appears to us without this apparition existing anywhere else than in consciousness. Dream and hallucinations add grist to the mill and this grist is not the product of our psychical activity. We dream of Peter and Peter is not the pure product of our dream work: there is a Peter, outside of us, whom the dream remembers with variable fidelity. Can we consequently put aside everything that is not the immanent content of the life of dreams, in the same way in which we can, as Husserl tells us, put aside all reality of the world? Do we therefore foster belief concerning what appears in the dream? The analysis of the dream tells us that the dream is interpreted by starting from what is exterior to it, hence for example the relations we maintain with Peter. Yet the analysis is posterior to the dream. One point is certain in any case.

The dream is lived. Although in a marginal manner, it is a real being in the world. And if Peter did not appear to me in the dream as he appeared to me when he visited me outside the dream, it is still the case that to some extent I live both appearances and that the former can only be lived (because there is nothing outside of consciousness). The time of the dream is not that of phenomenological work. Yet phenomenology can be instructed by the dream and by experiences that resemble it. The other (*Autrui*) can address me without this speech coming to me from outside of me. More exactly, consciousness can arbitrate words that are strictly immanent to it, that do not come from the outside, and that do not appear less as words of the other. I dream of Peter without "believing" when I dream that the content of my dream, images and words, is really exterior to me. Yet I "believe" sufficiently in the reality of my dreams for these to inspire fear in me, for example. "Believing," believing, can we abandon the quotation marks? That is not certain. A memory makes me happy or sad—I am here conscious of something else—nevertheless it does not imply any belief: I certainly believe in the existence of the world, but I do not believe that I remember. The memory is content to take possession of me. This taking of possession is its proper mode of appearing. And if the memory or the dream (and we know that the two are not totally independent) lead to the fact that we are addressed or that we address someone, such an event of speech escapes the opposition of the reducible and the irreducible. It is not reducible, because we are incapable of assigning it a place in the "world."[29] And it is not irreducible, because it is from us ourselves that both the dream and the words addressed to us in the dream originate. In many traditions the divine obviously encounters humans in dreams and the hypothesis cannot simply be excluded. But if this were the case, then we definitely "need" the word received within the dream to be an irreducible word. It therefore could not be contained or described without admitting absolutely that we cannot know anything about it without giving our agreement to its mode of appearing, which is that of being given to us from outside of consciousness and of appearing by certifying to consciousness that it really comes from this outside.

We have relinquished speaking of existence, that of the world, of its furnishings, of God, and by speaking of him with abundance we might create the impression that we have spoken in a univocal manner. "Existence" of God, "existence" of my pipe, can the two be said univocally? One perceives intuitively that the answer must be "no"; and thus that certain existences appear to us as "reducible" and others as "irreducible"; this intuitive certainty merits that one regard it as established. Barth, who is often right, remarks in his commentary on Anselm that the error of

Gaunilon is that of having believed that the existence of God is an existence among all others and a particular case of the general fact of existing.[30] The remark can be intensified, and we can observe also that it is really not certain that divine phenomenality, if there is a divine phenomenality, would be a particular case of the general fact of appearing. In respect to what kind of phenomena can we then say that they engage a divine initiative and responsibility? The beginning of a solution, or at least the conceptuality that puts us on the way to a solution, is found in Husserl himself. If "to every fundamental species of objectivities . . . belongs a fundamental species of 'experience,' of evidence,"[31] really only one step is necessary for suggesting that the Absolute does not appear to us without possessing a fundamental mode of phenomenality, and for enriching this suggestion by saying that such a mode of phenomenality includes irreducibility. An experience that we could not describe without being constrained to acknowledge the existence of what falls under the blow of this experience, such would be—would be—the coming of God to consciousness.

Nevertheless, suggestions and hypotheses do not have the value of demonstration, and they lead us to even more questions. Can we say first of all that we are familiar with God as our natural attitude makes us familiar with the world? And what there is of dysanalogy, does it reside in the fact that the existence of the world can be placed between parentheses while this cannot be done at all for the existence of God? It does not help (here) to appeal to spiritual experience. Our theology is never founded on the limited basis of our experience of God. We can feel his presence, or what we take as such, but we can just as much feel the presence of the "divine" of which Heidegger speaks, or worse, we can confuse one with the other. Emotions can act as consciousness, but they can despairingly lack identifiable and describable objects. God must not be assimilated too quickly to the sacred or to the numinous. When a supposedly "religious" experience takes possession of us, it will be a good existential and theoretical strategy not hastily to give the impression that something has happened that comes from the exterior of consciousness, on one hand, and on the other that it comes provided with a divine caution: one must first humbly ask what that thing was. And it is at this point that we see the possibility of a reduction reappear: On one hand as the spontaneous work of consciousness, on the other hand as the task of method.

(a) Does not experiential language presuppose the existence of God? It is clear that it does not do so, or in any case does not do so in all cases. The (sad) characteristic of "religious experience" is that it is always *my* experience, in a way that does not forbid that my experience might also be ours,[32] but that does not imply the integration of mine into ours in any way. And for as much as the religious human lives primordially "in" his or her experiences, the intentionality of religious consciousness does not lack objects—but the philosophies of religion are destined never to agree on the transcendent reality of objects. We have just said that it belongs to the group of elementary theological laws that our theology extend beyond our "spiritual" experience. Religious experience must be described (as any other experience must). It must be described as we describe any event that takes place within consciousness. Maybe I would be right to say that I have perceived a divine presence in a manner as convincing as I perceive human presences, hence presences that require being known as putting pressure on me from outside myself (and of which the description cannot be taken to the very end without conceding that we deal here with the irreducible), and all reduction would become impossible. But how can I (or can we) know that I have (or that we have) reason to appeal to the irreducible? We have only one coherent response at our disposal: confessing the limits of all religious contacts and ceasing to believe blindly in the witness of sensing (or of sentiment, and so forth). Phenomenology cannot be harmonized on this point with theology and the experience of the same is not an evidently theological given. Phenomena may seem supplied with a divine guarantee, but rarely are. It is not forbidden for the Absolute to "touch" the human, but the phenomenological criteria that would allow us to identify such "touches" are (almost) entirely lacking. And if "religious" experience furnishes us with ample provisions of phenomena, what they give us can be described without us really "needing" to attribute to it an extramental origin, and a fortiori a divine origin.

(b) Rather than believe ourselves engaged in an aporetic exercise, let us take a retrospective glance at Husserl's remark according to which the transcendent reality of the world is useless for us, does not respond to any "need," if we want to get to know the world philosophically. Do we, then, need God to exist in order to have (philosophical) knowledge of God? Or rather, is it necessary for us to accept the existence of God even within a phenomenological attitude, as we have seen that it is necessary to accept the existence of the other? We perceive this necessity intuitively. But we can also manifest the coherence with which it imposes itself. One reason, more important than any other: to place the existence of God between parentheses would not amount to placing "belief" (*une croyance*) in parentheses, but in placing a "faith" (*une foi*) between parentheses. When one speaks of faith, one certainly does not say less than belief. The logic of faith, however, exceeds that of belief, and it is here that one must score a point (a theological point that is also a phenomenological point). To a great extent our beliefs link us to the real that is outside us, to the world, to everything that populates it—and the great protophenomenologist Reid was right to insist on the fact that we are "believers" or "credulous" by virtue of birth. Yet we do not need much theology, or much philosophy, in order to notice that "I believe in God" says more than "I believe that God exists independently of experiences which manifest him to me," and that we cannot put faith between brackets as we can place belief within parentheses. "I believe in God" includes a judgment of existence: *there is* (*il y a*) a God, and this *there is* (*il y a*) is exterior to the field of consciousness. Yet there is more. Faith, in order to cite the classics, is a matter of illumination: what appears to us dictates the condition under which it can be perceived. And this condition is that "believing-that" cannot be disassociated from "believing-in" or, to say it more crassly, that we "need" God to exist if we want to say who he is. We can say that p is and even dissect p in placing between parentheses our belief that p is—after all, snow is white even if we abstain from believing in its extramental reality. Yet let us suppose that we believe in x (whether x is Peter or God). Can we then separate the identity of x (its *eidos*) and our belief in x, which implies (irreducibly) that x benefits from an extramental existence? We cannot do so—for if we could do so, we would make ourselves incapable of doing justice to the mode in which x, jointly, is and appears. We can describe the number x and put aside our belief in the existence of x: we have no "need" of this belief in order to carry out our work of description. But if x is Peter or God and, at the point where we are, if it is God, then an attempt at description that would forget that God appears to us as "credible," and that his credibility is essential to him, would be doomed to failure.[33] What we said of intersubjectivity is here essential again: We cannot speak of God rigorously without doing justice to a phenomenality that forbids all reduction. Barth was right: the existence of God is not "an" existence. If Barth reads Anselm correctly, which is probably the case, the existence of God is essentially irreducible. No "real distinction" of essence and of existence can be found to take place here. And the reason why it is good theological method not to ask "*an sit Deus*" before asking "*quis sit*" becomes clearer: demanding "*quis sit*" is the work of faith, and faith—is it really necessary to insist on this?—"needs" God to exist before speaking of him. No spontaneous reduction can find lodging here. In fact, a methodological reduction would be illegitimate, namely because it would be mistaken about a mode of appearing; its work would hence be that of a phenomenology unfaithful to its aim.

We are in no way already at the end of our brief inquiry. We have defended a thesis: What one understands by "experiences of God" can be reduced to the contents of experience, and the existence of God, of the gods, of the divine, and so on is then superfluous to the description—which therefore comes back to saying very classically that to describe an experience does not amount to describing the transcendent object of this experience. We have defended a second thesis: God is only known in the element of faith, and all description carried out by the government of a reduction risks missing a fundamental trait of our experience of God that is already obvious in the analysis of intersubjectivity: to know that what is at stake here is an encounter and, more precisely, an event of speech that requires response. We have always believed that there is a world (and have furthermore believed in the existence of the other), we have not always believed "in God." And to attempt to give an account of the type of phenomenon that "I believe in" represents, we discover that in this case reduction is impossible or would disfigure the phenomenon. The right description, in this case as in that of the intersubjective "encounter," requires the transcendent reality of what it describes. Neither the existence of the other nor the existence of God can be put aside: not due to a personal decision or by *petitio principii*, but because to call these existences phenomenologically indispensable to description is merely the right response to their proper mode of phenomenality. There is no doubt at all that our encounter with the other, our experience of "other words," and our encounter with God differ notably. The first two cases have to do with immediacy, and the third has to do with mediated experience. The belief in God is founded on texts, on indications, on motifs of credibility, and so forth, while the other human faces me in all transparency and evidence, or almost (not having seen this "almost" is Levinas's mistake). Yet in the two cases, what appears to us hence appears to us in the mode of an event of speech. "Do not kill me," "follow me," the two injunctions (of which we certainly do not pretend that they are the only two possible transcriptions of such an event of speech) have a lot in common. Was Levinas right to use an over-theologized vocabulary ("epiphany," "parousia") in order to describe an event that is not theological? Maybe—his idiosyncratic use suggests at least, and the suggestion is correct, that the encounter of human by human must be described in terms very close to divine-human encounter. We certainly do not encounter the other, whom we see, as we encounter God, whom we do not see—*latens deitas*. . . . It is maybe lawful to describe the presence of the other as "parousia-like" (nothing is concealed when the other human appears to me and whom I recognize as such), but it would be unlawful to describe the presence of God in these terms. Yet in both cases, presence and existence can only be thought as irreducible. And if we were to decide that we have no "need" for the God of whom we speak to be a God to whom we speak, the experience on which we were to base what we would say of God would be more than suspect.[34] The reduction has its domain, in which it carries its fruits. We have no other ambition than to draw attention to the limits of this domain (not all appearing lends itself to reduction) and to furnish an example or two of the phenomenological work that knows itself devoted to the irreducible.

Translated by Christina M. Gschwandtner

"it / is true"

KEVIN HART

Phenomenology, as properly practiced, is a response to what is given rather than a single procedure that can be perfected. Responses can take various forms—essays, treatises, paintings, conversations, narratives, plays, and poems—each of which has constraints that, whether respected or transgressed, inflect phenomenological observation in different ways. Literature certainly gives us a range of examples for understanding phenomenology. When reading Italo Calvino's *Invisible Cities* (1972) we see exactly what "free phantasy" is, and when watching *Othello* we grasp the *eidos* of jealousy far better than in reading a paper about that obsessive state in a psychology journal.[1] Yet literature also does phenomenology itself, though usually more implicitly than explicitly. Has any philosopher performed the *epoché* and phenomenological reduction more effectively than Franz Kafka, supreme artist of the opening sentence? When observing the world through K., we recognize that consciousness is implicitly founded by what it constitutes. Similarly, William Faulkner performs a startling phenomenology of time consciousness in *The Sound and the Fury* (1929) without knowing anything about Edmund Husserl's reflections on the topic in the ninth volume of the *Jahrbuch für Philosophie und phänomenologische Forschung* (1928).[2] And Francis Ponge, perhaps the closest we get to a poet explicitly interested in phenomenology, attends to the things themselves in *Le parti pris des choses* (1942).

I would like to thank Gerald L. Bruns, Geoffrey Hartman, Michael L. Morgan, Michael A. Signer, and Henry Weinfield for their comments on earlier versions of this essay.

The list could be continued, the names of the authors varied. We have competing analyses of the work of art from diverse phenomenological perspectives—Roman Ingarden and Martin Heidegger, Maurice Merleau-Ponty and Mikel Dufrenne—but we have still to learn all that we can from Husserl when in 1907, just before giving the lectures that would comprise *The Idea of Phenomenology*, he wrote of the closeness of the phenomenological and the aesthetic gazes.[3] I would like to center my reflections on this proximity. At the same time, I would like to touch on the "theological turn" that phenomenology is said to have taken in recent years, and to do so not with the question of divine transcendence in mind but with the central event for western religion of the last century—the unique horror of the Shoah—an event that unleashes many questions for Christian theology as well as Jewish thought, questions with which I will not directly engage here. Throughout, I want to remain close to one poem. Its title: "September Song." Its author: Geoffrey Hill. It first appeared in *Stand* in 1967, and it was placed in Hill's second full volume of verse, *King Log*, in 1968.[4]

Why this poem? Not because it was written out of an overt engagement with phenomenology or has been situated in its wake. To my knowledge, Hill has never quoted or alluded to Husserl or any of those who continue or redirect the philosopher's thought. Literary criticism, as he practices it, is a modification of British empiricism. I choose the poem because it is a "poem of our climate," if I may borrow an expression of Wallace Stevens's. We know that Stevens often composed with the Oxford English Dictionary close at hand, sifting through etymologies and unusual senses of words, and perhaps when he wrote "The Poems of Our Climate" he had in mind the Greek root of "climate," *klineio* or "slope."[5] Geoffrey Hill's "September Song" is a poem about the slope of our times, a precarious decline that falls in several directions at once. It is a poem of and about the "moral weather" of our culture, his part in it as well as ours. It is one of the first testaments to the Shoah in English, coming just a year after the publication of Richard L. Rubenstein's *After Auschwitz* (1966) and in the very year of the Six-Day War.[6]

SEPTEMBER SONG
born 19.6.32—deported 24.9.42

Undesirable you may have been, untouchable
you were not. Not forgotten
or passed over at the proper time.

As estimated, you died. Things marched,
sufficient, to that end.

Just so much Zyklon and leather, patented
terror, so many routine cries.

(I have made
an elegy for myself it
is true)

September fattens on vines. Roses
flake from the wall. The smoke
of harmless fires drifts to my eyes.

This is plenty. This is more than enough.[7]

ᘓ

"Literature has never been as 'philosophical' as it has in the twentieth century," says Merleau-Ponty; "never has it reflected as much upon language, truth, and the significance of the act of writing."[8] Why does Merleau-Ponty place "philosophical" in scare quotes? Presumably to respect the distance between literature and philosophy, and to allow a philosophical mode of activity that is not philosophy as such. Derrida would agree. He tells us that modernists share a common situation: "they are inscribed in a *critical* experience of literature," he says. "They bear within themselves, or we could also say in their literary act they put to work, the same one, but each time singular and put to work otherwise: 'What is literature?' or 'Where does literature come from?' 'What should we do with literature?'"[9] Modernist writing may not create concepts or adduce arguments but it folds questions of a philosophical type into the literary models that it receives and revises. As Derrida implies, the border between "literature" and "criticism" becomes blurred and divided in modernist writing; and if that is the case for Eliot and Joyce, it is all the more so for a belated modernist such as Hill, and especially so in a poem such as "September Song." Critical objections to writing poetry after Auschwitz, to the morality of representing the Shoah, if it is even possible to do so, must be engaged by the poem itself.

Derrida goes farther, and he talks about literature's rapport with philosophy in general and with phenomenology in particular. When he does so, he makes liberal use of quotation marks, sometimes to hold the word at a distance and sometimes to show that is a quotation:

Poetry and literature provide or facilitate "phenomenological" access to what makes of a thesis a *thesis as such*. Before having a philosophical content, before being or bearing such and such a "thesis," literary experience, writing or reading, is a "philosophical" experience which is neutralized or neutralizing insofar as it allows one to think the thesis; it is a nonthetic experience of the thesis, of belief, of position, of naivety, of what Husserl called the "natural attitude." The phenomenological conversion of the gaze, the "transcendental reduction" he recommended is perhaps the very condition (I do not say natural condition) of literature. (46)

Notice that Derrida begins by saying "Poetry *and* literature" (my emphasis). They are not one and the same. Literature becomes a way of framing poetry, prose fiction, and the drama only in the late eighteenth century, at least in Britain. It is a modern formation, and while it impinges on how we think of poetry, it is at heart alien to poetry, which is always a making although not always a fiction. Since I will be answerable to a poem, I will talk only of poetry, while remaining mindful that modern poetry, including modernist works, strives with and against its framing as literature.

We might wonder why Derrida places the word "phenomenological" in scare quotes. He does so because a poem performs the *epochê* and transcendental reduction without, in most cases, the author having any deep familiarity with either. A poet is already doing phenomenology as soon as he or she starts to write, for composition—at least the sort of composition we call poetry—suspends the natural attitude, and shows the writer's intentional consciousness to be concretely embedded in the horizons that "common sense" occludes. With the first line, the passage from mundane experience to phenomenological truth is already taking place. The poet is able to think in and with a given situation rather than to use thought to manipulate it to one or more ends. We might add, after reading Michel Henry, that a poet also does phenomenology in a non-intentional manner, in attending to the invisible, in responding to his or her auto-affection, in describing sensations and evoking the truth of feeling.[10] Derrida says nothing of this, confining himself to the experience of writing, of which literary inscription would be exemplary, and which is precisely what dislodges the phenomenology of Husserl, "self-presence of absolute transcendental consciousness or the indubitable *cogito*, etc."[11]

Let us grant that writing, in Derrida's sense of the word, does all these things. We might still wonder if a poem could dislodge classical phenomenology and yet open onto another formation of the discipline, one that is not entirely based on Franz Brentano's teaching that acts of consciousness depend on either presence or representation.[12] It might tell us something new about phenomenology, or might respond to the sorts of insights that the new phenomenology has developed. Henry's analysis of auto-affection is a case in point, Jean-Luc Marion's attention to saturated phenomena is another, and, as I have already stressed, we need not sharply separate these two from those who have bequeathed them questions and problems. Can we be sure that literary criticism has learned all it can from Levinas? I do not think so. We also need to recall that a poem will never be merely illustrative of a method completely foreign to it, if phenomenology is a method in the first place, since there can be no poem without *epochê* and a partial reduction. It would be better to think of reading a poem as an engagement between two styles, two practices, two itineraries, or two intensities, of phenomenology.

ﾞﾝ

"September Song": the title both situates the poem in time and characterizes it as a poem. It is a *song*, we are told, a lyric, heir to a tradition that in the West goes back to Alkman's "Maiden-Song" of the seventh century BCE, and, east of Europe, reaches back to the Song of Songs, which in turn has roots in the ecstatic poetry of Sumer in the third millennium BCE. Among the many songs in English poetry, we think first when reading Hill's poem of Blake's *Songs of Experience* (1794) and perhaps of one of the *Poetical Sketches* (1783), "To Autumn," with its evocation of the season "stained / With the blood of the grape."[13] No more than Blake does Hill naively celebrate the time of harvest. Indeed, any positive suggestion of "harvest," as well as celebratory song, is quickly put into question by the lapidary inscription beneath the title, which immediately adjusts our expectations of the genre of the work. Set in italics, the line reads, *"born 19.6.32—deported 24.9.42."* And so the poem is partly framed again, this time as an elegy, and another September is evoked, one twenty-five years before, when the child in question was deported. We do not need to labor the point that to be deported was a prelude to death by malnutrition, exhaustion, or execution, nor do we need to surmise why the child was deported. So this lyric will not inherit from songs addressed to a god or a great man, nor from drinking songs or folk songs, but from the memorial lyric addressed to the dead, such as Aristotle's paean for Hermias. As we shall see, the lapidary inscription is as important for what it does not tell us as for what it does. No name of the child is given, nor the reason why, out of all the children deported in 1942, this one is addressed.

Already, the lyric has folded poetic traditions tightly into itself, not by virtue of its form but by allusion to genres. It begins by addressing the dead child, using prosopopoeia, the figure for making a face. The figure is barely used, however, for the profile of the child that begins to appear does so entirely in terms of negatives. The child was "undesirable" but not "untouchable," certainly not "forgotten" or "passed over." If we needed more evidence than is given by the word "deported" that the child is Jewish, it is supplied in the allusion to the Passover (Exod. 12:12). This time, in 1942, the Lord did not pass over the child. He or she is "undesirable," a word for deportees that was in use long before the Second World War but here indicating a group deemed by the Nazis to be the *Untermenschen* or subhuman, namely Jews, Slavs, and Gypsies, male homosexuals, dwarfs, and the mentally retarded. Others, mainly communists and democrats, were also deemed undesirable, but only Jewish deportees marked for "resettlement" were classed *Rückkehr unerwünscht*, "return undesirable," and consigned to death camps such as Auschwitz-Birkenau, Gusen, Mauthausen, and Treblinka. The child was not "untouchable," however, the allusion being to the Hindu outcastes, the *Dalits*, downtrodden, or (as Gandhi proposed) the *Harijans*, children of God. If the child was deemed to be an outcaste by the Nazis, it was not because he or she could not be touched. On the contrary, the pollution the child represents for those who believe in the purity of the Aryan race renders him or her all the more vulnerable. He or she is well within the reach of informers, *Einsatzgruppen*, and the Gestapo. Not positively "remembered," which could happen only to an individual, the child is merely "not forgotten," one of many who fall within the scope of a government program, and we even hear the bureaucratic language of the time, and of all times, when told that there is a "proper time" for deportation to a camp.[14]

We continue to overhear a bureaucratic voice behind the poet's voice, "As estimated, you died." Not only does deportation imply death in the near future but also, and more chilling, the child is included in an approximate calculation as one of so many Jews judged to be living in Berlin or Munich, this part of Poland or that region of Romania. Yet the death of the child has already been announced, more quietly, in the changes of tense in the first stanza. We pass from "you may have been" to "you were" and then to the simple past tense, "Not forgotten / or passed over at the proper time." We see the child solely in terms of one horizon, the race laws. "Things marched," events and dehumanized soldiers alike, to the "end." This is not "the end of life," as the expression is commonly used, but an end as an outcome, the realization of a purpose; it is the direct consequence of a plan of social purification, *die Aktion*. As we know, in executing that plan responsibility was deflected from the self to others, whether superiors in the chain of command or abstract entities such as policy or government. If we read "September Song" in the frame of *King Log*, we will recall the opening poem of the collection, "Ovid in the Third Reich," in which Ovid says in the voice of one all too experienced in the ways of the world, "Things happen."[15]

Again, the discourse of official calculation is remarked by the word "sufficient," that which is adequate, competent, or—in a word we will hear later—enough. The stanza ends with a sentence without a verb, without the "you": "Just so much Zyklon and leather, patented / terror, so many routine cries." A precise amount of Hydrogen cyanide, a few blue tablets, is all that is required to poison the child and those with him or her. The guards performing the "fumigation" are "so much . . . leather," and with this image the word "untouchable" presses on the poem from another direction. Among Hindus, anyone associated with leather is untouchable, impure. Here, though, it is the German soldiers who are morally impure, not the child. The sudden reversal occurs in a slight shift from "so much" to "so many" which opens a cruel ambiguity. From the perspective of the guards, the "fumigation" generates only the usual number of cries within the twenty minutes it takes for death to ensue after the release of the gas. It is "patented / terror." The adjective, which recalls "patent leather," qualifies "terror." A metonymy distributes the qualification associated with the firm of Tesch and Stabenow, which manufactured the poison, to those who die inhaling it. Protected by the law, the cries are Nazi property; they are made "proper" to the regime. The reader knows at once that "so many" also means an unbounded number of cries, and that it would be inhuman even to think of counting them.

And so the child is murdered. A whole world of experience, as tenderly evoked in the "September Song" of Maxwell Anderson and Kurt Weill's *Knickerbocker Holiday* (1938), is denied the child.[16] And so he or she passes out of the poem. There is no more prosopopoeia, no more making of a face for the dead one, no more address to a "you." Indeed, the poem shifts from the "you" to the "I," and does so in a stanza that attracts notice, one that shows, as Merleau-Ponty would have it, reflection "upon language, truth, and the significance of the act of writing." Let us read it very closely:

(I have made
an elegy for myself it
is true)

ॐ

Set in parentheses, the third stanza seems to be in retreat from the rest of the poem; it is as though it turns away from the poet's public utterance in order to reflect on what has been said and how it has been said. In a poem in which lines are run on more often than not, this stanza has a particularly violent enjambment—"it / is true"—in which more than one philosophical issue is at stake. Yet the third stanza does not hide from the poem in all respects. The lapidary inscription announces that the lyric will be an elegy of a peculiarly modern sort, one in which "deportation" has become official jargon for "death"; but now we are quietly told that the elegy is for the poet who presumably has never been faced with horror.

Is this a moment of self-reflection, as in Wordsworth's lines about the "Boy of Winander" in *The Prelude*? Not quite: Wordsworth is more oblique, less self-conscious, than Hill, and the child's experience in "September Song" differs sharply from that of the boy who was "taken from his mates" and died "ere he was full ten years old."[17] Nor does "A Slumber did my Spirit Seal" seem an appropriate lyric for comparison; the "touch of earthly years" that the child Lucy does not seem to feel is a long way from her not being untouchable. Is Hill's a moment of judgment akin to Hopkins's gesture in "Spring and Fall"? There "a young child," Margaret, is seen to be grieving over "Goldengrove unleaving," and is told at the end of the lyric, "It is Margaret you mourn for."[18] Hopkins and Hill meet here only for a moment, if at all: Hopkins's child mourns nature and herself as a part of it. The mourning at work in "September Song," though, is the consequence of an atrocity, and Hill is led back from the mourning of the child by virtue of re-considering the imaginative identification with him or her and the rectitude of talking about it. Yet there is a reason why *this* child is mourned, and why Hill turns from him or her to himself. No one fully performs the reduction, Merleau-Ponty teaches, and certainly it is never completely achieved in a poem.[19] This poem can be seen to turn on a transcendent event that remains outside the world of the lyric. It is this: Geoffrey Hill was born on June 18, 1932, one day before the child who was deported in September 1942. That single day stands for the slight change of circumstances that, in bad outbreaks of history, can mean life or death, everyday existence or sheer horror, and it also helps to explain the emotional link he feels with this one child. That said, this empirical fact is of limited help in reading the poem. More significant, I think, is that the "you" of the poem, the Jewish child, remains somewhat abstract until the "I" appears to disown him or her; and, disconcertingly, the sheltered appearance of the "I" draws attention to something uneasy in the elegy and perhaps in all elegies.

Addressing the child in the first two stanzas, Hill is utterly powerless as a speaker. Because the child is not present, all he can do, strictly speaking, is report an empty intention. Yet he addresses the child nonetheless, and thereby turns the dead child into a phenomenon that is both invisible and irregardable. There is little for Hill to aim at, surely not a memory, perhaps only the memories of others. Only as a poet does he have power, a way of enchanting himself and us with words, with the elegance of a reversal such as that in the opening lines, and a rhetorical power over life and death. Only by way of prosopopoeia can the child be made to enter what seems to be the field of experience, even if it is not. Thus poetry becomes the means by which nonexperience is violently changed to counter-experience, and counter-experience is passed off as experience.[20] The prosopopoeia feigns a bringing back of the child to life, feigns too a relation between the poet and the child, an act that can be terminated by a shift of attention as required by the shape of the poem, in other words, by aesthetic ends. All the face can say, Levinas and Marion agree, is "Thou shalt not kill," a command to which Hill must respond as a poet as well as a man, a distinction that he would rightly distrust. In talking of the child, the poet is envisaged, as well as envisaging; his act of representation is "ruined," as Levinas puts it, by an ethical *Sinngebung* or bestowal of meaning that does not depend on a perceptual context.[21] Hill the poet has created a countergaze that accuses Hill the man in the very moment of calling it into being, since its re-creation is only momentary and, to a greater or lesser extent, intended for aesthetic ends. It is as though the child's face says, "Do not kill me again," as though the child knows with Stevens (but otherwise than Stevens) that poetry can kill.[22]

I recall another poem from *King Log*, "History as Poetry," with its talk of "The tongue's atrocities" and its wariness of poetry that "Unearths from among the speechless dead."[23] The first two stanzas of "September Song" do indeed exhume the child. Also, they allow us to "to think the thesis," as Derrida says, to suspend a thetic relation to reference, and in doing so they let us contemplate the suffering of an innocent as a theme, without being required to take any responsibility for the act. The contemplation of what happened, perhaps with even a degree of imaginative variation, is not in itself immoral. It can mark a disturbance of the making of a theme; the poem can be *itself* a relation with the dead child, a relation of unsaying, not simply of the said. Yet the contemplation can become immoral if it remains at the level of phenomenological description without a *reductio* such as happens in the third stanza. Eugen Fink alludes to the reduction as a passage from the natural attitude to a far more disinterested gaze, as though one has become like one of the gods, "the player of the world [*Weltspieler*]."[24] Long before then, Husserl had noted the proximity of the phenomenological and aesthetic gazes, as we have seen, but did not remark the moral danger of that closeness. In "September Song" Hill is finely alert to the threat.

The turn from the second to the third stanza is marked by parentheses. They indicate less a neutralizing of positivity than an awareness of the impropriety in continuing the poem by way of a purified gaze.[25] It is, if you like, a reduction of reduction. I doubt that I am alone in hearing an oblique acknowledgement of Dylan Thomas's well-known poem, "A Refusal to Mourn, the Death by Fire, of a Child in London" (1945).[26] Let us recall it:

Never until the mankind making
Bird beast and flower
Fathering and all humbling darkness
Tells with silence the last light breaking
And the still hour
Is come of the sea tumbling in harness

And I must enter again the round
Zion of the water bead
And the synagogue of the ear of corn
Shall I let pray the shadow of a sound
Or sow my salt seed
In the least valley of sackcloth to mourn

The majesty and burning of the child's death.
I shall not murder
The mankind of her going with a grave truth
Nor blaspheme down the stations of the breath
With any further
Elegy of innocence and youth.

Deep with the first dead lies London's daughter,
Robed in the long friends,
The grains beyond age, the dark veins of her mother,
Secret by the unmourning water
Of the riding Thames.
After the first death, there is no other.[27]

Thomas's child is also a victim of war, a German air raid on London late in World War II. Here, too, are Jewish references, though ones that have been thoroughly naturalized and neutralized—"Zion of the water bead," "synagogue of the ear of corn," and "valley of sackcloth"—as has the Christian reference to the Stations of the Cross. The lyric is a sustained instance of *occupatio*: in saying he will not mourn the child until his death, he does precisely what he says he will not do.[28] Yeats is a vanishing point in Thomas's poetic world, and even more than Yeats's poems, including his elegies, "A Refusal to Mourn" is a high-toned and supremely self-confident rhetorical performance, one that luxuriates in language and in the freedom of the poet to refuse to mourn, and yet to mourn, to involve both nature and himself in the event, to use biblical and ecclesial language while denying a central Christian teaching in the final line.

Nothing could be further from "September Song." Formally, the poem eschews the satisfactions of ripe stanzas of varying line length and intriguing rhymes. If we look at *King Log* we find that "September Song" is the fifth poem in the collection, and the first both to break with form and not to begin each line with a capital letter. Not only is the amplitude of a bardic voice declined but so too are conventional signs of its own status as a poem in conversation with a rich tradition. Notice too the rhetorical movement of the lyric: we pass from talking *to* the child to talking *of* the child, and before the poet could begin to talk *for* the child, as is done in many elegies ("Who would not sing for *Lycidas?*") or poems with an elegiac strain (James Dickey's "The Sheep Child," for example), he recoils from the very possibility, and not in the freedom of acceptance or refusal. Thomas may assure us that "I shall not murder / The mankind of her going with a grave truth" but he does so anyway ("After the first death, there is no other"). When Hill speaks of truth, it is in quite different ways, as we shall see. Yet before we can be in a position to judge what "true" means for Hill in this poem, we must recognize that the lyrical "I" here is less one that abides in the freedom of a *cogito* than in the responsibility imposed upon him by the other person, here the child.

What does the third stanza say, and what does it do? I will begin with the first part of the question. The first line and a bit are the least difficult: "I have made / an elegy." Notice that the "I" figures himself as a poet, while stressing the element of craft, that he is a *makar*. It is as though he is well aware of the claim of art to remove the artist from the world, to engage in what Jean Wahl calls "transascendance," a rising to the ineffable heights, and he insists on drawing attention to the element of craft in the work.[29] For the Levinas of "Reality and Its Shadow" (1948), this gesture is a first sign of ethics irrupting in the artwork, requiring it to make contact with the world. An older Levinas would see here a refusal to make the child a phenomenon, to allow him or her to remain an enigma, and also a reduction of the Said to the Saying. Yet we must respect the tense of the statement; it reads, "I have made," not "I am making." A division is marked between the first two stanzas and the third: the address to the child is an elegy for himself, and for the first time in the poem we have an explicit registration of a fulfilled intention. Does this change come about because Hill has been imaginatively identifying with the child but really writing about himself? Or has it come about because he has no right to speak as he has been doing of another's suffering? Both, I would say.

Only the first reason for recoiling from his own poetic stance brings Hill into relation with the poems by Wordsworth and Hopkins. The second reason is the more original and the more sobering, and it prompts us to reflect further on the expression "an elegy *for myself*" (my emphasis). For it also means that Hill has made an elegy, a poem, for his own aesthetic delight, for the enlargement of his poetic repertoire, and at the cost of erasing the child. Adorno's well-known remark, dating from 1949 and appearing definitively in *Prisms* (1967), comes to mind, "To write poetry after Auschwitz is barbaric [*nach Auschwitz ein Gedicht zu schreiben, ist barbarisch*]."[30] Of course, Adorno later resiled from the judgment, and observed, even before the essay was collected, in *Negative Dialectics* (1966), "Perennial suffering has as much right to expression as a tortured man has to scream; hence it may have been wrong to say that after Auschwitz you could no longer write poems. But it is not wrong to raise the less cultural question whether after Auschwitz you can go on living— especially whether one who escaped by accident, one who by rights should have been killed, may go on living."[31] There are many ways of escaping horror by accident, many sorts of contingency, and in "September Song" the difference of a single day is secretly felt by the author to be one of them. More pertinent for Hill than Adorno's reflections, I think, is Levinas's argument in "Reality and Its Shadow." In presenting itself, we are told, a thing produces both a phenomenon and an image, and attending to the latter leads us away from the world and the inexorable demands of justice for other people. Levinas's judgment on aesthetic delight is among the harshest in western philosophy. "There is something nasty, selfish, and cowardly in artistic pleasure," he writes. "There are times when one could be ashamed of it, as if carousing in a town struck by the plague."[32] Most writers will recoil from the judgment, crying "Unfair!" But the Hill of "Annunciations," "Poetry as History," and "September Song" would be in firm agreement.

It is easy to imagine a "new phenomenologist" seeking to interpret the brackets of the third stanza. One might say, following Henry, that here we have the invisible revelation of the poet's subjectivity. The poet's intentionality is unable to determine a relationship with the dead child, and so his mourning must be explained in another way. What Hill's concern for the child manifests is precisely itself—"I have made / an elegy for myself"—and the manifestation is invisible. Or, following Levinas, we might see the brackets as performing a reduction of the Said to the Saying, a leading of the speaker back from the world in which poetic declaration is one with a rhetorical freedom to create and observe, to a site where his speech is vulnerable and well aware of the wounds it can make. Yet the passage from ontology to ethics is not one that can ever be reassuring in a poem. The sacrifice of poetic power can always be a subtle way of gaining pathos, of laying claim to another, more legitimate sort of power, one that is infused with moral concern. There can be no assurances of moral purity in the world of poetry, a judgment that should not let us draw too sharp a distinction between the aesthetic and the ethical, and should not blind us to the testimonial power of high art. Celan's "Todesfuge" and Hill's "September Song" bear witness to the Shoah in ways that are more piercing than many films, many stories, many analytic studies, and their drive to satisfy aesthetic hungers are neither simply fulfilled nor simply refused. No one has a secure place to stand on this slope.

"Todesfuge" is not the only poem Celan wrote about the Shoah, and perhaps not the closest one to Hill's poetic sensibilities. A later lyric such as "Die Fleissigen" might be a more exact parallel in terms of a shared poetics.[33] Yet "Todesfuge" provides the sort of contrast that is needed here. Celan had to bear Adorno's judgment about poetry after Auschwitz, and his pain in doing so must be acknowledged, while Hill responds elliptically to that same judgment in the writing of his lyric. There can be no question of responding to "Todesfuge" here, or even considering in requisite detail what the question of response would entail, but let us at least recall its opening lines:

> Schwarz Milch der Frühe wir trinken sie abends
> wir trinken sie mittags und morgens wir trinken sie nachts
> wir trinken und trinken
> wir schaufeln ein Grab in den Lüften da liegt man nicht eng
> Ein Mann wohnt im Haus der spielt mit den Schlangen der schreibt
> der schreibt wenn es dunkelt nach Deutschland dein goldenes Haar
>   Margarete
> er schreibt es und tritt vor das Haus und es blitzen die Sterne er pfeift
>   seine Rüden herbei
> er pfeift seine Juden hervor läbt schaufelen ein Grab in der Erde
> er befiehlt uns spielt auf nun zum Tanz

> Black milk of daybreak we drink it at sundown
> we drink it at noon in the morning we drink it at night
> we drink it and we drink it
> we dig a grave in the breezes there one lies unconfined
> A man lives in the house he plays with the serpents he writes
> he writes when dusk falls to Germany your golden hair Margarete
> he writes it and steps out of doors and the stars are flashing he whistles
>   his pack out

he whistles his Jews out in earth has them dig for a grave
he commands us to strike up for the dance[34]

In its insistent, almost hypnotic rhythm, its surprising figures, its powerful juxtapositions and its imaginative reach, "Todesfuge" is a lyric in the high modernist manner. If it does not withhold its speech or reflect on its intensity, it is because of the "right to expression" of which Adorno spoke. Hill does not exercise such a right because it is not his to exercise. To speak in empathy for a dead child is one thing, to speak in the third person plural in the context of the Shoah is quite another. Hill could not be part of that "we," as Celan was, and his "I" is less hesitant about speaking of the Shoah (as impossible or immoral to represent) than about speaking of it in poetry.[35] On the one hand, Hill's poem evokes "what otherwise mocks every description," while on the other hand it restrains itself from saying too much.[36] "September Song," as Gentile speech, can be responsible only if it heeds Adorno's warning about "poetry," only if it expresses a reserve about speaking for the Jewish dead. "We grasp, roughly, the song," as he says in "Two Formal Elegies: *For the Jews in Europe*" (30), poems that should be read in close conjunction with "September Song." Roughness, here, would seem to be offered as an ethical gesture.

Which brings us to the enjambment, the "it" hanging at the end of the line without even a dash to keep up appearances. Hill says "it / is true," and we must ask if the truth claim refers to the *making* of an elegy for himself or if the elegy itself *speaks* the truth. In the latter case, are we being told that, if the elegy is for him, then it is true, and that the first two stanzas are presumably untrue. We might think of them as untrue, according to the logic of the poem, because the poet knows only the general circumstances of the child and nothing particular about him or her. We have heard much in a phenomenological key in recent years about the mourning of friends but little about the mourning of people one does not know.[37] Death cancels the relation one has with the deceased, but what if the relation is entirely general and abstract, as with someone never met and never known?[38] Proust evokes the danger of "posthumous infidelity" toward the end of *À la recherche du temps perdu*, and Hill courts a version of that specter, an infidelity to the memories of others about the child.[39] Perhaps Hill's affectivity is consequent on an intentional rapport with a photograph of the child, a story about him or her, or a sense of compassion for the suffering of another human being. Does this suffice to write an elegy in a responsible fashion? How does the death of another person impinge on me? In his 1975–1976 lectures on death and time, Levinas reflects on an issue that is prior to these questions:

The death of the other who dies affects me in my very identity as a responsible "me" [*moi*]; it affects me in my nonsubstantial identity, which is not the simple coherence of various acts of identification, but is made up of an ineffable responsibility. My being affected by the death of the other is precisely that, my relation with his death. It is, in my relation, my deference to someone who no longer responds, already a culpability—the culpability of the survivor.[40]

Hill may have no particular responsibility for the child's fate, but the child nonetheless burdens him with a responsibility to bear witness to his or her plight. The emotions that spur the poem are difficult to disentangle. Grief, to be sure, and guilt for surviving, but at least some of the affectivity is without intentionality, as Henry would say, because it is a relation with Hill's own death to come, which offers no response to him, no more than the child does, and which cannot appear as a presence or a representation.[41]

Not that "September Song" is a lyric of undiluted auto-affection, or that the third stanza offers such a moment. Compare it with W. S. Merwin's lyric, "For the Anniversary of My Death":

Every year without knowing it I have passed the day
When the last fires will wave to me
And the silence will set out
Tireless traveller
Like the beam of a lightless star

Then I will no longer
Find myself in life as in a strange garment
Surprised at the earth
And the love of one woman
And the shamelessness of men
As today writing after three days of rain
Hearing the wren sing and the falling cease
And bowing not knowing to what[42]

This poem is almost pure affectivity with limited intentionality, an "elegy for myself" that plays elegantly with knowing that death is certain but that, unlike birth, does not yield knowledge of its date. If "September Song" concerns a seasonal repetition after the fact (the recurrence of September), Merwin's lyric responds to an illegible repetition before the fact. The self is seen as other, enabling the poet to find a minimal intentionality ("in life as in a strange garment"), though one that multiplies pathos. To be sure, the lyrical "I" looks around and takes stock of "the shamelessness of men," but this is the notation of an observer who takes refuge in his inner life, and any inclusion of himself in that category is tacit. Like "September Song," the poem has a moment of self-reflection. Merwin indicates that he is writing now, presumably the very poem we are reading, and this introduces a complication into the lyric that becomes apparent only when another mode of non-knowing is declared in the final line. The poet bows in reverence but does not know to whom or what. Could it be God? Or Love? Or Life? Or Death? Or the poem we are reading? Or the poet's creativity that enables him to write the poem? Doubtless the lyric allows all these possibilities. Yet its mode of ambiguity is not self-lacerating in the manner of "September Song."

Let us return to Hill's poem. It addresses truth, not knowledge, though not in the straightforward manner of a thesis. We are not told of something that "it is true" but of each of more than one thing that "it / is true," which is hardly the same. For the third stanza puts at risk whether a truth claim is actually being made in the first place. The enjambment "it / is true," can mean, "I concede that the elegy, which seemed to be for the child, is in fact for myself." And it can also mean, "the elegy is true to life, it shows that we seek to speak for the Other even when we do not know what we are saying or even have the right to speak" or "the elegy is in good tune, a proper poem, despite appearances" or "the elegy shows loyalty, faithfulness, it is true to myself, to my feelings for the child, if not the child himself or herself and the child's inner experiences which are hidden from me." Inevitably, anyone interested in phenomenology will recall that "truth" here could mean correctness or disclosure. So "I have made / an elegy for myself" would be correct if it confirms the way things are, and true if it indicates a disclosure of a state of affairs, such as the poet recognizing that only he is present, not the child. Is this a poem that admits correctness or displays the truth? There is, I think, a prior question: Is the poem true in the sense of offering testimony? The lyrical "I" of the poem is unusual in that it assumes responsibility for the child it addresses, not just freedom to determine an aesthetic response to a situation, and, with this in mind, we might pose the question that Levinas has taught us to ask. What is primary, truth or justice?[43]

If this question takes us more deeply into the poem, it does so by more than one route. To be making an elegy for myself when apparently talking about another person might be true, although it might not be just, which for Levinas would mean that it revolves entirely in a world of aesthetic pleasures. Or to make an elegy for myself might be both true and just, which for Levinas would mean that it interrupts or retards its movement of self-transcendence.[44] The latter alternative fits with a high modernist insistence on the breaking of form, yet it has become such a familiar gesture in contemporary literature that it is difficult to credit it as having any ethical force, assuming in the first place that we believe that the aesthetic and the ethical are as distinct as Levinas takes them to be in "Reality and Its Shadow." Even if the third stanza enacts a movement from the Said to the Saying, it does not step far outside the order of meaning. Hill figures the ethical situation by way of difficulty, one of his favored words, and here "difficulty" is to be understood, as William Empson would have us do, in terms of ambiguities.[45] If asked what the third stanza does, the answer must surely be that it "unwrites" the poem as read so far, that it is an attempt to make the poet as well as the reader "lift his eyes from the page."[46] Also, though, the third stanza does other things. First, it enacts a passage from the Jewish child to the Gentile poet. Hill shares mortality with the child, yet he does not share the horror to which the child was exposed. The lyric that might have marked a place for Jewish-Gentile dialogue about the Shoah erases that place in its very performance. Second, the third stanza is an economical means of keeping the poem open to all intuitions. This is of course a desire of phenomenology, one remarked and revived by Marion. It has also been a desire of literature. In its multiplication of languages, and its passivity with respect to their interaction, *Finnegans Wake* (1939) allows all intuitions to be received by the novel above and beyond the intentionality of James Joyce or any narrators he might employ. It is one way in which modern literature has performed its desire to say everything, *tout dire*.[47] Hill may not wish to encompass everything in the manner of Joyce, or to say everything (including what is forbidden) in the style of the Marquis de Sade, but he does want to say everything, as Celan does, by staying within the confines of a lyric.[48]

༧

How can a poem continue once it has turned aside from itself, once it has disowned itself as poetry? Certainly Hill no longer speaks of the child, and presumably the remainder of the poem would aim to be responsible speech. There is no talk of the Shoah, certainly no appeal to theodicy. The poem seeks closure in five simple declarative sentences:

> September fattens on vines. Roses
> flake from the wall. The smoke
> of harmless fires drifts to my eyes.

> This is plenty. This is more than enough.

Unlike Christopher Ricks, I do not hear any hint of a fattening for sacrifice in the first of these lines.[49] The "fattening" is one of fullness, marked by the surprising conjunction in an English setting of "vines" and "roses" before we reach the deflation of "flake." The lines hint at a complacency in nature (and the cultivation of nature) far beyond the ripeness that Rilke evokes in "Herbsttag":

Befiehl den letzten Früchten voll zu sein;
gib ihnen noch zwei südlichere Tage,
dränge sie zur Vollndung hin und jage
die letzte Sübe in den schweren Wein.

Bid the last fruit to ripen on the vine;
allow them still two friendly southern days
to bring them to perfection and to force
the final sweetness in the heavy wine.[50]

The point of "September fattens on vines," rather, is the sharp contrast of Hill's September with the child's. A complex experience of time is marked in these lines. There is a repetition of September, underlining the fact that the poet has survived, not the child. Also let it be noted that the child's experience of time differs from the poet's: September is the month, in Gentile time, of two high Holy Days, Rosh Hashanah and Yom Kippur. And, as already seen, "September Song" may also retain an echo of Blake's "To Autumn" with its image of the season "stained / With the blood of the grape," and Hill's September is stained with the death of the child, as the "harmless fires" (in contrast to the fires of Auschwitz) and the suggestion of tears caused by the two sorts of smoke imply.

September is the month of fullness and decay, grapes ripening and roses fading, of leaves that are burned in bonfires. Such is Hill's world, the one from which he has never been deported, and which he has survived to take part in. It is his judgment on what he has just stated that makes the final lines responsible speech. The ordinary world he has inherited is "plenty," "more than enough." The final word might recall "sufficient" earlier; it might also make us think, with a bitter irony, of the "Dayenu" in the Passover Haggadah with its refrain that the Lord has done enough, more than enough, many times over, in bringing the Jews out of Egypt, in giving the Sabbath, and in giving Torah.[51] Certainly Hill has nothing about which he can decently complain. Yet the final line is also a judgment on the poem, on the presumption of talking to and of the child, of the failure of offering testimony for another's suffering. "I have said plenty," it says, "I have said more than enough about the child and about myself—I have risked an excess of poetry, I have both staged and queried 'the tongue's atrocities.' "[52] If the question "What should we do with literature?" is folded into the poem, as Derrida suggests, so too is an answer: we should be vigilant with respect to the proximity of aesthetics and phenomenology, lest the ethical be occluded. Adorno may have retracted his judgment about poetry after Auschwitz, but it has left its mark on Hill's poem.

PART II

Jean-Luc Marion

The Phenomenality of the Sacrament— Being and Givenness

JEAN-LUC MARION

I. At the Limit of Phenomenality

The question of the sacrament—or, more precisely, that of the sacramentality of the sacrament—undoubtedly first arises concerning theology. If one admits, at least as a formal point of departure for it one of its normative definitions, one will say with the *Decree of the Eucharist* of the Council of Trent: "Indeed the holy Eucharist shares in common with the other sacraments that it is a symbol of a sacred thing and the visible form of an invisible grace."[1] Starting from the Eucharist, one must pose and then formulate the connection between the sacramental symbol and that to which it offers access, the "sacramental thing" (*res sacramenti*)—the grace of Christ, such that it governs all the other sacraments, beginning with baptism. According to this connection of the sensible and grace in a unique symbol that joins the one with the other, everything refers to the original connection of the extremes, the one that the Incarnation of the Word accomplishes in our humanity. Henceforth, the flesh (the physical body and the conscious soul) is found hypostatically united at this point with the divine in Christ, such that it can display this unique communion in certain gestures and acts, which also are structured according to the symbol of the thing and of grace.

Nevertheless, as radically theological as it may be, the question of the sacrament does not any less call upon some of the terms which philosophy has appropriated for itself, at least in the case of one of its major movements for more than a century, a movement inaugurated by the *Logical*

Investigations of Edmund Husserl in 1900, which has developed ever since under the name of "phenomenology." In fact, by way of the doctrine of the phenomenonality of phenomena, phenomenology inquired regarding a basic and therefore in a sense very simple question: How can sensory or even intellectual appearance give rise to the manifestation of the thing itself, whether it is under the modality of the "true" or the equally determining modality of the "false"? Put otherwise, how does appearance find itself taking responsibility not for a simple misleading illusion but for a full and complete appearance, whose integrity in the end would offer the sole and final framework of manifestation—as much of the true as of the false? For in the end, certain knowledge is always determined by way of clarity and evidence, therefore in accordance with a particular manifestation. The formal methodological or discursive criteria, which will then possibly come to discern it, will only ever confirm its indisputable and originary authority. Whatever is or pretends to be will have to appear at the end. And no appearance could possibly fail to fulfill expectations, as long as it remains the unique attribute of the manifestation, therefore the unique agent of truth. Yet the question of the sacrament (and first of the Incarnation itself, which gives the paradox its currency) undoubtedly implements two terms arising from the phenomenological debate, since it very precisely combines the visible and the invisible, as the two inseparable faces of a single phenomenon: "a symbol of a sacred thing and a *visible form* of an *invisible* grace." We can therefore ask: must the sacrament be received as a phenomenon, and, consequently, which particular phenomenality does it concern?

The tradition indeed speaks here with a single voice, defining the sacrament in terms of phenomenality. Saint Augustine defines it thus: "The *visible* sacrifice is the sacrament, the sacred sign, of the *invisible* sacrifice."[2] Saint Thomas again picks up the same duality: "Sacraments . . . are *sensible* signs of *invisible* things by which man is sanctified."[3] The pair *sensible/invisible* is certainly equivalent to the Augustinian pair *visible/invisible*, since "*invisible* Divine virtue [operates] under *visible signs*."[4] In fact, the Tridentine definition lends itself straightaway to a sense of sacrament according to phenomenality: "The most holy Eucharist has indeed this in common with the rest of the sacraments, that it is a symbol of a sacred thing and is a *visible* form of an *invisible* grace." A double consequence follows from this audacious assumption of a visibility of the invisible. First, a positive consequence: since in any sacrament it is a matter of rendering visible the invisible grace of God granted to the Church in Christ, theological reflection cannot get by without a strictly phenomenological analysis. In particular, it will be necessary to inquire regarding the double phenomenality at work here: a visible thing that is one and the same (the thing one names a *sacramentum*) appears on the one hand as an already constituted phenomenon (a mundane thing—bread, wine, water, oil, and so forth), visible among the other visible things of the world. On the other hand, it appears also as the intermediary, not yet constituted as such, toward another term, which remained invisible (the "thing" accompanied by the sacrament, *res sacrimenti*, the sanctifying grace of Christ) and yet is supposed to constitute itself as a final phenomenon. One should first ask how the same phenomenality may be doubled in the visible "thing," in order to make of it, beyond its own mundane visibility (the appearance of itself), the visibility of an other, though supposedly remaining invisible (grace). Whence comes the first question: How may the same visibility serve two phenomena? Subsequently, on this basis, one cannot escape a second consequence, which is negative or at least aporetic: How can one conceive the visible (and moreover the *sensible* visible, not simply the intelligible) as being able "to act on" (and even "sanctify") the invisible, whatever it may be? How can one conceive that the same phenomenality—by definition visible—is extended univocally to the invisible? And the difficulty here does not result from the origin (in this case, theological) of this invisibility (the grace of the Christ), but purely and simply from the status of the invisible in general. For in phenomenology the fundamental correlation between the appearance and that which appears—such that it opens all possibility of phenomenality—always plays in principle between two terms that are rightly visible. On one hand, a first visible, or at least a first perceived one, the experiences of consciousness (the *data*, the *Erlebnisse*) that are not yet constituted in a phenomenon with full rights (the simple appearance). On the other hand, a second visible, the intentional object constituted around its noematic kernel that is fully phenomenalized (that which appears). Yet, in the very particular case of the sacrament, it would be a matter of an absolutely new correlation, that between a perceived visible and an "intentional object" (without doubt, an already inadequate term that one will employ here only with some reservation) destined to remain definitively invisible. The two faces of the sacrament therefore do not remain within the phenomenality of the visible, since the first one alone employs it, while the second one decidedly and definitively avoids it. In fact, the noematic kernel does not stop identically drawing itself even within the center of variations of fulfillment, variations that always illuminate it differently but determine it all the more visibly. On the contrary, the *res sacramenti*, the grace of the Christ, will never on the contrary appear as such in the light of this world. It will never be counted among worldly phenomena, even if sacramental acts are performed at each moment of our lives since our baptism—for their visibility will never extend beyond the intra-mundane things toward "that which the eye has not seen" (I Cor. 1:9).

Therefore, if one had to approach the sacrament according to the common requirements of phenomenology, it would be necessary to conclude that it belongs only partly to phenomenality, but in the last analysis it transgresses phenomenality in order to aim at an authority that is definitively resistant to the visible. According to this aporia, the sacrament would be subject to phenomenality precisely only in order to set up its limits and to distinguish itself from it—unless it does not admit in this way the limits of its own rational coherence.

II. Models of the Gap

Obviously, theology did not wait for this phenomenological aporia to attempt to join the visible with the invisible in the same and paradoxical manifestation. By schematically recalling several attempts made in this direction, one will note their limits but without criticizing them: indeed one could not reproach theologians for not having overcome an aporia they knew was insurmountable. When it proceeds from the sacrament, the question is never to reduce its terms to univocity, nor to integrate the invisible of the *res sacramenti* into the visibility of the *sacramentum*, but to comprehend as precisely as possible which models of intelligibility can clarify the paradox and what exceptions it imposes upon them in return.

The first model which theology can use to attempt to reduce the gap between the visibility and invisibility in the sacrament comes from the metaphysics of substance. Or more exactly from the relation of inherence between a substance and its accidents: accidents appear directly, substance appears only through their mediation. From this gap, one can conjecture a theological possibility: the same visibility of the accidents (aspects such as the whiteness of the bread, the redness of the wine, the translucence of the water) could change from an account of a mundane substance (bread, wine, water) to that of a non-mundane substance (body and blood of Christ, grace of filiation). As natural aspects of a substance, the same accidents become the non-natural species of a different substance. This model is characterized by two difficulties.

(A) A philosophical difficulty emerges only after its theological employment by Saint Thomas (unless this difficulty alone does not make this employment possible, by weakening it): One can much more legitimately consider the (theological) possibility of a transfer of the accidents of one substance to the other, in that in itself no substance can (philosophically speaking) appear directly as such, but must always go back indirectly to the visibility of its accidents. As such, no substance affects us immediately: In short, none appears to us in the highest degree as a phenomenon.[5] From that, the theological argument ensures less a phenomenality particular to the sacrament than that it replays in its own favor the metaphysical non-phenomenality of any substance in general. The sacrament does not find any way toward manifestation, but finds in a particular way the universal shortage of manifestation of the substance, already reduced to the level of the thing in itself.[6]

(B) The other properly theological difficulty can be formulated as follows: with what right can the body of Christ engage in person and irremediably in the accidents of a substance that is not only finite, sensible, and material, but also without relation to the individual human substance it assumes in its Incarnation? And this is the case especially in strict philosophy, in which the substance does not enter into its accidents but rather withdraws itself from them at the risk of no longer affecting us nor hence appearing to us. Theology could thus not legitimately assume that the (quasi) substance of the sacrament rightly appears as such in the form of accidents, except by presupposing an actual engagement of the *res sacramenti* in the visible. It would be necessary that what the sacrament claims to take responsibility for truly gives itself to sight: it gives itself visibly as invisible. In short, *it gives itself without withdrawal* to the point of abandon.

In order to try to fill the same gap in the sacrament, theology can borrow a second model from metaphysics: that of the invisible cause of a visible effect. For in philosophy one can perfectly admit that in certain (even physical) cases only the effect reaches phenomenality, while the cause that "explains" it (and so renders it rational) remains itself invisible—only "proven" in its existence by the effectiveness of the effect.[7] Yet assuming that this schema, which was initially formalized to explain the natural world, could legitimately be applied to the phenomenality of the sacrament (which is debatable), the distribution of the roles does not go without saying. No doubt, the matter of the sacrament concerns the visible, but one could not take it as an effect, since from *ex opere operato* it itself follows the sanctification of the faithful receiving of the grace (created) in him; the effect of the sacrament remains thus perfectly invisible. As for what must be understood as its originating cause, it concerns the invisible par excellence, since "the principal efficient cause of grace is God himself, in comparison with Whom Christ's humanity is as a united instrument."[8] The materiality of the sacrament remains an accidental instrument caught between a principal cause and a spiritual effect that are both equally invisible. How can theology all the same legitimately employ a causal schema? By assuming that God enters without reservation into the humanity of Christ as into his "joint instrument" and that Christ enters irrevocably into the materiality of the sacrament to the point of qualifying its visibility as the very invisibility of his fleshly body. Only on this condition can the sacrament traverse the difference between visibility (its matter) and invisibility (of the cause and effect). But, to satisfy this condition, it would be necessary once again that what invests the sacrament truly gives itself to sight: It gives itself visibly as invisible. In short, *it gives itself without withdrawal* to the point of abandon.

To ensure a phenomenality of the invisibility of the sacrament, theology finally has at is disposal a third model: semiotics—to interpret the sacrament as a *"sacrum signum"* (sacred sign).[9] Here the gap between the visible and the invisible should be able to be traversed by putting one's trust in the arbitrary but inseparable unity of the two faces of the sign. The duality of the sign without doubt can be understood here in two senses. (A) On one hand, by dividing the sign itself, in which case the matter of the sacrament *ex opere operato* would be like the signifier and grace like the signified.[10] Yet in this configuration there is strictly speaking no sign, since the sacrament does not unite a signifier with a signified, but a sensible being that is already real in the world (bread, wine, water, and so forth) with a being that is an insensible and invisible thing within the world (sanctifying grace). To intend the sacrament as a sign, it is thus necessary to widen this concept to a semiotic relation between two beings. In short, it is necessary to move to the consideration of the referent. (B) On the other hand, the distinction of the sign (taken as a whole) and of its referent: In this case, the sacramental act is equivalent to the sign and Christ applies to the referent, inasmuch as a sacrament memorializes him, manifests his grace, and announces his coming glory.[11] Of course, this semiotic model of the sacrament functions exactly in proportion to the connection between the sign and the referent within it. Yet with what right can one assign an invisible referent with a necessary connection to a sign—even only an invisible (unrepresentable) signified to a visible (representable) signifier? Who would have the authority? Certainly not the speaker (or the beneficiary of the sacrament). Would it then be the referent? Would it have to be requested that a referent comes in person to validate a sign while acting as its guarantor—by guaranteeing that, if the sign is said, then the invisible referent will be visibly accomplished in it? Does such an engagement of the referent in the sign have a theoretical sense and a probability of having happened? No doubt only theology itself has the means of supporting it. But in any case in order to validate this model, it would once again be necessary that what invests the sacrament as its sign truly gives itself to say and effectively to make in person: thus it gives itself visibly as invisible. In short, *it gives itself without withdrawal* to the point of abandon.

Three models are thus available (among others) to theology to think rigorously a continuity between the visible and the invisible in the sacrament: the relation of substance to the accidents, of cause to the effect, and of sign to referent. None of them can as such ensure the phenomenal coherence of the sacrament, apart from satisfying a condition, which cannot be shown, nor show itself—provided that the invisible (substance, cause, referent) delivers itself without withdrawal to the visible, that is, it not only invests itself there, but it also gives itself there until the point of abandon. To define the phenomenality of the sacrament, it would have to be conceived that the invisible translates itself within it and that it delivers and abandons itself to the visible to the point that it there appears as the invisible that it remains. To conceive this condition requires considering two questions. (A) The phenomenological one will ask whether the possibility of being given without withdrawal or return concerns the possibility of manifesting itself, whether to give itself allows it to show itself (section III). (B) The theological question will ask whether the kenotic abandon of the Word to its humanity and of Christ to death achieves—among other gifts—that of the phenomenality of the invisible, therefore of the sacrament (section IV).

III. To Give Itself; to Show Itself

The difficulties that have just emerged in the enterprise of defining the phenomenality of the sacrament certainly concern to a large extent the difficult and undetermined relation within it of the visible with the invisible. Undoubtedly they also concern a deceptive obviousness that disturbs the concept of the phenomenon in general. As succinct as it may be, its clarification could thus help to raise unjustified hypotheses as well as let the authentic difficulties declare themselves.

Without question, the elevation of the "phenomenon" in metaphysics goes back to Kant, who accords it the role of a central concept, in relation to which the thing-in-itself remains a marginal authority (a margin or more exactly a limit). No more remarkable than recognized, the phenomenon is immediately misunderstood by being equated with the object—within the universal framework of the division of objects into noumena and phenomena, under the aegis of the "supreme" concept of the transcendental object $= X.$[12] Is it self-evident that any phenomenon results in an object and falls under objectivity? The question is essential primarily, because it belongs to the objectity of the object to allow itself to be synthesized (thus produced) starting from another pole than itself, as it happens starting from the originally synthetic unity of apperception, that is, of the "I think," in short of the *ego cogito* raised to the rank of the transcendental *I*. This structural alienation of the object from the *ego* removes from the phenomenon the initiative of its appearing. More detrimental still than the "subjectivism" thus imposed on the phenomenon, this decision especially sanctions the solipsism of the *ego* in the field of theoretical reason: It knows what it produces only by synthesis—no exteriority approaches it beyond what it could truly know. Husserl inherits this restriction of phenomenality from Kant without disputing it in depth. Neither the widening of intuition to the categorial and to essences, nor the recognition of passive syntheses, nor non-objective intentionalities (the other, time, my own flesh, and so forth) will lead him to call into question "the precedence of the *primordial objectity* [*Urgegenständlichkeit*],"[13] as the ultimate horizon of phenomenality. It follows the same privilege of the transcendental *I*, which exerts its empire on all the phenomena by the constitution that it ensures them. From this also results the same difficulty of recognizing phenomena that could not be constituted by the *I*—the phenomenon of the other stands out first among these. Other than by way of a marginal exception, which implicates the ordinary mode of phenomenality—the phenomenon cannot occur to the *I* as an event, which would decenter it to accomplish or transform it.

These aporias are sufficiently known that we will not develop them. It is better to insist on their origin: the phenomenon, lowered to the level of the object, is alienated from the transcendental subject and, more radically, loses its initiative to appear. It no longer depends any more on the phenomenon to begin the process of its arrival at the visible; it must return to the synthesis (Kant) or to constitution (Husserl), in any case to the now uncontested transcendentality of the *I*. It fell to Heidegger to be the first to have dared to call this subjection of the phenomenon to the *I* into question by challenging its interpretation as simple object. This decisive revolution is achieved with the imposition of an unprecedented definition of the phenomenon, from now on defined as "that which shows itself in itself." What shows *itself* in itself does not receive its visibility from somewhere else, for example from the transcendental *I*, but properly from itself. It can also, at least formally, show itself *in* and *as* itself, since it comes *from* itself and *for* it alone. Phenomenology does not aim any more at constituting (even less synthesizing) an object alienated from the lived experiences of consciousness, starting from the apperceptive activity of a transcendental subject, but aims at "showing from *itself* what shows *itself* so that *itself* is shown from *itself*."[14] And in fact, *Dasein* phenomenalizes itself from itself, no longer under the yoke of a transcendental subject: either fundamental emotional tonalities (boredom, anxiety, care) come to it at their own initiative or it arrives at its own anticipatory resoluteness without deciding either the moment or the modalities of its initiative. And if—as is open to debate—a "phenomenon of 'being'"[15] can some day phenomenalize itself, it will obviously not do so by starting from a being (even the *I*) but under its own light, having emerged from it alone. Appearance no longer imposes itself on the phenomenon with the status of an object coming from a transcendental authority but rather erupts at its own initiative. The phenomenon appears in and by itself. It owes the crossing of the gap between the invisible and the visible only to itself.

Would it be necessary to accord a *self* to the phenomenon, to recognize for it an ipseity equal to that of the *ego*, in short to dissociate the ipseity from *egoity*? Without doubt, this would run counter to the entire movement of metaphysics. At the least, it is the grandeur of phenomenology to have attempted this in its Heideggerian moment. Yet can one conceive such an ipseity of the phenomenon and grant to it a *self*, other than metaphorically? Can one define such a *self* of the phenomenon, of which Heidegger says nothing? The response to this question will take shape—perhaps—if another difficulty is considered, one that Husserl identifies with the "essential correlation between *appearing* and *that which appears*."[16] In fact, phenomenality supposes that the appearance does not deceive us and does not amount to a simple appearance which would itself apply only to the visible and would conceal anything when it itself disappears. It thus assumes that the appearing takes charge of an appearance, which receives a visibility from this appearing, but fills it in turn with its still invisible reality. In order that appearance yields to phenomenality, there must thus be an originary correlation between appearing and its appearance, an engagement of appearance in appearing. How should we qualify this engagement? As the propriety of appearing to give to the appearance in the same degree to which the appearance is engaged in the appearing. On this model, phenomenality accomplishes itself in the full phenomenon insofar as the appearing gives the appearance and the appearance gives itself in its engagement in the appearing. It is a question of "two absolute givennesses,"[17] the givenness of the appearing and the givenness of what appears by and as this appearing. By givenness, it is necessary here to understand the ultimate accomplishment of phenomenality, indubitable because it is perfectly reduced to immanence, such that it makes it possible to calibrate and accommodate all the degrees of presence, evidence, reality, and actuality, without nevertheless itself being reduced to them. The phenomenon thus recovers the sovereignty of its appearance only while being phenomenalized of and for *itself*, in showing *itself* as from *itself*. Yet it attests this *self* only when the appearance engages itself in its appearing. It engages itself in and to the appearing only if it gives *itself*. Nothing shows *itself* that does not first *give itself*. This rule of phenomenality in general measures the legitimacy and the possibility for any phenomenon to show itself according to the measure of givenness.[18]

IV. The Phenomenality of the Sacrament as the Phenomenality of the Abandon

From such a redefinition of phenomenality, can we reconsider the preceding aporia—that of a visibility of the invisible in the sacrament, "the *visible form* of the sacred thing and of *invisible* grace"? Undoubtedly the specifics of a theological theme (in this case straightforwardly Christological in nature) must inspire in us a great methodological prudence; no doubt also phenomenology, even when pushed toward its new resources, cannot open up a complete intelligibility of the Christian mystery, anymore than metaphysics could. However, starting from the principle that nothing shows *itself* which does not first *give itself*, reasoning by analogy becomes possible and legitimate, provided that it leads us to better conceive what we will yet never be able to comprehend. We will thus briefly but clearly try to outline here an approach to the phenomenality of the sacrament by analogy with the phenomenology of givenness.

In fact (as we have seen in section I) the sacrament takes a certain mode of phenomenality. That is because it depends directly upon the manifestation of Christ—not of a manifestation that Christ would achieve only in the economy, at a moment of the drama of salvation, as an extrinsic act, but of a manifestation intrinsic to theology which defines the Son's person itself, throughout directed toward the manifestation of the eternal mystery of God in the Spirit.[19] Christ manifests himself as the Son under the title of "icon of the invisible God, first-born of all creation" (Col. 1:15). Icon, therefore visibility—of God, therefore of the invisible, eternal articulation of the visible by the invisible as such and which remains the same in its manifestation. So that the transition from the invisible to the visible— what phenomenology precisely intends to think as such—determines the person himself of the Word assuming flesh in Christ. The meditation of the Son joins the mediation of Christ in the same making visible the invisible. Certainly, the analogy with the question of the phenomenon directly concerns the sacrament—it manifests an invisible effect, grace, because "an instrumental cause, if manifest, can be called a sign of an invisible effect."[20] But it concerns initially what the sacrament comes from and from where it draws its only legitimacy, namely the eternal involvement of the God of Jesus Christ in the process of manifesting and showing *himself*. The sacrament is sent by the dispensation of God himself, not only as one of his effects, nor even of one of his gifts, but also of Himself. When he gives, God never gives less than himself. God causes in person: "God alone brings about the interior effect of the sacrament" and "the power of the sacrament is from God alone."[21]

We thus have a firm base: the sacrament accomplishes and reduces the intrinsic manifestation of the Son, the transition in it from the Father's invisibility to Christ's visibility spread by the Spirit in its Church. In fact, the Church consists only in permitting the Trinitarian mystery to show *itself*—to phenomenalize itself according to all figures of grace: the rhythms of the liturgy and prayer (*lex orandi, lex credendi*), the service of the word of Scripture and thus its infinite hermeneutics, the sacraments starting from baptism and the Eucharist, charisms ordained for the good of the community, and all the fruits of holiness, which result from it in faces without number and end. More than as a society of the children of the Spirit, the Church defines itself in the world as a unique place. According to the simultaneously visible and invisible work of the Spirit, it is within the Church that the manifestation of the invisible can be accomplished. Through it the holiness of God succeeds in showing *itself* against all verisimilitude, even through finitude and sin. It thus exercises an analogously phenomenological function—"I give you a new commandment, that you love one another. Just as I have loved you, you also should love one another. By this evidence everyone will know that you are my disciples, if you have love for one another" (Jn. 13:34). In the (obviously sacramental) communion of the faithful a unique charity shows *itself*, the charity they share because it unites them with Christ and connects them even to the union between Christ and the Father. In this union, God thus shows *himself*—theologically manifests his glory—to the eyes of the world: "as you, Father, are in me and I am in you, may they also be in me and I am in you, so that the world may believe that we are one" (Jn.17:21). The indication and accomplishment of salvation are shown in fact by the universal revelation, therefore by the phenomenalization of all the glory of God, according to the radical apocalyptic principle that "nothing is covered up that will not be uncovered, and nothing secret that will not be known" (Lk. 12:2). One can and must obviously speak here of phenomenalization. Yet, one can do so only with the reservation of an analogy: It is not that the phenomena of revelation show *themselves* less than those of the common mode of experience, but on the contrary, because they show *themselves* infinitely more. It is not a question here only of the constitution of objects starting from a transcendental subjectivity, which controls them by the initiative of intentionality and certifies them by the insurance of intuitive fulfillment, but of the reception of phenomena that show *themselves*, beginning with the intentionality of God, such as he reveals himself in and from Himself, contrary to our expectations, predictions, and intentions, according to the deployment of an intuition that is "too much" (Mk. 9:3), or too strong for our capacity, God's glory itself. Before such phenomena—phenomena saturated by the characteristic of revelation—the usual problems of constitution give way to otherwise more formidable difficulties of intuition and its limits. It is a question of admitting phenomena where the excess of given intuition exceeds the range of concepts that we would have at our disposal to constitute them as objects. Knowledge, since it is always necessary to go in that direction, cannot be confined to the processes of objectivation, but must be accomplished by exceeding itself, that is, in being assimilated to faith. Faith is the mode of knowledge appropriate to the saturated phenomena characteristic of Revelation.[22] Thus, it is advisable to situate the sacrament in the horizon of God's Revelation in his icon, Christ, and to apprehend it, by analogy with the phenomenality of the world, as a phenomenon that shows *itself* par excellence and in excess.

Yet can one maintain this analogy? With what phenomenological right may one admit that the sacrament shows *itself* to the point of manifesting God's invisibility? It certainly shows, but only what it gives to see as a phenomenon of the first degree—this bread, this wine, this water, this oil. By what right can one see here more than these simple things of the world, which furthermore are perfectly sufficient to fill a gaze, a hand, and a human desire, even that of an artist? By claiming that the invisibility of the kindness, the glory, and the grace of God shows *itself*, do we not yield in the best case to a symbolic overvaluation or in the worst case a magic delusion? This "enlightened" objection has its force, but also its fragility. Two decisive points must be considered.

(A) First, that anything of the world, when it shows *itself* truly, that is, when it appears in its plenitude and as such, instead of traversing our visual field during the short moment when we employ it for a purpose that remains foreign to it (whether by everyday tools or that of technique), makes manifest much more than its materiality or its immediate utility. Water cannot not appear initially as what saves my life (alleviates thirst, cleanses a wound) or threatens it (drowns me, carries me away); bread, as what maintains my strength, even poorly; wine, as what rejoices my spirit, even if it also blurs it for me; oil, as what comforts my flesh, embellishes it, or embalms it. That which signifies the things of the world already brings to visibility more than simply matter; therefore, it always renders manifest an invisibility (a sense, a promise). Anything already shows infinitely more than its materiality. It is not necessary for the gaze of a painter to give it some assurance—only an eye open to more than economic interest. And these moral and spiritual tonalities already appear at the outset, intrinsically, with the materiality of the sacrament, which thus implements a determination of the phenomena in general in a simply more radical mode. Here, as in all cases, that which the thing shows, at least when one allows it the freedom to show *itself*, depends on the width of our reception and the meaning it carries with it. But who or what gives it to the thing? That which gives it to us or we ourselves who accept it as given? What does *to give* mean here?

The second point follows from this. (B) If we wonder regarding who or what gives what we will see, to decide what we see there in fact, or rather what we have to see there (waiting to see there), before any analogy this question returns to strict phenomenology. For as we established earlier (section III), nothing shows *itself*, which does not initially give *itself* and to the measure in which it gives *itself*, since in effect a phenomenon can manifest *itself* only insofar as it is *itself* given in real-life experience, that it engages in the flesh and in person in the field of consciousness. If water and bread, oil and wine already manifest more than their materiality, it is because from the outset they present more than matter to human consciousness, always already a total experience of itself. And this excess already authorizes them to phenomenalize the invisible in its appearing. Can one not, by analogy, envision a case where what is given would give *itself* in fact so radically that it guarantees, even by this engagement with our consciousness, that *itself* shows effectively all that it says it will give to see—all that which is invisible that it promises to see, since it gives it? Should one not envision the hypothesis that what gives *itself* would give *itself* so definitively that all that it promises to show is *itself* really shown? In this context, the sacrament would show *itself* (would manifest the invisible within it) by virtue of the authority of what or who gives *itself* (or himself) within it: nothing less than the Spirit, such as Christ delivers by giving *himself* delivered on the Cross to the beloved precisely in his abandonment of love: "he said, 'it is finished.' Then he bowed his head and gave up his spirit" (Jn. 19:30). Only this givenness of oneself—the *kenosis* as abandon which engages irrevocably—actually immediately garners the authority, which qualifies water and blood as more than daily tools but as the matter of the sacraments of the Spirit: "one of the soldiers pierced his side with a spear, and at once blood and water came out. (He who saw this has testified so that you also may believe. His testimony is true, and he knows that he tells the truth)" (Jn. 19:34–35; see I Jn. 5:5–8). The phenomenality of what gives *itself* extends to the givenness of the invisible; in short, it qualifies the sacrament as a phenomenon by full right, although by analogy, because what gives *itself* gives itself to the point of death and of the death on the Cross, because what gives it gives *itself* absolutely. Christ gives *himself* enough so that even the invisible face of the Father can show *itself* among us.

That is enough to qualify the sacrament as a perfect and whole phenomenality.

Translated by Bruce Ellis Benson

The Human in Question

Augustinian Dimensions in Jean-Luc Marion

JEFFREY L. KOSKY

Most of the English-speaking audience was introduced to the new French phenomenology, the subject of this volume, through the work of Jean-Luc Marion. In particular, the translation of Marion's *God Without Being* was the first major work of these authors to achieve widespread attention. Because of this, the new French phenomenology is associated with a "theological turn." No doubt, *God Without Being* justifies being labeled a theological work. Its project was to give revelation or to think a transcendent God absolutely and unconditionally. The divine transcendence could be given by liberating God from those determinations, which, Marion argued, reduced it to immanence, or what he thematized as "idol." The idol (1) marks the farthest point reached by a human gaze, intention, or aim directed at the divine such that the idol (2) serves as a mirror that shows this gaze, intention, or aim to itself. In short, the idol tells more about the finitude of man than it does about the transcendent God. Its correspondence with a human intention only shows a human subject who he is, what he is capable of, and how far his limits extend.

In its opposition to idolatry, the theology of *God Without Being* evidences a negative judgment on the human. The idol, telling of human finitude, must be overcome in order to reach a theology in which revelation of divine transcendence is given as such. *God Without Being* therefore had recourse to Christian theology for figures of thought that provided what Marion called an "icon" of the divine. In particular, the mystical theology of Christian theologians such as Gregory of Nyssa and especially

Pseudo-Dionysius provided a model of theology in which human conceptions and constructions were overcome and the divine transcendence given. Accordingly, Marion adopted a set of distinctions that distinguished between theological thought of God and other, nontheological thoughts: "God" and GXd, theiology and theology, idols and icons of God.

The Question of God Becomes a Question of Man:
From Dionysius to Augustine

As the new French phenomenology is more widely read, it becomes important that readers (especially English-speaking readers) not let the frame established by *God Without Being* obstruct another question. That question is the question of man: Who is Man, and what marks the finitude of the human subject? This is the obvious concern of Jean-Yves Lacoste's *Experience and the Absolute*, whose subtitle makes it explicit: *Disputed Questions on the Humanity of Man*. And it is equally important to Jean-Louis Chrétien, who suggests that his own work has never stopped trying "to think finitude positively."[1]

This positive regard for human finitude is shared, I argue here, by Marion's later work. Whereas *God Without Being* called for eliminating consideration of human experience and the finite subjectivity it presupposes in order to give the divine as such, in the later work, the human (named "the gifted"), "inasmuch as finite, has nothing less than the charge of opening or closing the entire flux of phenomenality."[2] Since phenomenality "is always put into operation in the essential finitude of the gifted" (BG, 309), Marion's later work offers positive consideration of human experience—as what he calls "counter-experience," which does not "consist in annulling or overcoming the conditions for the possibility of experience, but . . . in exceeding or contradicting them" (BS, 398).

This shift in which increasing regard is paid to human finitude goes together with a shift from Dionysian models of thought to Augustinian ones, reaching the point that the essay in which Marion asks explicitly, "What is Man?" is oriented directly by Augustine's declaration, "Factus eram ipse mihi magna quaestio."[3] This Augustinian orientation might not be surprising as scholars have long remarked on the absence of accounts of experience in Dionysian theology (which prefers to explain the objectively mystical character of the universe) and, inversely, Augustine's marked preference for arguing on the basis of an account of the human subject.[4] Sometimes Marion's Augustinian models are explicit, as in his 2005 inaugural lecture as the John Nuveen Professor of the Philosophy of Religion and Theology at the University of Chicago and in his keynote address for a 2004 conference at Notre Dame dedicated to his work.[5] These explicit references come from Augustine's *Confessions,* a work that the influential Catholic theologian Hans Urs von Balthasar *disregards* because they "shift the emphasis principally to subjectivity."[6] Von Balthasar's reason for disregarding *Confessions* would appear to be Marion's reason for regarding it, owing most likely to the fact that he will find in subjectivity something more than just the subject solipsistically coincident with itself. Even when Augustinian models are not explicit in Marion, I would like to suggest, they are already operative, as is the case in *Being Given.*

In Marion's later work, Augustine serves as guide in developing an anthropology in which the human proves as incomprehensible to itself as the divine was in *God Without Being.* If *God Without Being* supposes that human thought and language must be overcome in order to give divine transcendence, this thesis rests on the assumption that human knowledge is ultimately self-knowledge, consciousness ultimately self-consciousness.[7] On this assumption, Dionysian theology seemed to offer the only way out. In Augustine, however, Marion will discover a model of the human subject in which there is more to man than what he can understand of himself, more to my experience than the experience I constitute for myself. When man does not know himself, he loses the ground on which his knowledge of the totality of being rests (*cogito* being *cogito me cogitare*). The target that *God Without Being* aimed to overcome vanishes.

Marion shares this adherence to an Augustinian model of thinking about the incomprehensible and excessive human with Jean-Louis Chrétien—who credits Augustine's self-examination in *Confessions* X as paradigm for his own exploration of the "almost unbearable test that a person becomes for himself, [a test that is] not at all related to evil or sin, but to the excess of a human being over himself, an excess of what one is and can be over what one can think and comprehend" (UU, 119). Indeed, Marion's anthropology will also suggest that the incomprehensibility or excess of the subject to itself is not the degrading of the human but rather its "privilege" or the "first bulwark" to the dignity of man (PU, 14, 20). From a limit to be put out of play in *God without Being*, human finitude has become not only inescapable but a privilege, the privilege of being what Chrétien calls "the place where there can truly be—though not transparently—a testimony to the infinite" (UU, 122).

This use of Augustine to articulate an originarily incomprehensible human or a human who exceeds itself will surprise those inclined to take Augustine's journey as one of self-discovery in a self-knowledge grounded in knowledge of God. These would include orthodox traditionalists, for whom Augustine's self-discovery is a model to imitate, and it would also include those postmoderns for whom Augustinian selfhood is a model of the human whose overcoming is the task of thinking. Among the latter, the influential work of Mark C. Taylor is notable. In *Erring*, Taylor sees Augustine as the origin of the western "epoch of selfhood spanning a period that extends roughly from Augustine's *Confessions* to Hegel's *Phenomenology of Spirit*."[8] The Augustinian subject, Taylor claims, like the absolute subject in Hegel, achieves full and total self-possession in and through the inward turn of reflective introspection or recollection. Recollection (the investigation of memory) is the activity of presenting self to self in order to gather together (or recollect) the scattered fragments of my self. Taylor states quite clearly the connection between recollection, self-knowledge, and the human subject's presence to itself:

> In the act of knowing, the subject re-members or re-collects what previously had been dismembered or dispersed. Insofar as the object of consciousness is the self itself, self-knowledge inevitably entails self-recollection. . . . Recollection [*Erinnerung*] involves interiorization or internalization. . . . According to its founder [Augustine], the aim of autobiography is the establishment of personal identity through the integration of the personality. In order to achieve this coherence, it is necessary to relate the multiple experiences the self has undergone in such a way that they constitute a comprehensive and comprehensible totality.[9]

On Taylor's reading, recollection achieves the total and transparent presence of the human subject to itself in self-knowledge. At the end, human finitude is overcome as all experience that remains foreign or alien to me is reduced by inwardizing recollection to what is my own or appropriate to me. "The activity of self-presentation constitutes a process of self-appropriation, through which the subject comes into possession of itself."[10]

Now, the model of human subjectivity that Taylor finds in Augustine is precisely that which Marion's anthropology will claim is subverted by Augustine. Invoking Augustine in order to conjure a human subject who articulates the privilege of human finitude, incomprehensibility, and inauthenticity, Marion's Augustine defends the greatness of a being human that, in excess over itself, does *not* achieve self-possession.

Incomprehensibility and Inauthenticity

Marion's Augustinian reflection on the question of man (his anthropology) is most explicit in his John Nuveen lecture: "*Mihi magna quaestio factus sum*: The Privilege of Unknowing." There he starts from a claim to both the impossibility and undesirability of human self-knowledge. If the human subject were to know himself, Marion argues, such knowledge would mean that I am "masked and lowered to the dishonorable rank of an object. Rather than giving me access to the man that I am, [it] forbids me from drawing near to the man that I am and disfigures the very stake of anthropology—the self of each human being" (PU, 4). Given that what knowledge knows, by definition, is an object, to know myself means knowing myself as that which I am not—namely, as an *object*, not as the human *subject* I am.[11] Hence man cannot "apply to himself his own knowledge in order to become his own object" (PU, 3). Our knowledge (and what we know today is tremendous, as the rise of gigantic computing power has produced an ever-expanding domain of scientific objects) does not let us know ourselves, however much this knowledge might include the human objects known in fields such as neuroscience, pharmacology, and molecular genetics.

What is more, it is hardly even desirable that man should know himself. "What would it serve a man to know himself through the mode by which he knows the remainder—the world and its objects. . . . What would it serve a man to know himself with a concept, if in doing so he lost his humanity or, in other words his soul?" (PU, 7). The suggestion here is that man is reduced to an inanimate (unsouled) object when he knows himself objectively, clearly and distinctly, perfectly and comprehensively—as perhaps in the new "sciences of the soul" (neuroscience, pharmacology, and so forth), which know us so well as to predict and even control and produce moods, states of mind, and the pulsations of desire. Indeed, Marion claims, human self-knowledge and the objective determination of the human prove more dangerous than the lack of such self-knowledge. "To claim to define what a man is leads to or at least opens the possibility of leading to the elimination of that which does not correspond to this definition," a possibility that Marion suggests is realized in ethnic cleansing, racial extermination, and so forth (PU, 13).

Rather than take this aporia of self-knowledge as the end of the discussion, Marion seeks instead to count it as an evidence indicating another way of experiencing myself besides objectively in self-knowledge. If my humanity escapes me precisely to the degree that it is known, then, Marion concludes, "I do not appear to myself as knowledge (an object), but instead as a definitive question" (PU, 5). Though Heidegger is not cited here, Marion's point resonates with the Heideggerian determination of man as that being whose way to be is to ask the question of Being—that being "which in its Being has this very Being as an issue."[12] If to be is to ask the question of being, then definitive answers put an end to the question that I am. This point is repeated, throughout Heidegger's writing, but is found clearly stated here: "The determination of the essence of man is *never* an answer but essentially a question."[13] Being human involves the irreducible risk and instability of repeatedly and endlessly exceeding whatever conception I, or others, might have of myself.

If Heidegger is not declared a guide here, Augustine is: "Factus eram ipse mihi magna quaestio [I had become to myself a huge question]" and, "In your [God's] eyes, I have become a question to myself [mihi quaestio factus sum]" (PU, 5, citing *Conf.* 4.4.9 and 10.33.50). Marion cites several examples from Augustine in which the human being in his own investigation of himself discovers that he is other, strange, or not coincident with himself.[14] Marion concludes that for Augustine, "In a single moment I discover myself to be someone other than my self, I am not what I am, I become a *quaestio* for myself. The experience of self ends neither in the aporia of substituting an object (the self, the *me*) for the I that I am, nor in the pure identity with self, but in the alienation of self from self—*I* am to myself other than I" (PU, 7).

The noncoincidence with myself that Marion describes here by reference to Augustine's self-experience is what the phenomenology of *Being Given* described, without explicit reference to Augustine, as the "fundamental inauthenticity" of the human subject as gifted (BG, 270). The "gifted" is Marion's name for the successor to the metaphysical determination of the human as representational subject. As gifted, the human receives itself from the given that it receives—hence the title "the gifted." The gifted no longer precedes events as that which constitutes their meaning, but comes after, emerging in, or better as, the meaningful response to events. Hence, Marion will speak of the work of being human as "responsal."[15]

Now insofar as the human as gifted comes to itself in response to a call that precedes it, one of its chief characteristics will be what Marion calls "the delay of the responsal" (BG, 287). I am not there before my own origin, which has two consequences: my response never measures up to the events that make me who I am, and the call that makes me myself remains of "indeterminate origin" (BG, 268). From the very beginning, then, the human, as gifted, cannot say who he is or know where he came from. The call does indeed identify him, "but this identification escapes him straightaway since he receives it without necessarily knowing it" (BG, 268), owing to the constitutive delay of his origin. My own identity appears to me as a question.

This implies what Marion calls the "originarily altered" identity of the gifted (BG, 268). The human gifted is not originally in full possession of itself, but rather begins only with this distance from his own origin. Indeed, authentic self-knowledge alienates the human from itself: "authenticity hides the fact of the call" (BG, 270). Self-possession, in which I could appropriate myself and "authenticate myself without remainder" (BG, 290), prove self-defeating for a subject that is born in, or better as, response to a call that is only received and therefore not proper to me. The inevitable "delay of the responsal" attests "the irreparable excess" of the call over and above every response, no response ever co-responding to the call—condemning the human to an "originary difference with itself as an I, therefore [to] inauthenticity" (BG, 270). The response that I am is only ever inauthentic and improper, never equal to my original calling because this calling does not come from me. If the human is to achieve "access to itself" as the gifted, this cannot happen in the self-possession of self-knowledge. Rather it must involve coming into "the inauthenticity that alone is originarily giving" me to myself (BG, 270)—the alteration that makes me me by differing from myself.

With his Nuveen lecture, Marion finds in Augustine a way for human being to "acknowledge a fundamental inauthenticity, originary inappropriateness, [an acknowledgement that] lets us reach the truth of the gifted. I is an other," such that the human subject has access to itself as a stranger or other, distant from himself (BG, 290).

An Excursus on Augustine

Closer investigation of Augustine's *Confessions* can help us see Marion's grounds for claiming that Augustine offers a way to make the acknowledgment of the originary inauthenticity and incomprehensibility of the human that is called for in *Being Given*. The "distance [that] arises in the I itself" (BG, 290) such that I never coincide with myself or correspond perfectly with my origin owing to "the irreparable excess of the call"—all this echoes the Augustinian declaration "I cannot grasp the totality of what I am. The mind [animus] is not large enough to contain itself" (Conf. X, 8).[16]

Initially it appears to Augustine that *memoria* is, as Mark Taylor suggested, the sphere of self-possession. Memory contains all the experience that would make me who I am. "This thing [memory] is the mind, and this thing is I myself" (X, 17). What is more, not only would *memoria* contain all that I am, but all that I am would be transparent and accessible to me: "When I am in this treasure house, I ask for some things to be brought out to me. . . . The thing that I want is discovered and brought out from its hidden place into my sight" (X, 8). Everything I am is myself, and myself is all that I am—this experience of self entails a perfect coincidence and correspondence with myself.

And yet, this memory, "this thing [that is] I myself," proves not just great (magna), but "excessively great (magna nimis)," or great beyond measure, so "vast and unbounded [amplum et infinitum]" that "the mind is too narrow to contain itself" (Conf. X, 8). Considering more carefully the inventory of what he finds in his memory, Augustine's *inspectio mentis* notes some surprising excesses flickering within, excesses that undo the perfect coincidence of self with self.

First, "when I remember forgetfulness, there are present both memory and forgetfulness" (X, 16) such that my memory escapes me. In the intimate depths of the human subject (namely, in *memoria*), Augustine finds in forgetfulness something that is not identical to the subject he is. Hence he observes: "My memory is incomprehensible to me [memoriae meae vis non comprehenditur a me], even though without it, I should not be able to call myself myself" (X, 16). What makes me me remains incomprehensible to myself such that the originary encounter with myself is one that sets me at a distance from myself, originarily altered. I become a stranger to myself, the more I come to know the memory that makes me who I am.

Next, the experience of beatitude or the happy life—that is, the desire for God. In the search for God, Augustine notes, he must "go past this force of mine called memory"; and yet he observes equally that "If I find you beyond memory, I can have no memory of you. And how shall I find you if I do not remember you" (X, 17). Accepting the aporia, Augustine concludes that the human subject, his *memoria*, again exceeds what it can remember. This idea (happiness or God, unlike the ideas of Carthage or grammar), one I must surely have insofar as I seek the thing, cannot however be characterized as belonging properly to that which I am, *memoria*, because I cannot remember where or when I acquired it: "Where then was it and when was it that I experienced my happy life so that I should remember it and love it and long for it" (X, 21). The origin of this idea remains lost to Augustine such that it appears like a stranger within him. He cannot remember this original state of enjoying the presence of God, a lost origin that would constitute his ownmost being as desire for God. The highly influential and well-known theologian Hans Urs Von Balthasar will even speak of Augustine's "lifelong refusal to offer a theory for the soul's origin in God"—as if human being were fundamentally alienated from the event that gives it to itself originarily.[17] In short, with his desire for God, Augustine has found within *memoria*, himself, the trace of an event (enjoying the divine presence) he cannot possess, appropriate as his own, or give to himself, but which is nevertheless the event that constitutes him most fundamentally (as desire for God).

The philosopher Charles Taylor has noted an instructive contrast here with Platonic notions of *memoria*, a contrast that helps us see the originary alteration and fundamental inauthenticity of the human subject in Augustine.

Augustine's memory is rather different from Plato's. In his mature philosophy, it has broken altogether away from an original vision of the Ideas, crucial to Platonic theory. In fact, Augustine's concept gets extended and *comes to include matters that have nothing to do with past experience*, including just those principles of the intelligible order which we have been discussing and which are somehow within us . . . *even though they were never presented to us explicitly in the past.* Augustine [takes] the Platonic notion of memory and [cuts] it off from its roots in the theory of prenatal experience [my emphasis].[18]

In attempting to explain how it is that we might search for something we don't know, Platonic thought has recourse to a prior existence of the soul: based on experiences had in a past life or prior to a fall into body, my memory includes a memory of happiness such that I know what it is implicitly, desire it, and can ultimately find it by recognizing it. Augustine, however, does not accept this solution to the problem—as Charles Taylor notes, "Going within memory takes me beyond. . . . While for Plato, the 'within' was only a way of recurring to a 'before,' for Augustine, it is the path to an 'above.'"[19] The Platonic solution explains the desire for happiness by respecting the coincidence of the human with itself; according to the Platonic theory of prenatal experience or the soul's intelligible existence prior to its fall into bodies, there would be nothing in me that is alien to me, nothing in me that exceeds me, because all that is in *memoria* could be remembered as an experience proper to me, even if belonging to the soul's previous existence, forgotten since birth but not lost irretrievably. Augustine, "refusing to offer a theory for the soul's origin in God," as von Balthasar notes, suggests an irreducible alterity, difference, or distance at the heart of memory insofar as the turn inward leads him not to a before but to an up, taking him beyond the past still present in *memoria* and exceeding the experience of perfect coincidence with himself.[20]

This perhaps is why Augustine comes to what seems to be the conclusion of the reflection on himself with the declaration, "Late did I love you, beauty so ancient and so new, late I loved you! And, look, you were within me and I was outside" (Conf. X, 27). How could the search for God not come too late when it is grounded in the memory of an immemorial event to which he was never present because it never happened in a past belonging to the present of *memoria*? This inevitable lateness or delay leads Augustine to declare, "You [God] were with me, and I was not with you" (ibid.). The desire for God that determines the Augustinian soul most fundamentally bespeaks an originary relation structured by the nonpresence or noncorrespondence of the self and God, one that stands in marked contrast to the Platonic supposition of souls that exist before their birth and so might be present before the call so that they can receive it comprehensively.[21]

To conclude: what Augustine finds when turning inward to consider the human being that he is turns out not to be perfect appropriateness to himself, but a truth that he cannot comprehend at the very origin of himself—namely, God, a presence that precedes his own presence to himself and so confronts me with what Marion calls the "undeniable facticity" of a call that claims the human subject before it is there to deny it (BG, 270). This undeniable facticity is the God who Augustine also claims is *interior intimo meo et superior summo meo* (more inward than my most inward inwardness, and higher than my highest) (Conf. III, 6). Confronting the fact of this truth, Augustine declares, "I would sooner doubt my own existence than the existence of that truth" (Conf. VII, 10). His introspection has produced not self-certainty, but the certainty of another, in whose light his own certainty of himself is rendered doubtful. What Augustine's introspective experience of himself demonstrates is that human reflection on the human leads not to giving oneself one's own certainty of oneself, but rather opens the human to the instability and trouble, incomprehensibility and uncertainty, that are fundamental to the human when seen with regard to its origin in a certainty that exceeds it: "In your eyes, I have become a question to myself (Conf. X, 33), as both Marion and Chrétien remind us.

Theological Defense of the Indefinite Human

It is worth remarking here that the human becomes a question, more and more incomprehensible and uncertain of itself, insofar as it relates to its origin in God, an origin that, far from giving it a final definition, renders it indefinite. Marion takes this pattern to be Augustinian and will mobilize it in his effort to preserve and maintain what he takes to be the "privilege," indeed "the sign, the proof, and the guarantee of [man's] humanity" (PU, 14–15): namely, his incomprehensibility.[22] Against any definition of the human, Marion opposes a theological indefinition in which human incomprehensibility is grounded in the incomprehensibility of a God in whose image this human is created: "The incomprehensibility of the human being remains . . . it is bound up with theology" (PU, 23). The biblical doctrine of man as *imago dei* serves as the basis for the incomprehensibility of the human. "Man remains unimaginable because he is formed in the image of the One who admits no image whatsoever" (PU, 15). This use of Scripture might be surprising to certain atheists or philosophers (Marion names Heidegger) as much as it might be surprising to orthodox theists, insofar as it does not find in Biblical Scripture answers to the questions of life or certain definitions for the essence of the human. As used by Marion, the Scripture "establishes nothing certain and pronounces no clear and distinct knowledge whatsoever; on the contrary, its revelation of man as created in the image and likeness of God institutes an unknowing that is all the more radical in that is founded in the incomprehensibility of God himself" (PU, 21). The "answer" Scripture gives, like the ontology or thanatology of Heidegger's *Being and Time*, opens, rather than closes, the question that is man.

Theology, then, far from securing the definition of the human or guaranteeing the possibility of knowing myself, renders the human indefinite and ultimately incomprehensible. Gregory of Nyssa states this perfectly:

> Since one of the attributes we contemplate in the Divine nature is incomprehensibility of essence, it is clearly necessary that in this point the icon [the *imago dei*, man] should be able to show its imitation of the archetype. . . . Since the nature of our mind, which is according to the icon of the Creator, evades our knowledge, it keeps an accurate resemblance to the superior nature, retaining the imprint of the incomprehensible [fixed] by the unknown within it.[23]

Indeed, as Marion reminds us, Adam might very well name and define everything, and thus know and dominate it, but he does not name himself or God. What is definitive of the human, constituting its difference from every other animal and thing in the world (finite and also definite, therefore knowable), as well as God (infinite and therefore unknowable), is thus its indefinition. This indefinition of the human confounds the clear and distinct opposition of the finite (world) and infinite (God). Indeed the excess of a human being over what it can comprehend of itself and its world articulates an irreducibly finite, yet forever incomplete (infinite?) and not definite character of the human being. Strictly maintaining the distinction would contradict the incomprehensibility of man by situating finitude on the side of comprehensibility. The theological indefinition of the human, by contrast, guarantees human finitude at the same time as it renders this finitude uncertain, unstable, forever a question to itself, undecided.

Situated between God and the animals, Man becomes what Nietzsche called "das noch nicht festgestellte Tier (the animal that is not yet stabilized)" (cited in PU, 20). Human instability (*nicht festgestellte*), a fragility to be guarded as well as a shifting definition to assume, means that man cannot be set in place (*-gestellte*) securely or firmly (*fest-*). The human, however finite, cannot be captured in a concept that would contain the human, solidify it and set it in place. One should read this citation from Nietzsche against Heidegger's worry that the modern determination of reality according to technoscientific enframing or emplacement (*Gestell*) was being turned against man himself, the human increasingly being treated as a resource to be secured (set in place) and managed effectively by representational thinking. The incomprehensibility of the human, grounded in the incomprehensibility of God, protects the instability (*nicht festgestellte*), both fragility and flux, of "the being who remains, for himself, to be decided and about whom one never ceases to be astonished" (PU, 20).

The Noncorresponding Response:
A Positive Sense of Human Finitude

What remains for me in this account of the human in question is to consider the positive sense Marion gives to human finitude. Highlighting the departure from what would seem to be the negative regard for human finitude in *God Without Being*, Marion makes clear in "The Banality of Saturation" that "the "finitude of the transcendental subject . . . is suffered and experienced as such in the contradiction that the excess of intuition imposes on it" (BS, 402).[24] Two connected theses prove crucial to understanding Marion's account of human finitude: (1) Human finitude is given by the phenomenal event of saturation in which it is given in excess of what it can receive; such that (2) this finitude serves as what Chrétien calls "the place where there can be—though not transparently—a testimony to the infinite" (UU, 122). The greatness or privilege of the human resides in its weakness or powerlessness to offer a response that corresponds with the call that constitutes its originary finitude.[25]

These two theses relating to human finitude come together when Marion thinks the human gifted in terms of the witness. The notion of witness means that the human subject does not make or constitute the event he witnesses, but is himself made by it into what he has become: witness.[26]

Equally important, however, is the claim that the human as witness serves as "the worker of the truth" or "the gatekeeper for the ascent into visibility of all that gives itself" (BG, 217, 307). Nothing that is given shows itself in truth except insofar as it is witnessed. The testimony of the finite witness thus serves as the "luminous screen" on which alone the excessive given shows itself. This testimony is his response to events, *responsal* being another name for the operation of the witness.

Marion articulates quite clearly the finitude or constitutive weakness of the human witness. Overwhelmed by the excessive event that gives him to himself, the witness experiences "its own powerlessness to master the measurelessness of the intuitive given" (BG, 216). The witness discovers its constitutive finitude in its incapacity to give enough meaning to the event it experiences. The event calls for more meaning than I can give in the concepts, intentions, or signs by which my testimony, like an idol, makes it appear. Owing to originary alteration and structural delay of the responsal, there is no exact correspondence between the meaning the witness gives to the event, which is the response in which the event shows itself, and the excess of the phenomenal event that constituted him. No one will ever know the horror, or the joy, of these founding events, and the witness falls silent or faints before the tale is told. "Most of the time, he does not even claim [to comprehend what he saw]; indeed he ends by plunging into silence" (BS, 408), well before any end of his testimony, however much repeated incessantly, has been reached.

This plunge into silence, and even the necessary idolatry of the testimony that does not correspond, markers of the witness's finitude and powerlessness to constitute the event that constitutes him, need not be read as defects or shortcomings. Indeed, Marion, like Chrétien, will take it as a "consecration of the gifted by what happens to him" (BG, 306). Powerlessness to respond in a way that corresponds to one's calling (the inadequacy and inauthenticity of my response) become the privilege of the human to show forth the measureless given that exceeds us and gives us to ourselves. The ever repeated yet ever insufficient response of the witness testifies in its very unendingness to an excess that can never be exhausted. The finite witness is thus summoned to respond infinitely, a vocation to which it can never correspond, but nevertheless in its falling short bears witness to that to which it could only ever fall short.

Decision and Will

Frightening questions now confront Marion: How can the human become witness to a calling to which no response could ever correspond?

How can the human subject assume this vocation to manifest the excess of the given? In addressing these difficulties in *Being Given*, Marion has recourse to notions of decision and will that obey a logic that proves, in "The Banality of Saturation," to be Augustinian.

Insofar as the finitude of the human is given by an event of overwhelming and unmasterable excess, the human subject emerges in what *Being Given* claims is givenness's "conflict with the gifted" (BG, 307) and what "The Banality of Saturation" analyzes more explicitly as *resistance*.

> This ordeal of excess is actually attested by the resistance, eventually the pain, that it imposes on the one who receives it. . . . The gifted verifies itself infinitely more when face-to-face with a saturated phenomenon than before an object since it experiences itself as such in the counter-experience that resists it. For resistance can go so far as to expose me to a danger, the danger of seeing too much. . . . This resistance imposes itself as suffering. (BS, 403–4)

Human finitude is constituted by the harrowing ordeal of witnessing more than one can bear. This overwhelming event constitutes the human subject as finite more irrevocably than does the manageable experience of objects known adequately; for in the latter experience, the human reaches no limit to his powers. Insofar as the human receives itself in an experience that is too much for it, indeed one that acts contrary to him or counteracts him (what Marion calls counter-experience), and brings with it pain and suffering, how could his originary experience not be resistance?

What this means is that the degree to which man assumes his privilege of witnessing the excessive call depends on how he handles his resistances. How long can I stand exposure to the inevitable tension, pain, and suffering—maintain my fragility—of being that "unstable animal" given over to witnessing what resists? In *Being Given*, Marion seems to suggest that humans gain full standing as the gifted "by exposing ourselves to the humiliation of never constituting and endlessly repeating the responses," which are "always partial and provisional responses, marking the irrevocable shortcomings of the gifted" (BG, 306). What *Being Given* calls "humiliation" echoes in what Marion later calls "reverential fear": a form of resistance whose "recoil before what it glimpses . . . recognizes its excess" (BS, 404). Most often, however, and inevitably, Marion claims, human resistance takes the form of denial. With denial, a human gifted has reached the limits of what he can witness. His finitude is affirmed here in that he cannot resist forever and settles the conflict with givenness—by cutting off reception of the infinite, and fearsome, excess of the event. If humility and reverential fear accept originary finitude and inauthenticity, denial is the experience of human finitude that represses what exceeds it, "a second-order resistance (resistance to the resistance, evade it), a denial, a refusal" to give oneself over to the humiliating experience of being made by the excessive event in which I receive myself (BS, 405).

With a notion such as "denial," Marion shifts his account of human finitude to matters that *Being Given* discusses in terms of decision and will. Just how far we fall short of corresponding to our calling is a matter of our deciding not to accept the humiliating experience in which we are gifted with incomprehensibility and inauthenticity—that is, the privilege of being human. This "introduces, in addition to the powerlessness of the gifted (already constitutive of the witness), his will not to stage the intuitive excess given to him" (BG, 314). The will of the gifted human is not the will of a heroic human whose will, accepting no world there, given before it, confronts nothing other that would resist it and therefore can reshape the world in accordance with ends he sets autonomously. Rather, the will of the gifted human always acts by making "a decision to desert, *not to resist,* an act of defeat, at the opposite extreme from a defiant will, a will to power, or a will to will" (BG, 314 [my emphasis]). Here the decisions made by human willing show our weakness, not our strength or our autonomy: they cut short reception of givens that precede and exceed us, and they mark the limit of our capacity to receive.

For the phenomenal event of overwhelming excess to be witnessed, Marion suggests, it must be "truly wanted, not denied or evaded" (BG, 305). At this point, Marion seems to suggest a form of will that is more fundamental than the will discussed a moment ago. Before the will is defeated and makes the decision to cut off excessive reception and settle on this or that, there comes what Marion calls "the will to see." "In order to see, one must first want to see" (BG, 305). Since the will to see "sees nothing before giving itself over to it" (BG, 304), this will delivers us to a state of "indecision" (BG, 306), where it wants to see without vision or reason deciding in favor of this or that to be seen. The will to see belongs to a human who "who does not know what it wants because it must first want in order to see, therefore, to know it" (BG, 306). In delivering us over to the indecision that precedes all decision, the will to see proves crucial in maintaining the definitive indefinition of that unstable animal, man, "undecidable to himself, who loses himself if he claims to decide about himself" (PU, 20).

Now, the will to see can be approached according to an Augustinian logic that becomes explicit in "The Banality of Saturation." When Marion makes the will the condition of seeing and knowing, he rejects what he calls the metaphysical principle according to which "the will wants what the understanding sees in its own light" (BG, 305). This rejection follows the well-known discoveries of Augustine in *Confessions*, where he finds that, put simply, knowing the truth is not enough to accede to it. However much the Platonists might have given him a concept and a path by which to know God (Book VII), Augustine finds that this is not enough to receive the phenomenal event of the divine. Indeed what he requires more basically than knowledge that would give him certainty of God is help for his broken will (Book VIII). "Non intratur in veritatem nisi per caritatem [we shall not enter truth except through love]," Augustine declares famously in *Contra Faustum* 32, 18. Indeed according to the logic of *Being Given*, it is also the case that for the given to show itself in truth, the witness must want to see—that is, love to see—before seeing the truth.

Now, in "The Banality of Saturation," this "will to see" operates with an explicitly Augustinian dimension. Just as assuming the privilege of gifted human being entails a will to see in which I give myself over to the humiliating counter-experience of receiving myself from an event that exceeds me, so too does Augustine discover a meaning of truth in which truth does not simply show me something but accuses (humiliates) me. This is the *veritas redarguens* that Augustine speaks of in Confessions X, 23: "They love the truth when it enlightens them, but hate it when it remonstrates with them [*amant eam lucentem, oderunt eam redarguentem*]. . . . They love truth when truth discloses itself, but hate it when it discloses them. . . . The human mind cannot hide from truth, but truth can be out of its sight" (cited in BS, 405). This truth that remonstrates must be distinguished from the *veritas lucens*, a truth that shows and illuminates. This is the truth in which Augustine is shown the certainties he comes to know in Book VII of *Confessions*. *Veritas redarguens*, by contrast, is a truth in which "the more the evidence discloses the thing the more access to it is shut, the more it becomes the object of a refusal" (BS, 405), precisely because the truth that is shown is a truth that accuses the man to whom it appears. Whereas the truth that illuminates is one the will happily follows after, the truth that remonstrates is one that we *do not* want to see (decide to evade after it is given) and so one that appears only to the degree that we *do* want to see (give ourselves over with a "will to see"). A truth that discloses me is one before which I recoil, seeing as the doubt it casts on the self-certainty I constitute for myself is too much for me to bear. The *veritas redarguens*, according to Marion, "can indeed almost inevitably must, lead the gaze to refuse what shows itself [se *montre*] only by remonstrating [*en remonstrant*] with this gaze" (BS, 406). The defeated will that decides to cut short reception of this excess (fainting and the fall into silence) follow inevitably from this excess, but only if we enter into the truth in which it appears.

If what is seen in the *veritas redarguens* is to appear, according to Augustine, it must be loved. According to Marion, Augustine's text "concerns loving the truth so as to bear it" (BS, 406), not to put it out of sight or deny it. Only by loving it do I reach this disclosure that undoes me, since I have no good reason to choose a truth that contradicts me or acts counter to me. Love thus maintains the human in its privilege as recipient of excess in the opening of a truth that remonstrates. What Marion in *Being Given* calls the "will to see" (the will that brings the human to encounter the humiliating excess that constitutes it as gifted, or not) here assumes an Augustinian name: Love.

The Poor Phenomenon

Marion and the Problem of Givenness

ANTHONY J. STEINBOCK

Today one can hardly speak of a phenomenology of givenness without approaching or coming to terms with Jean-Luc Marion's novel conception of the "saturated phenomenon." The saturated phenomenon is that which subverts, overflows, exceeds, and precedes the intentional sense-giving on the part of the subject.

According to Marion, there are four main modes of saturated givenness, what he calls the event, the idol, the flesh, the icon, and, encompassing all of them, revelation.[1] The phenomenological status of the saturated phenomena is relatively clear in Marion's work, and it has been the topic of many investigations. What remains extremely ambiguous, however, is the phenomenal status of what he calls the "poor phenomenon."

This essay determines the meaning and status of the poor phenomenon. The significance of the poor phenomenon is not simply an interesting point because it concerns the thought of Marion and the exegesis of his work. It is significant philosophically because it bears on the way in which we understand experiences of everyday life that fall outside of, or ostensibly fall outside of, religious, moral, and aesthetic life. Is the poverty of poor phenomena intrinsic to the things themselves? Are poor phenomena given uniformly? Is there a shortfall or corruption in givenness due to us, to our inattention, or to our inability to receive saturated phenomena? Are there degrees of poverty like there are of saturation? Are poor phenomena essential or contingent features of our existence? Are the poor (phenomena) always with us?

In the final analysis, I am critical of Marion's characterization of saturation and poverty, not because it is uncalled for, but because it tends to miss the implications of his own work whereby the poor phenomena are determined on the basis of saturated phenomena.

1. Saturated Givenness as Revelation

According to Marion, different kinds of phenomena can be categorized according to the different ways in which they show themselves. Something *shows* itself only insofar as it *gives* itself such that the showing can vary according to degrees of givenness.[2] Marion's work on *phenomen*ology therefore centers and must center on the problem of givenness.

Since the paradigm of givenness for Marion is the saturated phenomenon (because it marks the givenness from which it comes), let's approach the significance of poor phenomena through the meaning of saturated givenness. This is, in fact, Marion's approach: "My entire project . . . aims to think the common-law phenomenon, and through it *the poor phenomenon*, on the basis of the paradigm of the saturated phenomenon."[3] More than the complete fulfillment of an intention, saturation is marked by an excess of intuition over the subjective intention.

There are in the main four ways saturation takes place, and this corresponds to four types of saturated phenomena. Saturating the category of quantity is the "event." It is marked by its unanticipatable character, by its singularity, and by the fact that it is historically nonrepeatable. The "idol" is evident under the aspect of the "unbearable" and "intolerable" character of the phenomenon; it forces us to accommodate our gaze to it, and in this sense bedazzles the perceiver, overflowing his or her ability to master it. Further, the absoluteness of the saturated phenomenon absolves itself as "flesh" from the category of relation; in its radical immediacy of auto-affection, it remains irreplaceably "mine." Finally, free from any reference to the ego, the "icon" or "face" saturates the categories of modality. The saturated phenomenon as icon is irreducible and irregardable in the sense that the face (of the Other) gives me nothing to see, but nevertheless weighs upon me and is that from which I receive myself.[4]

What is the essential meaning of the event, the idol, the flesh, and the icon as modes of saturation? For Marion it is the "phenomenon of revelation," which concentrates the four types of saturated phenomena. Not merely being one among the others, revelation as the maximum of saturated phenomenality is the *essential possibility* of saturation and thus its phenomenal meaning.[5] For Marion, the privileged manifestation of the icon is Christ, and hence Christ is the example par excellence of revelation. But since, according to his own claim, Marion proceeds as a philosopher and especially as a phenomenologist, he brackets the reality of the world in order to liberate the phenomena and givenness (and kinds of givenness); this allows him to determine the meaning of saturation in terms of its essential possibility—revelation—without passing judgment on its existential claims. As the essential meaning of saturation, revelation is qualified by the "call," which bears the traits of the summons, surprise, interlocution, and facticity. The call, the undeniable par excellence, "in fact characterizes every saturated phenomenon as such."[6]

The blow of the saturated phenomenon on the subject, radicalized as the revelatory call, not only transforms the otherwise passive object into activity and more precisely the gift; it transforms what we formerly understood in phenomenology as the "giver of sense" into the "receiver," and further, the receiver radicalized now as "the gifted," the one who receives one's self from what gives itself.[7]

To sum up, the saturated phenomenon is the paradigm of givenness, whereby revelation becomes exemplary of the meaning of saturation. The essence of givenness is revelation received as the call whose transformative impact constitutes me now as the gifted one. Having all too briefly determined the meaning of the saturated phenomenon as revelation, we are in a position to examine the status of the poor phenomenon.

2. The Poor and the Common

Given that the saturated phenomenon is the paradigm of phenomena, and revelation is the paradigm of givenness, we might question the status of anything that is not a saturated phenomenon. For example, is everything else ultimately reducible to the saturated phenomenon? Is all givenness really just revelation, only at a remove? Are other phenomena derivative modes? Before determining the meaning of the poor phenomenon more critically in the final section of this paper, let me remain with Marion's explication of the topic.

According to Marion, there are other types of phenomena in addition to the saturated ones. They are called the "poor phenomenon" and the "common phenomenon." Far from being reducible to one another, he regards them all (the saturated, the poor, and the common) as *original figures of phenomenality*," which is to say, essentially distinct, irreducible types.[8] Allow me to describe the latter two types briefly and then address them in a more critical fashion.

A. *Poor Phenomena.* The poor phenomenon is initially defined as a phenomenon that is poor in intuition. In order to give itself, such a phenomenon does not need much more than its concept alone or its bare intelligibility; it need only admit an intuition that is formal. Since the poor phenomenon is merely formal, universal without content or material differentiation, it no longer need admit an experience that is uncertain. It is *undurchstreichbar*, as Husserl might say, not able to be crossed out through subsequent experiences. Such an abstraction from content and its unproblematic iterability makes it a perfect object for metaphysics, and in fact, this object-ness, this objectivity, becomes for Marion the privileged form of intuition and phenomenon proper to it. "They claim only a formal intuition in mathematics or a categorical intuition in logic, in other words, a 'vision of essences' and idealities."[9]

The poor phenomenon cannot become the paradigm of givenness, therefore, because the abstract epistemological certainty of the poor phenomenon does not allow there to be an "accomplished phenomenality," that is, real or individual intuition or temporalization.

B. *Common Phenomena.* Common (or common-law) phenomena are initially described as different in kind from poor phenomena. Here we are not concerned with eidetic entities that lack material individualization, but with everyday phenomena that might in principle be adequately given, but most often are given in an inadequate manner. In short, common phenomena are those that receive fulfillment (or are disappointed) according to how they are intended. In this case, a "maximum" of givenness could only be an intuition that perfectly measures up to how I intended it.

For Marion, the model of givenness is what we might loosely term the "pragmatic object." This covers not only the phenomenon encountered in the everyday context of use but also the object that can be predicted in use because of its weak intuition, "attaining a degree of certainty comparable to that of the poor phenomena."[10] Because of the deficit of intuition, it is susceptible to my mastery. Thus, I can have a concept of what is supposed to happen, or of what is supposed to appear before it actually does happen or appear. In this way, if I cannot prevent the infraction of my mastery on the part of the object, I can at least reduce the impact of things not going "my" way. Through my "foresight," or the preeminence of the concept over intuition, I can anticipate the object in advance as already given and in this way "delay" its givenness since its concept precedes its givenness. The techniques employed where common phenomena are concerned permit and demand repetition of the phenomena since they cannot tolerate innovations or modifications that are not governed in advance, which is to say, they permit nothing novel or unanticipated.[11]

In one respect, nothing could be clearer in Marion than these three types of phenomena: the saturated, the poor, and the common. Indeed, we already had a preview of them in his *Reduction and Givenness*. In that work, Marion described the kind of objectivity that was peculiar to the "first reduction," which he called the "transcendental reduction." This allowed what is known here as the poor phenomenon to be given. The common phenomenon is tied, though admittedly in a more complex manner, to the "second reduction," insofar as the latter does allow us to be led back to what has the structure of an object and the principal differences of ways of Being. The saturated phenomenon and revelation, likewise, is peculiar to the third reduction.[12]

Perhaps because he thought he had already treated extensively what became the poor and the common phenomena in *Reduction and Givenness*, he did not feel the need to revisit them in his subsequent work. (Marion has elaborated upon his notion of the saturated phenomenon, and the exemplary types of saturation, in a separate work entitled *De surcroît* or *In Excess* following the publication of *Being Given*.)[13] But what I find dissatisfying is that if the poor and the common have to be determined on the basis of saturated phenomena, then we need to revisit the issue, for surely in *Reduction and Givenness* their treatment only got us to the point of advancing the so-called third reduction.

Be that as it may, the treatment of the poor and the common in *Being Given* is nothing less than sparse. And this sparseness raises and leaves unanswered many important questions—questions that have to be treated on the basis of the givenness of saturated phenomena or revelation.

3. Poverty

For the sake of convenience when speaking of phenomena other than saturated ones, let me follow a trend initiated by Marion himself. I will now use the expression "poverty" or "poor" to refer to all types of phenomena that do not give themselves in a revelatory manner. Except for a few instances, Marion will press the poverty of givenness into service so broadly that "poor" comes to designate all those phenomena that give themselves as an object or anything that has the structure of an object. Even the subject, who takes itself as an object, is regarded as "poor."[14]

If we are to determine the poverty of givenness on the basis of revelation, as Marion suggests, then there are at least four types of phenomena that are not saturated phenomena, three of which rightly can be called "poor"—if we understand by "poverty" that which is not saturated in the manner in which Marion has described.

Under the general rubric of poverty, I make further distinctions, namely, between (a) the poor phenomenon proper, (b) the humble phenomenon, (c) the denigrated phenomenon, and (d) pride as the poverty of the gifted. Given the limitations of space, I cannot go into detail in each phenomenon, but I can sketch their significance in the following pages.

A. *The Poor Phenomenon Proper.* The poor phenomenon proper is the phenomenon of perceptual and epistemic experiences. In and of itself, there is nothing wrong with this kind of givenness.

Rather than focus on the epistemic object, since Marion has done this with respect to eidetic objects, let me emphasize the passive, perceptual ones. Husserl has described this kind of phenomenon in astonishing detail in his analyses of passive synthesis.[15] Although Marion mentions in passing the phenomenon of passive synthesis in the context of saturation,[16] let us be more precise, since aside from some similar characteristics, the passively given phenomenon should not be equated with saturation.

Descriptions concerning the experience of passive synthesis account for the fact that the constitution of meaning, and thus "givenness," is something more than the fulfillment or intuition of the object corresponding to the subjective intention. Sense occurs prior to the activity of the subject, prior to egoic constitution, and prior to judicative acts. Sense emergence is a veritable "constitutive duet," as Husserl terms it. Even when I intend an object or aspect of an object, there is a *plus ultra* of my intention when I discover in the course of perception that there is always more to see or to touch or to hear than my active and passive movements of sense-bestowal. According to Husserl, "Perception is a constant pretension to accomplish something that, by its very nature, it is not in a position to accomplish. Thus, it harbors an essential contradiction, as it were."[17] This is to say that it belongs to the structure of the transcendent object to be given in perspectives, to be given with a foreground and a background, with referential implications that guide the perceiver.[18]

Moreover, Husserl accounts for the fact that "pre-objects" can exert an affective force on me; they come into "affective relief," they exert their motivational force on the kinaesthetic body, and *they* can lure "me" into *their* active constitution. Husserl even speaks of this in terms of a "call" that resounds from the side of the object itself; the object or object-like formation instigates what I could later anticipate of it.[19]

As much as this may sound like Marion's notion of saturation in some respects, Marion means—or, at least, has to mean—something else. Saturation has to be more than the passive or active negotiation that occurs between the "subject" and "object." Certainly, we often detect an overflowing of intention on the part of the object, and even a precedence of the object over the subject. The difference between the former negotiation and saturation, however, consists in the fact that in the case of the latter, activity "falls to the phenomenon and to it alone." "Thus it does indeed show *itself* because it gives *itself* first—in anticipation of every aim, free of every concept, according to a befalling that delivers its self."[20]

The difficulty with Marion's analysis in this regard is that he does not account for the fact that the poor phenomenon proper *has its own integrity* as a nonsaturated phenomenon. The poor phenomenon as a perceptual and epistemic object should not be something that it is not. The poor phenomenon proper is just the way it gives itself in perceptual and, *mutatis mutandis*, epistemic experience.[21] We should not forget that even perceptual and epistemic experience is "authentic" insofar as and to the extent that we let it give itself. This is how we engage the world around us.

B. *The Humble Phenomenon.* Humble phenomena are those phenomena that give themselves with their own (perceptual/epistemic) integrity, but/and in the service of revelation. In Marion's schema, it is difficult to account for a wide range of religious experiences (from Saint Francis of Assisi to Rabbi Dov Baer to Ruzbihan Baqli). We need only cite one example from Saint Teresa of Avila's experience to illuminate this point.

When some of her novices were getting disturbed at being drawn away from contemplative prayer in obedience for the sake of menial, mundane tasks, Saint Teresa offered the following instruction: "Know that if it is in the kitchen, the Lord walks among the pots and pans helping you both interiorly and exteriorly."[22] My point in noting this short remark is that the "pots and pans" are not simply what Marion calls saturated phenomena. They are kitchen utensils, common objects, and they have all the identifiable characteristics of objects. Yet, even in their everydayness, there is more, not a quantitative more, but a qualitative surplus. In the everyday common experience, in the context of use, in the technology of cooking, God is present in the activities involving pots and pans. The pots and pans give themselves in "the epiphany of the everyday," to borrow a phrase from Kearney. True, Marion has accounted for how phenomena reveal, but he has not accounted for how otherwise poor phenomena can remain on the one hand poor proper, and on the other hand, how they reveal in and through their own proper "poverty." They simultaneously present themselves and reveal what is other than themselves.

One may argue that this is what Marion means by the "saturated phenomenon": for some the painting calls, for others it does not. I also realize that Marion is not giving us a list of things that are or are not saturated, but rather, describing a unique kind of givenness, revelation. Nonetheless, his descriptions of the poor phenomenon do not give us an account of how poverty can be poverty and simultaneously reveal. Otherwise, he would not limit the scientific or the technological objects to the scientific "mathematical" or to the technological, merely. To do this, he would have to be attentive to the "humble" phenomenon. The humble phenomenon, which does what it does and thereby "serves," modifies the very experience itself and the orientation to that particular sphere, say usefulness. Because the humble phenomenon "delimits," it opens to the infinite. Where, for example, pots and pans or cooking are concerned, we have in the humble phenomenon the possibility of the redemption (the delimitation) of the product, of the utensil, of the technical.

The fact that Marion does not treat mathematics or technology (or mathematical and technological objects) as possibly revealing in and through their poverty makes one wonder whether or not Marion himself is not limiting the "poor" merely to their poverty.

C. *The Denigrated Phenomenon.* This general givenness and movement of the humble phenomenon I call "delimitation" because in its specification as, say, scientific, technological, or utensil, it also simultaneously reveals what is more; it opens up "vertically" such that it is not limited to "its own" dimension of experience.

The denigrated phenomenon arises when the delimitation or specific orientation of an act or object is not simultaneously realized as a delimitation, when, for example, the technical life is restricted to the technical sphere merely, not allowing it to reveal in a delimiting manner. In this case, the poverty of the phenomenon is the poverty of experience in the sense that it arbitrarily limits the phenomenon to itself, merely. Not allowing the phenomenon to be all it can be, namely, revelatory of more than itself in its poverty, it denigrates givenness. Denigration, however, can only be named as such from the perspective of saturation.

Isn't the denigrated phenomenon what Marion really means by "poverty" determined from the essence of saturation? Doesn't Marion really mean by poverty what we would also have to call the "secularized" phenomenon? After all, if phenomena can reveal in the strict sense, then cutting revelation short could not amount to a neutrally given thing; rather, it would suggest an arbitrary deprivation of its ability to give itself in the mode of revelation. I say "arbitrary" because there are no grounds for cutting short the givenness. Anything short of revelation in its fullness is subjectively capricious, the exercise of the subject over the givenness of the phenomenon. It is to secularize revelation, which for him has to mean the denigration of saturation.

In this case, poverty does not belong to the structure of the object, but to our deficiency in being ready to receive the givenness, which is to say, to see it as saturated. We thus have two types of poverty: An essential poverty that is peculiar to every kind of seeing, and about which I think there is nothing we can do, and a poverty of self-imposition without reception, in which the saturated phenomenon as revelation, as call, is missed.

But there is also another kind of poverty, one whose violence is more evident, since it denigrates from the start what is properly saturated (in Marion's sense). We need not dwell on this point for the purposes of this paper. It is enough to evoke the significance of the "face" of the Other who is regarded merely as an object. We need not reach to the tragedy and evil of genocides, the Holocaust, misogyny, or racism for examples. We can take more prosaically the imposition of "assessment procedures" such as quantitatively measurable "learning objectives" and "learning outcomes" on students in otherwise creative educational situations. In Marion's words, "since intuition always comes after the fact and plays the role of actual confirmation of the plan's original rationality, and since it should make no difference ('flawless'), it should not tolerate any innovation, modification, or, in short, any event."[23] Something as seemingly innocuous as "assessment procedures" has as its goal the predictability, control, and repetition of student learning without surprise, interruption, creativity, or novelty. For the purposes, literally, of "accountability" students are reduced not even to consumers, but now to "products" of education. The denigrated phenomenon is therefore the saturated phenomenon creatively, historically, deprived of its ability to reveal.

D. *Pride as the Poverty of the Gifted.* We might ask ourselves how such denigrated phenomena could arise, how denigration could take shape in the face of revelation. Marion considers this problem with the description of the "responsal" and the "abandon."

i. *The Responsal.* The responsal is the process of "admitting" or "wanting" to receive the given. But it is more than that; it is also wanting to receive oneself from the given as given over *to it.* I have to give myself over to the given in order to see. In this way, the responsal transforms what gives itself into what shows itself since it sees nothing of the phenomenon before giving itself over to it.[24]

One could question Marion's problematic invocation of volition here by his use of the expression "wanting." But his point is clear enough: Someone who does not dispose himself or herself, who has not made an "immanent decision," will not see the given. The poor phenomenon, in the sense of the denigrated phenomenon, is what I see without wanting to see. I see in ordinary terms without receiving; I "merely" constitute it. I master it before I could receive it or "want" to receive it. The problem is not on the "side" of phenomenal givenness, but on the side of the "subject," a subject who has to be understood more fundamentally as the gifted.

ii. *The Abandon.* What is the root of this lack of wanting, this lack of self-disposal, of receiving oneself as given, and not allowing what gives itself to show itself? For Marion, the difficulty seems to be almost of neutral, impartial import. For example, Marion writes that "it sometimes happens that what gives itself does not succeed in showing itself," because the monstration of the given takes place "in the essential finitude of the gifted."[25] Because this finitude is essential, and because what gives itself is received only within the finitude of the gifted, it will always be the case that not everything that gives itself, and not all of what gives itself, can show itself. Essentially, the gifted cannot receive the given in the manner in which it gives itself, namely, "without limit or reserve."[26] Notice that this would seem to be a kind of essential poverty of the gifted. For the gifted in the responsal may "want" to receive the given, but essentially (because of our finitude) cannot do so "without limit or reserve."

In distinction, there seems to be yet another kind of poverty of the gifted, one more historically and ethically significant, whereby I "want" (or do not "want") to receive the given. Thus, we are faced with the "can/could" of receiving and the "want/would" of receiving. We read: "If the gifted always phenomenalizes what gives itself to him and receives himself from it, nothing establishes that the gifted always *can or wants* to receive *all* that is given. We can never exclude some cases in which a given would not succeed in showing itself because the gifted *could* or simply *would* not receive it; we can only imagine those unpredictable landings in which the gifted fails before the excess of the given or remains idle in its shortage."[27]

It is helpful to distinguish two types of gifted poverty here, the essential and the historical. In effect, however, these are not two different poverties, because it is not a matter of choosing or not choosing in any moment of time. We are pushed back, not merely to a historical "immanent decision" of Marion, but to what Derrida has called, drawing on Foucault, "*the* Decision."[28] We are faced with the *decisive* act, that fundamental "point," which is not a point in time, but a "temporal originality in general."[29] It is the point at which—in the words of Tarkovsky's Dimitri in his film *Nostalghia*—"we made the wrong turn," and repeat it anew, each time, in our immanent decisions; it is an originary decision that is decided each time, anew. In my finitude, I prepare myself or do not prepare myself to receive the given, and to be transformed into the gifted. The issue is not whether or not there are "limits" or "reserves," but whether or not these limits are or are not "delimiting."

There is something missing in Marion's depiction of the problem, and this is due to the fact that, after all, poverty does not ultimately get determined by him from the standpoint of revelation. Is it really, that is, most profoundly, a matter of a "could" or "would" or "idleness"? On the one hand, we have to put it in more appropriate terms, namely, in terms appropriate to revelation. Understood with respect to revelatory givenness, there is a "subjective" poverty here that is peculiar to the gifted: *the poverty of pride*. Pride is to be understood as the clinging to the self, as ultimate self-interest and so (purposefully or not) not allowing the given to show itself. We have to ask: Is the essential finitude just the way things are? Does it point us to the problem of sin as essential finitude, to the Fall? In my terms, this amounts to the problem of idolatry and not a mere "could not/would not" of receiving.

Notice that the given as it gives itself, and the requalification of the subject into the gifted, is ultimately not within my power. In some sense, "to want" to receive would also be an expression of pride. "What comes after the 'subject,' namely, the gifted, is characterized by the submission of its undeniable activity and live spontaneity to the passivity of an absolutely originary receptivity."[30] In the face of the given, the response (admitting it, and so forth) becomes more and more insufficient, and therefore endlessly repeated, but more and more fruitful. That is, through the excess of the given over the response, through a given that is more powerful than could have been anticipated, we, the gifted, become humble in the face of the given. The gifted receives and thereby receives itself.[31]

But can we or to what extent can we (actively) submit our activity to passivity? Can *we* accomplish the self-denial and attenuation of the self so that what gives itself can show itself? Or instead, cannot the self-disposal only be accomplished by an Other whom I serve? Is it not by being occupied by another—in religious experience, by God; in moral experience, by the Other person—that the self is called into question, and only in this way? Perhaps there is something we can do to dispose ourselves to allow what gives itself to show itself, or in other words, to rescind "the decision"? In my view, this would have to take place through a different kind of poverty, what the mystics call the "*poverty of spirit*."[32]

Thus, we encounter one more distinction that is made by nearly all the mystics of the Abrahamic tradition, the distinction between what can be accomplished by virtue of our own efforts, and what can only be received as a gift or in an "infused" manner. Marion does hint at the latter, though not in these terms. He writes of "a given that accomplishes itself on the basis of its irreducible self, therefore one that sometimes . . . is not governed by the receptive capacity of the gifted and thus frees itself of these limits." In other words, it is a matter of *grace* as a revelatory givenness that alone can exceed the "limits and reserves" of the gifted, whether or not the gifted can/could, want to/would receive. There is poverty, however, if we reverse the orientation of the giving. In my terms, this amounts to idolatry and not a mere "could not/would not" of receiving. To challenge poverty as denigration and pride, to see the significance of the poor proper and the humble phenomenon, we can point to the poverty of spirit and the phenomenon of grace.

Conclusion

My attempt has not been to theologize the problem of the given in Marion. It has been to problematize the poverty and kinds of poverty of the phenomenon, and to determine them from the perspective of revelation. To determine the meaning of the poor phenomenon in relation to the saturated phenomenon, four modes of poverty can be discerned: the poor proper, the humble, the denigrated, and pride as the poverty of the gifted. These are integral to the problem of the saturated phenomenon. To this we require a consideration, in terms of revelation, of the poverty of spirit and grace as ways in which the poverty of the phenomenon is challenged.

PART III

Michel Henry

Michel Henry's Theory of Disclosive Moods

JEFFREY HANSON

Michel Henry pursued throughout his career a remarkable, and remarkably consistent, account of disclosive mood. As a phenomenologist of affectivity, it is no surprise that Henry focused his attention on specific tonalities that reveal a privileged truth. Early in his career Henry emphasized despair as the privileged tonality, but later he dispensed with despair and instead preferred to speak of anxiety. Despite the change in vocabulary, however, in each case his interpretation of what the disclosive mood discloses is the same.[1] Beyond the sort of disclosure characteristic of any ordinary feeling, a disclosive mood, according to Henry, reveals the self to itself and ultimately reveals the self's identity with the absolute, its life as selfsame with the divine life. Early in his career Henry circumvented the influential account of anxiety provided by Heidegger and instead (sometimes avowedly, sometimes not) preferred a certain reading of Kierkegaard. Anxiety is thus a touchstone for Henry's unique philosophical anthropology, which posits a fully immanent self disclosed to the self in a fundamental mood.

That disclosive mood plays a central role is suggested by the fact that Henry situates his reading of *The Sickness Unto Death* at the very end of

---

I would like to thank Jeffrey Bloechl and David Sims for their helpful comments on drafts of this chapter. I would also like to thank the executive committee of the Society for Continental Philosophy and Theology, who hosted the conference where an early draft was presented, and those conference participants who raised questions at that meeting.

The Essence of Manifestation, at the conclusion of a long section on affectivity. In fact, it would be no exaggeration to say that, leaving aside the appendix, Henry ends his lengthy book with a discussion of Kierkegaard's treatise on the self and despair.[2] Significantly, this final chapter is entitled "The Essence of Affectivity and the Fundamental Affective Tonalities. Affectivity and the Absolute." So it is not an understatement to say that the entire discussion of affectivity culminates in Henry's treatment of the essence of affectivity and his specifying of the tonalities as "fundamental."

Heretofore Henry had established that the "how" and the "what" of affectivity's revelation are identical, making affectivity "its own content" (EM, 553 [692]). For Henry the content of life is the pluriform richness of feeling, including all feeling in every possible valence, but nevertheless ultimately unified in the fount from which joy and suffering coequally spring. For Henry, "What hate reveals is hate itself and nothing else; what love reveals is love, and likewise boredom reveals boredom, despair despair, fear reveals fear and anguish reveals, uncovers, exhibits and shows forth anguish and nothing else" (EM, 554 [693]). Even when we pass an axiological judgment on feeling, such as a condemnation of suffering as evil, the only meaning such a proposition can have is a seemingly tautological one, namely, that suffering is suffering, and its truth is not that it is one way or another apart from being the tonality of affectivity that suffering in fact irreducibly is. "For no meaning given to the Being of suffering can change anything in its regard or in any way diminish the weight of its presence or parody its 'truth,' viz. *this truth, which is consubstantial with it, which is its own revelation as constituted by its own affectivity and by the mode according to which the affectivity takes place in it*" (EM, 555 [695]). And while Henry acknowledges that every tonality of affectivity, every feeling correlates to a transcendent object, to something determinate that we regard as hateful or loveable or inspiring of indifference or boredom, the determination of this transcendent relation is so completely established by the essence of the tonality itself disclosed to itself in auto-affection that nothing in the transcendent relation to the thing can serve as "motivation" for the feeling itself or for grounds of its provocation, or any such "mechanical determination of the feeling by a reality exterior and foreign to its own reality" (EM, 564 [706]). So even here where we might reasonably expect to find a substantial unity between immanent auto-affective content of feeling, manifested in a number of ways corresponding to the transcendent objects of those feelings, Henry denies that this correlation is fundamental (EM, 562–63 [705–6]).

Furthermore, according to Henry's analysis, all specific feelings spring from the essential unfreedom determined by the inescapable bond that rivets the self to the self, wherein lie what Henry calls the fundamental tonalities.³ The fundamental tonalities that are anticipated by the title of §70 are not specific feelings determined a posteriori nor occasioned by experience of things in the world but are the primordial self-experiences of suffering and joy (EM, 557 [697]).⁴ "The essence of affectivity resides in suffering and is constituted by it. In suffering, feeling experiences itself in its absolute passivity with regard to self, in its impotence at changing itself, it experiences itself and has the experience of self as irremediably handed over to itself in order to be what it is, as loaded forever with the weight of its own Being" (EM, 658 [827]).

Needless to say, suffering is not a psychological phenomenon or an evanescent tonality provoked by hetero-affective experiences (EM, 658–59 [827–29]). Its status as essential is not challenged by the experience of "positive" tonalities either, for suffering is selfsame with joy: "The impotence of suffering is the Being-given-to-itself of feeling, its Being-riveted-to-itself in the perfect adherence of identity and, in this perfect adherence to self, the obtaining of self, the becoming and the arising of feeling in itself, in the enjoyment of what it is, this is enjoyment, this is joy" (EM, 660–61 [830]). Despite their apparent opposition, suffering and joy are conjointly born in the original phenomenalization of the essence of Being itself, and they can only be so if they are identical. All possible determined tonalities are the product of the unity of suffering and joy (EM, 662–63 [833–34]).⁵ This unity is not the product of a retrospective synthesis that attempts to hermeneutically liberate joy from suffering or a concurrence on different "levels" of affective experience of opposed tonalities but an "interior, necessary relationship" (EM, 675 [849]).⁶

In the final pages of Henry's analysis of this crucial topic he turns to Kierkegaard and his account of despair.⁷ He makes an explicit defense of his choice in an unusually lengthy footnote:

> Here we must reject categorically the assertion of Heidegger according to which Kierkegaard could grasp the problem of existence only as an *existentiell* problem such that "the existential problematic was so alien to him that, as regards his ontology, he remained completely dominated by Hegel and by ancient philosophy as Hegel saw it. Thus, there is more to be learned philosophically from his 'edifying' writings than from his theoretical ones."⁸ Because the determination of the fundamental affective tonalities of existence, i.e. of existence itself, is actually worked out by Kierkegaard, notably in his *Sickness unto Death*, i.e. a theoretical work, beginning with the internal

structure of immanence and in it, it is not merely invested with a manifest, "existential," ontological meaning, but actually presupposes a conception of ontology radically different from that of the Greeks and Hegel and even from that of Heidegger himself. (EM, 676 [851], n. 23)

The famously dismissive words from Heidegger are well known; what ought to attract attention here in Henry's rejection of Heidegger is his claim that Kierkegaard is like Henry himself a thinker of immanence. The theme that Henry isolates from Kierkegaard in the pages that follow and that he repeatedly places at the heart of his discussions of both despair and anxiety is the insight that despair cannot be grasped apart from the self-manifestation of the ego in its immanence. In much the same way that we regard the fundamental tonalities of joy and suffering as results of circumstances arising from exteriority, despair is misrepresented to ourselves as the result of an external provocation, as in the example of Cesare Borgia's despair over his inability to be Caesar. "Despair is related to the ego even when it seems to be related to something else, to the world and to that which in the world arouses and provokes it. For we do not despair for not having become Caesar, 'but he is in despair over himself for the fact that he did not become Caesar'" (EM, 677 [851–52]).[9]

By reading Kierkegaard as a phenomenologist of radical immanence, Henry claims him as an ally on a variety of interrelated fronts that converge in the following passage: "*The ego, says Kierkegaard, is the relationship to self . . . posited by another; it is the relationship to self insofar as he has himself not posited this relationship, that he has not posited himself, it is auto-affection as finding its essence in the original ontological passivity of Being with regard to self. . . . In the impossibility of surmounting this passivity, in the impossibility for the ego of breaking the bond which attaches him to himself, namely his relationship to himself, in the impossibility of escaping this suffering, resides his despair*" (EM, 677 [852]).

Two crucial, recurrent points can be extracted from this excerpt. First, Henry sees Kierkegaard as sharing his conviction that the self has its essence in a fundamental unfreedom, and he supports the parallel by reference to Kierkegaard's argument that despair is an impotent self-consumption that strives impossibly to rid itself of itself. "To get rid of his ego, to break the bond which attaches him to himself, this is precisely that of which the ego is incapable if the irremediable nature of this bond, the insurmountable character of the relationship to self of the ego in its absolute passivity with regard to self, if the impossibility for his surpassing himself in any way whatever, of separating himself from himself, of escaping himself, in short if the internal structure of immanence, as the problematic has shown, constitutes his very essence" (EM, 678 [853]).[10] The non-freedom then at the heart of the ego that Kierkegaard's examination exposes is its essential bond to itself, its "impotence," its "torment," its inability to extricate itself from itself (SUD, 18).

Second, Henry reads Kierkegaard as arguing that the self's eternity is its foremost identifiable quality, which flows from its non-freedom. That the indissoluble bond that relates self to self is the essence and condition of the self's despair means that sickness unto death is eternal. "The internal structure of immanence, the absolute unity which it encloses and constitutes, this is what Kierkegaard calls eternity, and this rightly so if such a structure is determined by excluding from it the time of transcendence, if positively, the unity which it encloses and constitutes, the interior and living unity of life, cannot be broken" (EM, 679 [854]).

This final association of eternity with the living unity of life, the theme at the heart of Henry's phenomenology, is where Henry's presentation of Kierkegaard ends, not least because this is where Henry himself ends his monumental book. Henry says straightforwardly, "Despair bears within it life, eternity" (EM, 679 [854]). As surprising then as it may appear, despair is renarrated by Henry as a positive mechanism for allowing the self to recognize itself as a lived identity with life itself. Despair is therefore a disclosive mood that does not remove the self from essential truth but capacitates its recognition of essential truth.

In the years that intervened between Henry's promotion of despair as the disclosive mood that allows the self to recognize its fundamental unfreedom in its bond to itself, its identity with life that it receives from life's own self-generation in the self, he seems to have changed his mind not about the essential operations of disclosive mood but about the name of the disclosive mood that he prefers to use. Henry is dismissive of Kierkegaard's theory of anxiety in the long footnote cited above. Just as he repudiates Heidegger's discounting of the theoretical works, he disputes Heidegger's evaluation of Kierkegaard yet again, only this time not in Kierkegaard's favor. At the end of the long footnote he writes: "Furthermore, this is why the thesis, whereby Heidegger would attribute to certain existential developments of Kierkegaard, notably those in his *Concept of Dread*, an ontological dimension which they do not have, must also be rejected" (EM, 676 [851], n. 23). So whereas Henry enthusiastically defends Kierkegaard's *The Sickness unto Death* from Heidegger, he dissents from Heidegger's approval of *The Concept of Anxiety*. There are only three other references that Henry makes in *The Essence of Manifestation* to *The Concept of Anxiety*, one of which is similarly disapproving.[11]

The significant point here is that as of 1963 Henry is clearly not that interested in the vocabulary of anxiety and seems to strongly prefer despair as the disclosive mood of paramount importance.[12] In much more recent interviews, however, Henry expresses his appreciation for Kierkegaard's theory of anxiety, and it is this term he clearly prefers to use in his later works, though again, the way he interprets the disclosive mood and the role it plays in his thought as a whole remains the same.[13] In fact, by the time of *I Am the Truth* Henry seems in a short passage to repudiate his prior interest in despair, with a single reference, now negative, to the Cesare Borgia example from *The Concept of Anxiety* where Henry is posing a question to himself regarding his account of man as son of God: "If men are really sons of God within Christ, how can we explain that so few of them know this and remember it? If they bear within them this divine Life in all its immensity . . . how can we understand why they are so unhappy? In the end, it is not the tribulations visited upon them by the world that oppress them; rather, it is with themselves that they are so discontented" (IT, 132).[14]

That men are not ultimately afflicted by external circumstances arising from the world but by themselves is not surprising, both consistent with Henry's earlier exposition of Kierkegaard and indeed with Kierkegaard's original theory as well. But the answer now according to Henry as to how men recover the sense of themselves as essentially living is not despair as the witness to man's eternal bond of self to self. Despair is now characterized as part of the problem, not the solution. "As Kierkegaard puts it: 'Consequently he does not despair because he did not get to be Caesar but despairs over himself because he did not get to be Caesar.' But how can one despair of this me if it is nothing less than the coming into us of God within Christ? Such despair is possible only if, one way or another, man has forgotten the splendor of his initial condition, his condition as Son of God—his condition as 'Son within the Son'" (IT, 123). It is with these words that Henry introduces his chapter on forgetfulness of one's self as son of God. The transformation then of the role of despair in his thought is now complete; despair is no longer the testimony of one's essential self but a blockage to it, an ally of forgetfulness. Anxiety now takes over as the disclosive mood that allows for overcoming of this forgetfulness.

Given the thrust of Henry's project as sketched so far and the concerns he emphasizes in his early treatment of despair, one could imagine the attraction for him that the concept of anxiety might hold: Anxiety is for the tradition that Heidegger called a "state-of-mind [*Befindlichkeit*]" (BT, 232), which "makes manifest 'how one is'" (BT, 233), that is to say, it is not a theoretical knowledge of the world or of entities within the world but a fundamentally disclosive mood, which Henry might prefer to call an affective tonality or *pathos*, that reveals the self's being to itself. And indeed, Henry does find occasion to speak of anxiety in *The Essence of Manifestation*, *The Genealogy of Psychoanalysis*, *I Am the Truth*, and *Incarnation*. Anxiety appears in these texts closely allied to his main thesis referred to above, that of the essence of the ego's identity with life itself. By reading a variety of important passages it is clear that for Henry anxiety reveals the ego's condition to itself: its inescapable unfreedom with respect to the imperative to be the self that it is, its totally immanent character as auto-affection and separation from the transcendence of the world, and its identity with life itself. Finally, it is possibly the case that anxiety simply seems more intuitive a candidate for a disclosive mood that operates entirely within immanence. According to even a casual phenomenological analysis it might seem that despair is, while maybe essentially about inwardness, never without some precipitation from exteriority, whereas anxiety might befall us without any triggering event.[15]

Beginning with *The Essence of Manifestation* there is a significant treatment of the topic of anxiety as formulated by Heidegger. Though it is a critical one, it is instructive inasmuch as it establishes the contours of Henry's own theory of anxiety in contradistinction to what he finds unacceptable in Heidegger. Of course for Heidegger anxiety discloses no specific object in the world but being-in-the-world as such, and thus makes possible *Dasein*'s face-to-face encounter with itself as being-in-the-world. As opposed to ontic emotions like fear, anxiety is a fundamental disclosure of self to self even when the self hopes vainly to avoid the self or to lose itself among entities within the world. And it is from *Being and Time* that Henry preserves the notion that anxiety reveals to the self the inescapable burden of being a self in his later discussions of anxiety in *The Genealogy of Psychoanalysis* and *I Am the Truth*.

Henry credits Heidegger with having seen the significance of affectivity and its meaningful link to revelation. "This meaning is immediately apparent and shows itself in the fact that affectivity is not merely taken as a power of revelation in the ordinary sense of the word, a power of revealing something, this or that thing, but precisely *the power of revealing to us that which reveals all things, namely, the world itself as such, as identical to Nothingness*" (EM, 586 [735]). This revelation, which is also a self-revelation, is exhibited in a special way by the phenomenon of anxiety. In distinction from other moods or tonalities like fear, anxiety is a fundamental disclosure of self to self even when the self hopes vainly to avoid the self or to lose itself among entities within the world. It is this theme above all others, the notion that anxiety reveals to the self the inescapable bond of self to self, that Henry will repeat throughout his later discussions of anxiety in *I Am the Truth*.

The description of anxiety as revelatory of the self to self is Henry's preferred locution in the majority of texts under discussion in this paper. It finds an antecedent in Heidegger, and thus on this score we find the most significant point of commonality between Henry's and Heidegger's respective interpretations of the phenomenon. "Dasein's absorption in the 'they' and its absorption in the 'world' of its concern, make manifest something like a *fleeing* of Dasein in the face of itself. . . . But to bring itself face to face with itself, is precisely what Dasein does *not* do when it thus flees" (BT, 229). At the same time, however, Henry seems to depart from Heidegger precisely where Heidegger conjoins fleeing with disclosure of the world: "To understand this talk about Dasein's fleeing in the face of itself in falling, we must recall that Being-in-the-world is a basic state of Dasein. *That in the face of which one has anxiety is Being-in-the-world as such*" (BT, 230). For Heidegger, anxiety discloses both *in-der-welt-Sein* and *Dasein* to itself, a coincident duplicity that seems to attract Henry's critical opposition.

Henry rejects this Heideggerean account of anxiety because it confuses manifestation with revelation, transcendence with immanence. As he puts it in this section: "When it is understood as the power of transcendence, the power of revelation particular to affectivity is lost—together with the very nature of affectivity as constituted by this power" (EM, 594 [745]). Though Henry cites no specific passage, something like this one from §40 of *Being and Time* would surely support his argument: "Anxiety individualizes Dasein and thus discloses it as '*solus ipse.*' But this existential 'solipsism' is so far from the displacement of putting an isolated subject-Thing into the innocuous emptiness of a worldless occurring, that in an extreme sense what it does is precisely to bring Dasein face to face with its world as world, and thus bring it face to face with itself as Being-in-the-world" (BT, 233).

It is just here that we find Henry objecting to Heidegger's interpretation, which he reads as grounding the revelation of the self to itself not in immanence but in transcendence, the venturing out of the self into the world to return to itself. "*To the extent that affectivity opens the world to us and places us face to face with Nothingness, its power of revelation resides in transcendence itself and is constituted by it.* The following evidence henceforth presents itself without delay: *The essence of revelation peculiar to affectivity and taking place in it is completely lost to Heidegger, confused by him with the essence of the ontological understanding of Being to which it nevertheless remains heterogeneous both in its structure and in its phenomenality"* (EM, 588 [737]).[16]

Earlier in the text Henry has told us, "The ego has no business at all manifesting itself in the milieu of transcendent Being, some day or other, sooner or later, in the course of a history whether individual or universal, or within the progress of philosophy, if it is true that it is henceforth present to itself at the heart of a revelation which owes nothing to time or transcendence, but is accomplished within the sphere of the radical immanence of absolute subjectivity" (EM, 42–43 [54]). Henry interprets the relation of *Dasein* to the Nothing as exhibiting the formal structure of hetero-affective object intentionality, apparently whether the Nothing is properly an object or not.[17] Because Heidegger makes self-revelation and manifestation of the world/Nothing consubstantial in anxiety, he has ultimately manifested the ego via transcendent Being, ecstasis.[18] But for Henry, "The affectivity of understanding resides, not in itself nor in the ecstatic structure which the understanding develops in each case, but in the anti-structure of this structure, in the anti-essence of transcendence" (EM, 598 [750]), namely, the immanence of auto-affection, the identity of ego with life itself.

This dominant thematic is underpinned by Henry's opposition of the truth of life and immanence to the nontruth of the world and transcendence, a dichotomy already established in *The Essence of Manifestation* and intensified in the later writings.[19] The truth of immanence is not intuited like an object in the world, and as such Henry does not hesitate to call it "invisible."[20] Because it does not appear in the world and has nothing in common with things in the world, nothing in the world is a clue to life, and nothing in the world provides a path to it. "Where there is no transcendence, there is neither horizon nor world. Far from being a universal structure of all manifestation, and consequently, of constituting the essence of the latter, the horizon of the world is, on the contrary, excluded from this essence considered in itself. A comparable exclusion is that of all intramundane reality in general" (EM, 281 [349–50]). Thus any definition of anxiety that interprets the disclosive mood as being precipitated by experience within the horizon of the world (even a privileged experience), by an uncovering of the horizon of the world itself, or by the revelation of the world as groundless nothing, must be disregarded by

Henry. The truth of immanence, of self, has nothing to do with venturing out into the world, and thus anxiety cannot either.

In keeping with his original treatment of the subject in *The Essence of Manifestation*, Henry's later examinations of anxiety continue to emphasize the notion that anxiety reveals the self to itself, disclosing the inescapable bond of self to self, and repeatedly underscore Henry's exclusion of exteriority and transcendence. Turning to *The Genealogy of Psychoanalysis* and his analysis of Freud, we find Henry again arguing that true anxiety's "leading characteristic is that it is not an anxiety before a real external danger, an anxiety before an object, but before the drives. But the drives in turn, especially the libido, are not, let us recall, provoked by any external stimulus; they are endogenous excitations, self-excitation—life itself" (GP, 311).[21] This passage brings into view a crucially important dimension to Henry's thought, both as a whole and with respect to anxiety in particular, namely, the identification of the essence of the self with the essence of life itself, from which the self receives the bond that ties self to itself. This is the central insight of Henry's phenomenology, and here we find it linked explicitly with anxiety. Again, from *The Genealogy of Psychoanalysis*, "Anxiety is the feeling of being, as life. It is the feeling of Self" (GP, 312) and "anxiety, at the very heart of suffering and its increase, is nothing but the feeling of not being able to escape itself" (GP, 313).[22] Anxiety reveals the self to the self, again without the aid of exteriority and in this selfsame revelation the self is revealed to itself as life itself.

Much the same interpretation is given in *I Am the Truth*, where once again the concept of anxiety is assigned a place of central importance, in the chapter entitled "The Paradoxes of Christianity." Announcing the advent of a "new series of paradoxes, which no longer rest on the duplicity of appearance but take their principle from Life itself and its own truth" (IT, 198), Henry claims that "The clear apperception of life's antinomic structure constitutes what we will call the second founding intuition of Christianity" (IT, 199). Anxiety, it turns out, is what reveals the antinomic structure of life, which is the basis of the paradoxes that together comprise the second founding intuition of Christianity; so again, anxiety makes its appearance at a pivotal stage in Henry's phenomenology.[23]

Speaking of the suffering that I as a self inevitably undergo in the experience of my ipseity, Henry writes, "From the suffering of this Self charged with self in the suffering of his ipseity there arises anxiety, the anxiety of the Self to be a Self—this self that he is without being able to avoid or escape this condition, the fact that he is a Self, and, even more, this particular Self that he is now and will be forever" (IT, 200). At the same time, however, this suffering is also joy, and "thus is disclosed to us the antinomic structure of life"[24] (IT, 200) which unites suffering and joy in the self's ipseity and serves as the foundation for the other paradoxes that Henry explores in this chapter, particularly those given expression in the Beatitudes and the Scriptural teaching that whoever loses his life will find it.

The contours of Henry's theory of disclosive mood remain intact in *I Am the Truth*. The bond of the self to itself is again in these pages interpreted as a form of unfreedom, inasmuch as all of the material from *The Essence of Manifestation* on the fundamental co-belonging of suffering and joy is recapitulated here and called by Henry the "second founding intuition of Christianity" (IT, 201–3). "Because the Hearing in which I hear the Word of life is my own condition of Son, my own life engendered in absolute Life's self-engendering, this Hearing has no freedom at all with respect to what it hears. It is not the Hearing of a call to which the person has license to respond or not. To be able to respond to the call, to hear it in an appropriate listening, but equally to turn away from it—it is always too late for all that. Life, thrown into itself, has always already thrown us into ourselves, into this Self that is similar to none other, that at no moment ever chose to be this Self that he is, not even to be something like a Self at all" (IT, 227–28).[25]

That this disclosure of the self to itself in its constitutive unfreedom has to take place in total detachment from the self's experience of the world is mandated by Henry's overall phenomenological theory. He rigorously rejects theories of anxiety that make transcendence the avenue of self-manifestation precisely because for Henry the world of transcendence does not and cannot reveal the essential truth of immanence.[26] So anxiety has to be a mechanism that operates entirely within the space of immanence, where its witness is wholly alien to thought, to the truth of the world. As a phenomenon revelatory of life anxiety, like all expressions of life, speaks only of itself; its truth consists in its auto-reference. "Because it is riveted to itself without being able to break this link that links it to itself, 'it is what it is'—which means: it experiences itself as it experiences itself. In this way of experiencing itself as it experiences itself resides its truth" (IT, 212).

This truth, heterogeneous to the truth of the world, perhaps even explains why Henry has chosen anxiety in the first place as the disclosive mood that testifies to the truth of the self. Though it is described in similar terms as suffering, Henry's theory of suffering and joy as fundamentally identical is counterintuitive at the very least. But anxiety is a phenomenon that arguably needs no explaining. According to Henry no hermeneutics of experience can deliver the truth of experience,[27] but in anxiety there is no need of hermeneutics at all. There is only the certitude of life as it is lived, "the fact that each of life's modalities, reduced to what it experiences when it experiences itself, is absolutely certain. Thus the ego goes about its life from certitude to certitude—even though it does not think about it and *because* it does not think about it" (IT, 212). Impenetrable to thought, inexpressible in language, irreducible to exteriority, anxiety is a voice crying out not in the wilderness of the world but in the enclosed garden within.

Can We Hear the Voice of God?

Michel Henry and the Words of Christ

CHRISTINA M. GSCHWANDTNER

The crackling of flames around the bush looked threatening in the dry desert. Where would he get water to extinguish the blaze? Yet this fire was peculiar: it didn't seem to spread. The barren branches were brilliantly illumined in the flickering tongues, but like a well-coordinated dance they moved back and forth without damaging the bush itself. A mysterious fire indeed.

His step was slow and hesitant; his feet almost stumbled under the weight of his grief. The mountain seemed impossibly high and yet the destination far too close. His son skipped ahead with firewood on his shoulder. How could he be so carefree? Had he no sense that this journey would be his last? That his young life and all his father's hopes and dreams would be snuffed out shortly?

The fleece was wet, soaking to be exact. He could extract an entire bowlful by squeezing it carefully and yet the ground around it was cracked from dryness. Just like the dinner that had not been eaten, but had burned when the strange messenger put his staff to it. The next morning brought the opposite result: the ground glistened with dew yet the fleece wool was so dry that it felt stiff to the touch. But was a dry fleece enough to win a war against the threatening enemy who had so long oppressed his people and destroyed their harvests?

With a startled expression, the young girl gazed at the shining figure before her, addressing her with mysterious words. She was to have a child, and yet no man would be involved. And the child would deliver God's people. A child

147

would deliver them from the immense power of the Roman occupation? How could that be possible? Or maybe the dazzling messenger meant even more than that?

Can we hear the voice of God? How would we identify it? How did Moses know that Yahweh was speaking from the burning bush? How could Abraham be sure that it was God and not a demon that ordered him to sacrifice his son? What convinced Gideon that it was indeed God who was calling him to deliver the Israelites? How did Mary trust that the angel truly carried divine words to her?

How do we know today? Is God's voice distinctive? Is it recognizable by form or content? Must a sign or an angel accompany it as confirmation? If a sign is provided, how would we interpret it? What if we do not receive a sign like Gideon's fleece or a burning bush that is not consumed?[1] Things are not always as clear as they were for Isaiah in the temple, where the only appropriate response to the overwhelming divine vision was, "Here am I—send me."[2] When no obvious sign is present, is not extreme caution in order? How often has God's voice been invoked to justify acts of violence and terror. How often have both sides of a struggle claimed divine endorsement. And how many have embarked on unjust and destructive missions in the name of God.

And yet, how can one hesitate when the divine voice speaks? What if Mary had laughed at the angel? What if Joan of Arc had ignored the voices she heard? What if Mother Teresa had been blind to God's beckoning in the eyes of the dying in Calcutta? In his final book, *Paroles du Christ*,[3] the late Michel Henry argues that we not only *can* hear the words of God, but that we can hear them *as* words of God, that we can know that they proceed from a divine source. He previews his argument in an earlier text:

> There exists another word than that spoken by people. This other word speaks otherwise than do human words. What it says is other than what human speech says. Because it speaks otherwise, it says something else. Because it speaks otherwise, the way it should be understood differs, too, from the way one understands people's words. This other word, which speaks otherwise than human speech and says something else and is heard in another way, is the Word of God.[4]

We *can* hear the voice of God and it *can* be distinguished from merely human words. That is Henry's fundamental contention.

I begin by examining Henry's proposal that in the words of Christ we can phenomenologically distinguish the voice of God. Showing the connection with arguments proposed already in *I Am the Truth* and *Incarnation*,[5] I explicate his depiction of the divine word as complete immediacy in its auto-revelation. In the second part of my discussion, I go on to deplore the implied dismissal of hermeneutics in this emphasis on complete immediacy and propose that much greater hermeneutic care is required for hearing the "divine voice." I urge that despite the immediacy of revelation, interpretation is required in order to hear the voice of God and to identify it as divine.

I. The Words of Christ

Henry begins by analyzing the words of Christ in the Scriptures. Throughout his argument Christ's words form the basis of his discussion and his text is replete with references to the Gospels. That Christ is speaking these words is taken at face value.[6] Central to Henry's discussion is the mystery of the dual nature of Christ. While Christ claims to speak as God, he does so as a human being.[7] His words are therefore *both* human and divine. This leads us to a difficult paradox: If Christ or the Scriptures are truly divine revelations or words of God, how can they reach *human* ears? And if they are human words comprehensible to human beings, then how can they maintain their *divine* nature? Henry asks: "How could this revelation, made accessible to people in human speech, revealing itself to them in the form of their own speech, prove its divine character? How, beyond its human nature, is such speech in a position to attest that it comes from God?"[8] If a voice is truly divine, how could we hear it, we who are limited human beings? And if we can understand it, how can it be more than human? How could we confirm or even identify its divine character? Unraveling this paradox is the central task of *Paroles du Christ*.

Leaning heavily on his earlier work that had outlined how in Christ we have access to the divine life of God, Henry takes seriously Christ's assertions to speak as God and from God. His argument proceeds in the following steps: First, he considers the words of Christ as the words of a human being addressing other humans in their own language and speaking about their own experience. He suggests that central to this message is a fundamental distinction between humans and the world, which highlights the unique nature and worth of humanity. This distinction is exemplified, for Henry, in a "radical opposition" between the visible (objects or bodies in the world) and the invisible (the immediate experience of human flesh) or what he calls "Life." The words of Christ challenge our common interpretation of the world and displace the human condition from the realm of the world to that of relation with God through divine revelation. Second, he interprets the words of Christ insofar as they are human words spoken to human beings in their own language, but instead speaking about Christ himself and his identity. Henry shows how Christ does indeed claim divinity by showing himself to be grounded in the divine life. Christ's divine condition is constituted by his claim to have direct access to the divine Life of God. Third, Henry looks at the words of Christ as divine words, as speaking the Word of God, and examines their legitimacy. Who would be able to testify to the authenticity of the divine claim and how would we verify such testimony? Finally, he wonders how we can hear this divine Word and identify it as coming from God. I will focus in particular on these final sections for my analysis.

Henry draws a fundamental distinction between human speech and the divine Word.[9] Human words imply distance: they signify that about which they speak but are removed from its experience. We can hear about the barrenness of the desert and the flickering of the flames, but we are not there, we do not witness them ourselves. Human language, according to Henry, is always a kind of lie, since it never gives direct access to what it seeks to designate in its speech. He observes several central failures in what he calls the "words of the world": While human speech only depicts events instead of making them happen, it can posit events that did not happen and are not true.[10] Human speech refers to a reality different from the words and hence requires verification that such reference is true. Language itself has no responsibility for what it designates. Because it is incapable of giving access to reality, it misrepresents and misdirects.

This failure of language is evident even within Scripture. Although Henry's text is replete with references to the Scriptures, his relation to the text is rather ambivalent. He points out the difficulty that we only have access to Christ's words through the record of the evangelists and that consequently "the word of the Scripture has become similar to the words spoken by men; it is a collection of unreal significations incapable in themselves of presenting a reality other than their own" (IT, 214).[11] We might acknowledge, for example, that a particular text claims that Christ broke bread and lifted a cup of wine and said: "This is my body. This is my blood." Yet, churches have split and wars been fought over what those words mean, to what they referred then and what they signify now when a priest repeats the words at the table. Very often they have been interpreted as a statement of fact, where the words "this is my body" designate a reference to the bread and a claim about the truth (or falsity) of this reference. The mere assertion that this bread in some way is Christ's body is not seen to have the power to accomplish such transformation by itself, which is why many people remain skeptical that it is more than theatrical performance or sentimental memory. The words of the priest, by all appearances, do not seem to change anything. Human words, in Henry's estimation, are powerless, unable to bridge the triple distance they create: their difference from what they signify, their indifference to what is being said, and their inability to effect or create that of which they speak.[12]

In contrast, according to Henry, Christ's words contain no such distance. They do not *refer to* God but are themselves the auto-revelation of the divine life that flows in each one of us. In Christ's words we have direct and immediate access to the life of God; they are not characterized by delay, absence, signification, separation or interpretation.[13] The divine word does not produce or establish any correspondence between its content and the things of the world. It speaks the divine life that generates all other life and thus is the voice of life flowing within me, "the sound of my birth."[14] These words express the immediacy of our experience and of our suffering.[15] This word of life is prior to any word of the world and anybody who wishes can have immediate access to it, since God speaks through the direct experience of our lives and our flesh. God's word, then, for Henry, cannot be heard with our ears or in any audible sense (PC, 134). Rather it is heard in and by the heart, in our impressions, desires, and emotions. While the speech of the world separates word and action as two different things, the divine word is inseparably linked to action: "God spoke and it came to be." The divine word is characterized by power (even omnipotence). It immediately accomplishes what it speaks; its very word is action.

Humans hear the word of God by responding to it and accepting the salvation and eternal life that is offered within and by it. The words of Christ are the words of God because they are the auto-revelation of the divine life and thus of the Truth. No further proof is necessary because no distance exists between the word and life itself. The Word itself is Life. To hear the voice of God only one thing is required: receiving Christ's words as divine self-revelation. Such reception implies rebirth into the divine life; thus only the one engendered by the divine life is capable of hearing and identifying the word of God. God inhabits our flesh and enables our faith which allows us to hear the divine voice. It is our heart that gives us such direct knowledge of God and permits us to hear the divine voice.[16]

The language that gives access to immediate experience does so only because it speaks the reality of the divine life in us. In this way Henry bases his discussion of the divine word on his previous analyses of the "Truth of Christianity" and the access to life which it grants. In his earlier work he makes a strict division between the "truth of the world" (which is that of the science inaugurated by Galileo or of Western philosophy in general) and the "Truth of Christianity" (which is the phenomenology of life and direct experience of the flesh). The truth of the world is dual in nature: it assumes a separation between "what shows itself and the fact of self-showing" (IT, 13). The world is always external to us and its truth different from us, a product of our vision or imagination. Things do not give themselves in their reality, but only as an image or appearance or phenomenon. Henry suggests that any form of truth is passing, except that of Christianity which is a pure phenomenological truth.[17] Christianity's Truth is manifestation and phenomenality itself. It implies no distance. The Truth of Christianity is self-revelation or, as Henry will call it later, auto-affection. "Christianity is nothing other," he affirms, "than the awe-inspiring and meticulous theory of this givenness of God's self-revelation shared with man" (IT, 25). We cannot access divine Revelation through our physical vision or through thought. It does not appear in the world as a phenomenon, but rather is Life revealing itself. According to Henry, it is the only access to life that we have, the only true reality there is, and the only place where we could fully experience love and enjoyment. Henry consequently rejects the "truth of the world" as inadequate and even false because it is always distanced from reality, from the concrete and immediate experience of the flesh in suffering and joy. In contrast, Christianity speaks of an authentic phenomenological experience of reality and is able to establish the sole valid phenomenology of the human person as a "son of God," a participant of the divine life. Although this life is ours as human beings from the beginning, we have rejected and ignored it and must recover this experience through a new birth and salvation in Christ.

Hence in order to hear the voice of God, we must recognize ourselves engendered by the divine life and receiving all life solely from it. We must believe in Christ's identity as the first-born son who enables us to enter within eternal salvation through the salvation he grants. We all hear the voice of God in the secret of our hearts and the immediacy of our suffering and joy (and the life that ultimately sustains them): an inner fire of recognition illuminates them (PC, 152). In this way for Henry the phenomenon of religious experience justifies itself. The deeds we do in fulfilling the will of God "prove" the word of God, because they make us one with Christ (PC, 153). Religious experience liberates from the failures and lies of ordinary language. While the word of the world keeps us away from the divine Life that has originated us and encourages us to do evil, the incarnation breaks the vicious cycle in which evil prevents us from hearing the truth that would set us free from it. We can now hear the words of God because they are spoken by the human voice of Christ. Christ not only assumes our flesh but gives us his flesh. By partaking of it we are enabled to receive salvation, to return to the source of life and claim our divine sonship.

It is not that a historical text designates bread and wine as elements that really signify something else, namely body and blood linked obscurely to a death about two thousand years ago. Rather, our flesh and our very life itself are sustained by the divine life, communicated by what the Fathers called "the food of immortality." Henry insists repeatedly that only our real communion in Christ's flesh enables us to participate in the divine life and to transform our finitude. The words of institution, then, do not signify but vivify, they do not refer us to another reality, but they transform our reality: "The institution of the Eucharist which the synoptic Gospels describe, exhibits this power: 'This is my body.' Since then from an uninterrupted memorial of this institution across the centuries, it is, repeated by the priest, the sovereign word of Christ who sanctifies the offering."[18] These words are not "words of the world" that refer to or designate some reality external to it. Rather they are the divine Word himself who comes to meet us in the Eucharistic action and communicates his life to us. To identify with Christ's flesh is to enter eternal Life, to participate in the very life of God.

II. Does the Truth Require Interpretation?

Henry claims, then, that the voice of God can be heard and identified by its immediacy and that it requires no interpretation. The need for interpretation, instead, points to the word of the world which is characterized by reference and distance. Hermeneutics consequently becomes a deeply un-Christian (and un-phenomenological) endeavor. Divine speech is in no need of interpretation or hermeneutic judgment of any kind, in fact, such need would indicate precisely that the word in question is not divine. At times Henry is extremely dismissive of any hermeneutic exercise. In a criticism of Heidegger's analysis of *Dasein*, for example, he concludes: "Such is the obscurity of the call and the gratuitousness of the response that, between the Word and its hearing, a primal Gap has slipped in that separates them forever. So in effect it comes down to interpreting them as one can and wants. In any case, *phenomenology has given way to hermeneutics and commentaries, or rather, to endless hypotheses.*"[19] Hermeneutics is mere "commentary" or "hypothesis" and thus an endeavor external (and blind) to actual reality. It is an exercise of the "world," since it is concerned with interpretation, reference, signification, and authentication.

In contrast, Henry repeatedly emphasizes that Christianity, or the "Truth" of "Life" justifies itself and requires no outside proof. The Scriptures are in no need of any exterior referent or confirmation because God speaks in them directly and we are able to hear them in our hearts. Although they are not identical with our joy and suffering, they embrace these feelings and desires and in them we can hear the divine.[20] While normal human language finds credible what corresponds to an exterior reality and rejects what does not seem to do so, it cannot ever justify or prove that reality (nor confirm the correspondence of language to it). Yet Life itself is immediate to our existence and requires no further proof precisely because we live it. We know that we have not given ourselves this life, but that it is a gift from the source of life. Thus our very life is direct proof of the divine life flowing in us. The divine word at work within us both justifies the legitimacy of Christ's words and the validity of the Scriptures.[21] The spirit testifies within us to the truth of this word (even while evil attempts to convince us otherwise). The phenomenon of religious experience thus certifies itself and cannot be invalidated.[22] It requires neither verification nor interpretation.

This rejection or at least suppression of hermeneutics I find deeply troubling. There are three important problems I see in Henry's dismissal of hermeneutics and emphasis on complete immediacy. First, the intense immediacy of the divine word in Henry's account seems to eliminate the possibility for any meaningful response to it. Second, a dismissal of interpretation does not mean that no interpretation is present, but opens itself up to dangerous misinterpretation(s). Any "immediate" sensation of the heart appears able to take the place of the divine. Finally, the absolute immediacy of this revelation seems to lead to a type of solipsism. If the divine life is more or less identical with our feelings and sensations, it cannot be communicated. There is little possibility for the community to interpret *together*.

First, by rejecting the need for interpretation Henry also seems to eliminate the possibility of free response to this word. He claims that the "truth of the world" separates call and response by introducing a fundamental gap between them and continues: "In the Word of Life, by contrast, the difference between Word and Hearing, the call and the response, has disappeared. Because the Hearing in which I hear the Word of life is my own condition as Son, my own life engendered in absolute Life's self-engendering, this Hearing has no freedom at all in respect to what it hears. It is not the Hearing of a call to which the person has license to respond or not. To be able to respond to the call, to hear it in an appropriate listening, but equally to turn away from it—it is always too late for all that" (IT, 227). Despite all the problems with positing an autonomous and free subject as the paradigm of what it means to be human, eliminating all freedom and the very *possibility* of response seems equally problematic. If there is no room for interpretation, if one cannot wonder about how to understand and what to do in response, if one has no freedom even over whether to listen at all, then the divine word becomes dictatorial and absolute. To what extent would Abraham's trial still have been a "test" of his faith, if God had dragged him up the mountain and forced his hand to sacrifice his son?

Henry tries to avoid this difficulty by speaking of the divine as the life of pathos in us. It is not something separate controlling us, but our inner-most self at the very core of our existence. But since it is the divine life, he is only consistent in saying that ultimately this life does not belong to us (PC, 122). This, however, either leads to a complete identification of the divine and the human that leaves no meaningful distinction between them—and thus amounts to a sort of pantheism[23]—or it eliminates one by replacing it with the other (so either God is reduced to designating merely the innermost reality of human life or humans are mere pawns for the divine life to express itself). In either case, some kind of hermeneutic distance seems required here, so that the two do not become collapsed into each other. And, in fact, Henry does want to maintain a distance. He clearly speaks of Christ as a real person, as the Son of God who took actual human flesh and in whom it is required to believe in order to gain access to eternal life. The divine life does not merely refer to our inner-most feelings. Yet the distinction between Christ's sonship and human sonship, God's Life and our life, often becomes nearly impossible for him to maintain. Maybe hermeneutics would help us at least to begin to sepa-rate them?

Second, as Richard Kearney has convincingly argued, hermeneutic judgment is necessary in order to distinguish a God of love and justice from the monstrous or demonic.[24] Such hermeneutic judgment does not constitute a human limitation imposed upon the divine (in an idolatrous or blasphemous hubris that would interpret God as always confined to our categories) but rather acknowledges the fundamental human limita-tion of recognizing the divine and thus the continual need for interpreta-tion. Henry is analyzing the *words* of Christ and in that, it seems to me, is engaged in a hermeneutic endeavor which he often fails to acknowledge. Henry claims that interpretation involves distance while Life (and hence the divine) is experienced immediately, without any distance or separa-tion.[25] This immediacy is precisely the "proof" of its divinity and authen-ticity—it is so immediate that no proof (and hence no hermeneutic interpretation) is needed. One knows its Truth in one's heart. Yet this "knowing" seems a very dangerous one without hermeneutic judgment guiding one's interpretation of the message of the heart. Emotions maybe more than anything require interpretation.

For Henry apparently all immediate experience arises directly out of Life without differentiation. Yet how can both exhilarating joy and excruciating pain equally be a sign of the divine life flowing in us? Does it not matter significantly whether we are experiencing the one or the other? Does the intensity, immediacy, and uncommunicability of torture become a sign of God's presence? Of course what Henry says about the Christian ethic prevents some of these more serious misreadings. Henry does emphasize the importance of ethical action in Christian faith (even as he does not want to reduce Christianity to ethics). Yet is not his guide in discovering and explicating this ethics precisely the interpretation given of Christianity by the Scriptures and especially the tradition of the Church over the past two millennia? Does it not matter, then, what *kind* of action the message of the heart proposes? And do we not need some guidance even in understanding this message and in putting it into action? Henry identifies the action of Life with love and thus summarizes the Christian ethic as following the command of love. This love is grounded in our "feeling" ourselves "to be sons" of God. Yet is feeling really sufficient here? What if we misinterpret the message of the heart? What about the religious fanatic for whom the message of the heart is indeed not only loud and clear but utterly immediate and compelling, fueled by intense emotion and pathos? What helps us choose love and compassion over hatred and deceit?

This leads to the third difficulty. The immediacy of the divine message seems to make any meaningful communication with others impossible. Yet must not the community help us to discern what feelings to follow, which to ignore, what feelings to combat, and which to fuel? Henry defies the very idea of the need for any kind of reference. Reference itself, in fact, is the problem. Yet is not some measure of reference necessary for communication? It is certainly true that the immediate experience of pain cannot be shared, that we cannot truly feel the other's suffering or joy. And yet do I not need someone to hold me when I am wracked with grief, someone to acknowledge my pain, someone to exult in my joy? Emotions, as solitary as they may be when we experience them, can destroy us if they cannot be shared. Henry emphasizes repeatedly how we feel God's voice within our heart, how it speaks directly to us in our emotions, and therefore seems to imply that this immediate experience cannot be communicated, since it would employ again the lie of worldly speech. This is somewhat ironic, however, since so much of his analysis depends on Christ's communication of the divine life to all human beings. And the only context in which he can envision relation to others, then, really is when he talks about this divine life "flowing in each of us." It is only through Christ that we can have any sort of relation with each other (PC, 61), but even then it seems more an undifferentiated participation in the divine life than the possibility of any real communication. Such a monadic interpretation of pathos is not only unsatisfying, but does not reflect the Christian tradition's emphasis on the common work of liturgy and communal worship (nor does it do justice to Henry's own references to the Eucharist).

The hermeneutic process of discernment and judgment, then, is not only essential in itself, but must involve dialogue with and accountability to others to preserve it from becoming an individualistic spirituality that loses connection with the real body (or flesh) of Christ which Henry is so fond of emphasizing. The hermeneutic judgment that it was indeed Yahweh speaking to Moses in the burning bush is confirmed by the communal experience of the liberated people worshipping at the foot of that same mountain. Gideon's fourfold attempt to misunderstand God's command to liberate the Israelites is foiled only by his leading men into battle and routing the Midianites. Mary's acknowledgment of the angel's message as coming from God is "validated" by the child in her womb, by that child's life and death, and by the ecclesial affirmation of her as the *theotokos*, the one who gave human flesh to the divine. And even partaking of the bread and drinking from the cup is an essentially communal activity, a sharing in the ecclesial and Eucharistic body of Christ that provides a hermeneutic understanding of what such participation means and entails. Can we hear the voice of God? Maybe. But this hearing does require interpretation and response by the listener and by the community of faith, regardless of how immediate and close to our hearts it might be.

Radical Phenomenology Reveals a Measure of Faith and a Need for a Levinasian Other in Henry's Life

RONALD L. MERCER JR.

Jean-Yves Lacoste reminds us in "The Work and Complement of Appearing" that things exist inasmuch as they invite themselves to us. Were we but able to render an account of this invitation, were we only to perceive that it is not in disguise that things appear to us, and were we, finally, to know the conditions under which consciousness is open, all the work of philosophy would be, by right, achievable.[1] "Were we"—a contrary to fact conditional. If we *were* to have made these accounts, perceptions, and conditions—but we have not—then all of philosophy's work would be achievable, but it seems as though it is not. Whenever philosophy flags, phenomenology trumpets the need to go back to the beginning, so we must return to ask a better question. Since "all the work of philosophy" as such is beyond the scope of this essay, let us focus upon that work that endeavors to move from the immanent to the transcendent, the move at the heart of the essays in *Phenomenology and the "Theological Turn": The French Debate.*[2]

Transcendence, in this context, must mean something more than the "not-I." In simple terms, all worldly objects that can be classified as "not-I" are transcendent to me; however, these objects are reducible to a realm of immanence, my conscious field. The transcendence we seek must be classifiable as "other-than-I," irreducible to my conscious field while yet integrally related to my consciousness in such a way that the practicing of phenomenology can bring the "other-than-I" into relief.

Dominique Janicaud surely lies in wait. I must be making reference to God, having invoked the terms "transcendence" and an irreducible "other-than-I." To begin with the notions of phenomenology and God is surely to castigate Janicaud, prompting him to call for further denuding of the transcendental I, which I have dressed up in the antithesis of the emperor's new clothes—meaning clothes that everyone can see but they pretend the clothes are not there.[3] If this were the case, I must admit to being in good company: with Emmanuel Levinas, whom Janicaud finds to be the master-weaver of the theological covering; and Jean-Luc Marion and Michel Henry, who are most likely to don the inappropriate material and be chided by Janicaud, who plays the part of the bothersome but well-intentioned child in our tale. Beginning again, we must ask a question that both sides would allow, one that starts at the beginning, at immanence.

To propose a question relevant to achieving a sense of transcendence from immanence, I will adapt Lacoste's third condition for the proper working of philosophy: "What are the conditions, what is the structure, of human consciousness such that it is open to the invitation of transcendence, if an irreducible transcendence could give such an invitation?" This question strikes at the heart of Pope John Paul II's challenge to philosophy to "vindicate the human being's capacity to know this transcendence."[4] In Biblical terms, we are seeking the very ground of Saint Paul's "measure of faith," an openness to transcendence. Exegetically, Paul's reference to a "measure of faith" in Romans 12 is restricted to Christian believers; however, phenomenologically I will show that we can argue for a constitutive structure that grants a universal possibility of faith. Of course, after quoting a pope and Saint Paul, there seems little chance that Janicaud would endorse my question; however, let us not forget that according to his own assessment of the "Contours of the Turn" he is not entirely averse to discussing a "dimension of height," only the idea that this height must lead to a "Most High."[5] I will answer our question by looking at Michel Henry's work, but insofar as I believe Janicaud can be appeased, I will argue that Henry's transcendent does not account for any measure of faith. I will then add a corrective based on Levinas's discussion of the transcendent other.[6]

In order for a Levinasian corrective to be added, however, it must first be the case that Levinas and Henry are engaged in the same game, a game that I have claimed involves the rules of understanding transcendence. There should be little debate as to whether or not Levinas concerns himself with such material, for the other person has often marked a paradox of transcendence in his works. On the one hand, the other, while transcendent to me in a bodily fashion, appears well within one's conscious field as an object. Does one not see the other's face and body, smell the odor of clean soap or lack of deodorant, and hear the words when the other speaks? On the other hand, however, the other person is never reducible to any definitive totality within the conscious field on account of the ego's inability to know the other's experiences from the viewpoint of the other person effectively negating the possibility of sharing in any unmediated way the meaningfulness of the world from the other's perspective, preserving the transcendence of the other.

Henry, however, clearly wants to distinguish his work from any discussion of transcendence as something ultimately beyond the conscious ego. He will claim that God, whom Henry equates with Absolute Life, is experienced in a straightaway phenomenological fashion. Nevertheless, Henry is careful to distinguish this experience from the simple intending of an object. God does not appear out of the bright light with the long robe and glowing hair. This straightaway fashion must also not be confused with the act of protending. Protention is the cognitive filling-in consciousness does with each adumbrated viewing of an object, and even though the protended aspect of an object (for example, the backside of a mirror) is necessarily absent in viewing, one can always take up a position such that what was merely a conscious protention becomes what is intentionally viewed. God, while absent, is not hiding behind Calvary's cross or in a cave on Mount Sinai in such a way that one can merely walk around and find God hiding in those shadows. Absolute Life, as we shall see, acts upon the living in a transcendental way such that Life is ever-present, but forever unobjectifiable.

Consequently we now have a solid link between Levinas and Henry that can be expressed in transcendent terms. As the other person acts in transcendental fashion by conditioning the human in terms of substitution but doing so in a way that cannot be objectified, so acts Henry's Life, which constitutes the human condition as living but also cannot be made into an object of consciousness. As nonobjectifiable transcendental conditions, these conditions remain transcendent to my conscious field.

Any phenomenology that involves some indication of transcendence must be regarded as, in some sense, radical. The problem with laying out a brief explanation of radical phenomenology is that everything after *Ideas I* must look like radical phenomenology to someone like Janicaud.[7] However, it is not just Henry, Marion, and the other new phenomenologists who discuss Life, the gift, and the call, or even Levinas and Derrida, who discuss the other and *différance*, who have radicalized phenomenology.

Husserl's protégés, Heidegger and Fink, also moved beyond Husserl's central period with discussion of world horizons, the absolute, and the meontic. Fink, as Husserl's confidant during the last years of his life, moved Husserl to radicalize himself.[8] Radical phenomenology begins with the movement from the description of a viewed object to a comprehension of the conditions necessary for that object to be viewed, and this entire process of analysis, which must be supplemented by reanalysis, constitutes the phenomenological reduction itself. These conditions are transcendent insofar as they are not perceptible, for they are that which we are always already in and no position can be taken up "outside" these conditions such that a proper viewing can take place. Consequently, they can only be suggested, hinted at, or metaphorically named.[9] Henry and Levinas both attempt such a radical phenomenology that reaches for such conditions of the human experience, Life in the former case and the other in the latter, and each finds reason to name (perhaps metaphorically or perhaps not) their respective conditions as God.

Henry, God, and Absolute Life

Our investigation of Henry will begin with his recognition of the Gospels' assertion that we are "Sons"; however, this sonship does not resemble in any way the biological notion of offspring.[10] To be a biological child is to be begotten into the world, originating from the genetic material of a woman and a man, growing in the womb, replicating cells and ordering cells in a human fashion. When born, the expectation of biology is that the parents have made a new life, but Henry finds a disparity between the description of various biological processes and being alive. The formation of the body is the formation of an external manifestation, the rules of which do not guarantee that the body be any more than a cadaver: a body reduced to its pure externality.[11] Parents, then, are not the originators of the new life but simply two who participate in Life. This Life, which receives a capital "L," the sign for Janicaud that a term is about to get a divine designation, is indeed defined as the very essence of God such that the living are more truly the offspring of God than of parents.[12]

As a living child, the only true parent is God, such that "*no man is the son of a man, or of any woman either, but only of God.*"[13] The extraordinary universality of this claim that all are somehow children of God should alleviate some of the pressure of charges that Henry is directly linking his philosophy with one form or another of Christian dogmatism. Take for example the conversation between Jesus and the "Jews" in John 8:41–44 (NRSV): "They said to him, 'We are not illegitimate children; we have one father, God himself.' Jesus said to them . . . "You are from your father the devil, and you choose to do your father's desires." Consequently, Henry's understanding of a universal progeny need not be related to doctrinal questions of inclusion or exclusion. This clearly seems to be the case when Henry argues that the one living as a child of God is able to experience the condition as straightaway phenomenological and, thus, as something discoverable in immanence.[14]

The assertion that living as a child of God is something universally phenomenological already seems to have two strikes against it. On the one hand is the religious claim that evidence of God is not secularly manifest but divinely revealed, while on the other hand is Husserl's prescription, of which Janicaud is so fond of reminding the new phenomenologists, that any notion of God as an object of phenomenology must be bracketed off. Both of these objections, however, begin with the idea of God as a being in the world, existing in some special way such that God is in hiding and will not come out except under miraculous circumstances, but as Henry explains, the Truth of Christianity is not about God as a being but about "a transcendental phenomenology whose central concepts are Father and Son," God and Christ.[15] The essence of God as Life, then, is not only transcendental but absolute, being fundamental ground for the very goings-on of the living of lived experiences. At this point, we see the need for a radical phenomenology to be performed within immanent life, for while that which is absolute is integral to the coming to pass of living, it does not appear in the world as an object; therefore, it is not observed in the manner of things. Life is also not observed in the manner of the ontologically disclosed, wherein a regression is made from what is manifest to the conditions of manifestation. What we mean here is clearly evidenced at the seminal stages of a phenomenology of life when we see Husserl introduce his widely applauded concept of the *life-world*, that analytic concept used for disclosing the experienced "being-in-the-world." Emphasis has been placed continually on the side of the *world*, leaving underdeveloped and *presupposed* the investigation of life.[16]

A study of life would have to mean a phenomenology that is essentially aware of itself. Inasmuch as phenomenology is expected to be that philosophy of disclosure of an object intentionally grasped in lived experience via acts of analysis and reflection, a phenomenology aware of itself is more insofar as the acts of reflection and analysis do not just reveal the lived experiences of a consciousness but reveal instances of *living* itself. In the doing of phenomenology, we find some of the intricate goings-on of life, and if we recognize that reflection and analysis are but parts to the whole of living, then it becomes apparent that all conscious intending consists of *acts of life* that find fulfillment in the apprehending of an object. The self, then, is a Son, in Henry's terms, "generated in absolute phenomenological life" because the self is grounded in life in an absolute sense, meaning the self does not partake of a portion or even of all of life.[17] A self is a corporal instance of life engendering itself as a person, which Henry expresses in the double claim: "Life self-engenders itself as me. . . . Life engenders me as itself."[18] If we can say that God is Life, and we are only hinting at our readiness to make this statement, then we can now see why Henry so often invokes Meister Eckhart who echoes the double claim about life wherein "God is begotten as myself. . . . God gives birth to me as himself."[19]

Have we gone too far? Surely Janicaud's concerns are validated, and Henry's priestly robes, supposedly locked up in the closet of the *epochê*, were never truly discarded.

Let us turn to two nondoctrinal sources that suggest Henry's equation of God to life is not a violation of phenomenological bracketing: a Hebrew-English lexicon and the work of Eugen Fink, who would never be confused with the new phenomenologists or with any theological preoccupation. What we will find is that Janicaud presupposes the term "God" to be necessarily laden with religious assumptions. The word "God," however, to suit Henry's purposes, only needs to represent the absolute origin of life, names for which, Husserl has reminded us, we only have metaphors. The meaning of God's name, the Tetragrammaton, is philologically debatable, but recent scholars tend to agree that YHWH represents a lost causal form of the verb "to be" (Hifil 3rd masc. sing.). Therefore, without any orthodoxy attached, YHWH suggests the "one who brings to pass," an equation with the origin of life.[20] Echoing this absolute usage is Fink, whose work centers on the methodology of disclosing and the disclosing of that which is originally constitutive of lived experience. Fink writes that even though the absolute cannot be brought directly into view, phenomenology transforms philosophy such that "philosophy is the manifestation of God in us. God is not a transcendent idol, but rather is the me-ontic depth of the world and existence."[21] In this disclosure of the manifestation of God, there is an "un-nihilating of the Absolute," which Fink recognizes as "true theogony."[22] In essence, the disclosure of the Absolute is linguistically compatible with watching the birth of God, simply describable in the equation of God and Life.

Janicaud's accusations that Henry has done nothing more than disclose a transcendental ego already dressed in religious raiment seems untenable given that the conception of God as life appears a well-accepted term for the very origination of life. However, it is not necessarily the case that we have found that structure of the human that guarantees the possibility of a connection to the transcendent. Can we in any way consider his work as actually *Toward a Christian Philosophy* or actually fulfilling the task set forth in this essay to discover the possibility of a connection between the human and the transcendent? Henry's absolute life is transcendent in that it is forgotten as I exercise those capacities that it enables. It is ever behind what I do, while never being present. However, as argued, this transcendence is the very essence of immanence itself, which determines that "[Faith] is simply a name for the unshakeable certainty that life has of living. . . . Faith does not come from the fact that we believe, it comes from the fact that we are the living in life."[23] In essence, faith is no more than the recognition of our ultimate phenomenological ground, an orientation in perception such that the absolute is brought to relief by radical phenomenology. Such faith is, radically put, a faith in oneself as much as it might be a faith in God, such that every move toward transcendence brings one back to immanence.

The charge against Henry could be couched in terms of Gnosticism. Has Henry forsaken any recognition of a personal relationship with God, a relationship that appears presupposed in any discussion of sons and daughters, for a speculative grasping of God as absolute origin, which is reducible to an understanding of the transcendental conditions of the self as living? Henry seems to avoid this charge, at first, in his reconceptualization of salvation, for salvation is not in terms of any special knowledge but is achieved through acts of mercy that reorient the ego, which has forgotten its engendered origin in absolute life.[24] We should not fall into debates of salvation by works or by grace here, for salvation is also reconceived as less than theological. Salvation is the process of making the self aware of its dependence upon Life; it is a recovery from the fall that is the forgetting of sonship. The ego forgets its origin on account of its active life wherein each individual ego is aware of those powers it controls: feeling, movement, and thinking. In the exercise of these powers, the ego forgets the conditioning of life, the affective life that makes these powers possible on account of the ego's mastery of its powers in effective living. "In the action of the ego as action, supposedly issuing from itself and aimed only at itself, the very essence of absolute life is ruled out."[25] The reorientation necessary for bringing the ego back to itself in the light of its origins does not occur in Gnostic speculation but in the doing of acts of mercy.

If it is the case that Henry's divulgence of the absolute is not accomplished in the speculative sense, then we must discover how deeds of mercy awaken the self to its proper origins. For examples of these deeds Henry refers us to medieval theology's seven works of corporal mercy, which include such acts as feeding the hungry, clothing the naked, and caring for the sick. In these cases, the one who performs these services still acts from the ego's ability to effect changes in the world, but the meaningfulness of these acts will also affect the performer in such a way that the condition of Life in which the action is done is disclosed. For Henry, such a merciful act realized as part of the absolute occurs in the book of John in the example of Jesus' healing on the Sabbath.[26] While it was accepted that working on the Sabbath was forbidden, Jesus' justification was that his deed was not his alone but that he was always at work just as God was also always at work. The connection between Jesus' act of healing and God's perpetual work as Life, for Henry, is in the realization that the act of mercy is simultaneously an act of life affirmation. That Jesus was aware of the overlap between his particular deed and the very possibility of Life that exists in God is the proof of Jesus' ultimate claim to sonship.

What becomes ultimately problematic for Henry is the way in which the deeds of mercy do not take one beyond the self but firmly return the self to the absolute Life of which the particular ego is already an expression. One can be reoriented to engendering Life by performing life-affirming acts; however, the reorientation that occurs is not toward anything absolutely other but toward something absolutely immanent, as Henry asserts in the following:

> One who is born of life finds actions capable of satisfying him only if this action suits his condition. The action can only suit the condition of Son if it comes from that condition and returns to it. *Its coming from the condition of Son is what makes it possible in the first place.* There is no "I Can" except in life.[27]

We have already remarked that our discussion must begin from the immanent to be properly phenomenological, but in order for our analysis to be anything toward a philosophy of Christianity, there must result a sense in which the transcendence in immanence points one beyond the conditions of the ego, which Henry's reciprocal engendering between God and self appears to deny. The unfortunate consequence is that either the accusation of Gnosticism must be revisited, or worse, that transcendence reveals what is ultimately intelligible and as intelligible does not allow entry into anything theic.

I do not in any way disparage the impressive discussion of life and the absolute and the human's position as child of life. Nevertheless, is faith in Henry's absolute "Father" not more properly Christian faith when placed in *Abba*, daddy?

A Levinasian Corrective

Levinas's concept of the same haunts Henry's transcendence revealing the idea to be insufficient for describing the life of the human being, the new conception of which was Henry's goal. Levinas agrees with Henry insofar as transcendence "is the very life of the human," and in this case, Levinas recognizes that transcendence "is used without any theological presupposition." However, that life must already be "troubled by the Infinite."[28] What is insufficient in Henry's work is that life as the field into which living being emerges is not specific enough in its essence to describe the living *human* being. Inasmuch as life acts as a coming to oneself, a wakefulness open to the world, the transcendence of life does not assure that the living "I" will acknowledge the right of anything else to awaken into the world as different. If living things are the very essence of God and the very essence of God is my essence, then all living things and I are essentially the same. Everyone is me.

It would appear that Henry's reading would run afoul of Levinas's harshest comments for Christianity. Levinas critiques the Christian tradition for having succumbed to the influence of the Western tradition's penchant for totalization: "Christianity too is tempted by temptation, and in this it is profoundly Western."[29] What he means here is that Christianity sees itself caught in a struggle with the tempter, caught in a struggle with temptations, and as Nietzsche and Hegel correctly surmised, this corporate and individual conflict acts as a high motivator for Christians to evolve in the world, constantly overcoming new challenges, conquering, and assimilating. Any time Christianity constructs a new totality, reduction to the same, whether political or intellectual, as we have in the case of Henry, Levinas would almost certainly point to Christianity's own scriptures that point the way to the transcendent God through ethical human action for the other. Without religious misgivings, he willingly quotes from the Gospel of Matthew where those condemned for their lack of attention to God's needs ask: "Lord, when did we see you hungry or thirsty or a stranger or naked or sick or in prison?" God responds, "Truly, I say to you, whatever you did not do for one of the least of these you did not do for me" (Matthew 25:44–45).

Levinas, however, also appears to support Henry when he asks, "Is not transcendence to God?"[30] The important difference of course is the recognition that transcendence as a nontheological concept delivers us a-Dieu rather than reveal the essence of God itself. The human, as such, not only emerges at its foundation in life, but it is also fundamentally conditioned in the face-to-face, the immanent meeting of one person with another.

The otherness of the other, absent in the presence of its face, is also a transcendent that receives a divine appellation, but just as in the case with Henry, it is difficult to see how the other, as God, represents anything of God to whom we pray. Nevertheless, it is within these ideas that I believe lie phenomenology's greatest service to religion. The importance of the other's description as God is not in the revelation of the divine but in the orienting of the self toward transcendence. Even if we grant, as I will, that the otherness of the other person in no way equates with the God of the philosophers or with the God of Abraham, Isaac, and Jacob, the otherness of the other person conditions the human such that the human being is constituted as devoted to that which is incomprehensible, ineffable, and transcendent to experience.

Devotion to the other leaves one without Henry's grasp of God, but realizing the problematic nature of such a grasp, it is enough that such devotion leaves one with the sense of holiness. Derrida notes Levinas's remark, "One often speaks of ethics to describe what I do, but what really interests me in the end is not ethics, not ethics alone, but the holy, the holiness of the holy."[31] This sense of holiness that so interests Levinas originates in the emerging of the I into the world as ethical, the very event of which he declares would also be "first theology."[32] Such a theology, however, is not one of conceptual/Gnostic proportions in which the deity is grasped in concept but in which the deity is brought "to just and human efforts, as one brings the light of day to the human eye, the only organ capable of seeing it."[33] Through ethical human efforts, the human situation clarifies the idea of God, not in terms of conceptual grasping but in terms of familiarity, a drawing near to holiness.

To call out Abba, daddy . . . mommy, is to reach away from oneself in the ultimate hope that that which is absolutely other than I will respond in some way. However, such a reaching out must begin with a measure of faith, a possibility within the very structure of the human being that is always already oriented toward the transcendent. Regardless of how much Henry's description of Life is necessary for uncovering the absolute foundation of the living being, it is simply not enough to account for the desire to reach God. A fuller description of all the conditions that structure consciousness is necessary. However, with the beginnings of this description in hand and the condition of devotion to the other disclosed, one can turn back to Henry's analysis with an affirmative answer from Levinas's question. Indeed, transcendence does lead us to God, but only if we begin with a measure of faith.

The Truth of Life

Michel Henry on Marx

CLAYTON CROCKETT

With the translation of *I Am the Truth*, Michel Henry has emerged in the English-speaking world as one of the Christian phenomenologists associated with the turn to religion on the part of contemporary continental philosophy. Henry's previous phenomenological books, such as *The Essence of Manifestation* and *Philosophy and Phenomenology of the Body*, can be read as significant philosophical works in themselves or alternatively as leading toward his later, more explicitly religious writings.[1] Whether in his dense phenomenological reflections or his intense religious meditations, Henry's language is provocative, and I would like to second Jean-Luc Marion's initial negative reaction. Referring to *The Essence of Manifestation*, Marion relates that the book "fell from his hands."[2] I had the same response to *I Am the Truth*. In this book, Henry's language appears hyperbolic in its rhetorical opposition of the Truth of Christianity to the degraded nature of science and the modern world, where men and women are reduced to the status of machines.[3] At the same time, as Mark Wenzinger points out, Henry "uses apophantic logos to do violence to apophantic *logos* itself. . . . The violence that Henry inflicts on the *logos*, however, is in fact intended ultimately to *renew* rather than *suppress* thought, language, or the text."[4] Logos is apophantic because it is not self-sufficient. Language is secondary to life, but it can be used to stimulate life if reconnected to the Logos that is the source of Life and Truth. Henry stages an oppositional conflict of language in order to spur thinking to new heights of living.

So just as Marion later revised this negative impression and praised Henry's "example of philosophical probity,"[5] I have also come to admire the depth and rigor of Henry's thought and appreciate this apophantic use of language. At the same time, I still want to elaborate my critique: in his rhetorical excessiveness, Henry verges on a Gnostic rendering of Christianity, which sunders humanity from the world. According to Henry, "living is not possible in the world," but only outside the world, "where another Truth reigns."[6] My negative reaction to the language of *I Am the Truth* is supplemented by an appreciation of Henry's subtlety in *The Essence of Manifestation* and other works, especially his reading of Karl Marx. My reading of Henry's book on Marx will enable me to develop my critique more carefully and less superficially, and I will connect his interpretation of Marx back up to his theological justification of a Christian philosophy in *I Am the Truth*.

A supreme example of Henry's philosophical probity occurs in his two-volume treatment of Marx, abridged and translated into English in one volume entitled *Marx: A Philosopher of Human Reality*. Marx would seem a strange philosopher for Henry to champion, and his reading is not a critique but an affirmation of Marx's thought. At the center of Henry's reading of Marx is a profound focus on life as living labor. Henry develops a reading of Marx that counters the traditional interpretation of Marx as a fundamentally economic thinker. In fact, according to Henry, Marx criticizes the capture of modern humans by economic relationships and realities.

A theme that emerges most insistently in Henry's entire oeuvre is life. In an interview from 2001, Henry explains that "living is above all having the sensation of oneself, feeling oneself."[7] The sensation of feeling oneself is auto-affection, or affectivity, which is the pure immanence of life. In *The Essence of Manifestation*, Henry says, "that which is felt without the intermediary of any sense whatsoever is in its essence affectivity."[8] The essence of manifestation in phenomenology is the revelation of this pure affectivity. The source of affectivity is "life itself, it is the transcendental life of the absolute ego insofar as it is the ultimate foundation."[9] Furthermore, Life is explicitly identified with God in *I Am the Truth*: "God is Life—he is the essence of Life, or if one prefers, the essence of Life is God."[10] This theme of life is found not only in phenomenology and Christian philosophy but also, strikingly, in the work of Karl Marx as well.

I want to draw out Henry's reading of Marx in order to show where he locates the essence of life in Marx's thought, and then relate this notion of life back to *I Am the Truth*. My argument is that whereas Henry brilliantly illustrates Marx's notion of praxis as resolving the separation of theory and practical action, he goes too far in opposing them, which leads to his overblown and quasi-gnostic theological claims in *I Am the Truth*. Nevertheless, Henry's reading of Marx opens up an important avenue for theological and religious reflection, and I will conclude by raising the question of a more faithfully Marxist theological materialism, partly in relation to Antonio Negri's reading of Marx.

Marxian Praxis of Life

In *Marx*, Henry sets up a philosophical and phenomenological reading of Marx over against more conventional political readings of Marx from Friedrich Engels to Louis Althusser. Henry critiques the caricature of Marx in Marxism that crystallizes very shortly after Marx's death, which is "a tragicomic story in which the incompatibility of Marx's philosophical thought with Marxism is at once revealed and hidden."[11] One reason for this political misreading of Marx is the fact that his more explicitly philosophical texts were not published until the twentieth century. Marxism as an interpretation must be suspended in order to recognize that "the fundamental concepts of Marxism—are by no means the fundamental concepts of Marx's thought."[12] The reason that Marx is continually misunderstood, according to Henry, is paradoxically because Marxists reduce Marxism to a theory, a vision of reality that must be then brought into reality. Instead, "thought, in Marx, is the vision of being, whose internal structure is irreducible to the internal structure of this vision, irreducible to theory: it is praxis."[13]

Henry develops his philosophical and phenomenological reading of praxis as life through a careful explication of Marx's philosophical texts, especially Marx's working out of his own ideas in relation to Hegel. In Hegel's *Philosophy of Right*, the individual becomes the manifestation of civil society, a particularization of a universal State. For Hegel (not for Marx!), "the essence of the individual is the political essence."[14] In the 1843 *Critique of Hegel's Doctrine of the State*, Marx turns to Feuerbach's notion of species to resolve his dilemma with Hegel. "It is the Feuerbachian concept of 'species' which is to make possible and to show the unity sought with respect to civil society and the State, the individual and the universal, the finite and the infinite."[15] Marx is searching for a way to relate the individual and the universal, and he uses Feuerbach's philosophy to oppose Hegelianism, but he later realizes that this is a dead end.

The concept of species fails to do justice to the individual. Later in the 1840s, Marx realizes that the metaphysical notion of species, like those of history and society, is an objectification. There is no essence of history, or society, or even humanity as a species; rather, "the reality of history is to be sought outside of it," in "living individuals."[16] Marx rejects the very reality of society and history. Society and history in the 1840s, and economy in his later work, are abstract notions divorced from individual life. These objectified abstractions then alienate living individuals from the conditions of their concrete existence, their immediate and productive labor. "The originary founding nature of life," concludes Henry, "characterizes all of its determinations, need, production—precisely—and labor."[17] Marx then turns to the concept of class, which is "that of an ensemble, of a totality which alone is concrete and real," as an alternative. The difference between class and these other concepts is that class does not exist before the individuals who compose it. For Marx, according to Henry, class "is reduced to the individuals that already compose it despite their absolute dispersion."[18]

Marx turns to the concept of class not as a simple substitute for prior notions of society, species or history, but in order to oppose the abstractions involved in these other concepts. Abstraction as objectification then brings about the alienation that is essentially identified with capitalism. Henry follows Marx's development of economic theory as a radical critique in the *Grundrisse* and *Capital*. Henry claims that for Marx, "alienation, as identical to abstraction, is the originary founding act of the economy and, precisely, of its transcendental genesis."[19] Capital is the master-name for this process of substituting other, alienated realities for the primary reality of living labor, or subjectivity. This is why, ironically, on Henry's reading of Marx, "considered in itself, reality is nothing economic."[20]

Henry turns Marx's detailed economic analyses and prescriptions against the reason and source of Marx's protest, which is living labor, the essence of subjectivity. Living labor and its productive process is then objectified in its product, and appropriated by capitalism as capital, alienating life from itself in abstract processes of economic and political relationships. Capital is essentially connected to theory; it is "a medium of objectification" through which is realized "the givenness of a being which makes it an object."[21] For Henry, this is why the *Theses on Feuerbach* is crucial, because it demonstrates the reduction of praxis to theory by most thinkers. Abstraction, and hence alienation, proceeds from the eye of man, who "elevates himself above the earth only with the eye."[22] The eye of theory objectifies appearances under its gaze and constrains practical action. The essence of being is not theory, but praxis understood as action. "For action, being means acting," which is prior to theory.[23] Being is not objective, but is radically subjective.

Marx works out this insight in a complicated engagement with Hegel and with Feuerbach, but ultimately he performs a reversal of the essence of theory. Hegel's philosophy of action "is not really action; it is only the production of consciousness and exhausts itself there, in theoria."[24] Feuerbach appeals to the action of sensuous intuition to counter Hegel's speculative idealism, but Marx realizes that Feuerbach's sensuous action is objective, and still essentially theoretical: "'sensuous activity' means praxis as it is presented to the gaze of theory."[25] In the *Theses on Feuerbach*, Marx designates praxis as the ground of being. Being "is" only in action, as it is practiced. Henceforth, "the power of revelation belongs . . . exclusively to doing: only he who does something knows, by this doing and in it, what being is about."[26] The valorization of praxis effects a reversal of the relationship between theory and practice and puts praxis in the place of the living connection with being.

In light of this reversal, what is left for theory? Theory can no longer describe or designate truth, but can only "summon it and invoke it" in a prescription. This status of prescription frees the religious word from its constraint to an objective reality, and it thereby becomes a divine word. "Absolute, divine, the word is bound to nothing, has no extrinsic justification."[27] After Marx, according to Henry, theory can only take the form of normativity, because normativity expresses "the decisive limitations of theory."[28] Any descriptive, scientific function of theory would separate theory from practice and open up a space that is necessarily ideological.

Theories of Marx

One must be impressed by the force of Henry's powerful reading of Marx and the ideas that it opens up. One can also note an affinity with transcendental neo-Thomism, especially that of Joseph Maréchal and Karl Rahner. Maréchal contrasts Kant's philosophy of the knowledge of static being with Saint Thomas's emphasis on knowing in act, whereas Henry reads praxis as action in the texts of Marx in order to oppose them to traditional philosophy and its scientific knowledge of being.[29] I do not want to do any more than briefly indicate a genealogy for Henry's reading of Marx, nor am I evaluating the accuracy of Henry's reading in scholastic, Marxist, terms. In the space that remains in this essay, I would like to engage Henry's results.

According to Henry, Marx's emphasis on praxis reverses the relationship between practice and theory. Practice must be understood as action, while theoria is necessarily limited and truncated—only normative theory serves action, because it prescribes activity. Action is the activity of life, of living labor, and this is the source of all productivity, in a Marxian sense and more generally. Marx's calls for political change must be heard in light of this emphasis on normativity. At the same time, this transformation opens a vital space for theology, because it frees the religious word from theoretical contemplation of what is, and allows it to speak. Language is ripped from the world, and seen in its essence as Word, as a productive call of life. Here is the connection to Christian theology explicitly worked out in *I Am the Truth*.

For all its impressiveness, however, Henry's reading goes too far in its opposition of action to theory, and it, too, is ideological because there is still a gap. For Henry, theory is a shadow of real action, but it can range ahead of action in order to lure and guide it. Even in its normative form, theory maintains a force that is separate and essentially disconnected from action, because it is still seen as something other than action. If praxis deconstructs the opposition between theory and practice and dislodges theoria's superiority over action in the *Theses on Feuerbach*, Henry privileges theory by assigning it a normative power. That is, in its objectified form, theoria is chastened and restrained, but in its normative, prescriptive form, it possesses a divine power beyond action to reconnect with the source of action, Life. Henry overstates the opposition at the heart of Marx's philosophy, and then ironically repeats it, and this result leads to the trivialization of Marx's later work on political economy.

In *I Am the Truth*, Henry claims that Marx is one of the greatest thinkers of all time, who shows the true essence of economic reality. "Behind all these so-called 'economic' and 'social' activities," Henry writes, "what is acting . . . is the transcendental ego, whose every power is given to itself in the givenness to itself of this ego, such that this fundamental I Can is alone capable of walking, lifting, striking—of accomplishing each of the acts implicated in each form of labor."[30] The transcendental ego, as the core essence of Life, underlies and explains the appearance of the world and its economy. Apart from the world, it is the being of Christ as the "Arch-Son" that connects man to "the absolute Life of God himself."[31] According to Henry, Christ is the Arch-Son who relates man to God as Son, and it is this fundamental relationship that absolutely distinguishes man and God, as transcendental ego, from the world. Henry insists upon "the phenomenological, and hence ontological, heterogeneity of the transcendental Arch-Son in relation to the world and its truth."[32]

It is life, or Life, that establishes the relationship between humanity and divinity, and it is living labor that provides Marx with his critique of capitalism. Human action disrupts static being and its reification of all theoretical, social, and historical categories. Henry's analysis in his book on Marx feeds into his theological claims in *I Am the Truth*. But just as his reading in the latter is quasi-gnostic and ends up dualistically opposing Life and the world, his reading of Marx also retains an opposition between theory and praxis. Henry subordinates theory to praxis, but his relegation of the normative Word to theoria, and its elaboration in *I Am the Truth*, provides theoria with an uncanny power to speak, because the Word speaks the Truth of Christianity: "When Christ himself speaks, it is the very Word of God that we hear spoken, and this is so because Christ is defined as God's Word, his Spoken Word."[33]

Conclusion: A Theological Materialism?

Although I question his conclusions, Henry develops a rich phenomenological reading of Marx, just as Antonio Negri provides an important contemporary interpretation of Marx in his book *Marx Beyond Marx*. In some ways, Henry is close to Negri in following the Marxian reversal of theory and practice without jettisoning the important philosophical implications of Marx's thought. Henry and Negri both emphasize the subjective aspect of Marx's thought, as opposed to any objective, scientific determinism. The main difference is that Negri is committed to materialism, while Henry dismisses materialism as a "fetishism." According to Henry, Marx affirms "the identity between materialism and idealism," and rejects both.[34] The question remains, can you have Marxism without materialism? No, which is why Henry chooses a Marx purified of Marxist dogma, whereas Negri conducts a more complex and faithful reading.

Negri claims that the *Grundrisse*, which is also important for Henry (although Henry focuses more on Marx's earlier writings from 1843 and 1844), "represents the summit of Marx's revolutionary thought."[35] Negri, like Henry, affirms the subjective power of living labor, but he does not reduce labor to an individual expression of life to the extent that Henry does. It is rather "abstraction, the abstract collectivity of labor" that "is subjective power," which is the revolutionary force of "creative worker activity."[36] The subject of labor, the worker, comes into existence by making a radical leap of opposition to capitalism and its alienating objectivity.[37] This act is praxis rather than theoria, but Henry loses the tension and force of this action by denying the significance of objective worldly reality, which produces a troubling dualism that does not occur in Negri's reading of Marx.[38]

The question is whether a theological materialism is possible, that is, is it possible to affirm the material world of human praxis without succumbing to the trap of theoretical abstraction? Or, can we value action, living labor, truth, and language, including the language of scripture, without slipping into a transcendental idealism, as Henry seems to do? Henry's theology criticizes classical German idealism, but in some ways this is because Christian theology would like to substitute for idealism as an alternative explanation of reality. What is needed is a radical theological materialism, or a materialistic theology that would be directly productive, or practical. That is, theory is always already praxis, it is active and productive, provided we do not get entranced by its spectacle and forget this. Henry's phenomenology reminds us of this insight, but it veers away from it to take refuge in normativity in its flight from the world. In a similar way, despite his emphasis on immanence in *The Essence of Manifestation*, Henry equates immanence with transcendence to such an extent that the reader loses any clear sense of what immanence entails and wonders whether Henry is simply trying to have it both ways, or whether the term immanence is really a mask for transcendence.

What is wrong with transcendence? Theology would seem to require transcendence in order to be operative, but transcendence threatens to dissipate the efficacy and importance of political action by locating the source of meaning and value outside the world. If ethics and politics are based on transcendent values, then that grounds ethical and political action in a foundational manner, but at the same time, it reduces politics and ethics to a program or imitation of that transcendence. For example, in his essay on "Materialism and Transcendence," John Milbank argues that "if matter is to be more than inert, and even capable of subjectivity and meaning, then it must be forcefully self-transcending."[39] A political materialism cannot function effectively unless it is grounded in something outside itself, which is supplied by Catholic (in a broad sense, not Roman Catholic) Christian theology. The problem is that if this orthodox theology is true, then it diminishes rather than reinforces political action, because it swallows up materialistic socialism in transcendent Christian love. Milbank imagines "a desiring love that ineffably blends us with the other insofar as we come to realize how both our imagining desire and the other's symbolic presence blend beautifully as a remote participation in a real plenitudinous infinite."[40] This sounds wonderful, if somewhat incredible, but it sublates socialist materialism in a way analogous to Henry's sublation of Marxist philosophy. Furthermore, Milbank's Catholic orthodoxy both predetermines and co-opts the "new debate" between theology and "the political" in hegemonic fashion.[41]

Henry separates transcendent value—life—from the world. The separation of the source of life from the world institutes a new idealism, which dissipates the political force of Marx's thought. On the other hand, Antonio Negri's Marxist reading of Spinoza in *The Savage Anomaly* demonstrates the force of Marxist antagonism in a political and metaphysical sense. According to Negri, Spinoza's metaphysics is his politics, which culminates in his unfinished *Political Treatise*. The key is that Negri, following Deleuze, reads Spinoza as a philosopher of radical materialism, where antagonism produces real, constitutive change because it is not mediated or referred to a vertical world of transcendence. Mediation allows political force (*potentia*) to dissipate, being replaced by hierarchical or sovereign power (*potestas*).[42] According to Negri, the bourgeoisie create modern capitalist society by means of "a mystification of value" that defines all relations in terms of mediation by or through the State, whereas "Spinoza's thought is the preliminary [to Marx!] demystification of all this," because of his "denial of the concept of mediation."[43] Milbank substitutes God for the State as the source of real, harmonious mediation, replacing the State's violent, false, and alienating mediation. Henry presents his phenomenology as a pure immanence, but this immanence is not radical enough, because God as Life mediates meaning and value, whereas the world is completely deprived of any significance. The challenge is to think a radically immanent theology that is also a radical political theology, and to delink theology from its seemingly necessary connection with transcendence, in order to powerfully think and effect real change in a contested and violent world. What would a theology look like that takes materialism seriously, that forsakes transcendence for immanence, not as a ruse to appeal to or restore transcendence at a later time, but all the way? What if the material world is all that is the case, and there is no other, ideal world, even if this world is always other? Such a radical political theology could function with or without God, but if we are to save the name of God, we have to take Derrida's advice: "We should stop thinking about God as someone, over there, way up there, transcendent . . . capable, more than any satellite orbiting in space, of seeing into the most secret of the most interior places."[44] God is rather "the name of the possibility I have of keeping a secret that is visible from the interior but not from the exterior."[45] Then the challenge would be to think the material conditions and nature of this very possibility, as well as its political significance. Michel Henry directs us toward immanence, life, and the interior, but he then cuts off pure affectivity from dead matter in order to connect life back up with a transcendence-in-immanence, which is not of this world. But for Marx, Negri, and a radical political theology, the truth of life is in the world, not in another, otherworldly reality, even if all of our conceptual language about it risks reification and abstraction.

PART IV

Jean-Louis Chrétien

The Call of Grace

Henri de Lubac, Jean-Louis Chrétien, and the Theological Conditions of Christian Radical Phenomenology

JOSHUA DAVIS

It is always useful to repeat that there is a wrong way of defending the truth and that, in spite of apparent results, a false method can never give genuine and solid support to religious doctrine.

Maurice Blondel

Nemo te quaerere valet, nisi qui prius invenerit (No one values seeking you unless he has already found you).

Saint Bernard

This essay investigates the theological issues associated with the so-called theological turn in French phenomenology.[1] The burden of the inquiry is threefold: to question the terms of the debate as elaborated by Dominique Janicaud; to suggest a possible reason for the stalemate in the debate that has developed in response to those terms; and to present a more *theologically* attentive perspective that can overcome this deadlock from within specifically phenomenological strictures. The claim will be advanced that Christian radical phenomenology tacitly and illicitly deploys the theological categories of grace and the supernatural, leading to unwarranted claims about manifestation that occlude the force of its keenest insights.

Although the following argument unfolds in conversation specifically with the work of Jean-Louis Chrétien, the appraisal equally pertains to the work of Marion, Lacoste, and Breton.[2] The reasons for this commonality are laid out in the first section, which argues, drawing upon the work of Christian Yves Dupont, that the controversy over the theological turn is the manifestation of a tension between two disparate trajectories inherent to the French appropriation of phenomenology: the religio-philosophical phenomenologies of Maurice Blondel and Henri Bergson, and Husserl's transcendental analysis of consciousness.[3] The explicit conflict wrought by this tension stems from the implicit (and often unrecognized) theological disputes over the themes of nature and grace as they came to be associated with the religious appropriation of what Dupont has isolated as the Blondel-Bergsonian legacy in French phenomenology.[4] The second and most important section explores the significance of these themes as they relate to phenomenological intelligibility. This is explored through comparative analysis of Henri de Lubac's theology of grace and Jean-Louis Chrétien's meditation on the call and response. This section seeks to show that Chrétien's reflections are finally only conceivable on the theological presuppositions of the unity of nature and grace as analyzed by Lubac. The third section brings theology to bear upon these issues, suggesting that the unintelligibility highlighted in the prior section stems from incoherent application of those theological assumptions. This section makes certain suggestions as to the basic contours of a Christian radical phenomenology that could avoid these mistakes, and anticipates certain objections.

The French Appropriation of Phenomenology and the Theological Turn

James K. A. Smith keenly draws a connection between Dominique Janicaud's description of the recent phenomenological interest in religion as *le nouvelle phénoménologie* and the same kind of doctrinaire severity that led the neoscholastic Garrigou-Lagrange to decry Henri de Lubac and his companions for creating *le nouvelle théologie*.[5] This is certainly a shrewd observation, with implications reaching beyond those discussed by Smith. Indeed, insofar as Janicaud isolates the beginnings of the so-called swerve to theology with Levinas's *Totality and Infinity*, Smith's parenthetical observation points to a much broader genealogical trajectory.[6] It is not my goal to dispute that *Totality and Infinity* is of monumental importance for the development of radical phenomenology. I only wish to point to the fact that, if Jeffrey Kosky is right in stating that the one of the decisive questions regarding Janicaud's claim is whether an immanent methodology necessarily excludes the perception of transcendence, then, as Christian Yves Dupont has shown in detail, any assessment of that question is incomplete if it neglects the influence of the work of Maurice Blondel and

Henri Bergson.[7] Dupont's study, *Receptions of Phenomenology in French Philosophy and Religious Thought, 1889–1939*, shows that although both thinkers' influence on the development of Husserlian phenomenology is slight, they each remained a subaltern stimulus to much of the appropriation of phenomenological method in French philosophy and religious thought in the 1920s.[8]

Dupont's argument is, in part, that the Blondel-Bergsonian and Husserl-Heideggerian lines of phenomenology represent two tributaries of the French reception of phenomenology and that these diverge in their assessments of philosophy's scientific status.[9] He argues that in the Blondel-Bergsonian trajectory, philosophy achieves a scientific status only through a final appeal to religion, whereas in the Husserl-Heideggerian line, this status demands a purely immanent construal.[10] Insofar as Marion, Lacoste, Breton, and Chrétien's projects are, finally, as equally indebted to this Blondel-Bergsonian trajectory as to the Husserl-Heideggerian, Janicaud is certainly not wrong to recognize a religious impulse informing their phenomenology. Nonetheless, this genealogy itself destabilizes his apologia for some "pure" phenomenological method, untrammeled with questions of transcendence. For, if Dupont's claim is correct (and it appears to be), then the very religious elements Janicaud seeks to remove from phenomenological consideration are in fact endemic to how the French appropriate those elements.

And yet, this does not mean Janicaud's claim is altogether wrong. The real force of his critique persists. After all, as he claims, any phenomenology of the *in*-apparent must at least be open to the charge that it is doing nothing more than evading phenomenality by imposing theological categories upon the phenomenon.[11] But, as his adversaries insist, restricting the appearance of phenomena to the finite horizon of the ego is itself exemplary of just such an evasion, precisely insofar as it refuses to acknowledge a disclosure that exceeds that appearing.[12] Thus, prima facie, the terms of this dispute are quite clear; but, by pressing them a bit further, we can see that the reasoning of both sides is a bit tortured.

There is a certain irony at work here. On the one hand, if Janicaud is right that a turn to theology directs the conclusions of radical phenomenology, then he is implicitly arguing that *theological* rather than phenomenological categories must be given priority in the discussion. The claim that "phenomenology and theology make two"[13] also entails, at least in this instance, that only theological discourse is properly equipped to adjudicate the phenomenological status of transcendence as perceived by radical phenomenology.[14] What is at issue is not whether a phenomenological method can or cannot perceive transcendence; it is rather a matter of whether what radical phenomenology claims to perceive is, in fact, what theology understands as the appearance of transcendence. This is tantamount to arguing that dogmatic theology—and not simply a fundamental theology that "played the role of a propadeutic to theology"—must guide phenomenology on this matter in much the same way biology guides the medical profession.[15] But, conversely, if the counterclaims of radical phenomenology are accurate, as they are developed, then Janicaud's objections are only reinscribed insofar as a fundamentally Husserlian understanding of perception remains the benchmark for both camps. That is, each presumes what Heidegger described as the priority of *Offenbarkeit* (revealability) over *Offenbarung* (revelation) such that—even as the transcendence of the phenomenon is preserved by an intentionality dispossessed by *kath'auto* (givenness) —manifestation is itself constrained by what can be legitimately asserted on the basis of the sheer bestowal of phenomena as such.[16] This kind of perception cannot evade the possibility of reduction once again to the finite horizon of the ego, and this is exactly what Janicaud does.[17]

Nonetheless, as I want to argue, this is not necessarily detrimental to radical phenomenology provided it restricts its claims simply to demonstrating the possibility of prioritizing transcendence in manifestation. Indeed, the difficulties Janicaud finds with the discussion really only arise at all because of the attempt to show that transcendence is both *necessary* to and *accessible* from within manifestation as such.[18] As a result, it is difficult to see how the dispute does not boil down to two antinomous *judgments* regarding the very nature of the experience of experience.[19] It is much like Private Witt's observation in Terrence Malick's film adaptation of James Jones's novel *The Thin Red Line*: "One man looks at a dying bird and thinks there's nothing but unanswered pain—that death's got the final word, it's laughing at him. Another man sees that same bird, feels the glory, feels something smiling through it."[20] That difference is, ultimately, a matter of judgment about the nature and content of experience, and not something given in and with experience as such. And if the phenomenological recognition of transcendence only occurs under such conditions, it is all the more difficult to justify the application of religious categories such as revelation (Marion), prayer/liturgy (Lacoste), and election (Chrétien) to illumine the problem.[21] In fact, one can very easily empathize with Janicaud's objection that the persistent invocation of such categories is disclosive of the surreptitious specter of theological assumptions at work in the investigations. But, for this very reason, it is not enough simply to arraign radical phenomenology for undertaking a "quest for divine transcendence," because one must also inquire after the nature of those theological assumptions informing these judgments.[22] This, though, would be to claim that Janicaud has gotten the matter backwards. It is not that radical phenomenology represents a turn from phenomenology to theology, but rather a turn from theology to phenomenology. And that makes all the difference. What is needed, then, is clarification of the theological issues at stake in this question, since the debate cannot advance as a dispute about phenomenological method.

These brief observations have yielded three conclusions, the consequences of which I will unfold in more detail in the remainder of this essay. First, insofar as Janicaud overlooks the Blondel-Bergsonian trajectory of phenomenology traced by Dupont, he is unwarranted in taking Husserl as a phenomenological benchmark. The thinkers he critiques do not represent a deviation from a supposed phenomenological orthodoxy, but are instead elaborating upon an integral tributary of the French appropriation and development of phenomenological method in which religious concerns were integral. Second, this fact is no more apparent to or goes unacknowledged by practitioners of radical phenomenology, who continue to take the Husserlian account of perception as axiomatic in their analyses even as they seek to overturn it. Third, through recognition of this legacy, we are in a better position to appreciate the nature of and be critical of the theological component of radical phenomenology. The following section isolates this in the single example of Jean-Louis Chrétien by way of comparison with Henri de Lubac. My concern is to show that the theological presupposition of the unity of nature and grace is the condition for Chrétien's analysis of the call-response structure of manifestation. This will open a door to draw certain conclusions as to the legitimacy of Chrétien's approach from a theological perspective.

Grace and Beauty in Lubac and Chrétien

The thrust of Henri de Lubac's work has recently come to be broadly well known in North America, particularly as it relates to the nature of his opposition to the neoscholasticism that dominated Roman Catholic theology throughout the late nineteenth and early twentieth centuries. Until recently (and still to some extent), the various aspects of this dispute remained arcane to mainstream theological concerns. But as many of the most fundamental assumptions of modernity came to be questioned, Lubac's work on the relationship between nature and the supernatural has also begun to gain a broader audience. This is especially so regarding his concern to combat the idea of a fundamental separation between creation and grace, which he understood to be enshrined in the modernist conception of the world that divorced the supernatural from nature in such a way that God was rendered alien to human experience and superfluous to human meaning—two claims, he argued, explicitly denied by the authoritative voices of Augustine and Aquinas. He openly acknowledged his debt to the work of Maurice Blondel in inspiring his reflections on these matters.[23] However, unlike Blondel, Lubac's approach was not phenomenological, but historical and theological. He wanted to recover for contemporary theology that patristic and high medieval vision of grace that, according to him, was viewed as an integral component of creation. His claim was simple: prior to the sixteenth century, human beings were always understood to be, as intellectual creatures, fundamentally oriented toward union with God as the source and goal of their existence. Lubac was here reiterating the dominant Platonic and Neoplatonic themes of patristic theology.[24]

A paradox lies at the heart of his schematic: while the orientation to seeing God is *constitutive* of humanity, the beatific vision is not *owed* to humanity. Because the existence of anything at all is gratuitous, the desire for God that is displayed in creation is neither a matter of intentionality nor potentiality since the dynamism of subjectivity and the structure of nature as such derive their very being from God's free choice to create as well as the free choice to inscribe upon that creation an orientation to communion with God.[25] The human intellect cannot negate this orientation, nor does it contain a power that is the condition for its realization. With the former claim, Lubac is denying that subjectivity is *causa sui*, and with the latter he is rejecting the neoscholastic interpretation of the *potentia obedientialis* as articulated by Cajetan. In contrast, he insists that humanity *is* simply "called" by the divine.

As he specifies in *The Mystery of the Supernatural*, three abstract moments characterize this call, although it is itself one act. First, there is the gratuity of the world's creation, which includes spiritual being; second, there is the instillation of that spiritual being's necessary desire for what is inaccessible to its natural capacities; and, third, there is the equally gratuitous offer of the means to fulfill that orientation. In the earlier *Surnaturel*, Lubac had claimed that the inscription of the call upon the being's nature did not mean that God was obligated (*exigence*) to meet the creature's demand (*exigence*) for God because the very necessity of the desire for God was an experience of the creature's obligation to its creator.[26] In the later *The Mystery of the Supernatural*, Lubac emphasizes the logical distinction between the gratuities of creation (first moment) and the inscription of a supernatural destiny upon the creature (second moment). He also chose to highlight in the third moment the fact that, although the call is given everywhere in creation, elevation to its fulfillment is itself an act of grace inasmuch as it is the providential outworking of that call in history. Yet in both cases, a second paradox results: namely, that God's call is only heard in response to it since the call founds the possibility of response.

Turning attention to the first chapter of Chrétien's *The Call and the Response*, we see an almost seamless recapitulation of this paradigm, bringing it to bear upon a discussion of the origin of speech.[27] Here, he agrees with Heidegger that the reduction of language never encounters "a pristine and first call," but only "what is already an answer"; yet, he recognizes a demand for transcendence that Heidegger does not: if the call establishes the possibility of response, then it is impossible for the response to correspond to the call.[28] Chrétien concludes then that speech begins with the impossibility of corresponding to the invitation to speak. This is analogous to Lubac's second paradox of grace insofar as it underscores the infinite priority of the call as the condition of possibility for the response.

By appeal to Plato's *Cratylus*, Chrétien develops his argument through an etymological meditation on the Greek word *kalon* (5). He highlights the significance of this word as a responsive naming of the "power to call and to name"—an act displaying continuity between consciousness, speech, and manifestation (7). Chrétien unfolds the logic of self-predication: consciousness names (*kalein*, calls) the objects of appearance; beautiful objects are named by consciousness; consciousness, therefore, must be beautiful since it names the beautiful. This is consistent with Heidegger, who claims that, in the call, "the things that are named are called to their being as things."[29] "Beautiful" (*kalon*), Chrétien says, is the name we give to what summons (*kalein*) us to nomination. The call *of* manifestation must exceed all calls given *within* it: because manifestation calls (to) us, we are summoned to a vocation of naming. Chrétien quotes Claudel on this point, stating that "the eye listens," and this, he says, is the origin of speech.[30]

But Platonism—and we can presume also Levinas's *il y a* and Heidegger's *es gibt*—only hears "the blank voice of beauty's splendor." Chrétien contends that this is the "neutral and impersonal *par excellence*"—far too inadequate to express the summons to a vocation of naming (16). Only in Christian theology, where categories of election, creation, and redemption are invoked, is the significance of founding *kalon* in *kalein* realized. There the call's excess is linked to the absolute, rendering the origin and goal identical. This unity stems from the thought of Saint Paul, who connects creation to redemption (Romans 4:17), and it is further developed by Denys, who says God "calls all things to himself, and this is why he is called *kallos*, beauty."[31] Since we are summoned to name the *excess* of manifestation, the first—and perhaps only—response is our own existence. This, Chrétien insists, is the meaning of Saint Paul's claim that election precedes creation.[32]

The correlations between Lubac and Chrétien are striking. It is clear that Chrétien is indebted to a phenomenological approach seeking to isolate nature's orientation to transcendence. The priority of the call over the response, which "refers back to a prior call" of the absolute, is consistent with Lubac's argument that grace is constitutive of human being (16). This is reflected in his statement that the call "includes the possibility of our response and constitutes it," which is also consistent with Lubac's refusal to understand subjectivity as a *causa sui* (11). For each thinker, because the call precedes—and, in the case of God, constitutes—consciousness, the orientation of the ego must be determined outside of itself and prior to its intention. Chrétien concludes that the humanity *is* sheer openness to what lies outside self-consciousness, and this mirrors the content of Lubac's rejection of the *potentia obedientialis* (11). Lubac would echo Chrétien's assertion that "nothing is alone what answers the call because it cannot answer it" (22).

However, the most important correlation pertains to their appeals to paradox. In Davenport's words, for Chrétien, paradox is "the precise phenomenal form under which the infinite disproportion that characterizes the religious call-response structure appears" (xv). Paradox is the excess "gripping us by the throat," compelling us to speak; it is where the source of all possibility is found to arise out of a more primal impossibility (32). Likewise, paradox is the crux of Lubac's theology of grace. For, while the orientation to the beatific vision is constitutive of humanity, there is no rightful natural claim upon it. The structure is very similar to the way Lubac describes the exigence of the desire for God as the expression of our obligation to God.

What bearing do these observations have on assessing Chrétien's relation to theology? The answer, as suggested earlier, pertains to the predominance of Husserlian assumptions about the nature of perception, as reflected in his adherence to Heidegger's distinction between revealability (*Offenbarkeit*) and revelation (*Offenbarung*). This is apparent in the moment in Chrétien's etymology where the notion of *creatio ex nihilo* gives content to the "blank" voice of beauty's splendor, naming it "election." Although Janicaud would understand this as a theological diversion, Chrétien argues that the vocational content of the call is *given* within language and manifestation and is therefore perceivable within both, as the condition for the possibility of their appearance. This is clearly a phenomenological, not a theological, assertion; it is in keeping with the Heideggerian observation that the structure of revealability precedes revelation. It is further consistent with his claim that existence, as an expression of beauty, is the first and only response to the call. In James K. A. Smith's terms (appealing to the Barth/Brunner debate and siding with Brunner), existence constitutes a "capacity" (*Offenbarkeit, potentia obedientialis*) for revelation that makes revelation possible.[33] This is what Chrétien means by saying that the response is a "nothing" that "cannot answer" the call, even as it does not cease responding.[34]

The appeal to *creatio ex nihilo* pivots on a reversal of the priority of revealability and revelation in the argument. Chrétien admits this when he states that, between Plato and Denys, stands Saint Paul whose doctrine of election solicits the insight that the call of beauty is a summons, an election. Does this not mean that "election," as a mediating concept, is not *given* in manifestation as such, but is rather a particular judgment made about the experience of manifestation? Does this not mean that "election" must be *independently related* to manifestation precisely as a non-phenomenological category?[35]

Paradox is apparently intended to account for the convertibility of revealability and revelation, but the difficulty remains. On the one hand, while Chrétien is right to question Heidegger's mutual reduction of call and response, his counter-argument only justifies holding open the *possibility* of prioritizing the call.[36] It is the *paradox* of the call's relation to the response that is irreducible—not, as he argues, the call itself.[37] On the other hand, Chrétien fails to see that his way of locating the excess of the call over the response implies the opposite. Asserting the call's irreducibility furtively privileges the response as the condition for the recognition of the call's priority, which is tantamount denying it—mere contradiction, not paradox. This second problem is simply an extension of the first. Chrétien believes his analysis yields the *necessity* of affirming the *accessibility* (possibility) of the *inaccessible* (impossible) when all he has really shown us is that it is *necessary* that we affirm an *inaccessible possibility*. Any attempt to move beyond the latter remains reducible to immanence. The significance of this point should not be missed. The point is not that a phenomenon does not appear that is not reducible to an immanent horizon, but that such appearing is not *given* in, with, and according to the structure of manifestation as such. It rather precedes, conditions, and determines it. Such appearing, then, irreducibly includes the reality of the perceiver as an agent, through judgment and action, in the very reality it discloses. This is not merely hermeneutical, as Ricoeur suggests, a way of talking about the cultural and linguistic mediation of the experience of phenomena.[38] It goes much farther, suggesting that the *act of judging* a phenomenon as revelatory is inseparable from the revelation itself. It is to insist that what is revealed simply *was-not* prior to and apart from its *reception* as revelation, apart even from the cultural and linguistic factors that shaped that reception.

This means that Chrétien's appeal to theological categories (for example, creation, election) can, then, only be justified on grounds other than those of phenomenology. Such categories express not the structure of the appearing of the things themselves, but *a certain experience of the determination of the experience of manifestation.* Chrétien's mistake is in arguing that this determination of experience is simply given in manifestation itself. But, what is important for my concerns here is to point out that it is only a theological structure like Lubac's that could authorize the deployment of these theological categories within the phenomenological field in just this way.[39] It is just such a theology of grace, which interprets the call of God as constitutive of the human experience of the world, that could understand the determination of experience as expressed in those categories to be something given in manifestation as such. Reliance on such a notion is true not only of Chrétien, but for the similar phenomenological projects already named. And, although in this regard it is possible, with Janicaud, to accuse such projects of perfidy, this subtle shift in registers—to the priority of revelation over revealability, to the priority of the theological over the phenomenological—may simply be the result of the incoherent application of theological categories within that field.[40] A poor deployment of phenomenological method in support of theological claims very well may be, in this case, the result of bad theology. Because we have noted that religious questions are not unrelated to phenomenology, and because the theological turn represents, not a turn *to* theology but *from* it, this possibility must be explored more closely.

On the Theological Conditions of Christian Radical Phenomenology

If the ontological unity of nature and grace is the conceptual precondition for certain Christian radical phenomenologies, the most pressing issue for those projects is not phenomenological method, but theological consistency with regard to the application of the category of grace.[41] The requirements for this consistency are threefold. First, Christian radical phenomenology must explicitly return to and develop the insights of the Blondel-Bergsonian trajectory of its inheritance. This would serve to challenge both the preponderance of Husserlian assumptions regarding perception, and the tendency to treat religious experience as a purely epistemic matter of correctly discerning what is given in manifestation as such. Second, Christian radical phenomenology must cultivate a refined understanding of the issues entailed in affirming the unity of nature and grace. This would help to surmount the immanence/transcendence distinction that has deadlocked the debate, opening the door to a reinvigorated discussion of the phenomenological status of the inaccessible, which theology understands as the *donum perfectum* of the supernatural. Third, these points converge on the centrality each ascribes to the will, especially as genetically analyzed by Blondel.[42] This final point is intimately connected with the above observation concerning the constitutive role of the act of reception in the event of revelation, and should be elaborated upon briefly as to its importance for the prior two points.

The problematic of the will is integral to a proper assessment of Lubac's thesis.[43] Against what Pierre Rousselot called "those who would reduce the whole desire for the intuitive vision . . . to a secret transformation effected historically in man by grace," Lubac insisted that the desire for God was a constitutive component of the human being as an actually existing creature of God.[44] However, as Lubac insisted, this did not imply that grace was somehow "historically" coincident with creation, as the principle of its vitality, propelling it toward its goal.[45] That Lubac rejected this is displayed in his third "moment" of grace (elevation), which implies, at least implicitly, recognition that the illumination of the *intellect* alone is insufficient to constitute a response to God's call. Rather, the relational logic of gratuity entails that grace *appear* as an extrinsic force for the *will*, provoking not simply the intellectual recognition of a truth, but the concrete, historical, and material production of an act—and, in this case, an act in excess of the will's natural potencies (that is, the supernatural).[46] Because Christian radical phenomenology is preoccupied with the epistemic investigation of the conditions necessary for phenomena to appear, this integral role of the will has been almost wholly overlooked.

That this role of the will cannot be so easily obviated is due to its centrality in Western Christianity's theories of grace. As Saint Thomas states, the "principle and root" of nature's elevation to and cooperation with the supernatural is, first, a quality of being, and, second, a principle of action.[47] As Lonergan has shown, this is what Aquinas means when he speaks of grace as *habitual*, a divinely infused nonnatural basis for rendering a person capable of producing an act that exceeds its natural capacities: namely, one adequate to Godself.[48] Insofar as God alone initiates this transformation this grace is *operative*, and insofar as the creature participates in the transformation this grace is *cooperative*.[49] This requires an affirmation that this qualitative transformation is not given in experience as such, and is itself the principle of action whereby knowledge of the Source of the true, good, and beautiful is attained. By referring to the third moment of grace as "elevation," Lubac points to the necessity of upholding this distinction; yet, the fact that he does not name this distinction—or the even the prior and more complex distinction of *actual grace*[50]—is suggestive of the distance he wants to put between himself and neo-scholasticism.

The centrality of the will and the importance of the notion captured in the idea of habitual grace support our previous assertion that the phenomenological recognition of transcendence is an event that determines, includes, and alters the action of the perceiver as an agent.[51] The failure of Christian radical phenomenology to account for this fact, preferring instead to focus on what is given to be perceived in the things themselves, has resulted in the ultimate unintelligibility of its respective projects, especially with regard to its implicit affirmation of the contradiction that the inaccessible is accessible. However, by recovering a Blondelian emphasis on the role of the will in the perception of transcendence and by recovering the theological significance of the designation of operative habitual grace Christian radical phenomenology can correct this contradiction and open out onto a true phenomenological paradox. Such a recovery would involve undertaking the phenomenologically intelligible and theologically coherent task of demonstrating the *necessity of affirming an inaccessible possibility* upon which one can only pass judgment.[52] Just as Blondel states in his *Letter on Apologetics*, phenomenology can point to what is united to but not confused with nature (that is, the supernatural) insofar as it presents itself in the mode of a demand to act with regard to an essential and unattainable possibility.[53] What phenomenology cannot do is confuse that possibility with a capacity or condition (*Offenbarkeit, potentia obedientialis*) of manifestation as such, which requires an affirmation of the contradiction that the inaccessible (impossible) is accessible (possible).

This proposal, and the criticism upon which it is based, is likely to solicit three objects. First, the nature/supernatural distinction seems to be subject to Hegel's critique of the limit.[54] As Hegel expressed it, "Something is only known, or even felt, to be a restriction, or a defect, if one is at the same time *beyond* it."[55] There is a limited sense in which our argument agrees with this supposition. We have argued that there is no justifiable reason to inquire into the *in*-apparent if one has not already perceived it. This is precisely the thrust of our emphasis on habitual grace. There is a further sense in which the recognition of these limits necessarily implies the presence of the supernatural to it; our previous arguments are consistent with this. However, insofar as Hegel's critique intends to demonstrate the immanent and necessary accessibility of what transcends the limit, the claim requires a more adequate response. Borrowing from Paul Guyer, we can note that, just as there is no reason to suppose that the possibility of doubt entails the supposition that one exists who does not doubt, so upholding the possibility of a natural limit does not *require* positing the necessity of a supernatural.[56] As we have argued, the supernatural appears to consciousness as a possibility for judgment and action—a possibility that is paradoxically both essential for thought and unattainable to it. It is only after having acted in judgment regarding that possibility that its presence is recognizable as such.

Second, one could argue that our critique misreads radical phenomenology, indicting it for claims not made.[57] Specifically, one could point to the fact that many of the thinkers here cited insist they are only doing precisely what is here advocated: namely, preserving the phenomenological possibility of holding open the question of transcendence.[58] This is particularly the case with Marion, whose notion of "givenness" would appear to sustain a wholesale reversal of the structure of revealability (*Offenbarkeit*) and revelation (*Offenbarung*) inasmuch as he refuses to admit any a priori delimiting conditions preceding possibility.[59] However, in the foregoing critique, everything is decided on the locus of that reversal: whether it is understood to constitute the conditions necessary for appearance as such; or, whether that reversal occurs at the level of judgment regarding the experience of appearance. For example, when Marion claims the third reduction is irreducible and that this is where God could appear were God to appear, he understands the third reduction as an analytic necessity that itself preserves the possibility of God's appearance therein.[60] That the structure of revealability (*Offenbarkeit*) is prior to revelation (*Offenbarung*) is here displayed; and, the attempt to reduce this structure to revelation only yields the contradiction of an accessible inaccessibility, which—as reiterated in the prior discussion of Hegel—is wholly subject to a reduction to pure immanence. A genuine perception of "givenness" then requires a reversal in the priority of revealability (*Offenbarkeit*) and revelation (*Offenbarung*) such that demonstration of the openness of revealability is superfluous; to be properly irreducible, *givenness* can only present itself as a possible judgment regarding the experience of manifestation.[61] Furthermore, as implied in our discussion of the a priori status of the theological assumptions required for the a posteriori deployment of such arguments, the priority of revelation (*Offenbarung*) is here preserved insofar as any judgment in favor of the givenness of phenomena always already presumes and includes God's appearance (revelation). And, in contrast to Chrétien, *this* is, in fact, the true meaning of Saint Paul's claim that election precedes creation.

Third, one must address the charge that theological issues of nature and grace have no immediate bearing on the phenomenological task itself. Specifically, one can contend that phenomenology proceeds quite independently of whatever theological categories bear upon it. This critique can be levied in two ways. On the one hand, one could argue that phenomenology is indifferent to the supernatural insofar as its concern is solely with the nature and structure of appearance; thus, should something like the supernatural appear, it would be but another phenomenon for analysis. In response, we should claim that this argument mistakenly assumes that the supernatural is convertible with transcendence. We have shown the unintelligibility of asserting the irreducibility of transcendence, and have instead highlighted its status as a demand to affirm the necessity of judging as to the reality of the inaccessible possibility presented by the category. The supernatural then is not transcendence; it is that to which transcendence is referred when a positive judgment is made regarding the reality of that possibility. What is supernatural appears then as the realization of an *act* of perception—not *within* perception—that is wholly inexplicable according to the immanent structure of manifestation as such, that is, a mystery.[62] However, insofar as Christian radical phenomenology has not offered an intelligible account of this act, or demonstrated the necessity of this judgment, the criticism remains valid. The burden of this section has been to highlight the ideas necessary to overcome this charge.

On the other hand, one could contend that the phenomenologist is disinterested in such matters, not because she has no investment in them, but because her task is simply to produce good philosophy; and, since the Christian phenomenologist implicitly trusts that all good philosophy displays the *desidarium naturale videndi Deum*, such matters are finally inconsequential.[63] We must respond that our previous arguments have shown that failure to designate the phenomenological status of the theological meaning of supernature inevitably conflates the category with transcendence, thus producing a philosophy that is subject to the prior critique. In this regard, any Christian radical phenomenology that does not clarify this matter first in the discursive domain of theology remains fixed in the quagmire that has been the subject of this essay.

Conclusion

This essay occupies the liminal space where theology and philosophy meet, mutually informing and illuminating one another. We have shown that this meeting is the hinge upon which the debate concerning the theological turn pivots. This is displayed in the history of the French appropriation of phenomenology where, prior to Husserl, issues of religion and phenomenology were thoroughly imbricated; and, it is exhibited in the theological assumptions regarding nature and grace that are the condition for the possibility of Christian radical phenomenology. Regarding this, we have proposed ways in which Christian radical phenomenology would benefit from greater attention to the theological coherence of the categories of nature and grace, specifically as to phenomenological analysis of the will and the theological distinction of habitual grace.

Because theology names revelation as the summons of mystery, a theological turn within phenomenology is impossible. But, because theology knows Being as a directive to embrace God's new creation, phenomenology is capable, in and of itself, of isolating the demand for this transformation. As such, revelation cannot be thought of as bedazzlement; it must be invoked as transformation. In this light, Christian radical phenomenology would do well to heed strictly Lubac's warning: "What might quite rightly seem, after the event . . . as having been a 'preparation for the Gospel,' is also, and in fact primarily, an obstacle to it."[64]

Between Call and Voice

The Antiphonal Thought of Jean-Louis Chrétien

JOSEPH BALLAN

Although the book itself offers no substantial development of its marvelous title, Paul Claudel's *The Eye Listens*[1] is often cited by Jean-Louis Chrétien as a pithy formulation of an important phenomenological principle. In addition to the observation of artworks (the topic of Claudel's book), itself impossible without the silence of listening, the concept of a listening eye applies more generally to the relations of the individual sense faculties to one another in their common, worldly labor. Seeing and hearing, touch and sight, cannot be separated one from the other but, rather, bespeak a "radical unity of sense,"[2] a oneness constitutive of the body's engagement in the world as a corporeal unity, a ground of the diverse human modes of perception. Following Proclus, Chrétien suggests that there exists "a modality of addressing and calling" that persists even in the absence of an auditory call (CR, 62). Reversing the traditional formulation of the relation between self and world as a subject-object relation, Chrétien suggests that the visible world, for instance, can be said to call us, soliciting our gaze and compelling our attentive listening. Like Merleau-Ponty, who showed the senses to be intertwined and inseparable in their work of perceiving "a unique structure of the thing, a unique way of being, which *speaks* to all my senses at once,"[3] Chrétien claims that our sensory encounters open upon a meaning, a *logos*, however obscure.[4] That is to say, our engagement in the world is not a one-way operation, where the (passive) things surrender themselves to our prying eyes (and bodies), but is rather that aspect of our existence in which we are made to halt, to listen, and to find ourselves addressed by things. To hear what in the visible might be speaking to us requires an audible silence and tactile stillness that undermines philosophical and theological accounts of the senses that would make vision the standard measure for knowledge and truth, rendering hearing and touch peripheral and derivative.

On the line of thought we pursue here, the optical does not trump the auditory, nor is the opposite the case, but hearing and seeing are, as in Merleau-Ponty, "interlaced,"[5] a relationship expressed in Chrétien's often-used chiasmic figures of listening eye and visible voice. Can one claim for these undeniably appealing images the status of phenomenological truth? Does Chrétien's "unity of the senses" imply a synesthesia that gives an unwarranted mystical sense to the kind of analyses of sensory intertwining offered by Merleau-Ponty?[6] Or do the images of listening eye and visible voice articulate a "rigorously phenomenological principle of human sight" (CR, 33)? Even those in the phenomenological tradition who have given up the search for a phenomenology that would meet the requirements of a "rigorous science," as Husserl had dreamed, might raise a suspicious eyebrow at these kinds of claims about the senses. No less suspicious than these claims are the sources used to support and substantiate them: Paul Claudel and Proclus, as we have seen, accompanied by other Platonists of various stripes, forgotten seventeenth-century French Catholic mystical theologians, Greek tragic dramatists, German romantic poets, biblical and patristic writers, and a whole host of other, similarly questionable characters. Chrétien is a historian of philosophy who writes poetry as well as phenomenological analyses (often blurring lines between two kinds of writing destined to have been brought into closer proximity), and the singularity of his voice receives perhaps its best description as a particularly eloquent version of what Adriaan Peperzak has described as "hermeneutical phenomenology." Such an orientation draws (critically) upon historical traditions of thought that, to varying degrees, offer the possibility of guiding us in the endeavor to understand and describe the phenomena, opening our eyes to aspects of the phenomena that the purportedly presuppositionless mind might have passed over.[7] Chrétien presses this unique philosophical style into the service of a phenomenology whose content also differs, in significant though not all respects, from many of the most important thinkers within that tradition. Effecting what Jacques Derrida describes as "a break from the phenomenology of carnal auto-affection," Chrétien's account of the senses and their (inter)relations emphasizes transitivity rather than reflexivity (without denying the place of the latter in a complete account of sense perception), opening and *autrui*-affection rather than pure immanence and auto-affection.[8] Derrida's characterization of the opening onto excess, which Chrétien describes in his essay "Body and Touch"[9] as a mode of transitivity, shows itself to be an apt one, accounting not only for an encounter (with things, people, artworks) but also for the moment of *consent to* this encounter, of affirmation of and response to the event.[10]

To speak, then, of "call" and "response" is to appeal not only to sensory metaphors, but also to the sense experience that gives meaning to these metaphors, making of mundane sensory encounters the occasion for understanding the vocation for listening and singing which all the senses share. This essay represents an attempt to follow the interpretations of sensible experience through Chrétien's analyses of the various modalities of call and response: the silence which characterizes vision, the musicality of the work of art, the labor of listening, and the voice, which erupts out of silence into responsive song. As we shall see, drawing as much upon literature and theology as he does upon a close attentiveness to the texture of experience, Chrétien seeks to redescribe the world as a provocation, as that which not only calls but which, more specifically and in a stronger sense, pro-vokes, calls *for* and calls *to*, awakens, and beckons forth response. The experience of *thauma* (marvel or wonder) which both Plato and Aristotle claim lies at the origin of philosophy signifies, for Chrétien and his understanding of the orientation of thought, "nothing other than the world itself" (AS, 116–17). His work grows out of the question, raised anew for us: Can phenomenology, as the thought of what appears in the world and its mode of appearance, be born in wonder? And, perhaps more controversially, can it issue in gratitude and even praise?

Silent Music

Not unlike the "listening eye," the first figure we consider appears paradoxical at first glance, but Chrétien will use the tension of the paradox to call attention to a dimension of visual experience that may not have otherwise suggested itself to a "minimalist" analysis. As with Claudel's image, Chrétien seizes upon the phrase "silent music" from Saint John of the Cross's *Spiritual Canticle* and applies it to contexts reaching far beyond those in the original text (although he does provide a commentary on the use of "silent music" in the *Spiritual Canticle*, a discussion to which we will have cause to return later). For instance, the idea of "silent music" plays a role in one of his essays on visual art, "Silence in Painting." Here Chrétien first establishes the way the "eye listens" to the work of art: by becoming still, by "entering into the active silence of attention."[11] In a kind of antiphony of silences, to cite another metaphor favored by Chrétien, we offer our own silence—the stilling of our voices and the quieting of our passions—to the silence innate to the painting. Moreover, this offering of silence does not necessarily issue from an act of volition; one can say, to the contrary, that certain artworks (those whose silence is particularly palpable and arresting) *command* our silence, literally taking our speech away and imperiously drawing our attention to what is taking place therein (HH, 19).

Do these appeals to a silence in painting amount to anything more than rather obvious observations regarding the nature of the plastic arts? What could be more apparent than the fact that paintings and sculptures don't make noise? As in Vladimir Jankélévitch's discussion of silence *in* music (that is, that silence which charms us away from the distraction of "universal noisiness" and draws us into contemplation), which differentiates between silence and auditory nothingness,[12] the silence of which Chrétien speaks—when he characterizes the silence of paintings as a "communicative," welcoming silence—is a silence that can be described as having veritably musical qualities. If we focus upon the specifically auditory qualities of the act of attending to a particular painting, we discover that the silence of the art work is not that of a simple lack of sound, but presents a silence characterized by a "singular density," a density which becomes palpable only upon approaching the work of art in its auditory, even musical dimensions (HH, 21). Awakened to the density of the art work's silence, we can no longer conceive of silence in painting or in music as a lack, but rather as that which, lying "underneath the banal, busy plenitude of daily life," reveals "a more dense, more inspiring plenitude,"[13] to quote Jankélévitch. Chrétien illustrates the density of silence present in all beautiful works of art by way of an exposition of paintings that portray solitary, abandoned instruments, such as Picasso's and Braque's guitars (HH, 31–38). Like Plotinus's wise man, who has abandoned his lyre in order to sing more beautifully but who nevertheless keeps it close by his side,[14] Braque's guitars "no longer serve to play music, but are the silent song of music itself" (HH, 37). In the realm of instrumental music, one thinks of the restrained, concentrated expressiveness of Frederico Mompou's *Musica Callada* series for the piano, a series that takes its title from the same poem by John of the Cross.

One of the finest expressions of this phenomenology of silence in art is provided by John Keats in his "Ode on a Grecian Urn." Possessing the power to "express a flowery tale more sweetly than our rhyme," exposing the limits of even poetic speech, the urn Keats apostrophizes also embodies a kind of silent, more profound music:

Heard melodies are sweet, but those unheard
Are sweeter; therefore, ye soft pipes, play on;
Not to the sensual ear, but, more endear'd,
Pipe to the spirit ditties of no tone.[15]

Of this poem, Chrétien remarks that "at issue in this silent music is not an oxymoron but, rather, the essence of music;" the music that has been "interrupted and immobilized by the image . . . becomes for Keats a perennial and uninterrupted music, the music of silence itself" (HH, 23). In what way could silence constitute "the essence of music"? In that, by virtue of its silence, every work of art (including sonorous ones) gives itself to be *heard*. Moreover, and as every musician knows, the manipulation of silence by means of pauses and rests, of decrescendo and ritardando, is as crucial to a piece's performance as the clean execution of passages requiring virtuosic skill. Could any piece of music be either performed or received without silence? From the perspective of both the producer and the receiver of an art work, silence shows itself as the outcome of a discipline, on one hand as the discipline of reticence, modesty, restraint (even in the most tumultuous scherzo or the most frenzied display of color and texture), and on the other hand, as the discipline of hospitality, the hospitality of listening. As is the case with the work of writing, which Chrétien will describe as one of "ferr[ying] words from silence to silence" (AS, 39), the music of silence is that out of which each song (poem, painting, and so forth) emerges and to which it returns, granting to its observer the space in which to listen to and contemplate it. Keats's "unheard melody" is a figure for the *call* that issues from the (in this case) visible artwork, bidding us to become silent and attend to its voice. The Grecian urn sings "unheard melodies" that solicit the contemplative engagement of the viewer, inviting her to "the active silence of attention."

The Event of the Beautiful

In all the multitudinous forms it assumes, beauty (*kalon*) is always, on Chrétien's account (and here he appeals explicitly to the Platonic and later Platonic traditions), that which calls (*kalein*) and charms (*kélein*) our senses. If the paradigmatic mode of the call is that of the spoken word and that of charm, the musical song, one can conclude that "the event of the beautiful lies in the fact that the origin calls out *audibly in the visible*, calling us back to the origin" (CR, 9; emphasis mine). The call, a theme that recurs and resounds throughout Chrétien's oeuvre, cannot be discussed without granting sufficient attention to the sensory qualities of *every* call, be it the visible call of a beautiful painting or the silent, wounding call of God. On the most elementary level, even the world of everydayness that appears before us, to which we awaken anew every morning, has the structure of a call: we see the world only by responding to the call of the visible (CR, 14). Shifting the discussion to the sphere of the aesthetic (if, indeed, we are not there already), Chrétien posits that visible beauty is properly visible only when it *speaks* to us, that is, when it gives itself to our hearing (CR, 35). The effect of this line of argument is not to subsume all artistic or religious phenomena under a rubric of the auditory; indeed, the visible itself presupposes no one particular "organ ready to receive it; rather it creates in us the conditions of its reception. The visible speaks when unforeseen" (CR, 41). According to Chrétien, *no* sense is adequate to the reception of beauty. The beautiful always overwhelms our capacity to foresee it or to take its measure by noting its effects upon eye, ear, or skin. Acknowledging this failure of the senses amounts, however, to more than recognizing a simple breakdown; instead, it constitutes the beginning of true listening. Indeed, listening is that form of silence which grows out of the experience of having been exceeded and overwhelmed: "knowing how to listen is discovering at my expense that my available silence and my empty welcome . . . never suffice . . . that there is more to be heard than I can listen to."[16]

While Keats begins his poem by addressing the Greek urn ("Thou still unravish'd bride of quietness"), he ends by finding *himself addressed* by the "silent form" which "dost tease us out of thought" by a silence whose music affects him viscerally, "that leaves a heart high-sorrowful and cloy'd / A burning forehead, and a parching tongue."[17] We have here an example of a situation where "that which was addressed itself comes around, through patience, to address us" (HH, 24), as in the closing line of Rilke's poem inspired by an early-fifth-century BCE statue: "You must change your life."[18] To cite the title of an early work (*l'Effroi du Beau*), beauty imposes itself upon, commands, and shocks us. That is to say, sensory, worldly beauty is "in the strictest and strongest sense of the word, phenomenal . . . it is a self-manifestation, it is that which manifests itself of its own accord, and it is only thus that it calls" (AS, 79). To ascribe beauty to any given phenomenon is to attribute to it a twofold excess innate to its phenomenality. First, beauty appears in disproportion to what is required by usefulness or rationality, in the sense that "the rose is without why." Likewise, in the later Platonic tradition on which Chrétien draws so often, the beautiful, though inferior to the Good, appears as that which exceeds itself in its procession from the Good, which gives beauty by making it "live and shine, [making it] something entirely excessive and surprising" (AS, 88). Secondly, the beautiful phenomenon presents itself as exceeding any possible object for which we might have been seeking. It does not conform to our expectations. As with human conversation, where we truly listen only when we listen "to and towards the impossible," when "I do not know any more than the other about what he is saying to me" (AS, 9–10), beauty bears the phenomenological structure of impossibility:[19] the beautiful object appears as beautiful to us only insofar as we could not possibly have foreseen it, only insofar as it was utterly absent from our horizon of expectation until the moment of its miraculous appearance. Any response to such beauty cannot be other than belated and deficient. It must begin by listening in a silence we have not chosen to that which is unheard-of and unanticipated.

Given the frequent use of figures of excess, shock, and wound, the question presents itself at this point: In what measure, if any, might Chrétien's account of beauty actually be a thought of the sublime?[20] Like Heidegger, Chrétien prefers to speak of "beauty" and has little to say about the sublime as such, but this does not exclude the possibility that he translates the concept of the sublime into a different vocabulary (as Heidegger also does).[21] We can be reasonably certain that, in any case, Chrétien's is not, strictly speaking, a *Kantian* thought of the sublime. By virtue of his silence on the question, Chrétien seems to refuse the distinction between the sublime and the beautiful on which Kant's aesthetics is predicated. Would the "merely beautiful" be worthy of the name "beauty," with all the significance Chrétien attaches to it? Moreover, Kant does not make frequent appearances in his texts[22] and, as we have emphasized throughout this section, Chrétien's understanding of beauty is heavily informed by an extended engagement with texts from the Platonic traditions. These works, and not those of post-Kantian aesthetics, in large part set for him the terms of his discussions of beauty and its manifestation. Yet, interestingly, he does not seem to share the Platonic preoccupation with matters of form and conformity, of mimesis and representation. Rather, Chrétien focuses upon the *event* of the beautiful, describing in his work the contours of the *encounter* with beauty. That is to say, he seeks to give an interpretation of the appearance of beauty as call and provocation.[23] In this respect, he betrays a certain proximity to Kant, whose analytic of the sublime treats of the fact or event of presentation rather than presentation itself. For Kant, sublimity does not name a property of an object (that is, it does not describe a noumena), but rather the way an object appears to a subject. One can speak of a sublime feeling or a sublime phenomenon, but not of a sublime object.[24]

More significantly, as Jean-Luc Nancy notes, the sublime in Kant throws the regular (that is, auto-affecting) functioning of the affections radically into question, making necessary

> a double analytic of feeling: one analytic of the feeling of the appropriation, and another analytic of the exposition: one of a feeling through or by oneself and another of a feeling through or by the other. Can one feel through the other, through the outside, even though feeling seems to depend on the self as its means and even though precisely this dependence conditions aesthetic judgment? This is what the feeling of the sublime forces us to think.[25]

It is also, as we noted at the outset of this essay, what the work of Jean-Louis Chrétien challenges us to think. While insisting on reflexivity (most especially, the reflexivity that determines the sense of touch, "the most fundamental and universal of all the senses") as the only adequate starting point for any phenomenology of human life (see CR, 84–86), Chrétien refuses to make auto-affection the last word of such a phenomenology. He is more concerned with Nancy's more difficult "analytic of exposition," with the explication of the fact that "sensation does not send us back to an autarchic life of self-feeling and self-gratification; rather, it opens the realm where life risks itself and ventures out" (CR, 98). This very orientation toward the other that Chrétien would seem to share with a Kantian thought of the sublime, however, also marks the point at which he parts ways with the latter. For, as William Desmond argues, "The *seeming otherness* of the [Kantian] sublime really serves as a *mediating detour back to ourselves* and the self-confirmation of our moral superiority."[26] Where the sublime in Kant becomes reincorporated into the circle of subjectivity as it makes us "conscious of our superiority to nature within us, and thereby also to nature outside us,"[27] Chrétien describes an encounter with beauty an element of which always remains excessive and unmasterable.[28] Far from confirming in us a sense of moral superiority (who would need the beautiful or the sublime for that?), the call of the beautiful wounds us more deeply than Kant's sublime, shattering our identity while granting us life and purpose (CR, 19), stirring in us the vocation to the risky ventures of speech and responsibility, ventures which share, at their core, a nudity that determines and constitutes them.[29]

The Glory of Manifestation (or, *Hiersein ist herrlich*)

Earlier, we mentioned that the origin of Chrétien's "silent music" lies in stanza 15 of Saint John of the Cross's *Spiritual Canticle*:

The tranquil night
At the time of rising dawn,
Silent music,
Sounding solitude,
The supper that refreshes, and deepens love.[30]

In the Christian tradition, the silence named in this poem is the highest silence—that of the union with God—and directs us to a music older than Keats's unheard melodies: "It is here [in the *Spiritual Canticle*] the whole world that sings God and sings in God" in a kind of "cosmic eucharist" (AS, 72–73). This silence is not "highest" in the sense of being most removed from the world; on the contrary, its superiority lies in the degree of its recognition of "the glory of being here."[31] As with Plotinus, one of whose spiritual exercises consists in directing his students to begin by imagining the visible universe in all its diverse, varied splendor in order to properly contemplate the beauty beyond beauty of the One,[32] Chrétien holds that beauty's transcendence, "far from forcing us to leave our dwelling place, constitute[s] the most urgent of invitations, not to say initiations, to the 'here'" (AS, 80). Bonaventure's *Itinerarium Mentis in Deum* famously describes this movement as one which leads from the natural world, "perceived through sensation," to the contemplation of God "in all creatures."[33] Though close in many ways to the Franciscan thought to which Bonaventure gives remarkable expression, Chrétien proposes that the opposite movement can also take place: "to be listening out for God in silence may lead one to finally hearing the true song of the earth" (AS, 72), to being (re-) awakened to a world where everything speaks (CR, 14). Not entirely unlike many who work in the environmental phenomenology (for example, John Llewelyn) and environmental aesthetics (for example, Allen Carlson) movements, Chrétien wants philosophy to hear the (visible) voice of the natural world and to hear this voice as an "appeal for compassion" whose call sounds forth without being drowned out by the all-too-human dronings of natural theology and proofs for the existence of God (AS, 128, 130). The human voice (which includes, presumably, the speech of action) has a role to play in responding to this decentering, de-anthropomorphizing call: "we have to speak on behalf of things, and not only behalf of one another, as if the world were merely human" (AS, 136).

Futility of the Sonorous

At this point, we could perhaps modify the statement quoted above to read, "to be listening out for God in silence may lead one to *joining* the true song of the earth." This song (or, perhaps better, this chorale) does not need our voice. Indeed, it presents itself as a splendor which lacks nothing but which somehow, nevertheless, stirs us to sing (EB, 73) and to speak. Chrétien describes this responsive speech as forming an "ark" that, reminiscent of Francis of Assisi's "Canticle of the Creatures," welcomes and gives expression to the beauty of the world whose speech is of another order than language (see AS, 113). Likewise, "human art offers its voice to that which has none, and presents to all things that are held prisoner to silence the universal escape of its fragile word" (HH, 163). This does not imply that Chrétien would make of representationality the measure of an artwork's significance. Rather, his work on art and his interpretation of speech share in common an understanding of the human response as a phenomenon determined by its relation to silence. In the case of art, it is not necessarily a matter of giving voice to the silent things that make up the landscape of the natural world; like speech, much art gives expression to the "silence within events." To the extent that speech and art arise from this place (call it the "unheard-of"), such endeavors will be risky, venturesome, and "strong only in [their] weakness" (AS, 13).

In our own silence, we learn that that which gives itself to be heard exceeds our capability of listening to it, but that beauty (in art, in the world), far from being indifferent to our response, beckons it, provoking the almost imperceptible movement in which listening becomes speaking and singing. Following a formulation of Joë Bousquet, Chrétien suggests that the voice offered in singing is a kind of translation from silence: the "silent music" which John of the Cross experiences in contemplation does not seal his lips in muteness but opens them for praise. This opening of the lips is nothing other than a wound (EB, 78). Song does not compensate for the deficiency of all listening (even the most silent and attentive), but expresses this deficiency with abandon. The voice welling up out of silence, granting "asylum" to the "suffering and beauty of the visible" (CR, 43), is, of necessity, a naked, faltering voice, but in its nudity and stammerings lies its perfection. Rather than offering in speech and song nothing but its own act of speaking and singing (self-expression of auto-affectivity), the naked voice offers the world, which is to say, it gives what it does not have, what it has only received. Additionally, to offer the world in one's naked speech and song is not only to pronounce this opening to the other, this receiving, but it is to speak and to sing *to* another person (or, perhaps, to God). "The soul is naked only in dialogue, but the nudity of dialogue forms, not a spectacle," but rather an exposure to the other, a denudation required to truly listen and speak *to* her.[34] This denudation resembles what Chrétien describes as the first movement of true prayer, namely, the confession that one does not know how to pray, a confession that nevertheless can only take place in the act of prayer, in a(n impossible) dialogue with God (AS, 27).[35]

As seen earlier, beauty approaches the human subject as a shock and a wound; it "grips our sight," sometimes even "closing our eyes shut." Yet, by virtue of this dazzling of human sight, the call of beauty "summons our voice" (CR, 44). Where we can no longer see or even hear, we sing. One is reminded here of the concluding pages of Jacques Derrida's *Memoirs of the Blind*, where we discover that "deep down, deep down inside, the eye would be destined not to see but to weep. For at the moment they veil sight, tears would unveil what is proper to the eye."[36] The true vocation of the eyes becomes apparent only at the moment of breakdown, at the moment when the presumption to perfect vision and absolute knowledge is revealed to be illusory. In the same way, the voice fulfills its proper, human role, not when it produces self-possessed, self-assured, commanding tones, but when it breaks and falters, betraying its nudity and dispossession.

We arrive here at the defining mark of Chrétien's thought. In a 1999 retrospective covering his work of the preceding twelve years, Chrétien describes his overarching project as one of describing the "*excess* of the encounter with things, other, world, and God," that is, an encounter which calls "most imperatively" for our response and "yet seems at the same time to prohibit it."[37] This gap between the insistence of the call and the impossibility of an adequate response is inscribed on human bodies—by means of the effects of beauty upon the senses as well as the shattering of the voice that endeavors to sing it—and has a name in Christian spirituality: humility, which for Chrétien is the "touchstone" of Christian mysticism.[38] All of the senses, indeed the entire body, have a role to play in the vocation for humility, but the auditory experiences of listening and singing (experiences which, nevertheless, cannot be separated from visual and tactile encounters and feelings) provide particularly good examples of the encounter Chrétien describes, as well as a helpful point of entrance into his thought. We have found this to be especially true in this concluding section: with what better metaphor could we describe the always faltering, necessarily inadequate response of humility than that of an unadorned, human voice? As Jankélévitch has put it, "of all forms of appearance, the form of appearance assumed by sound is the most futile,"[39] but in the context of the encounter with shocking, imperious beauty or with the gently overwhelming advent of the divine, such futility is most proper. It refers us back to the silence out of which every response grows, the silence that is at once an attentive listening to what in the world speaks and sings and an exposure to what in the world shocks and wounds. The merit of Chrétien's work, exemplified here in his (hermeneutical) phenomenology of listening, consists in giving expression (in a unique style both phenomenological and poetic) to the beatitude of this wound, the fecundity of this shock (EB, 88). It accomplishes this project by demonstrating that, to refer once more to Jankélévitch, "existence, with distracting irony, assumes paradoxical form, as a chiasmus"[40] where the eye listens, the visible speaks and sings, and the most futile of appearances, the most naked voice constitutes the most perfect of human responses.

Chrétien on the Call That Wounds

BRUCE ELLIS BENSON

Only at the very end of Jean-Louis Chrétien's remarkable essay on prayer do we discover why he thinks of prayer as "wounded":

> Why call it "wounded word"? It always has its origin in the wound of joy or distress, it is always a tearing that brings it about that the lips open. And it does so as it is still and otherwise wounded. Wounded by this hearing and this call that have always already preceded it, and that unveil it to itself, in a truth always in suffering, always agonic, struggling like Jacob all night in the dust to wrest God's blessing from him.[1]

It is striking to think of prayer in terms of "wounding." After all, prayer is so often depicted as a moment of peace and tranquility—we even sing (at least in many Protestant traditions) of the "Sweet Hour of Prayer." In the words of that treacly hymn, prayer is depicted as act in which consolation is found and "I view my home and take my flight." On this model, prayer is anything but agonic in nature.

Yet Chrétien would have us think otherwise. Perhaps there is consolation, *too*, but that comes only in the midst—or perhaps at the end—of an agonic struggle. Is Chrétien right that prayer is "always agonic"? How we answer that question will have much to do with what we *mean* by the term "agonic." Much more striking, still, is the way in which this nature of wounding is so central to Chrétien's thought. One could argue, of course, that wounding is the central metaphor of the essay on prayer and that it again comes to the fore in his text *Hand to Hand*. To be sure, Chrétien himself claims that this wounding and its effect "are the locus of meditations at the heart of *Corps à corps*."[2] But it is likewise to be found—even if not nearly as clearly or forcefully as in *Hand to Hand*—in his text *The Call and the Response*.[3] Indeed, one might argue that something like this structure of "wounding" is at the heart not just of Chrétien's own "theological turn" but also of the theological turn in phenomenology in general.[4]

In this chapter, though, I limit myself to considering the wound in *The Call and the Response*, "The Wounded Word," and *Hand to Hand*. Although the most obvious locus of the wound is in the encounter with the divine, it is clear that Chrétien thinks that all of our encounters with any others are wounding ones. We must consider exactly what kinds of "wounds" these are, as well as whether speaking of prayer and encounters with the other as "wounding" is the right language to use. In what follows, I trace the notion of the wound in terms of (1) the call that comes to us before we are even aware of it, (2) the agonic nature of the call and the response, and (3) the surprising way in which the English verb "to bless" ends up being related to the French term "*blesser*" (to wound). Although Chrétien does not simply *bless* "blesser," he patiently considers how they are so often entangled. Since he constantly uses the metaphor of struggle, it should not be surprising that any engagement with his thought means that one struggles alongside of him, with him, and with his thought. The end result is *not* that all becomes clear. If anything, Chrétien's gift may well be that he has a brilliant ability to comflexify what might be viewed in much simpler terms and also the sheer unwillingness to settle for those simpler terms or anything like a quick or neat resolution. In that respect, Chrétien's thought is much like the Socratic dialogues, which so often result in no *conclusion* but simply end. The result is a struggle with an issue without feeling the need to a reach a point of definite resolution.

Always Already

Central to Martin Heidegger's early phenomenology is that *Dasein* always finds itself *already* at home in the world, in the midst of language, and with tools ready to hand. The phrase "*immer schon*" (always already) is like a leitmotif in *Being and Time,* and it plays a similar role in Chrétien. After citing Heidegger's claim that we are able to speak only because we have "always already [*toujours déjà*], listened to speech,"[5] Chrétien goes on to say: "We are entangled in speech as soon as we exist, before we have ever uttered a word, and in this sense we have always already listened and obeyed."[6] Such is true of speech, but it is likewise true of the call (*l'appel*) in general, which is closely connected to speech itself. "We speak only for having been called, called by what there is to say, and yet we learn and hear what there is to say only in speech itself."[7]

Whence comes this call? One could say that it begins the moment "God said, 'Let there be light'" (Gen. 1:3). God speaks and suddenly light comes into existence. The response, then, is the very appearance of the light itself. And these calls into existence continue throughout the creation narrative, in which the phrase "let there be" echoes over and over again. Yet are these truly the first calls? Might there not be ones that preceded even them? The clue that raises at least the possibility comes in the portion of the narrative in which humankind is brought into being. In a dramatic departure from the previous refrain of "let there be" we find a "let *us* make humankind in *our* image, according to *our* likeness" (Gen. 1:26, italics added). Whether the use of "us" and "our" is itself truly an indication of the Trinity is less important than the doctrine itself. For, if God is not one but three, then there is reason to think that some sort—however it might be conceived—of "call" and "response" goes back and forth between these three persons. Moreover, if God is eternal, then it makes little sense to speak of a "first" call. The relationship of the persons of the trinity has been eloquently described by the fourth-century Eastern fathers Gregory of Nyssa and Basil the Great in terms of *perichoresis* (in Latin, *circum-incedere*, from which we get "circumincession," which means "to move around in"). *Perichoresis* is the divine dance of the persons of the trinity in which they move around, with, and in each other. But surely that *perichoresis* could likewise be thought in terms of a call and response, not a divine dance but a divine discourse of ceaseless calls and responses reverberating and interpenetrating each other.[8] And, should we read the "let us" as simply God speaking of the celestial hierarchy (a common enough reading of this passage, even among Christians), we also find evidence of calls that precede that of the calls of creation. John speaks of the "four living creatures" in the heavenly realm who sing "day and night without ceasing": "Holy, holy, holy, the Lord God the Almighty, who was and is and is to come" (Rev. 4:8). This is truly a continual call, a call that continues throughout eternity. Moreover, John is echoing something already found in the Hebrew Bible: in responding to Job, God says "that the morning stars sang together and all the heavenly beings shouted for joy" (Job 38:7). John does not tell us exactly what the "response" of God is to these calls. Perhaps it is already God's *existence* that is the response, let alone all the things that he says. Of course, there has been a call prior to those of the heavenly beings. As their creator, God had already called them into existence.

In either case, by the time the call reaches us, it is never the first call. Yet that feature of not being first also implies that every call that comes forth is a composite of all the calls and responses that went before. Chrétien maintains that "every voice, hearing without cease, bears many voices within itself because there is no first voice."[9] It is not coincidental—nor due to a stylistic feature so common in French writing—that Chrétien begins many sentences with the pronoun "we." For both the call and the response are composed of multiple voices. Chrétien opens *The Call and the Response* with a quotation from Joseph Joubert: "In order for a voice to be beautiful, it must have in it many voices" (CR 1). When we speak, it is never simply "I" that speaks. Rudolf Bernet puts this quite beautifully when he writes: "Only somebody who must hold a lecture discovers that he or she is continually paraphrasing other authors and speaks as well in the name of colleagues and friends."[10] Having had Bernet as my doctoral advisor (or, to use the Flemish term, "*promotor*," the meaning of which is self-explanatory), I have often found myself speaking in his name and paraphrasing from him.

Yet is not this always the case? Perhaps it is not "only somebody who must hold a lecture," but all of us who reflect even a little on the nature of discourse discover that we are constantly speaking by repeating, restating, and paraphrasing. All of language is a kind of improvisation upon that which has been said and resaid. We are always already caught up in the improvisatory movement that makes language possible. To speak is to be part of an ongoing conversation and also to be part of an ever-evolving hybridity of both speech and self (Chrétien speaks of an "altered voice," CR 44). It is here that questions of identity and ownership not merely arise but are stretched to their limits. What exactly of what I say is "mine"? How many times do I have to repeat something said by someone else before it becomes in some sense mine? And how long can I hold on to something as "mine" when it is being said in the mouths of others? We can hardly adjudicate such issues here, though they raise complex questions not just regarding intellectual property (which might be worked out in court) but ontological issues (for which there is neither court nor court of appeal). The "said" may have an identity and perhaps even an ownership, but it is hardly simple or fixed. As someone who speaks with many voices, *I* am not simply my own voice but a polyphony of voices. Thus, the *I* for Chrétien is no "self-contained" or "self-constituted" *I*. Instead, it is composed of multiple voices. But, if the *I* has the polyphonic character, then it has always already been *wounded*. "Each new encounter shatters us and reconfigures us," says Chrétien, citing Hugo von

Hofmannsthal.[11] There is no way of receiving the call, of being open to the other, without not merely the possibility but always the probability that we will be wounded—that is, changed or reoriented or perhaps rebuked. But one thing is certain: if we truly hear the call, we will not be the same as before we heard it. We will return to the way in which the *I* is wounded by the call in the following section, but it is important to note early on that the call always has this quality.

Perhaps polyphony, though, is not quite the right word—or perhaps it is not *enough*. True, it brings out the nature of multiple voices, yet it also at least implies a kind of "blending" in which those voices produce simply a beautiful chorus. But, if we are to be true to the phenomena, we must challenge any such reading. John Milbank is almost right when he speaks of a community in which there is "an infinite differentiation that is also a harmony."[12] In such a community, says Milbank, "the possibility of consonance is stretched to its limits, and yet the path of dissonance is not embarked upon."[13] Those familiar with Milbank's work know that it relies upon notions of harmony taken from Augustine's *De musica*. Although he grants that such harmony may be stretched "to its limits," harmony remains the dominant metaphor. For the ancient Greeks, *poluphônia* carried the idea of multiple tones and *poluphônos* multiple voices. To describe a community as one of multiple voices is indeed right. Yet it does not go quite far enough. In juxtaposition to (that is, *in addition to*) the notion of polyphony, we need to set the notion of heterophony—both descriptively and prescriptively. First, whereas polyphony provides the aspect of a *multiplicity* of voices, heterophony emphasizes the *otherness* of those voices. If there is to be true otherness, then we cannot—and should not—have a beautifully blended polyphony. Indeed, one can argue that this lovely notion of polyphony is all too liberal and modern, for it wishes to smooth over the difficulties and the dissonance. Second, heterophony emphasizes the idea of differing voices that do not simply blend or produce a pleasing harmony but remain distinct and sometimes dissonant, sometimes precisely when we would rather they were not.[14] This is not to say that now dissonance takes center stage; rather, it is to say that dissonance—sometimes eventually resolved and sometimes not—is simply part of that conversation. Only if there is true heterophony can there be the expression and existence of otherness. Without such openness to such dissonance, we would not have the late Beethoven quartets or Stravinsky's *Rite of Spring*. Harmony may *arrive*, but that arrival may well have to do with a change in *us* as listeners, and perhaps a radical revision of what counts as "harmony" (as in the case of Peter's vision, in which God says something new).[15]

All of this becomes even *more* complicated, because for Chrétien the structure of the response is never simply that of answering the call. For one "also calls out in turn and appeals to other calls."[16] That structure of not simply returning but also furthering the call is for Chrétien simply part of the nature of speech. We are given the gift of speech and, in turn, we both give back and disseminate that speech. Hence arises the question of the gift. For Chrétien, though, the gift is not a problem to be worked out but rather a phenomenon to be *lived* out. He assumes that, in gift giving, there is a fundamental inequality of gifts that is precisely what makes giving possible. He insists that "no response will ever correspond. The perfection of the answer will lie forever in its deficiency, since what calls us in the call is from the start its very lack of measure, its incommensurability."[17] Of course, the logic here seems problematic. On the one hand, if gifts were unable to be measured, then the problem of gift exchange would not seem to arise—or at least not with the same force or degree. True, *that* gifts are exchanged would seem to set up a reciprocity. But it is a reciprocity that can never be worked out in terms of measurement, of gifts being equal or unequal to one another. On the other hand, if perfection of the response is found in insufficiency, then must there not be some way of "measuring" gifts and thus declaring their insufficiency? While Chrétien does not explicitly work out this problem, what he goes on to say about nothingness would seem to provide a kind of answer. He asks: "Where does nothingness find these inexhaustible resources, if not in the fact of possessing nothing except the fact of possessing nothing, and in the fact that this very lack is given to by a request that transfers to it the open fault line of promise?"[18] If the gift comes to my nothingness and I can never possess it—but only respond and pass it on—then I can neither "possess" it nor measure it (since I have "nothing" to measure it *with*). And, if everyone else is in this same situation, then the gift always remains incommensurable. We can now see how the gift exceeds us, even though it cannot be measured. For, if we possess only nothingness, then anything that comes our way as a gift always already exceeds us.

How do we live out this gift giving? Chrétien responds that it is by way of translation. The call always comes to us in need of translation, rather than having been translated in advance. Moreover, the call only is what it is *in* being translated. In other words, "the translation therefore does not refer back to an original language given before it and outside of it. The original is given only in the translation itself."[19] Translation is thus the possibility condition for the call to have its appeal. Of course, Chrétien realizes that this immediately poses a problem, namely that of immediacy. If I must translate the call, then it can only be accessed in a mediated form, which would seem to mean that we relate to one another only in a mediated way in which there is distance between us. But here Chrétien counters by citing Fichte, who actually reinforces what we have already seen: "You and I are not separated. Your voice resonates within me and mine echoes it back within you."[20] In other words, mediation only becomes a problem if we assume a self-contained *I*. If, instead, the self is always intertwined with the other, my call with the call of the other, my call intermingled with multiple calls, then selves are always already connected. It is not just the child who "is always already caught up in a speech that exceeds him," but all of us (CR 80). To speak is to join in a conversation that has been going long before one and that is made possible precisely because my voice is never truly my own. Understandably, then, "other voices are at once the past and future of my own voice" (CR 81). Other voices make my voice possible and also keep it sounding.

But how does all this relate to wounding? As already noted, if one's voice is indebted to all of the other voices, then one is already "opened up" to those others. Chrétien puts it as follows: "Someone who takes up speech, by so doing, opens himself to more than himself and to others."[21] Yet the dimension of wounding goes considerably deeper than that, since the call and response is always agonic in nature.

Always Agonic

Here we need to return to certain key features of the citation with which this essay began. Chrétien tells us that prayer has the effect of "wounding" in the sense of both "tearing" open and "suffering." Moreover, prayer is "always agonic," and it will turn out that the very structure of the call and response is agonic. Each of these features needs to be considered in turn.

Chrétien begins "The Wounded Word" by saying: "Prayer is the religious phenomenon par excellence, for it is the sole human act that opens the religious dimension and never ceases to underwrite, to support, and to suffer this opening."[22] One might first wonder if this is not far too strong a statement—prayer as the *only* way to the "religious dimension"? Yet "prayer" for Chrétien covers a multitude of acts, not simply "prayer" in its narrowest definition. The same could be said for the "wounding" that "opens" and the sense of "suffer" that Chrétien assumes. We naturally think of wounding and suffering as "bad" things to be avoided. And, of course, there are many sorts of wounding and suffering that truly *are* bad—not to mention *evil*—and worth avoiding at any cost. However, not all species of either phenomena are necessarily to be avoided, if Chrétien is correct.

The wounding that takes place in prayer is essentially a kind of opening of the self to the other. Prayer "exposes him in every sense of the word *expose* and with nothing held back."[23] To pray is to say, "here I am." In this regard, it is remarkable how similar are the responses of Moses and Samuel to God's call. God calls out from the burning bush, "Moses, Moses," and Moses responds: "here I am" (Exod. 3:4). This "here I am" is to say "I am at your disposal." And the formula that Eli gives to Samuel is: "Speak, Lord, for your servant is listening" (I Sam. 3:9). What takes place in these exchanges is a crucial reversal that Chrétien is certainly not the first to note. Emmanuel Levinas puts it as follows: "Here I am (*me voici*)! The accusative here is remarkable: here I am, under your eyes, at your service, your obedient servant."[24]

Opening oneself to the other is likewise connected to "suffering." While we normally think of suffering in terms of pain or discomfort, the word "suffer" comes from the ancient French *suffrir*, the basic meaning of which is "to bear up." So its primary meaning (and that of its modern equivalent in French, *souffrir*) is "to submit to" or "to endure."[25] It is in *that* sense that one "suffers" in prayer, for prayer is a kind of submission to God in which one becomes a "subject" before and to God. "All prayer confesses God as giver by dispossessing us of our egocentricism," writes Chrétien.[26] In prayer, we recognize that we are not our own, that we are subjects in relation to God. Of course, we can find this same movement in Levinas, who thinks such takes place in the relation between myself and an other: I become a "subject" who is "subject" to the other. But this reversal—in which I am no longer at the center—causes suffering of the other sort. It is *painful* to think of myself as not being the center of the universe. Moreover, it is actually quite *difficult* to truly see one as subject to either the human other or to God, for it requires a change in *us*.

It is not surprising, then, that in his later work Levinas resorts to increasingly more brutal sorts of metaphors—such as "trauma"—to describe how the other affects me. Given what Chrétien has already said regarding the call and its constitution of the self, the trauma is not so much to break through the shield of protection surrounding the self but the always already *having broken through*. Or, perhaps better yet, there is no need to break through precisely because there is always already an interconnection. In any case, Levinas is not alone in using such strong, even combative language. Chrétien speaks in a similar—if not even stronger—way regarding the call: "In order to constitute, the call destitutes. In order to give, it takes away. In order to create, it deletes all that would boast of self-sufficient being, prior to the call and independently of it."[27] The call wounds us, causes us to suffer in multiple ways, and thoroughly upsets our neatly ordered world.

For Chrétien, prayer is the ultimate agonic struggle. One reason is that prayer is a struggle (*combat*) for and "with the truth."[28] Although speech is already a struggle for and with truth, the speech that addresses itself to God is all the more so, for to speak to God is to speak to the author of truth, the ultimate *truth*. To depict that struggle, Chrétien turns to the admittedly strange and difficult passage in which Jacob struggles with a man/an angel/God. On the night before he was to meet with his brother Esau, after having sent his family and everyone away, Jacob curiously meets up with someone with whom he struggles throughout the night. It is literally a night of hand-to-hand combat.[29] Presumably, Jacob has the upper hand, for the person with whom he wrestles (first identified as a "man" and then identified by Jacob as "God," though often taken to be an angel) finally asks him to let go, at which point Jacob asks for a blessing in return. We turn to that "blessing" in the following section, but here the concern is for the fact that Jacob's encounter with God is not one of safety and security but *risk*. Moreover, it is a *violent* encounter, in which the striving continues on until daybreak. One could counter that other exchanges between God and humankind in the Hebrew Bible are more benign, such as when Abraham welcomes the three strangers in Genesis 18. Yet, even that passage contains a kind of "struggle," albeit in the guise of laughter: for Sarah laughs upon hearing that, at an advanced age, she will yet bear a son. What ensues is an "argument" in which God mentions Sarah's laughter, she denies it, and God asserts it again ("you did," "no, I didn't," "yes, you did"). But the struggle is also that of whether God can overcome human expectations. As the text has it, "is anything too wonderful for the Lord?" (Gen. 18:14).

Perhaps not all encounters with the divine are agonic in nature, though it would seem that all would have at least been preceded by an agonistic element. For, if prayer or even simply hearing the word of the Lord that a woman advanced in age can have a child requires that one recognize that God is God, then a struggle has already taken place. One certainly doesn't *begin* thinking of oneself already as a decentered self, willing and ready to recognize an obligation to an other—whether human or divine. Instead, one begins with a world in which oneself is always already the center. Or such is what one supposes. Yet, if Chrétien is right about the constitution of ourselves being so closely connected to the constitution by others, then it is really more of a question of how we *think* about ourselves than how we truly *are*. To think otherwise is always a struggle, though not the sort of struggle in which one finally *wins* but rather the sort in which one continually *engages*. In that sense, all of our encounters with the other are struggles in which we are constantly *trying* to love God or our neighbors as much as we love ourselves, let alone to put the neighbor or God *first*. If Chrétien is right, then there is a certain kind of violence that is not merely present but *necessary* in our encounters with the other. Unfortunately, the violence often has to be done *to* us, even done *by* us, precisely for the sake of the relationship with the other. The agonic aspect of our relations to others, then, may not be the *only* aspect, but it is certainly one that must be present.

Not surprisingly, then, Chrétien does not see all violence as simply gratuitous and thus always to be avoided. In fact, he links the wound of the call with the giving of the gift. On his view, one cannot have one without the other. But, then, what exactly connects them?

Sometimes *Amis*

Every French teacher who works with English speakers knows that one particularly dangerous set of *faux amis* (false friends) are the English verb "to bless" and the French verb *blesser* (to wound). But they turn out to be not just friends at times but even relations. "Blêtsian," from which comes the verb "to bless," was an Anglo-Saxon term that meant "to make 'sacred' or 'holy' with blood." When Christianity arrived in England, it was chosen as the word to translate both the Latin term *benicere* (to pronounce a benediction) and the Greek *eulogeô*, to bless, a word largely used to translate the Hebrew *barak*, which means both "to bless" and "to kneel."[30] But "blêtsian" is most likely also the source of the French *blesser*, which remains more clearly tied to its Anglo-Saxon origins than does the English "bless."[31]

While there is no reason to think that Chrétien has this etymology in mind, there is good reason to think he sees the two words as being connected. In his "Retrospection," he writes that *Hand to Hand* is concerned with "the fact that the wound [*la blessure*] can bless [*bénir*] and that benediction can wound [*la bénédiction blesser*, which could just as easily be translated as "the blessing can wound]."[32] Yet how exactly can blessing and *blesser* be related? The reference in this quotation is—once again—to Jacob's struggle. It is immediately after being wounded—when Jacob's adversary puts his hip out of joint—that Jacob asks for a blessing. What he receives is a change of name: "Then the man said, 'You shall no longer be called Jacob, but Israel, for you have striven with God and with humans, and have prevailed'" (Gen. 32:28). While the text goes on to say that Jacob received a blessing, it is not clear that this change of name *is* that blessing. In any case, Jacob could hardly have been expecting to get what he received. For what he is given by way of a name is in effect a new self, a different identity. Chrétien writes that "the meaning of call and response is radically transformed when the call actually creates the respondent."[33] Here we have a perfect example of that. Jacob simply asks for a blessing and instead he receives a new identity—Israel. For Chrétien, Jacob is the "eponym" for wounds that bless, for struggles that affect both the body and one's identity. Such wounds "one must not heal, for they are the source of our loving intimacy."[34] Precisely in the *opening* of the wound one is further *opened* to another. While our natural tendency is to see wounds as necessarily bad and always to be avoided, Chrétien wants to insist that the story is more complicated.

Yet this struggle raises a further question: "Who is the victor? Who is the vanquished?"[35] Chrétien realizes that the interplay between these two figures is striking in many ways—and that it also raises many complications. If the one with whom Jacob wrestles is truly God, then who really "wins" in this case? God pleads with Jacob for him to let go, and then goes on to bless him. Who, then, has given in to whom? One can argue the case either way. But, then, that is precisely Chrétien's point. It is far too simple to speak of "victor" and "vanquished." Jacob receives a blessing and also a wound. God both inflicts himself upon Jacob—in every sense, God "sets him up" for the fight—but then allows Jacob to "win" the fight. It is here where Chrétien's point becomes particularly uncomfortable. For he claims that "we are each new Jacobs, assaulted by God, and his perseverance should be for us a constant source of confidence."[36] "Assaulted by God"—and that is supposed to be good (let alone give us "confidence")? If that were not enough, Chrétien goes on to say something even *more* difficult to hear:

> To unfold its movements, love's violence has as much need of the faraway as it does the close-up. Love lights up the proximate with the faraway to continue to be love; and love opens the faraway in the proximate to continue to be an approach, and the sudden shock of an approach, an everyday, common miracle.[37]

"Love's *violence*"? Could these words possibly be associated with one another, let alone said in the same breath? Anyone suspicious of theodicy—in which it would seem that evil is often all too easily explained away or made too "good"—would be apt to read these words with the same suspicion. It is that suspicion with which James's exhortation, "whenever you face trials of any kind, consider it nothing but joy" (Jas. 1:2) is likewise read. Even more warily is the line from Hebrews heard: "the Lord disciplines those whom he loves and chastises every child whom he accepts" (Heb. 12:6). Even if we are willing to agree with Paul that—somehow, in some way that we cannot and, in many cases, *dare not* explain—"all things work together for good, for those who love God" (Rom. 8:28), those things *themselves* may not be good.

Yet here it must be remembered that Chrétien is not giving a theodicy but a *phenomenology*. That is easy to forget, given how grounded his thought is in distinctly theological—and, more explicitly, *Christian*—sources. Chrétien tells us very clearly that his is an attempt at thinking about

> loss, wound, and passivity, as well as forgetting and fatigue, which are phenomena where the trace of the excessive shines through, outside of the idealistic and dialectical language of "negativity" in which everything is as if vanquished and surmounted in advance. There is no philosophical parousia.[38]

Given this formulation, it would seem that Chrétien is trying to avoid two extremes. On the one hand, there is the danger already considered of glossing over evil and loss as if there *were* a philosophical parousia. Thinking through these experiences without thinking them away is what Chrétien attempts. As to exactly what a *theological* parousia would look like, that is a question that Chrétien leaves unanswered. On the other hand, there is the danger of thinking of "loss, wound, and passivity, as well as forgetting and fatigue" as wholly unrecoupable, irredeemable, gratuitous. Chrétien is unwilling to go in that direction precisely because he thinks it is *phenomenologically* incorrect. Thus, without simply embracing evil as good or loss as gain, he is willing to attend to the complexities of both. For, without a philosophical parousia, *neither* of these extremes can be embraced. *Either* to assert that all phenomena of loss and wound can be "justified" *or* to assert that they simply cannot be good in any sense would require a philosophical parousia.

Lacking that, we are left in the phenomenological middle, in which there are complexities at every turn—good that is mingled with evil of various sorts and degrees; evil that somehow manages to produce good of various sorts and degrees; and the problem of not always being sure which is truly good and which truly evil. This is why Chrétien insists that we need both the "faraway" and "close-up" views to truly *see* the phenomena for what they are. The difficulty, to be sure, is that we are often faced with evil that is dressed up so beautifully, so seductively that we assume it cannot be anything but good. We are likewise faced with good that comes to us so unattractively, so bruised and broken, that it hardly looks remotely good. And we are left with human to human, human to animal, and human to divine encounters that not merely range across a spectrum but also come so freighted with entanglements that they are often hard to rate as simply "good" or "evil." We all know the worn-out examples of what would seem to be truly unadulterated evil or else absolutely radiant good. But most of our lives consists of a struggle somewhere between these extremes in a much more complicated middle ground where goods compete with each other and loss, wounding, and pain are simply part of the package. Looking back, we can sometimes (though certainly not always) see that what was perceived at the time as either good or bad turns out to be somewhat different than what we originally thought.

It is with a fitting—though somewhat surprising—twist that Chrétien concludes his meditation upon Jacob's struggle by turning to the struggle of the "nonbelieving painter" Eugène Delacroix.[39] Painting *Jacob Wrestling with an Angel* in the Church of Saint Sulpice was a constant battle that occupied him from 1854–1861. The painting has often been cited as emblematic of the very struggle that constitutes his life. He writes repeatedly of the difficulty of the task. Yet it becomes a labor of love. What Delacroix writes about his struggle is so striking that it can only be left in his words:

> To tell the truth, the painting badgers me and torments me in a thousand ways, like the most demanding mistress . . . what from a distance had seemed easy to surmount presents me with horrible and incessant difficulties. But how is it that this eternal combat, instead of killing me, lifts me up, and instead of discouraging me, consoles me and fills my hours when I have left it.[40]

Delacroix himself experiences the wound that blesses, which he calls the "torment" that "consoles." Such an experience can only be known *through* experience. It cannot really be told or described—and certainly not "reduced" to an essence, any more than a painting can be reduced to a description. Moreover, Chrétien notes that Delacroix depicts Jacob as stripped to the waist and reads this as Jacob's giving up his defenses and entering into the fray unarmed. It is, on Chrétien's read, precisely this disarmament that enables one to be open to the other. In any case, Delacroix manages to capture the delicate balance of two figures in battle without settling the question of who is the victor and who the vanquished.

Chrétien closes his essay abruptly by saying that "the imminence of a blessing is already a blessing. It is a violent imminence."[41] Before such a thought, one can only *tremble*.[42] As Chrétien speaks of the difficulty Delacroix has in painting these hands clasped—in battle and perhaps in love—he says, "let us leave these hands silently vibrating in the immi-nence of the word."[43] As much as one would like to bring such a discus-sion to a conclusion, one can only really bring it to an end, not an end that explains the final *telos* of suffering or struggling but simply a breaking off. One could hardly *conclude* a discussion on struggling and suffering, for it would be to go against the very nature of the phenomena them-selves. Lacking a philosophical parousia, one simply continues the struggle.

Embodied Ears

Being in the World and Hearing the Other

BRIAN TREANOR

> With his gentle hand he wounded my neck
> And caused all my senses to be suspended.
> **Saint John of the Cross,** *The Dark Night of the Soul*

Philosophers thinking in the wake of Emmanuel Levinas—that is to say *all* of us working at the intersection of continental philosophy and theology—tend to construe the relationship of the self to the other in terms of one of two sensory metaphors: the visual or the oral/aural.

The mainstream philosophical tradition of the West is characterized by a marked preference for the visual metaphor. Plato, for example, analogizes knowledge and vision explicitly in his attempt to describe the role played by the Good (*agathon*) in intellection (either *noesis* or *dianoia*). "As the good is in the intelligible region with respect to intelligence and what is intellected, so the sun is in the visible region with respect to sight and what is seen."[1] On this account, the relationship between the mind and its objects is the same as the relationship between vision and its objects. Hence the commonplace, "Do you *see* what I mean?" However, critics of the visual metaphor point out that it has a disturbing tendency to encompass otherness, reducing it to a mere modulation of the same. It is typical of this tendency that Plato ends up asserting that there is nothing that is *truly* other: "the soul is immortal . . . there is nothing which it has not learned."[2]

In contrast, the oral/aural metaphor is favored by many postmodern critics of modern and premodern epistemologies that employ the visual metaphor. The oral/aural metaphor is Hebraic rather than Hellenic and, championed by Levinas and those influenced by him, it has become the common currency for speaking of otherness in contemporary continental philosophy. Thus, while Husserl, whose account was accepted more or less wholesale by many continental philosophers, "transforms relations into correlatives of a gaze that fixes them and takes them as contents"[3] (an example of the visual metaphor and its attendant problem), Levinas seeks to describe a relationship that does not grasp or dominate the other. Language, articulated in the oral/aural metaphor that Levinas favors, provides just such a relationship. "Language, which does not touch the other, even tangentially, reaches the other by calling upon him or by commanding him, or by obeying him, with all the straightforwardness of these relations."[4]

However, the fourth study in Jean-Louis Chrétien's *L'Appel et la Réponse*, "The Body and Touch," suggests that both these metaphors might be derivative insofar as our seeing or hearing anything presupposes our being there to see or hear.[5] If post-Levinasian philosophy critiques the Hellenic visual metaphor by recovering the Hebraic oral/aural metaphor, Chrétien complicates the situation, fruitfully I will contend, by focusing on another sense: touch. Ironically, Chrétien's account, which suggests the possibility of describing our relationship with otherness in terms of a tactile metaphor, is based on another Hellenic text: Aristotle's *De Anima*.

In one sense, each of these metaphors is merely a trope for describing the relationship of the self to the other; however, this does not mean that there is nothing at stake in the difference between these varied expressions. The metaphors we use to describe our relation with otherness are indicative of deeper assumptions about the relationship of the self to the other, and the nature of otherness itself. Thus, the visual metaphor is used in philosophies that assert a correlation between the knowing or experiencing self and its objects. Phenomenology, for example, posits a correspondence between *noema* and *noesis* in its quest to return *zu den Sachen selbst*, which attempts to address things as they appear before being placed in a predetermined theoretical construct. The oral/aural metaphor, in contrast, tends to be employed by philosophers who call into question our willingness "to let that which shows itself be seen from itself in the very way in which it shows itself from itself" and the ability of visually oriented philosophies to do so.[6] The oral/aural metaphor stresses instead the passivity, receptiveness, or responsiveness of our relationship to the other (*autrui*) in order to emphasize that ethical openness to the other must be radically nonjudgmental and conscientiously noninvasive.

I hope to show how Chrétien's account of touch can contribute to contemporary accounts of otherness by recovering a well-known but underemphasized truth about human beings: we are embodied. In emphasizing our embodiment, Chrétien provides us with a warrant for restoring our contact with the lived world, something conspicuously absent in some contemporary discussions of otherness. I suggest that Chrétien's insights provide a needed supplement to, rather than replacement of, contemporary accounts of otherness that use visual or oral/aural metaphors, one that helps to give a fuller account of the encounter with the other.

The Primacy of Touch

In order for the ecstasy of sight and hearing to even be possible, must there not first be the immediacy of sensing, of a self-sensing that is prior to any speech, to any request? And if we posit a silent immediacy of this kind, does it not considerably reduce the scope of what follows after it and would, in any event, presuppose it? Does the call . . . not indeed always come too late, if it finds us already constituted without it, before it, in the silence of a sensing that is originally turned toward the self, even when the self is affected by another?[7]

Contemporary continental philosophy, under the influence of Levinas's incisive critique of the visual metaphor, overwhelmingly speaks of the encounter with the other in terms of a call to which the self responds. Could it be that the call of the other, rather than constituting the subject as Levinas claims, arrives to find the subject *already* constituted? Are we first and foremost visual beings (as Plato implies), auditory beings (as Levinas argues), or are we, perhaps, fundamentally tactile beings? Which of our senses represents our most fundamental engagement with others and the world? Chrétien's analysis suggests that an encounter with the other through any of the senses presupposes a tactile being; hearing the call of the other presupposes feeling oneself in the world. Feeling (touch) is coextensive with being and, therefore, only an embodied, tactile subject can hear the call of the other.

However, if touch is, or may be, primary, we need an analysis of touch that engages the postmodern debates surrounding the question of otherness, where the visual and oral/aural metaphors have enjoyed almost exclusive attention from philosophers. What exactly is touch? How does it work? And how does it shed light on the relation of the self to the other?

The first relevant point Chrétien makes is that touch is universal in at least two senses. To begin with, touch is always operative. All the other senses can be disengaged; however, "the sense of touch is inseparable from life itself: no animal is deprived of touch without also being deprived of life."[8] Standing on the earth, our feet touch the ground and, by virtue of "contact" with a "place," the sense of touch is engaged even in sleep.[9] Moreover, touch is not merely coextensive with being; it is tied to the maintenance of being. "Touch does not record sensible qualities; it grasps and immediately feels their useful or noxious character, their relevance to the preservation of our being."[10] Touch seems to sense either pain or pleasure in a less mediated fashion. For example, while we might say that a certain piece of music "pains" us, we do so only by analogy and only after making a culturally mediated judgment about what makes a piece of music harmonious or dissonant, a judgment that might very well be different if we were born into another culture or educated about the foreign scale. However, pain transmitted by the sense of touch, as when a child touches the proverbial hot stove, is immediate and incontrovertible. Because of this, Chrétien claims that, "touch constitutes animal life as such, the first act of animal life is tactile; and the joy of being, simply of being alive and of exercising a living act or life acts, resides first and foremost in the joy of touch."[11] This first sort of universality and its connection to the "maintenance of being" immediately raises problems—at least for this inquiry, which takes seriously the postmodern preference for the oral/aural metaphor. This is because the ethical relationship to the other is, by most accounts, supposed to rise above the selfishness of the *conatus essendi* and the hunger of *jouissance*.[12] The ethical relationship precisely transcends the desire to maintain one's own being in favor of the being of the other.

Deferring for the moment an analysis of the relationship of touch to the *conatus essendi*, we can note that the omnipresent quality of touch confronts us with additional aporias concerning the nature of touch, which point to another sense in which touch is universal: it is present throughout our bodies. If the first aspect of universality is temporal, so to speak—because it points out that as long as I am, touch is operative—this second aspect of universality is spatial because it asserts that touch is unlocalizable. That is to say, unlike other senses, touch is not located in a specific organ and, because it is nowhere specific, we can also say that it is everywhere at once. Certainly we feel with our skin; however, we can also feel things internally, such as the beating of our hearts. In fact, upon reflection, neither the proper location nor the proper object of touch is immediately clear.

Chrétien's second important point regarding touch, conceived as this sort of general sensitivity, is that touch is not only prior to the other senses, it founds them as well.

Touch is not primarily and perhaps not even ultimately one of the five senses: for Aristotle, touch is the necessary and sufficient condition for the emergence of an animated body, the perpetual basis for the possibility of human life and therefore eventually also of additional senses, which will always belong as such to a tactile body.[13]

We might note that the dependence of other senses on touch (and thus, the extent to which it is "foundational") is borne out by our modern understanding of the senses, at least if we think of touch in terms of contact. To see is to have photons "touch" the rods and cones on the back of our eyes. Hearing is the result of sound waves "touching" our eardrums. To smell is to have certain molecules "touch" our epithelium and taste requires that molecules "touch" our taste buds. To live is to touch and to be touched. Any subject who sees or hears is already a subject who feels. This is the crux of the argument in terms of the priority of the tactile metaphor over the oral/aural metaphor. In the following passage, I have intertwined Chrétien's comments about sight (the favored metaphor for knowledge) with my own bracketed comments concerning hearing (the favored metaphor for ethics).

Touch is "more necessary" even if sight is "more perfect" for knowledge [or, I might note, hearing "more ethical" for relating to the other]. There is, however, a difference in level between the two, since one is the condition of the other. Touch is "in some way the foundation of the other senses." It is absurd and vain to set up a competitive rivalry between the founder of something and that which it founds. The nature of their respective perfection is by definition distinct and cannot be reduced to the same scale. Touch is the condition of the possibility of sight [and hearing], and sight [and hearing] cannot do without it. If sight better than the other senses enables our knowledge to increase . . . knowledge nonetheless is the act of a living being and therefore of a being endowed with touch. [Likewise, if hearing better than the other senses enables us to encounter the other ethically, ethical response is the act of a living being and therefore of a being endowed with touch.] Touch is always already included in every act, in every pleasure, in every knowledge, [and in every ethical response] since without touch we ourselves would not be there. Our predilection for sight [or hearing] thus presupposes touch, inseparable from life itself.[14]

Touch and the Other

So it appears that touch is more primordial than seeing, hearing, or speaking and, therefore, that there ought to be some consideration of the tactile metaphor for describing our relationship to the world and our encounters with others. If the tactile metaphor has some priority over the visual and oral/aural metaphors, should we replace the latter with the former when discussing ethics, or should we preserve the ethical priority of the oral/aural by drawing a distinction between being constituted as an empirical body (where touch may well be primary) and being constituted as an ethical subject (where the oral/aural metaphor is more appropriate)? Given the usefulness of the oral/aural metaphor, the former option seems rash. However, the latter option also proves problematic because, while such a response no doubt disarms the tension between these two metaphors, it ignores some of the more subtle aspects of Chrétien's analysis.

How does touch fare with respect to the concerns that cause philosophers to reject the visual metaphor—and, hypothetically, the tactile metaphor—in favor of the oral/aural metaphor? Philosophers who favor the oral/aural metaphor tend, with rare exceptions, to have a dim view of "contact." Thus, Levinas's insistence that the otherness of the other is so radical as to preclude a shared border that separates the other from the self (the border, as shared, being a point of contact) and his assertion that language, as developed in his thought, does not touch the other, even tangentially.[15] Likewise, for Derrida, the other always remains *a-venir*—hoped for but never arrived—and thus contact is out of the question. Of course, these criticisms of contact are directed at philosophies employing a visual metaphor for knowledge or the relationship to the other. However, if contact raises the specter of "contamination,"[16] "grasping,"[17] and "comprehension"[18] in the context of a tradition framed by the visual metaphor, how much more would this be the case if the metaphor were tactile?[19] Touch seems even more likely than vision to be a matter of contact, contamination, and acquisition.

Without painting in overly broad strokes, we could say that thinkers who favor the oral/aural metaphor are suspicious of equating knowledge and vision because: (1) such models imply a grasping, acquisitive relationship to the object of knowledge (that is, the other); (2) such an orientation is fundamentally self-centered and therefore leaves no room for the other qua other; and (3) lacking an orientation toward the other, a visual model of knowledge cannot account for transcendence.[20] Are such criticisms applicable to the tactile metaphor? Surprisingly perhaps, no.

First, according to Chrétien, touch is about contact, not grasping, and therefore not acquisition. Some of the confusion results from the ambiguous distinction between *touch* and *tact*. Certain thinkers have suggested that the former is one of the five senses—located in a definable organ, the skin—while the latter corresponds to what is sometimes called "general sensitivity." While on this account tact may refer to a sort of general sensitivity of living beings, it is distinct from touch, the function of which is to handle or grasp. Such distinctions seem to introduce some ambiguity with respect to the preceding account of touch as universal. This ambiguity is evident, for example, in the conspicuous absence of any robust account of "fingering," the excellence of the hand, in Aristotle's analysis of touch.[21] However, Chrétien maintains that the absence of such an account is not accidental: "What matters to Aristotle *is* the universality of touch—what in touch founds all of the other senses. Consequently, *contact is privileged over grasp.*"[22] In fact, doesn't the etymological derivation of tact, as "sensitivity in dealing with people," from the Latin *tactus* (the sense of touch), suggest a complicity between touch and ethics?

However, even if we exclude the desire to grasp and dominate from our account of touch, the mere suggestion of contact raises problems in a post-Levinasian philosophical climate, where the distinction between contact and grasping seems tenuous at best. Within such a framework, the other must remain rigorously other and so beyond contact. But Chrétien challenges this claim and, having undermined our assumptions regarding touch as grasping and acquisitive, argues that there is no necessary reason to equate touch and contagion. Building on Aquinas's commentary on the *Metaphysics*, Chrétien points out that love "leads touch to its highest possibility."[23]

Contact with the infinite must necessarily involve a whole other order beyond contact with the finite. Yet touch, in its finitude and based on it, is already open precisely to a presence without image or representation, to an intimate proximity that never turns into possession, to a naked exposure to the ungraspable. The excess over me of what I touch and of what touches me is endlessly attested in the caress.[24]

Although Chrétien is speaking of God in this instance—he also references Aquinas's *Disputed Questions on Truth*—in the contemporary landscape the infinite applies equally well to other people.

This association of love and touch is not without precedent. Chrétien points out that Bonaventure saw a correspondence between the senses and the theological virtues: "faith calls forth sight and hearing, which it perfects, hope corresponds to the olfactory sense, and love to touch and taste."[25] Touch is also an important metaphor in various mystical testimonies. Saint John of the Cross is full of references to contact, although we can only speculate as to what a completed commentary on the later stanzas of *The Dark Night of the Soul* would reveal.[26] *The Spiritual Canticle* and *The Living Flame of Love* also abound with images of touch and contact, the latter describing God's touch as "so delicately strange." Similar images characterize the biblical Song of Songs, where we can find a description of love involving all the senses.[27]

Because Chrétien insists that there is an "excess over me of what I touch," touch never grasps what it touches. However, pursuing this point, we find that touch is further insulated from charges of grasping and contamination by the fact that it, paradoxically, never really touches. Levinas resorts to language in order to establish a relationship without contact. "Absolute difference, inconceivable in terms of formal logic, is established only by language. Language accomplishes a relation between terms that breaks up the unity of a genus."[28] However, while touch, more than vision or hearing, may appear to be in immediate contact with its other, Chrétien assures us that this is not the case. "Aristotle shows the interval is never abolished, only forgotten. There always remains an intervening body between our flesh and what it touches, a three-dimensional layer of air or water."[29] Therefore, not only does touch fail to *grasp* the other, *touch never touches the other per se.*

Second, touch is not a reflexive relationship of the self to the self, as some thinkers have suggested. It is true that the general sensitivity of the body seems to rest on a principle of proprioception. "The sensuous body, tactile in the broadest sense of the term, is such only because it feels itself."[30] It is for this reason that Merleau-Ponty claims "to touch is to touch oneself."[31] Indeed, I have noted that Chrétien's account established the primordial nature of touch conceived as general sensitivity, which seems to imply that the proprioceptive aspects of touch would exist more fundamentally than the relationship of touch to its other. However, Chrétien calls into question this conclusion. "Is touching oneself the truth of touch, or is the opposite true? Pradines says rightfully: 'The hand . . . obviously does not have at its function to touch itself: its function is to touch *things*.'"[32] While touch is no doubt proprioceptive, this function is not its most essential characteristic. "To feel oneself is not a beginning, but a response to the appeal made by a sensible that is other than myself and elicits the exercise of my act. I never start by saying 'I,' I start by being 'thou-ed' by the world."[33] Self-touch is, in fact, not the truth of touch.

> From the start, the exercise of touch is indistinguishable from the experience of touch, since touch delivers us to the world through a unique act of presence: in order to see one must be visible, yet seeing is not immediately to be seen by what I see. The same holds true of the other senses, whereas to touch is immediately to be touched by what I touch.[34]

This aspect of touch is striking when compared to sight or hearing. While the mutuality or reciprocity of touch does risk totalization due to its (mis)association with grasping, it also assures that tactile contact is forthright and without subterfuge. The tactile sense distinguishes itself immediately from the visual and oral/aural, which do allow clandestine operation. *There can be no "Gyges of touch."*[35]

Third, because touch is not primarily about grasping, is not immediate, and is fundamentally extrospective rather than proprioceptive, we can also say that touch harbors a kind of transitivity. Touch is indeed associated with the *conatus essendi*. Nevertheless, without diminishing the danger of this association, we should note that the noxioceptive character of touch does not manifest itself in a purely self-centered concern. "Sensation does not send us back to an autarchic life of self-feeling and self-gratification; rather, it opens the realm where life risks itself and ventures out."[36] Touch is not reflexive, but is dependent on the other.[37] Moreover, because touch "implicates itself in what it perceives," it is oriented toward difference in a manner unlike the other senses.[38]

> The organ of touch . . . is itself immersed in the tangible realm, and nothing is tangible that is neither hot nor cold, dry nor moist. The mean that we are is the measure of extremes, discerning extremes and differentiating them: the hot is always hotter than us, the cold is what is colder than our flesh, and similarly for the hard and the soft. *What is like us is not perceived; we feel only that which exceeds us.*[39]

While touch certainly has the potential to be used violently (when it attempts to grasp the other) or selfishly (as it supports the *conatus essendi*), it also harbors characteristics that seem less appropriate for, even inapplicable to, those ends.

Contributions to a Philosophy of Otherness

So touch is significantly more complex than we suppose. It appears to underlie and make possible the other senses; it is coextensive with life. Indeed, for Aristotle the sensible and the tangible are synonymous.[40] However, neither grasping nor proprioception is the essence of touch; rather, touch is characterized by, among other things: (1) its universality; (2) its "restraint," or at least its limited scope, due to the presence of an intervening body between it and its object; and (3) its affinity for difference rather than sameness. At this stage, having considered the ways in which touch is something more than it appears, we should consider what touch *contributes* to the picture of how we relate to others. As I suggested at the outset, the main benefit gleaned from reassessing the sense of touch is an appropriate reminder of a fact too frequently neglected in contemporary discussions of otherness: We are embodied and it is our embodiment that involves us in the world. Following Aristotle and Aquinas, Chrétien goes so far as to assert that "to have a more refined touch is to be as a whole more thoroughly delivered into the world, exposed to it—to respond to it better, through the whole of our body and therefore through the whole of our soul."[41]

Precisely for the reasons we have considered, touch "delivers us to the world."[42] Flesh—and therefore touch, which is coextensive with it—is inscribed in and inscribes us in the world. This world is not of our making; it is a world of others, in which we are actors rather than mere spectators. Touch accomplishes this engagement. "The sense of touch, far from making the living organism into a mere spectator, pledges it to the world through and through, exposes it to the world and protects it from it."[43] To touch is to participate in the world and, importantly, such action and participation are directed at more than self-sufficient *jouissance*.

> Sensitivity is given to itself only in the profusion of the world, it receives itself through the other and by means of the other. . . . I experience the joy of seeing, of touching, of hearing, of attentively exercising the diverse possibilities that are mine always by seeing, touching, hearing something other than myself, out in the world. . . . The joy of being is of another order than the self-sensation and self-enjoyment. Every joy is fueled by a pure yes, rising like a flame, without curling back on itself. One never says yes to oneself, which is why one is never truly oneself except in saying yes.[44]

If touch is so central to our experience and understanding of the world, then failing to account for the role played by touch amounts to a kind of abstraction.[45] The problem with such abstraction is that it obfuscates the way in which we encounter the other rather than clarifying or purifying it. So, while the visual and oral/aural metaphors help to describe essential aspects of how we relate to certain others, the tactile metaphor reminds us that we relate to those others in, and only in, the world we inhabit. We cannot "*see* the truth" or "*hear* the call of the other" without first *feeling* ourselves in the world in which we see the truth or hear the other.

This does not mean that we should simply replace the oral/aural metaphor with the tactile metaphor when speaking of transcendence, ethics, or otherness. The former metaphor clearly has been and will continue to be useful. Chrétien's analysis, however, does suggest that considering touch alongside hearing and vision may well provide us with a richer, more robust picture of the way in which we encounter others. The tactile metaphor need not replace the other sensory metaphors that have become common currency in philosophy, but it can and should supplement them.

The Witness of Humility

NORMAN WIRZBA

Nothing before God belongs to us as our own, if not our ability to say
thank you. What may appear as the most tenuous, the most slender of all
possibilities is in truth the highest and most extensive: the praise that *re-sponds* to the divine giving is the essence of human speech. It is in speech
that the gift is received, and that we can give something of our own, in
other words ourselves.

Jean-Louis Chrétien

There is no task more difficult than to be faithful and true to our creaturely condition. Whether out of fear, blindness, suspicion, arrogance, or
rebellion, our abiding temptation is to evade, dissimulate, or distort each
other and our place in the world. Rather than patiently and honestly living up to our need before others—by taking full account of, and then
honoring, the breadth and depth of the relationships we live through—we
deform need into fantasy and remake the world to suit our own desires.
Rather than being grateful for the fact that others contribute to our well-
being and joy—through acts of friendship and nurture as well as sacrifices
of food and energy—we destroy (often in the name of self-preservation!)
the very sources of life upon which all depend.

My thanks to Merold Westphal, Bruce Benson, and Adam Glover for reading an earlier
draft of this essay and for offering helpful suggestions for improvement. This essay doubtless would have been better had I followed all their advice.

There is lunacy in this attitude, a lunacy that we, for the most part, do not appreciate because of the disordered character of every fearful, blind, insecure, arrogant, and rebellious mind.[1] What our lunacy demonstrates, however, is a failure to be human, a failure to be honest about who and where we are. It is to forget that our being testifies over and over again to a primordial hospitality in which, as Jean-Louis Chrétien says, "We have been listened to even before we speak."[2] In a fundamental sense, all true speech is a response to the call of others—other people, history, habitats, the world, and God. When we fail to listen[3] and respond appropriately to this call, we bear witness to a spiritual malfunction of the highest significance.

As I will argue here, one of the best ways to understand our failure is in terms of the loss of humility, or perhaps more precisely, our *rebellion against* humility. Humility is central to human life because it is through a humble attitude that we most fully approximate our true condition as creatures dependent on others, daily implicated in the ways of creation, all together sustained by the gifts of our Creator. It is in terms of humility that we express the understanding that we do not stand alone or through our own effort, but live through the sacrifices and kindnesses of others. Humility, in other words, takes us to the heart of an embodied and spiritual life that is true to the world as a place of belonging and responsibility.

This is a thesis that needs clarification and defense. To accomplish this goal, I will refer to Chrétien's phenomenological descriptions of the call-response structure to human life. Abstraction is the great danger in any discussion of humility and creaturely/spiritual life. By attending to the concrete ways in which every human life is always already a life that has many other lives deeply implicated within it, lives that we are far from being able to name completely (let alone comprehend), we come upon the fresh possibility of encountering and engaging the world as the site of grace and hospitality and mystery. As we have yet to see, Chrétien's phenomenological descriptions play a key role in giving richness and depth to various theological themes that develop as the meaning and sense of humility dawns on us.

My essay will begin with a brief account of the central significance of humility for human life as religiously conceived. What a humble disposition entails is here contrasted with the pride that is our perennial temptation. Criticisms of and challenges to humility as a virtue are also presented. My essay then turns to an investigation of embodiment and creaturely life—and the memberships and responsibilities our embodied creatureliness entail—as a fresh opening for understanding humility. In particular, I appeal to phenomenological descriptions of touch as a profound lens through which to appreciate and understand humility's wide significance. The deep theological significance of touch and humility are then made clear through an understanding of Christ as the archetype of proper relationality. Christ, in other words, shows us practically what it is to be a creature (by modeling a life of attention and compassion), and thus is our inspiration for authentic humility. Humility is hereby shown to be central to the life of humanity because it is a reflection of God's own Trinitarian life, a life we are invited to witness to by participation.

Contrasting Humility

We can learn about the character and pattern of our collective malfunction if we turn for a moment to the prophet Isaiah. Babylon has overtaken Israel, but the prophet assures us that in the eyes of God the days of the Babylonians are numbered. Though they have exhibited great power for a time, their power is pathetic and destructive because it is without mercy or kindness. Having already been turned against others, it is a self-aggrandizing power that must finally turn against itself (a people devoted to self-interest will finally undermine themselves in the name of that interest). As Babylon begins to crumble, we are left with the desperate and absurd image of a people trying to save the gods they have themselves created.[4] They will not be saved because they are blind to their true need and closed to all genuine help. They are too comfortable and secure in themselves, believing they will never know widowhood or the loss of children.

The arrogant presumption that as a people they are without need and beyond judgment (Isaiah suggests that they did not believe anyone to be in a position to see, let alone condemn, their wickedness) lies at the heart of their failure. Isaiah puts the matter precisely: "Your wisdom and your knowledge led you astray, and you said in your heart, 'I am, and there is no one besides me'" (Isaiah 47:10). This confident, though utterly naïve and destructive, sentiment is the root from which all mockery and disdain for humility grows. The delusional belief that for life we need only ourselves—*I am, and there is no one besides me*—that our associations with others are of a purely voluntary nature, and therefore that we need not be attentive to or responsible for anyone else, takes us to the height of human folly. Should not a moment's honest and detailed reflection alert us to the fact that we are not the self-standing, self-legitimating, autarchic beings we often present ourselves to be?

History shows us that folly is notoriously difficult to teach and correct. Our temptation, still, is to believe that we can take the world by force and without regard for the needs of others. Centuries later, whether by intention or by consumer proxy, we still adhere to Francis Bacon's zealous project that the realms of nature be bound and enslaved, made to do our bidding and satisfy our every wish. Not surprisingly, technology has thus become for us the new sacred and the new sublime.[5] Through it we will bring more and more of the world, even the rudiments of life itself, under the stamp of our desire and control. The results of our control—wasted communities, blown-up mountains, poisoned and eroded soils, oceanic "dead zones," biological and viral "super pests," war upon war, and workers' anxiety—are getting harder to ignore.

To this arrogant, and finally destructive, path we should contrast the humble way suggested by Saint Bonaventure. In *The Journey of the Mind to God*, Bonaventure describes the path of contemplation whereby the follower of Christ can enter into union with the Supreme Good, the Maker of all that is. He invites us to join him on this path, even as he extends several cautionary notes. To embark on the divine way of peace we must combine reading with fervor, speculation with devotion, investigation with admiration, observation with exultation, industry with piety, knowledge with love, study with grace, and understanding with humility. In an important sense, we cannot really approach the former if we do not practice the latter, since it is through the exercises of devotion, exultation, piety, love, and humility that "the mirror of our soul [is] cleansed and polished."[6] Bent over as we are by sin, we have become blind and dark, violent and destructive, devoted primarily to our own obsessions, and thus unable to see the light of heaven that calls us to our own and creation's peace and good. We need the grace of charity and truth that has been revealed to us in the person of the crucified Christ. With this divine aid we can be lifted up into supreme knowledge and wisdom, and into the enjoyment of our Creator.[7]

Bonaventure is describing a reorientation of the person that has humility at its core.[8] For this reorientation to be true and authentic, however, it must grow out of the realization that we are creatures who are dependent upon each other and on God as our Creator. Bonaventure describes our complete dependence in terms of the nothingness of creation: "Therefore, since all things, which have been made, abide by the one principle and were produced from nothing, that man is truly wise who really recognizes the nothingness (*nihilitatem*) of himself and of others, and the sublimity of the first principle."[9]

The link between the understanding of our interdependent creatureliness and the realization of true humility is of decisive significance. The mind must be cleansed and polished of its sinfulness—which, in one of its definitions, means the prideful refusal to be a creature and instead to prefer the status of a sovereign, independent god—so that it can see honestly and desire properly. His assumption is that without this cleansing we will continually be infected with the hubris that places ourselves—our wants, fears, vanity, ambition, and anxieties—at the center of value and significance. This is why he says near the end of this book that the mind's journey to God will require us to become "oblivious to ourselves." A pure mind, one that is clothed by the theological virtues, demands that we "transcend ourselves" and our attachments to things, for it is precisely in holding to ourselves that we forgo Christ and the flame of God.[10] When we so transcend ourselves, we begin to see the world as it truly is: as nothing apart from God's vivifying and sustaining care. For the first time we also begin to enjoy it truly, as God does: as the created, concrete manifestation of divine love.

Contrasting the paths of the Babylonians and Bonaventure we can now begin to appreciate how humility grows as the capacity to see ourselves and creation honestly and truly. We cannot be humble so long as we persist in the belief that we can stand on our own, and that the significance of others resides primarily in how they signify for us. In a fundamental sense, humility is the natural outgrowth of persons fully aware of themselves as creatures made dependent upon each other and upon God, called to serve in the hospitable manner modeled by Christ, "the archetype of all relation." When we fail to appreciate the creatureliness of life we also inevitably fail in our understanding of humility.

As a capacity and disposition, however, humility is notoriously difficult to describe and develop because the person whose vision is clouded is not in the right position to sense or appreciate the full extent of the defect. We are all naturally predisposed to think that our vision is legitimate and clear, even when others around us challenge the ways we frame and picture reality. It takes honest self-awareness to admit and remove the logs in our own eyes that distort our vision and disfigure the world (cf. Luke 6:42). Our trouble is that by putting ourselves into the line of sight we cannot see things for what they are. We see as we want to see, which is to say that we engage reality in terms of its ability to satisfy, flatter, and glorify ourselves. Humility confronts this perennial temptation to self-aggrandizement by getting our ambition and arrogance, our fear and anxiety out of the line of sight. Iris Murdoch said it simply and directly: "The humble man, because he sees himself as nothing, can see other things as they are."[11]

Clearing a Space for Humility

It is precisely the call to see ourselves "as nothing" that has caused pleas for humility to be met with resistance, even scorn. What the call means is easily misunderstood (as when people mistakenly equate creaturely nothingness with worthlessness). That it can be abused is also readily observed (in power ploys that keep people down or subservient). If we are to rehabilitate the sense and the practice of humility we must, therefore, attempt a fresh characterization of its ways and inspiration. We should ask, how does the humble acknowledgment of our own nothingness relate to the nothingness (creation *ex nihilo*) that informs all of creation? What is it to be a creature created from nothing, and why is the proper attainment of our creatureliness of such significance for our spiritual development? In short, why and how is authentic humility the practical correlate of being a creature? As we will see, Chrétien's phenomenological description of the call/response structure of existence, precisely because it helps us to appreciate the nature and extent of creaturely interdependence, can serve as an excellent entry point into an account of authentic humility. But before we can consider his contribution we first need to attend to objections that invariably arise whenever humility is recommended as an indispensable virtue.

First, there is the problem of false humility. Experience shows us that room for deception abounds as we are tempted to feign meekness and thus turn our professed lowliness into an empty, and perhaps manipulative, show. Who has not seen the potential for self-advancement through false posturing? Insincere flattery of others, though suggesting the sense of one's inferior rank, actually turns into mockery as we play the insecurity of others to our own advantage. Whatever advantage we achieve, however, turns out to be a sham since it is generated through the debasement and corruption of ourselves and others. What makes this humility disingenuous is that it is premised on a hubristic disposition that would elevate or magnify the self at the expense or demotion of another.

Humility has also been roundly criticized as an unworthy attribute and goal because it leads to a rather depressing view of human potential and achievement. Critics, ranging from David Hume to Friedrich Nietzsche, routinely deride spiritual writers who, in their calls to humility, refer to the sinfulness and contemptibility of the human race. Norvin Richards is representative when he asks, "If humility is low self-esteem, where does this leave the rather *splendid* among us?"[12] On this view, humility is a vice and a blemish on the strength, daring, ingenuity, and dignity that elevate us as a species. It is the surest and most miserable sign of self-imposed decadence, and therefore ought to be rejected as a valued character trait. Failure to banish humility from a list of virtues will inevitably lead to forms of self-hatred and self-loathing that have done much personal and social harm. What Richards's criticism overlooks, however, is that self-hatred of this sort misrepresents people as creatures who, though nothing *in themselves*, nonetheless are called to and maintained in their being by God's love, and thus are of *inestimable worth*.

A subtler, and perhaps farther-reaching, impediment to the realization of true humility has to do with practical developments within modern and postmodern culture. As we have developed societies and built environments through the unparalleled use of powerful, now-ubiquitous technologies, we have constructed a world in which we often see reflected little more than our own desires. The "natural" or created world, now engineered and redesigned by us, signifies primarily as the idolatrous reflection of our own ambition, and has ceased to be an "iconic" realm of deep mystery and sanctity pointing beyond itself to God.[13] Societies, in turn, are manipulated through media and marketing campaigns that enrich the few but deceive the rest by assuring them that consumer acquisition is what life is all about. In a world of the "spectacle" (Guy Debord), humility cannot make an appearance because the rule of the "image" determines virtually every aspect of personal, social, and economic life. Rather than trying to see ourselves and each other for what we truly are—as creatures dependent upon each other and on God—we are busily projecting and purchasing "styles" and "brands" that will signify success.

Given these pitfalls and difficulties that are inherent in any exploration of humility, how are we to proceed? This question is more difficult than it seems because the very means to an answer—human speech and reasoning—are often implicated as being antithetical to authentic humility. Those people that we might identify as truly humble are known to shun unnecessary talk and prefer quiet, opting to let their actions, however inadequate, speak for themselves. After all, what could be more ridiculous than to argue for one's own humility? And so the genuinely humble avoid boisterous crowds where people (inevitably?) jockey for position. They eschew the clamor of self-justifying lips because they understand that there are depths of anxiety, fear, and hubris that, while worked out in what we say and think, are not immediately or clearly evident to others or to us. For instance, a deeply rooted sense of insecurity may (unwittingly or unintentionally) issue in claims that are false, presumptuous, or simply grandiose. The problem is not only that we will deliberately misrepresent ourselves to others but also that we will be self-deceived. If we understand humility as beginning in a detailed and honest estimation of ourselves, as when Bernard of Clairvaux defined humility as "the virtue by which a man recognizes his own unworthiness because he really knows himself,"[14] how, given our propensity for either self-promotion or self-deprecation, are we to arrive at such honesty and clarity?

One approach would be to follow Socrates, who was also compelled by the need and desire to "know himself." His method, based as it was on the tireless questioning and cross-examination of others, yielded a most noteworthy, if unpopular, result: namely, that we do not know as much as we think, nor do we fully believe or even understand the things we outwardly profess. Many of the beliefs we hold about ourselves and the world are simply false or entail consequences that, upon further consideration, are unacceptable or in contradiction with other, more deeply held beliefs. An equally important outcome of Socratic conversation and interrogation, however, was that his interlocutors could just as well be left speechless, without any "positive" result, and not understanding what they should do or believe. As Plato has Socrates put it in his *Apology*, "human wisdom is worth little or nothing" (23a) because we are so prone to speak when we should be silent or parade when we should retreat. In other words, we have great difficulty knowing and then respectfully observing the limits of our capacities and abilities. Fearful of our deep ignorance and weakness,[15] we presume too much for ourselves, and in our presumption we speak and act as arrogant fools.

The Body: An Opening into Humility

If we are to talk clearly and honestly about humility we must, therefore, be as attentive as possible to the practical, concrete contexts of our humanity and the limiting factors they may suggest.[16] We need to determine precisely where and what the limits are, and then how they should be drawn and understood. We should consider if a perceived or proclaimed limit is truly a limit and not artificially (or falsely) self-imposed. Given the great potential for self-deception, and our propensity to falsify and distort experience through personal fancy or fear, we may do better to approach authentic humility through our bodies rather than our minds. Though we might readily deceive with our ideas and words, our bodies, in a sense, speak for themselves. Though we might lie about our bodies, it is much more difficult to lie *through* them. Moreover, bodies are fundamental: it is in terms of them that we participate in and most basically approach reality. Whatever we know, believe, or experience, and thus also profess, depends upon points of access that each have their root and inspiration in a living body.[17]

In his remarkable essay "Body and Touch," Chrétien (following Aristotle) says, "The most fundamental and universal of all senses is the sense of touch. . . . While touch is separable from other senses . . . the sense of touch is inseparable from life itself: no animal is deprived of touch without also being deprived of life" (CR, 85). Touch, in other words, is coextensive with a living being. It defines us as creatures that must touch and be touched in order to be. Bathed in the mystery and complexity that life itself is, touch alerts us to what is so primordial as to elude our best efforts at comprehension.[18] We simply cannot imagine a human being without touch altogether. Obviously not all touch is intentional or conscious of itself as touching. This is why a person in a comatose or vegetative state is still (in the minimum activities of respiration and digestion) "in touch" with the world. As humans we are tactile beings immersed and embedded in a world of bodies. It is in terms of the vast and deep memberships of creation, what ecologists call "webs of interdependence," that we derive our nurture and inspiration, our very being. We live *through* others and could not possibly live alone.

This insight is of immense, but now mostly forgotten, significance. It is reflected in ancient spiritual traditions that recognize and celebrate rocks, trees, mountains, and springs as receptacles of a life-giving spirit, and in the Hebraic pronouncement in Genesis 3:19 that we come from and will also eventually (upon death) return to the soil. Indeed, the intimacy and ubiquity of our touching earthly bodies is conveyed in etymologies that identify humanity (*adam*) with the humus or life-giving layer of soil (*adamah*) that makes the earth come alive. Humility is the feature of a life that has adequately taken into account this body/earth relationship by honoring and strengthening the memberships of creation.[19] Preindustrial cultures, because of hunter-gatherer and agricultural patterns of life, would have understood more readily (even if they did not always honor) the intimacy and practicality of relationship that joins us to the world.[20] In the periods of modernity and postmodernity, as urbanization, industrialization, individualism, and consumerism come to dominate the practical shape of cultural life, the mass forgetting of our material, bodily interdependence—what we can call an "ecological/biological amnesia"—becomes much more likely.

Another way of putting this is to say that a proper understanding of humility depends upon an honest estimation of how we are placed in a physical and social world.[21] It includes a detailed and thorough accounting of the possibilities and responsibilities that follow from our placement. The humble person asks, "Being here, in this particular place, what is the proper and fitting (because attentive and respectful) thing for me to think and do?" When we let our arrogant or fearful foolishness control us, we are prevented from fully appreciating the precise nature of human limits that accompanies our being embodied in a place and embedded in a community. A sense for humility, or more precisely, the humble sense that follows from a deep and honest reckoning with our embodiment and embeddedness, is not something that we work ourselves into through an effort of the mind or tongue. It is rather a disposition and way of being that grows out of our faithful and nonevasive acknowledgment of our (material and spiritual) dependence upon others (worms, bees, chickens, photosynthesis, family, friends, teachers—the list goes on and on). When we are most honest and faithful, we bear witness to the many gifts from others of sustenance, inspiration, nurture, and sacrifice that are working themselves out in our lives. Failing this attention to and responsibility for our embodiment, we run the risk of misunderstanding, and thus also misrepresenting, humility.

What does our creaturely embodiment and embeddedness reveal about us, and how does this revelation contribute to an honest and true account of humility? Following Chrétien, we can describe the revelation as an encounter with excess, with "the excess of a human being over himself, an excess of what one is and can be over what one can think and comprehend."[22] It is simply impossible for us to name and know the myriad of bodies, ranging from microorganisms in the soil to stardust in faraway galaxies, which feed into our being. To be in a world is to be "exposed" to countless others, and to find oneself in a position wherefrom we must "respond" to them: have I honored their presence or compromised or violated it? Our exposure reveals the lie in every account of oneself as self-standing and alone, as self-justifying and autarchic. To respond to others, as Derrida notes, alerts us to a fundamental transitivity in all human life: "The sense of touch is first of all, like the sense of every sensation, a sense of consent; it is and has this sense: *yes, to consent*, which always, and in advance, implies transitivity (*yes to, to consent to*)."[23]

Our problem, however, is that we can never adequately or sufficiently account for or address what exceeds our comprehension or power. Our response forever falls short: we could never say "Thank you" or "I am sorry" enough. Chrétien is quick to point out that our falling short is neither a "contingent deficit nor a regrettable imperfection." "It is the very event of a wound by which our existence is altered and opened, and becomes itself the site of the manifestation of what it responds to."[24] Life is a perpetual passion play, an unfathomably costly drama in which vitality, suffering, and death inform, close, and again open possibilities. The wounded character of our speaking, a wound we experience intimately and inescapably through our eating and corruptible bodies, is the mark of our finitude and our dependence upon others. Through it we encounter ourselves not simply as a question (Augustine) but also as a paradox. I must appear to myself as impossible, since I could not bring about my own existence or the existence of the world in terms of which I live. Human experience is thus permeated and formed by a fundamental disproportion or incommensurability between itself and that which brings it about.

What is revealed in our embeddedness is a fundamental inability to objectify and comprehend our being placed. The conscious ego cannot constitute its place because it is always already, and overwhelmingly, constituted *by* place. Our bodies, understood as the bearers of speech, are thus the concrete site in terms of which we respond to an appeal from another that exceeds our powers to master and predict it. The highest possibility of speech, speech that is maximally attuned to our embeddedness and embodiment, would therefore be an act of praise in which we affirm and give thanks for the life-giving places that (inexplicably) make our being possible. "Our task is not to give an answer that would in some sense erase the initial provocation by corresponding to it, but to offer ourselves up as such in response, without assigning in advance any limit to the gift" (CR, 13). Our lives and our world are gifts. That we exist at all, and the dynamic set of possibilities that our lives represent, are features of how we have been "called," quite gratuitously, into existence by a creative word and a continually expressive creation.[25] The fitting, humble response is first to listen, and then to offer our lives as gifts to others in return.

When we offer ourselves we are not simply returning the gift. Self-offering is not of the same species as repayment, which presupposes economies of exchange in which we can estimate what sufficient repayment would be. Faced as we are with gifts that are inestimable in their being given, what we aim to do through our offerings is acknowledge and work to overcome the hubris, naiveté, or aggression that would claim the world as a possession or right. The offering of ourselves through humble service is thus a path of ascesis and purification leading us to our true creaturely humanity.

Life is a miraculous, inexplicable grace. It exceeds all economies of exchange. We all stand and eat within it, beggarlike, unable to receive it fully or properly because whatever we would take or claim already exceeds our longing and comprehension. In offering ourselves we do not often know what we are doing. Nor can we predict or control what our offering will accomplish. But in our acts of careful attention and humble thanksgiving we show ourselves to be mindful of our need, and the many gifts of creation available to meet it. We take seriously and respect the memberships of creation, and make the commitment to be faithful to them.

The Christological Relation

Our brief analysis of touch has shown us that "to be" is always already "to be in relation" with others. Life simply is being in relation. Those who are humble recognize this to be the most basic truth about their living, and so do what they can to honor the relationships they live through. It is simply wrong to presume too much for oneself, not because of some infection of self-loathing but because presumption represents a distortion and falsification of our place in the world. I have also suggested that an appreciation for interdependent life leads us into an understanding of people as creatures. What this means we now need to develop.

We should begin by observing how many people fear being in relation. It is easier and less threatening to assume the role of spectator, keeping others at a comfortable distance. Moreover, we are suspicious of the idea that we are fundamentally dependent on others because there is in this dependence such great potential for abuse. Others, as we well know, can turn our dependence to their advantage. And so we cling to the myth of a self-standing, self-regulating being, all the while ignoring the fact that what most needs our attention is the correction of relationships that have been distorted by sin. In other words, what we need is an account of how relationships are disfigured and how they can be made whole. The fact that we live in and through relationships does not automatically guarantee that we will live through them properly. We need an account of proper relationality.

For this account we can turn again to Bonaventure, who saw in Christ the archetype of all relations. Why, theologically speaking, is Christ this archetype? Most fundamentally it is because "All things came into being through him, and without him not one thing came into being. What has come into being in him was life, and the life was the light of all people" (John 1:3–4, cf. Colossians 1:15–20). Christ is the Word through whom all things are created. Given that this Word became flesh, we know that God remains profoundly in touch with creation: the world comes to be through the Word that has itself come into the world, which means that there is an intensity of intimacy at work between God and the world that surpasses all our imagining. What the incarnation of God communicates is that the relationships that constitute creation do not achieve their perfection until they approximate the intimacy and care that marks the relation between God and creation. The salvation of the world, as many of the early church fathers argued, depends upon a process of theiosis or divinization where we enter more deeply into the divine way of being. "Human beings are not truly themselves, are not truly flesh, until they have become flesh as he became flesh."[26] The pattern for proper relationality, in other words, is to be found in God's own ways of relating.

To appreciate this insight we must move beyond monarchical conceptions of creation that see the creative act as some sort of divine imposition. Rowan Williams has observed that we have misunderstood the logic of creation. As the creator of everything God does not exercise power over things, most basically because there is "nothing" (*creatio ex nihilo*) for God to exercise power over: "What creation emphatically isn't is any kind of imposition or manipulation: it is not God imposing on us divinely willed roles rather than the ones we 'naturally' might have, or defining us out of our own systems into God's. Creation affirms that to be here at all, to be a part of the natural order and to be the sort of thing capable of being named—or of having a role—is 'of God'; it *is* because God wants it so."[27] In other words, to be a creature means that we exist because of our relation to God, and depend upon God for our existence. How we choose to exist is not a feature of God's imposition but the result of our freedom to either acknowledge or refuse that relation.

Because God creates out of freedom and not through struggle—God's creative act is not an act of negotiation or domination (as in other creation myths)—we do not need to worry that God is somehow behind the scenes pulling strings. Rather, God's delight in the freedom of creation to be itself is grounded in God's own freedom. "With God alone, I am dealing with what does not need to construct or negotiate an identity, what is free to be itself without the process of struggle. Properly understood, this is the most liberating affirmation we could ever hear."[28] Because God did not have to create, the fact that there is a creation at all means that the divine creative action is to be understood as the work of love. God's way of being is a way that is "for others." To be God is to make room for others to be. What this "making room" for others, this hospitality, looks like in the flesh is most clearly to be seen in the ministries of feeding, healing, exorcism, forgiveness, mercy, and celebration as modeled for us in the life of Christ. To say that Christ is the archetype of relation, the one through whom the full potential of touch is best realized, is to understand that creation achieves its redemption when its memberships are characterized by vitality, health, justice, and freedom. Relationships that share in this redemptive work thus become the pattern for all right relationships.

If we think now again of how relation at its most fundamental level occurs through touch, then we should be able to appreciate how the practices of love and compassion must be the origin, medium, and goal of our living. As Chrétien puts it, "Only a thought of love . . . gives the flesh its full bearing of intellect and leads touch to its highest possibility" (CR, 129).[29] It is the touch of compassion that most properly leads us into the world and that most fully defines the character of our relationships, for in this touch we participate in the ongoing creative and sustaining work of the Creator.[30] This is work that is marked by detailed attention to the needs of all creation:

> You visit the earth and water it,
> you greatly enrich it;
> the river of God is full of water;
> you provide the people with grain,
> for so you have prepared it.
> You water its furrows abundantly,
> settling its ridges,
> softening it with showers,
> and blessing its growth. (Psalms 65:9–10)

This work is also marked by such Christological virtues as friendship (Jesus' concern for the family of Lazarus in John 11), tenderness (Jesus' healing of the hemorrhaging woman in Mark 5), mercy (Jesus' promise of paradise to the criminal in Luke 23), forgiveness (Jesus' unfailing welcome of Peter), and restoration of relationship (Jesus' healing of the lepers in Luke 17). God's intimacy with creation, as manifested in God's daily and sustaining touch, is the context that models and inspires all proper relationality.

The Flesh of Humility

It is not enough to characterize the humble person as one who appreciates the interdependence of created life, as one who understands that living is made possible through the receiving of gifts, and that speaking is always a responding to a primordial call. We need also to think more carefully about the character of our response. If it is true that we have been gripped by a world that speaks to us from all sides, how should we speak in return?[31] How should we speak through our bodies, put flesh on humility, since "there is no voice but the bodily voice" (CR, 83)? We cannot bear witness to humility in the abstract any more than we can speak without the organs of the body.

Chrétien tells us that the bodily voice is a "resounding voice that puts me, body and soul, in my entirety, to work in the world" (CR, 78). To appreciate the depth and revolutionary significance of this claim we must see it from the perspective of the relationships that characterize all created existence. Too often we confine speaking to the action of a mouth or think of our speaking as something we choose to do. We presuppose, in other words, that we could just as well not speak. But on Chrétien's and our theological reading, our not speaking is an impossibility. This is because we cannot choose not to be in relation any more than we can decide not to be in touch with others. As Aristotle put it long ago in *De Anima*, touch is coextensive with life itself (and death). Reality through and through is constituted by relationality.[32]

If this is true, then our dwelling and working in the world does not simply place us alongside others, as if we could choose to be with this or that other. Rather, from time immemorial, and for good or ill, we have always already participated in the life of others. We do not touch each other as spectators. Our relationships with others, whether we admit it or not, are far more intimate and involved than that. It is the nature of this participatory touch that we now need to understand.

Touch is unique among the senses because it entails reciprocity and reversibility (though not necessarily symmetry). When I touch another I am at the same time being touched. Touch thus has the peculiar quality of enabling me to feel myself. "I feel myself only by the favor of the other. It is the other who gives me to myself insofar as the return to myself and my own actions or affections always supposes this other. . . . I never start by saying 'I'" (CR, 120). Moreover, I discover another and feel myself not through any particular, isolatable sense organ. As Aristotle put it, "touch is not a single sense but many" (*De Anima*, II:11). We cannot control or direct the sense of touch since we are always already immersed in a world beyond our knowing and comprehension.

Our immersion in touch should not be taken to mean that the difference between self and other is therefore obliterated. When I reach out to another, as when I grab another's hand, there is still a gap: "proximity always includes some minimal remoteness" (CR, 88). Besides being a warning against all claims to complete comprehension, this distance or gap is of the highest significance for understanding the character of our relationships. Graham Ward has put it well when he observes, "Only when there is space, where there is distance, where there is difference, can there be the love that desires, that draws, that seeks participation."[33] We need the space between self and other so that we can learn to act on another's behalf, learn to suffer with others in their struggles and share in their joys. When we obliterate the boundaries between self and others, we destroy the prospect of any self-possession, which could then open up into "a free dispossession for the sake of the other"—the very mark of compassion.[34]

The movement between self and other is difficult for us to understand because we have grown so accustomed to thinking of persons first as freestanding agents who then decide to enter into relationship. But if we start with relation, as our treatment of the call/response structure of experience compels us to, then we discover that all selves are constituted by the exchange itself. Who I am is a feature of the relationships that exist before I can self-identify. "I never start by saying 'I.' I start by being 'thou-ed' by the world" (CR, 120).

Again, the best way to understand this is theologically. Creation is the concrete manifestation of the Creator's own Trinitarian life.[35] Insofar as we exist at all we participate in the ways of grace. The intimacy of relation that grace communicates can be better appreciated when we remember that the Hebrew word for grace (*hen*) carries the connotation of the life-giving womb (*rehem*). The fetus depends entirely on the womb for its life, participates fully in the life of the mother, but is not dissolved into the mother. The fetus remains itself, though not as a self-standing being. That it is and what it is are a feature of the relationships it lives through. In a similar way, our existence is womblike to the extent that it is "in" God that we move and have our being (Acts 17:28). Without God's continuous, intimate, life-giving Spirit and breath, we all would, as the Psalmist said, "die and return to their dust" (Psalms 104:27–30).

This way of speaking should not surprise us since it is the reflection of God's own Trinitarian life.[36] As theologians struggled to make sense of God's life as reflected in God's involvement with creation, they found the term *perichoresis* particularly helpful. *Perichoresis* means something like reciprocal participation or interpenetration. The three persons of the Trinity do not exist alongside each other. If they did we would move quickly to a notion of Tritheism. The Three are so closely related that they form a single divine dance. Father, Son, and Holy Spirit perform a work together. Their togetherness is so intimate that we cannot really speak of any of the members as individuals. What we have here is a fellowship of love, the sense that relationality is the very core of the divine way of being.

While this talk about the Trinity may seem abstract, it yields a most practical and revolutionary insight: "In God, there are no individuals; the Three dwell in each other so completely that we cannot divide them, one from another. And so we too are called to live lives of mutual participation, in which our relationships are not just something that we 'have,' but are what constitute us as human beings."[37] The early Christian communities understood something about this practicality since it led them to set up economic practices of sharing and benevolence that would not have made sense if they did not see the identity of each member in terms of the well-being of the whole (cf. Acts 2:44–45). These early Christians understood that they do not exist as individuals, and so were willing, even saw it as "natural," that they should sell what they have, give it to the poor, and live economically in such a way as to hold things in common.

When we learn to appreciate how our relationships with one another constitute our being, then we can understand why the apostle Paul stressed the importance of the upbuilding of the body of Christ. As he repeatedly states, to become a follower of God means that the self no longer lives as a self-standing, self-justifying being: "I have been crucified with Christ; and it is no longer I who live but Christ who lives in me" (Galatians 2:19–20). As ones who have "the mind of Christ" (I Corinthians 2:16), Christians are to live in such a way as to manifest and continue the healing, feeding, and forgiving work modeled by him. The focus of human life is thus shifted to the noble but practical and mundane work of protecting and strengthening the relationships we live through.

What we can now see is that flesh of humility is the sort of life in which our bodies are sympathetically in tune with the bodies of creation. The humble person is one who has grasped the "nothingness" of solitary life. There is no life apart from relation, apart from our mutual participation in the life of each other. This is why humble people do not try to stand out from others. They realize that an appropriate human life is one dedicated to serving others. Our attempts to stand out represent denials of the fact that we need each other and are constituted through the gifts we daily receive and can then share again. Because we are constantly in touch with each other, we bear the marks of each other in our bodies. Or as Chrétien would put it, we each carry the voices of the whole world within our own voice. What we need to do is learn to carry the voices of others in a way that respects them and brings honor to their Creator. "To sing the world is to try and concentrate its profuse and confused choir in the tremulous clarity of our own voice" (AS, 129). For us to sing the world our speech must first become hospitable by participation in the primordial, divine hospitality that continuously creates times and places in which the members of creation can thrive.

Owing to the presence of so much sin in the world, of so many disordered and assaulted relationships, the song we sing will often have the character of the lament. Lament presupposes that we have first become attentive to others, see their pain and suffering, and so can exercise compassion. If we are attentive to each other, as humble persons must be, then we will appreciate that suffering with others is an essential ingredient of current creaturely life, not because we prize the suffering but because we resist the distortion and violence that undermines creation. Our suffering, however, is not without hope, since it is "joined with all the living" (Ecclesiastes 9:4). If we lived as individuals, like the Babylonians who proclaimed "I am, and there is no one besides me," then our suffering would indeed be one long, bleak night. But humility rises out of a primordial and communal[38] affirmation of the goodness of relation and sees in our relatedness cause for gratitude and praise. "Only praise can make lamentation possible, for only love can really suffer. If there were nothing in the world for which we could give thanks, a lament would merely form an empty vociferation. Only the light shows the darkness as darkness, only beauty can be the index of ugliness" (AS, 145).

Touching/Witnessing God

One of the defining and most important features of a humble life is that it bears witness to the interdependent character of all life. Humble people demonstrate through their attention and kindness that we are all the beneficiaries of gift upon gift, and that the most fitting and honest response is to name these gifts and then honor them by cherishing and caring for them. Gratitude, praise, and celebration are the marks of the humble worship that grows seamlessly out of a life that is faithful to the many memberships of creation. Through our compassionate touch we bear witness to the divine, creative, sustaining compassion that is continually in touch with the world.

What this means is that love and compassion as touch's highest possibilities are never simply or merely of profane or pragmatic significance. Commenting on Thomas Aquinas, Chrétien observes that the transitivity of touch leads beyond the finite to the infinite. The touch of love moves from physical contact to the grace of God at work in all created things. As Aquinas says in *De Veritate* 28:3, "God himself touches the soul by causing grace in it." There is therefore, in our proper handling of creation, a touching of God, or mutual contact between Creator and creation (CR, 129). The witness of humility is therefore, and at the same time, a witness to God.

If this is the case, then we should not be surprised to hear the Psalmist say, "O taste and see that the Lord is good" (Psalms 34:8), or discover mystics who turn bodily senses into spiritual faculties for the discernment of the divine. In *The Journey of the Mind to God*, Bonaventure offers a remarkable meditation on precisely this theme. In order for the soul to be purified and perfected it must pattern its life on the ministry of Jesus Christ, the Word through whom all creation is what it is. Following this conformity to Christ the senses of hearing, sight, smell, taste, and touch are themselves reformed so that we can enjoy sweet communion with our Maker. Bonaventure is clear that the senses, what he calls "the experience of the affections," count for more than the considerations of the mind. When our senses have been restored by Christ we are enabled "to see what is most beautiful, to hear what is most harmonious, to smell what is most fragrant, to taste what is most sweet, and to embrace what is most delightful."[39] Because the Word has become flesh, we are through love made capable of touching the Word (CR, 129–30).

Though God is not the sort of being that can literally or physically be touched, it still makes sense to employ the language of touch in this context. The reason the refinement of touch is so important is that it better opens and attunes us to the grace of God at work in the world. Only as we give ourselves over completely to others, body and soul—is this why sexual intimacy and vulnerability are taken by scripture to be the high point of knowledge?—do we become maximally sensitive. Without such fine sensitivity Aquinas argued that we cannot have a fine intelligence. What our study has shown is that the ground for such sensitivity and intelligence cannot be prepared without the disposition of humility. Humility trains us in the art of being creatures. It does so by teaching us to be honest about our need, grateful for the gifts of others, and faithful in the service of healing the many memberships of creation. As an indispensable disposition in every spiritual life, humility prepares us to welcome our Creator and enter into our highest calling—friendship with God.

Notes

Introduction
Bruce Ellis Benson

1. Dominique Janicaud, "The Theological Turn of French Phenomenology," in Dominique Janicaud et al., *Phenomenology and the "Theological Turn": The French Debate* (New York: Fordham University Press, 2000).

2. The conference on the theological turn was held at Samford University, in Birmingham, Alabama, in 2006.

3. Edmund Husserl, *Cartesian Meditations: An Introduction to Phenomenology*, trans. Dorion Cairns (The Hague: Martinus Nijhoff, 1973), 57.

4. Edmund Husserl, *Ideas Pertaining to a Pure Phenomenology and to a Phenomenological Philosophy: First Book, General Introduction to a Pure Phenomenology*, trans. Fred Kersten (The Hague: Martinus Nijhoff, 1982), 44.

5. Edmund Husserl, *The Idea of Phenomenology*, trans. Lee Hardy (Dordrecht: Kluwer, 1999), 63.

6. Edmund Husserl, *Introduction to the Logical Investigations*, trans. Philip J. Bossert and Curtis H. Peters (The Hague: Martinus Nijhoff, 1975), 27.

7. Jacques Derrida, Jean-Luc Marion, and Richard Kearney, "On the Gift: A Discussion between Jacques Derrida and Jean-Luc Marion," in *God, the Gift, and Postmodernism*, ed. John D. Caputo and Michael J. Scanlon (Bloomington: Indiana University Press, 1999), 66.

8. Janicaud, "The Theological Turn of French Phenomenology," 27.

9. Peter Jonkers and Ruud Welten, *God in France: Eight Contemporary French Thinkers on God* (Leuven: Peeters, 2005).

10. As Hent de Vries would have it; see his *Philosophy and the Turn to Religion* (Baltimore: Johns Hopkins University Press, 1999).

11. Jean-Luc Marion, *God Without Being*, trans. Thomas A. Carlson (Chicago: University of Chicago Press, 1991).

Continuing to Look for *God in France:* On the Relationship Between Phenomenology and Theology
J. Aaron Simmons

1. Peter Jonkers and Ruud Welten, eds., *God in France: Eight Contemporary French Thinkers on God* (Leuven: Peeters, 2005). See my review of this book in *Bulletin de la Société Américaine de Philosophie de Langue Française* 15, no. 2 (Fall 2005): 99–105.

2. Dominique Janicaud, "The Theological Turn of French Phenomenology," trans. Bernard G. Prusak, in *Phenomenology and the "Theological Turn": The French Debate* (New York: Fordham University Press, 2000), originally published as *Le tournant théologique de la phénomenologie française* (Combas: Editions de l'éclat, 1991).

3. Although he is not included in *God in France*, we should add Jean-Louis Chrétien to this list.

4. Janicaud, "Theological Turn," 99ff.

5. Elsewhere I have used some of the ideas in this section (viz., that phenomenology does not prima facie exclude God-talk) to advocate the importance of a particular type of God-talk for contemporary continental *political* philosophy. See J. Aaron Simmons, "Is Continental Philosophy Just Catholicism for Atheists? On the Political Relevance of *Kenosis*," *Philosophy in the Contemporary World* 15, no. 1 (Spring 2008): 94–111. The quotation here is from Peter Jonkers, "God in France: Heidegger's Legacy," in Jonkers and Welten, *God in France*, 1–42, 8.

6. Bernard G. Prusak, "Translator's Introduction," in Janicaud, *Phenomenology and the "Theological Turn": The French Debate*, 3–15, 3–4.

7. See Martin Heidegger, *Four Seminars: Le Thor 1966, 1968, 1969, Zähringen 1973*, trans. Andrew Mitchell and Francis Raffoul (Bloomington: Indiana University Press, 2003).

8. Edmund Husserl, *Ideas Pertaining to a Pure Phenomenology and to a Phenomenological Philosophy: First Book, General Introduction to a Pure Phenomenology*, trans. Fred Kersten (The Hague: Martinus Nijhoff, 1982), §24.

9. Husserl, *Ideas*, §58.

10. Janicaud, "Theological Turn," 26.

11. Ibid., 27.

12. John Rawls, *Political Liberalism* (New York: Columbia University Press, 1993), 134–35.

13. Guido Vanheeswijck, "Every Man Has a God or an Idol: René Girard's View of Christianity and Religion," in Jonkers and Welten, *God in France*, 68–95.

14. Johan Goud, "This Extraordinary Word: Emmanuel Levinas on God," trans. Lydia Penner, in Jonkers and Welten, *God in France*, 96–118, 99.

15. Ruud Welten, "God Is Life: On Michel Henry's Arch-Christianity," in Jonkers and Welten, *God in France*, 119–42.

16. Ruud Welten, "The Paradox of God's Appearance: On Jean-Luc Marion," in Jonkers and Welten, *God in France*, 186–206.

17. Heidegger, *Four Seminars,* 80.

18. I am indebted to Scott Aikin for helpful suggestions on the previous two paragraphs.

19. Namely, Kant's Sublime. See Jean-Luc Marion, "The Saturated Phenomenon," trans. Thomas A. Carlson, in *Phenomenology and the "Theological Turn,"* 176–216 (*De sucroît: Etudes sur les phénomènes saturés* [Paris: Presses Universitaires de France, 2001]).

20. This fact leads Welten to contend, "Phenomenologically speaking, such 'theological remains' land Marion in trouble in *God Without Being*" ("The Paradox of God's Appearance," 198).

21. See Jean-Yves Lacoste, *Experience and the Absolute: Disputed Questions on the Humanity of Man*, trans. Mark Raftery-Skehan (New York: Fordham University, 2005) (*Expérience et Absolu: Questions disputes sur l'humanité de l'homme* [Paris: Presses Universitaires de France, 1994]).

22. See Jean-Louis Chrétien, "The Wounded Word: Phenomenology of Prayer," trans. Jeffrey L. Kosky and Thomas A. Carlson, in *Phenomenology and the "Theological Turn": The French Debate*, 147–75.

23. Jonkers, "God in France," 7.

24. See Hent de Vries, *Philosophy and the Turn to Religion* (Baltimore: Johns Hopkins University Press, 1999); and *Religion and Violence: Philosophical Perspectives from Kant to Derrida* (Baltimore: Johns Hopkins University Press, 2002).

25. Jonkers, "God in France," 8.

26. Chris Doude van Troostwijk, "Phrasing God: Lyotard's Hidden Philosophy of Religion," trans. Maarten Doude van Troostwijk, in *God in France*, 165–85, 165.

27. See Emmanuel Levinas, *Otherwise Than Being or Beyond Essence*, trans. Alphonso Lingis (Pittsburgh: Duquesne University Press, 1997), 160–62.

28. Emmanuel Levinas, *God, Death, and Time*, trans. Bettina Bergo (Stanford: Stanford University Press, 2000), 204.

29. Levinas, *Otherwise Than Being*, xlviii.

30. Levinas, *God, Death, and Time*, 224.

31. Jacques Derrida, *The Gift of Death*, trans. David Wills (Chicago: University of Chicago Press, 1995), 108.

32. It could be argued that this decidedly religious concern is only present in Derrida's later writings and, hence, that Jonkers's contention is rightly more applicable to Derrida's early work. Although I cannot adequately consider this division in Derrida's authorship here, it should be noted that an argument can be made for understanding the religious aspect of Derrida's thought as more properly being an ethico-political trajectory. If this is indeed the case, then Derrida's contestation of an ethico-political turn in his thought is strikingly relevant. As Derrida writes in *Rogues*: "there never was in the 1980s or 1990s, as has sometimes been claimed, a *political turn* or *ethical turn* in 'deconstruction,' at least not

as I experience it. The thinking of the political has always been a thinking of différance and the thinking of différance always a thinking *of* the political, of the contour and limits of the political, especially around the enigma or the autoimmune *double bind* of the democratic" (*Rogues: Two Essays on Reason*, trans. Pascale-Anne Brault and Michael Naas (Stanford: Stanford University Press, 2005), 39.

33. Welten, "God Is Life," 125.

34. Welten, "The Paradox of God's Appearance," 197.

35. Ibid., 206.

36. Goud, "This Extraordinary Word: Emmanuel Levinas on God," 99.

37. Ibid., 98.

38. Ibid., 112.

39. I am indebted to J. Caleb Clanton for some of this terminology. He applies the terms "separatist" to thinkers, like John Rawls, who advocate an elimination of religion from the public square, and "reconstructivist" to those, like Richard Rorty and Cornell West, who allow religion back in, but provided it is substantially stripped of its doctrinal particularity (Clanton, *Religion and Democratic Citizenship: Inquiry and Conviction in the American Public Square* [Lanham, MD: Lexington Books, 2007]). Robert Audi and Nicholas Wolterstorff also use the term "separatist" to describe the predominant liberal attitude regarding religion in the public square (*Religion in the Public Square: The Place of Religious Convictions in Political Debate* [Lanham, MD: Rowman & Littlefield, 1997]).

40. Janicaud, "Theological Turn," 27.

41. Schaeffer was one of the most influential twentieth-century advocates of a distinctively Christian "worldview." See Francis Schaeffer, *How Should We Then Live? The Rise and Decline of Western Thought and Culture* (Old Tappan, NJ: Fleming H. Revell, 1976).

42. Rico Sneller, "God as War: Derrida on Divine Violence," in Jonkers and Welten, *God in France*, 143–64, 163.

43. Ibid., 154.

44. van Troostwijk, "Phrasing God: Lyotard's Hidden Philosophy of Religion," 184.

45. Ruud Welten, "The Paradox of God's Appearance," 195.

46. Jonkers, "God in France," 38.

47. Joeri Schrijvers, "Phenomenology, Liturgy, and Metaphysics: The Thought of Jean-Yves Lacoste," in Jonkers and Welten, *God in France*, 207–25, 225.

48. Merold Westphal, *Overcoming Onto-Theology: Toward a Postmodern Christian Faith* (New York: Fordham University Press, 2001).

49. I am not saying that one must be a Christian to appropriate Christian themes. Rather, I am simply saying that far too often borrowing from a tradition can simply mask an unwillingness to actually engage a tradition on its own terms.

50. Importantly, I am not saying postmodernism *is* patronizing. I am merely raising the awareness of the dangers that accompany *all* reconstructivist strategies.

This danger is an ethical reality and it should continue to press upon all post-modern philosophy of religion. The worry about patronizing religious believers is really a worry that reconstruction can too often become merely a hidden variant of separatism. I do want to note that the work of Levinas and Derrida in particular offers crucial resources for addressing this worry. Due to their affirmation of the reality of responsibility, Levinas and Derrida recognize the ethico-political stakes that accompany all discourse. This ethical awareness is something that is lacking, for example, in Richard Rorty's reconstructivist approach to religion in the public square. Levinas and Derrida attempt to rethink how to take religious belief seriously after the death of metaphysics and thereby allow a renewed engagement with religious believers. For Rorty, however, reconstruction is just another way of excluding certain people from public discourse. This can be seen when Rorty's essay "Religion as a Conversation Stopper" (in *Philosophy and Social Hope* [London: Penguin Books, 1999]) is read alongside his more recent collaboration with Gianni Vattimo in *The Future of Religion*, ed. Santiago Zabala (New York: Columbia University Press, 2005). In the former essay, Rorty is a thoroughgoing separatist. In the latter, he appears to have revised his position and actually allows for religious belief if it has been properly reconstructed. Despite all appearances, however, Rorty has merely allowed for religion *if* it is understood as a certain brand of pragmatic social hope. We should notice that this social hope was the very thing that Rorty advocated in the former essay without explicitly terming it "religion." So, the apparent transformation in his thought is really only a change in rhetoric and not in substance. This is what I mean by the dangerous patronizing aspect that can accompany a discussion of religion that maintains its form without any of the substance. I am thankful to John Caputo for suggesting I make this clarification.

51. Plato, *Euthyphro*, trans. G. M. A. Grube, in *Plato: Complete Works*, ed. John Cooper (Indianapolis: Hackett, 1997), 14c.

52. It should be noted that Adriaan Peperzak argues for the continued relevance of "natural theology." See *Reason In Faith: On the Relevance of Christian Spirituality for Philosophy* (New York: Paulist Press, 1999), Chapter 5.

53. What this apologetic enterprise would look like and how it would operate can be sketched only briefly here. However, I do want to note that it is something of an open question whether this apologetics could actually be a positive defense rather than a negative limit. For good examples of what a positive trajectory might entail, see Merold Westphal, *Overcoming Onto-Theology: Toward a Postmodern Christian Faith*; James K. A. Smith, *Speech and Theology: Language and the Logic of the Incarnation* (New York: Routledge, 2002); Deane-Peter Baker and Patrick Maxwell, eds., *Explorations in Contemporary Continental Philosophy of Religion* (Amsterdam: Rodopi, 2003); and James H. Olthius, ed., *Knowing Other-Wise: Philosophy at the Threshold of Spirituality* (New York: Fordham University Press, 1997).

54. Peperzak, *Reason in Faith*, 129.

Being Without God

Jeffrey Bloechl

1. This has been Jean-François Courtine's characterization of the impact of Derrida. See D. Janicaud, ed., *Heidegger en France. II. Entretiens* (Paris: Albin Michel, 2001), 53.

2. A third possibility ought not to be overlooked, though it undoubtedly calls for separate attention. When the early Heidegger assimilates genuine thinking with philosophy, which for its part can supply faith with every necessary critical corrective, it should asked whether on his account theology *needs* to think. The better-known view (*Being and Timet* §10) that theology, as anthropology, is only an ontical science is uninteresting because it dispenses with all of the genuine difficulties. For a subtle examination of these difficulties, see the translators' commentary by J. Hart and J. C. Maraldo in M. Heidegger, *The Piety of Thinking* (Bloomington: Indiana University Press, 1976), 108–19.

3. See Martin Heidegger, "On the Essence of Truth," in *Pathways*, ed. W. McNeill (Cambridge: Cambridge University Press, 1998), 149–150.

4. E.g., *Philosophy of Right*, §6.

5. For exemplary clarification and analysis, see T. Sheehan, *Karl Rahner: The Philosophical Foundations* (Athens: Ohio University Press, 1987), 110–18.

6. Jean-Luc Marion, *God Without Being* (Chicago: University of Chicago Press, 1991), 37–49.

7. Jean-Yves Lacoste, *Experience and the Absolute* (New York: Fordham University Press, 2004), 200–201, n. 9. My analysis of this feature of Rahner's philosophy of religion and certain consequences drawn in my subsequent two paragraphs follow Lacoste.

8. Here one finds cause for new interest in Heidegger's suggestion, in his reading of Hölderlin, that "Nature" is an alias of the Sacred. See, e.g., Martin Heidegger, *Elucidations of Hölderlin's Poetry*, ed. K. Hoeller (Amherst, NY: Humanity Books, 2000), 85.

9. Karl Rahner, *Hearer of the Word* (New York: Continuum, 1994), 9 and 138. Rahner is far from insensitive to the phenomenon that prompts this thought. See, e.g., 135, where it is observed that: revelation transpires only in the lived history of "*some* individual human beings" (his emphasis).

10. Parenthetically, if there is anything like a guiding impulse for the specifically French approach to these matters, it seems to me to lie here, in a long engagement with the complexities of a form of life and way of thinking that make no appeal to faith, and a deep sensitivity to the fact that they are sustainable not only in concepts but also as culture. This has been explored in a lifetime of work by the religious sociologist and historian, Emile Poulat.

11. He did of course offer such a word, and more than once. As he said in a 1951 conversation with students in Zurich, "God and Being are not identical, and I would never attempt to think the essence of God according to Being. . . . I think very modestly of Being with regard to its suitability for thinking the essence of God theologically. With Being nothing can be done in this area." The

text of this conversation seems to have been published only in limited circulation. I cite Jean Beaufret's report in *La Quinzaine littéraire* 196 (1974): 3.

12. As I have shown elsewhere, the correspondence contains an interesting resonance. Each of the three theological virtues—faith, hope, love—reappear in Heidegger's philosophy during the period of his *Beiträge*, only to flesh out a way of life that is oriented to accepting the implications of godlessness. See Jeffrey Bloechl, "Being and the Promise," in Neal Deroo and John Panteleimon Manoussakis, eds., *Phenomenology and Eschatology* (London: Ashgate, 2009), 121–130.

13. Arguments to this effect include, most forcefully, Emmanuel Levinas, *Existence and Existents* (Pittsburgh: Duquesne University Press, 2001).

The Appearing and the Irreducible
Jean-Yves Lacoste, translated by Christina M. Gschwandtner

1. *Husserliana: Edmund Husserls Gesammelte Werke* (The Hague: Martinus Nijhoff, 1950), III/1 and III/2. Henceforth cited as Hua; Eng. trans. F. Kersten, *Ideas Pertaining to a Pure Phenomenology and to a Phenomenological Philosophy: First Book, General Introduction to a Pure Phenomenology* (The Hague: Martinus Nijhoff, 1982).

2. Notably Hua XXXVIII (*Wahrnehmung und Aufmerksamkeit: Texte aus dem Nachlass (1893–1912)*, 3–123.

3. See, for example, Hua XXXIV (*Zur phänomenologischen Reduktion: Texte aus dem Nachlass (1926–1935)*, 8, 10.

4. Hua III/1, §24.

5. To my knowledge, Husserl never discusses the Aristotelian concept of existence. "Existenzurteil," however, is a term he employs often. See, for example, Hua III/1, 62; *Ideas*, 58.

6. Hua III/1; *Ideas*, §49.

7. See, for example, Hua XXXVII (*Einleitung in die Ethik: Vorlesungen Sommersemester 1920 und 1924*), 65 (in regard to moral works, which are binding on both angels and humans).

8. See, for example, Hua XXXIV, 11. It is here a matter of a transcendental reduction that permits us to reach pure subjectivity and not eidetic reduction. But the work on this topic is identical in both cases.

9. Hua III/1; *Ideas*, §27.

10. Hua III/1 63, line 23; *Ideas*, 58.

11. Ibid., line 32; ibid., 59. Husserl does not know how to describe the process that puts us into the natural attitude differently. See Hua XXXIV, 9–15.

12. Hua III/1; *Ideas*, §27.

13. See note 2.

14. The equivalence between "belief" and "persuasion," *Überzeugung*, is affirmed for example in Hua XXXIV, 14, which affirms clearly that we do not abandon them when we engage in an act of reduction, but that we are content with not using them.

15. Hua III/1; *Ideas*, §24.

16. One should not forget here that *Experience and Judgment*, published post-humously in 1939, was compiled by Landgrebe with the help of manuscripts of which the majority are not "late," and that this book can serve as well as an introduction to the phenomenological project as the *Logical Investigations*.

17. An excellent illustration of this distinction is found in Hans Burkhardt and Barry Smith, eds., *Handbook of Metaphysics and Ontology* (Munich: Philosophia, 1991), 365–71, who find it necessary to have different authors treat "the early Husserl" and "the late Husserl."

18. Hua III/1, 104; *Ideas*, 110 ("*Vernichtung der Dingwelt*") ("annihilation of the world of physical things").

19. See Hua XXXVII, for example, 68.

20. Hua III/1; *Ideas*, §29, does not say that intersubjectivity is "in fact" in the world of the natural attitude. But he does speak of a "naturally intersubjective world."

21. The best exposition of this myth is found in the Sixth Cartesian Meditation due to Fink (Hua Dokumente II/1 and II/2). On Fink's "contribution" to Husserl's philosophy, see Ronald Bruzina, *Edmund Husserl and Eugen Fink: Beginnings and Ends in Phenomenology* (New Haven: Yale University Press, 2004).

22. Hua III/1; *Ideas*, §32.

23. Witness of these efforts Hua XII (contains *Philosophie der Arithmetik*, trans. Dallas Willard, *Philosophy of Arithmetic: Psychological and Logical Investigations* (Dordrecht: Kluwer, 2003), XIII, XIV (vols. 1 and 2 of *Zur Phänomenologie der Intersubjectivität*). Useful commentaries (and interpretations different from mine) in Natalie Depraz, *Transcendance et incarnation: le statut de l'intersubjectivité comme altérité à soi chez Husserl* (Paris: Vrin, 1995).

24. See *Die Idee der Phänomenologie: Fünf Vorlesungen*, Hua II, 62: "möglichst wenig Verstand, aber möglichst reine Intuition. . . . Und die ganze Kunst besteht darin, rein dem schauenden Auge das Wort zu lassen"; Eng. trans. Lee Hardy, *The Idea of Phenomenology* (The Hague: Martinus Nijhoff, 1999): "as little interpretation as possible, as much pure intuition as possible. . . .The whole trick here is to let the seeing eye have its say" (46–47).

25. The Heideggerian *Fürsorge*, in fact (see *Sein und Zeit*, §26), comes without requiring language, whose presence is not essential. But Heidegger's point of departure is radically different from Husserl's: the presence of the existing other (of the other *Dasein*) is admitted axiomatically and the phenomenological task is to describe the concrete modes of *Mitdasein*; *Being and Time*, trans. John Macquarrie and Edward Robinson (New York: Harper & Row, 1962).

26. The only Wittgensteinian parallel to Husserl's embarrassment with intersubjectivity is his discussion of "private language" (Ludwig Wittgenstein, *Philosophical Investigations*, trans. G. E. M. Anscombe [New York: Macmillan, 1953] §§243ff—but Saul Kripke has the discussion begin at §202).

27. Hua III/1, 32; *Ideas*, 27. Noting, however, that speaking of the transcendence and of the immanence of God in respect to conscience, Husserl specifies

that one must here admit the reality of other modes of immanence and of transcendence than those which are given in the appearance of things, hence of the world (Hua III/1, 109; *Ideas*, 116–17). But it remains clear that the transcendence of God, phenomenologically speaking, can be put aside (ibid., §58).

28. Olegario González de Cardenal, *Dios* (Salamanca: Ediciones Sígueme, 2004).

29. It becomes in any case reducible when "reduction," sliding from the status of eidetic reduction to that of transcendental reduction, ceases to have as goal the best knowledge possible of the other than itself and assigns itself the goal of reaching consciousness in all its purity. See, for example, Hua XXXV (*Einleitung in die Philosophie: Vorlesungen 1922/23*), §§15–25, or Hua XXXIV.

30. *Fides quaerens intellectum*: *Gesamtausgabe* II/13, 97; *Anselm: Fides Quaerens Intellectum* (Richmond, VA: John Knox Press, 1960).

31. *Formale und transzendentale Logik*, Hua XVII, 169; Eng. trans. Dorion Cairns, *Formal and Transcendental Logic* (The Hague: Martinus Nijhoff, 1978), 161.

32. See Jean-Yves Lacoste, "Liturgie et coaffection," in *Présence et parousie* (Geneva: Ad Solem, 2006), 45–61; Eng. trans. Jeffrey L. Kosky, "Liturgy and Coaffection," in *The Experience of God: A Postmodern Response*, ed. Kevin Hart and Barbara Wall (New York: Fordham University Press, 2005), 93–103.

33. Hans Urs von Balthasar, who claimed not to owe anything to phenomenology, gives an exemplarily precise lecture on this: see *Glaubhaft ist nur Liebe* (Einsiedeln, Switzerland: Johannes Verlag, 1963), 49–71; Eng. trans. D. C. Schindler, *Love Alone Is Credible* (San Francisco: Ignatius Press, 2004). This booklet permits us to posit one further thesis: the existence of the one whom we love could not be placed between brackets without ipso facto being misconstrued.

34. One could complete this with the aid of Bultmann's classic analyses in "Welchen Sinn hat es, von Gott zu reden?" in Rudolf Karl Bultmann, *Glauben und Verstehen I* (Tübingen: Mohr Siebeck, 1933), 26–37; Eng. trans. Robert Walter Funk, *Faith and Understanding I* (London: SCM Press, 1969).

"it / is true"
Kevin Hart

1. See Italo Calvino, *Invisible Cities*, trans. William Weaver (New York: Harcourt Brace Jovanovich, 1974). For "free phantasy," see Edmund Husserl, *Ideas Pertaining to a Pure Phenomenology and to a Phenomenological Philosophy: First Book*, One: *General Introduction to a Pure Phenomenology*, trans. Fred Kersten (Boston: Kluwer, 1983), §70.

2. See Claude Romano, *Le chant de la vie: Phénoménologie de Faulkner* (Paris: Gallimard, 2005).

3. See Husserl, "Une lettre de Husserl à Hofmannsthal," January 12, 1907, trans. Eliane Escoubas, *La part de l'oeil: Revue annuelle des arts plastiques* 7 (1991): 14. Also see Martin Heidegger, "The Origin of the Work of Art," in *Poetry, Language, Thought*, trans. Albert Hofstadter (New York: Harper & Row, 1971);

Roman Ingarden, *The Literary Work of Art: An Investigation of Ontology, Logic, and Theory of Literature*, trans. George G. Grabowicz (Evanston, IL: Northwestern University Press, 1973); Maurice Merleau-Ponty, "Eye and Mind," in *The Primacy of Perception and Other Essays on Phenomenological Psychology, the Philosophy of Art, History and Politics*, trans. James M. Edie (Evanston, IL: Northwestern University Press, 1964); and Mikel Dufrenne, *Phenomenology of Aesthetic Experience*, trans. Edward Casey et al. (Evanston, IL: Northwestern University Press, 1973).

4. "September Song" first appeared in *Stand* 8, no. 4 (1967): 41. The poem was revised a little for publication in *King Log*. In the magazine publication there is a semicolon between "been" and "untouchable" in the first line, no commas around "sufficient," and "zyklon" is not given a capital "Z." Also, the lapidary inscription is divided by a semicolon rather than a dash; in the later version it resembles more closely dates of birth and death.

5. See Wallace Stevens, "The Poems of Our Climate," *Collected Poems* (New York: Knopf, 1954), 193.

6. See Richard L. Rubenstein, *After Auschwitz: History, Theology, and Contemporary Judaism*, 2nd ed. (Baltimore: Johns Hopkins University Press, 1992). See in particular Rubenstein's reflection on the first edition of 1966 in his new preface.

7. Unless indicated otherwise, all quotations from Geoffrey Hill's poetry will be from his *Collected Poems* (London: Penguin, 1985). "September Song" was originally collected in Hill's second volume of verse, *King Log* (London: André Deutsch, 1968).

8. Maurice Merleau-Ponty, "Everywhere and Nowhere," in *Signs*, trans. Richard C. McCleary (Evanston, IL: Northwestern University Press, 1964), 157.

9. Derek Attridge, "'This Strange Institution Called Literature': An Interview with Jacques Derrida," in Jacques Derrida, *Acts of Literature*, ed. Derek Attridge (New York: Routledge, 1992), 41.

10. See Michel Henry, *The Essence of Manifestation*, trans. Girard Etzkorn (The Hague: Martinus Nijhoff, 1973), section IV.

11. Jacques Derrida, *Speech and Phenomena and Other Essays on Husserl's Theory of Signs*, trans. David B. Allison (Evanston, IL: Northwestern University Press, 1973), 46.

12. See Franz Brentano, *Psychology from an Empirical Standpoint*, trans. A. C. Rancurello, D. B. Terrell, and L. L. McAlister, 2nd ed. (London: Routledge, 1995), 198.

13. David V. Erdman, ed., *The Complete Poetry and Prose of William Blake* (Berkeley: University of California Press, 1982), 409.

14. The point was first made by Jon Silkin in his "The Poetry of Geoffrey Hill," first published in 1972 and reprinted in Harold Bloom's anthology *Geoffrey Hill* (New York: Chelsea House, 1986), 20. I am thankful to Silkin for introducing me to "September Song" in 1974, and to Bloom for conversations about Hill.

15. The epigraph of "Ovid in the Third Reich" is taken from Ovid's *Amores*, III, xiv. It reads, "non peccat, quaecumque potest peccasse negare, / solaque famosam culpa professa facit," which Guy Lee renders as follows, "Any woman who pleads Not Guilty is innocent; / only confession gives her a bad name," *Ovid's Amores* (London: John Murray, 1968), 175.

16. The lyrics to "September Song" are as follows:

Well, it's a long, long time
From May to December.
But the days grow short,
When you reach September.
And the autumn weather
Turns the leaves to gray
And I haven't got time
For the waiting game.
And the days dwindle down
To a precious few
September, November
And these few precious days
I spend with you.
These precious days
I spend with you.

17. William Wordsworth, *The Prelude: A Parallel Text*, ed. J. C. Maxwell (Harmondsworth: Penguin, 1971), V, 389–90. In the 1805 version the boy is not quite ten, while in the 1850 version he is not quite twelve.

18. Gerard Manley Hopkins, *Poems and Prose*, ed. W. H. Gardner (Harmondsworth: Penguin, 1953), 50. Hill evokes the poem several times in his *The Orchards of Syon* (Washington, DC: Counterpoint, 2002).

19. See Merleau-Ponty, *Phenomenology of Perception*, trans. Colin Smith (London: Routledge and Kegan Paul, 1962), xiv.

20. For counter-experience, see Jean-Luc Marion, *Being Given: Towards a Phenomenology of Givenness*, trans. Jeffrey L. Kosky (Stanford: Stanford University Press, 2002), 215–16.

21. See Emmanuel Levinas, "The Ruin of Representation," in *Discovering Existence with Husserl*, trans. Richard A. Cohen and Michael B. Smith (Evanston: Northwestern University Press, 1998), 121.

22. See Stevens, "Poetry Is a Destructive Force," *Collected Poems*, 192–93.

23. Hill, "History as Poetry," *Collected Poems*, 84. Also see "Tristia: 1891–1938," in which Hill declares of Mandelstam, "The dead keep their sealed lives," 81.

24. Eugen Fink as quoted by Ronald Bruzina in his *Edmund Husserl and Eugen Fink: Beginnings and Ends in Phenomenology, 1928–1938* (New Haven: Yale University Press, 2004), 354.

25. On Hill's use of brackets, see Christopher Ricks, "'The Tongue's Atrocities,'" in Bloom, *Geoffrey Hill*, 67–68.

26. See, for example, Jahan Ramazani, *Poetry of Mourning: The Modern Elegy from Hardy to Heaney* (Chicago: University of Chicago Press, 1994), 7.

27. Dylan Thomas, "A Refusal to Mourn, the Death by Fire, of a Child in London,'" *Collected Poems* (London: J. M. Dent, 1952), 94. It would be possible to identify poems of the same period that evoke children in the camps. Randall Jarrell's "In the Camp There Was One Alive" (1948) is an example. See his *The Complete Poems* (London: Faber and Faber, 1971), 405–6. See also R. Clifton Spargo's "The Bad Conscience of American Holocaust Elegy: The Example of Randall Jarrell," *The Ethics of Mourning: Grief and Responsibility in Elegiac Literature* (Baltimore: Johns Hopkins University Press, 2004), Chapter 6.

28. The earliest reference to "A Refusal to Mourn" is in a letter Thomas wrote to Vernon Watkins on March 28, 1945. It is linked to "Ceremony after a Fire Raid," and it is worth citing Ralph Maud's note that "An alternate title for part II of 'Ceremony after a Fire Raid' is written on the Texas manuscript of that poem: 'Among Those Burned to Death Was a Child Aged a Few Hours,'" in *"Where Have the Old Words Got Me?" Explications of Dylan Thomas' Collected Poems* (Montreal: McGill-Queens University Press, 2003), 41. "A Refusal to Mourn" appeared in Thomas's collection *Deaths and Entrances* (1946).

29. See Jean Wahl, *Existence humaine et transcendance* (Boudry-Neuchâtel, France: Éditions de la Baconnière, 1944), 37.

30. Theodore W. Adorno, "Cultural Criticism and Society," in *Prisms*, trans. Samuel Weber and Shierry Weber (Cambridge, MA: MIT Press, 1981), 34.

31. Theodore W. Adorno, *Negative Dialectics*, trans. E. B. Ashton (London: Routledge and Kegan Paul, 1973), 362–63.

32. Emmanuel Levinas, "Reality and Its Shadow," *Unforeseen History*, trans. Nidra Poller (Urbana: University of Illinois Press, 2004), 90.

33. See Paul Celan, "Die Fleissigen," *Threadsuns*, trans. Pierre Joris (Los Angeles: Sun and Moon Press, 2000), 112–15.

34. I take the German text, as well as the translation, from Michael Hamburger, *Paul Celan: Poems, A Bilingual Edition* (New York: Persea Books, 1980), 50–53.

35. On this issue I refer to Jean-Luc Nancy's essay "Forbidden Representation," *The Ground of the Image*, trans. Jeff Fort (New York: Fordham University Press, 2005).

36. I quote from a poem by Hans Sahl, a riposte to Adorno, that Nancy discusses in "Forbidden Representation." The relevant lines read as follows: "Wir glauben, dass Gedichte / überhaupt erst jetzt wieder möglich / geworden sind, insofern nämlich als / nur im Gedicht sich sagen lässt, / was sonst / jeder Beschreibung spottet." Fort's translation runs, "We actually believe that poems have only now become possible again, insofar as only the poem can say what otherwise mocks every description."

37. See, in particular, Derrida, *The Work of Mourning*, ed. Pascale-Anne Brault and Michael Naas (Chicago: University of Chicago Press, 2001).

38. See Maurice Blanchot, "Friendship," in *Friendship*, trans. Elizabeth Rottenberg (Stanford: Stanford University Press, 1997).

39. See Marcel Proust, *Time Regained*, trans. Andreas Major and Terrence Kilmartin, rev. D. J. Enright (New York: Modern Library, 1993), 309.

40. Emmanuel Levinas, *God, Death, and Time*, trans. Bettina Bergo (Stanford: Stanford University Press, 2000), 12.

41. See Levinas's reference to Henry in *God, Death, and Time*, 17.

42. W. S. Merwin, *The Lice* (New York: Atheneum, 1977), 58.

43. See Emmanuel Levinas, *Totality and Infinity*, trans. Alphonso Lingis (The Hague: Martinus Nijhoff, 1979). Levinas might well remind us that Heidegger published his essay "Plato's Doctrine of Truth" in 1942, the year in which the child was deported.

44. See Emmanuel Levinas, *De l'oblitération: Entretien avec Françoise Armengaud à propos de l'oeuvre de Sosno*, 2nd ed. (Paris: Éditions de la Différence, 1990).

45. Consider Hill's interview with Carl Phillips: "Human beings are difficult. We're difficult to ourselves, we are mysteries to each other. . . . Why is it believed that poetry, prose, painting, music should be less than we are? Why does music, why does poetry have to address us in simplified terms, when, if such simplification were applied to a description of our own inner selves, we would find it demeaning?," "Geoffrey Hill: The Art of Poetry, LXXX," *Paris Review* 154 (2000): 276–77. For Empson's views on ambiguity and complexity, see his *Seven Types of Ambiguity* (Harmondsworth: Penguin, 1972) and *The Structure of Complex Words* (London: Hogarth Press, 1985). Also see Hill's essay on Empson, "The Dream of Reason," *Essays in Criticism* 14, no. 1 (1964): 91–101.

46. I take both expressions from Yves Bonnefoy. See his "Baudelaire contra Rubens," in *Le Nuage rouge: Essais sur la poétique* (Paris: Mercure de France, 1992), 79; and "Lifting Our Eyes from the Page," trans. John Naughton, *Critical Inquiry* 16, no. 4 (1990): 198.

47. See, for example, Blanchot, *The Book to Come*, trans. Charlotte Mandell (Stanford: Stanford University Press, 2003), 45, 122; and Derrida, "This Strange Institution Called Literature," 36–40.

48. It must be conceded that some of Hill's recent works are more garrulous. See *Speech! Speech!* (Washington, DC: Counterpoint, 2000) and *The Orchards of Syon*.

49. See Ricks, "The Tongue's Atrocities," 67.

50. Rainer Maria Rilke, *Selected Poems*, trans. C. F. MacIntyre (Berkeley: University of California Press, 1940), 39.

51. I am obliged to Michael L. Morgan for reminding me of the Dayenu in this context.

52. Unlike Susan Gubar, I do not think the "This" includes the killing of the child. See her *Poetry After Auschwitz: Remembering What One Never Knew* (Bloomington: Indiana University Press, 2003), 212.

The Phenomenality of the Sacrament—Being and Givenness
Jean-Luc Marion, translated by Bruce Ellis Benson

1. Session XII, c.3, canon 3, H. Denzinger, *Enchiridion symbolorum*, ed.31, 1960, n. 876.

2. *De civitate dei*, X, 5; Eng. trans., Augustine, *The City of God*, trans. Henry Bettenson (London: Penguin, 1972), 377 ("Sacrificum ergo *visibile invisibilis* sacrifi sacramentum").

3. *Summa theologiae*, IIIa, q.61, a.3, reply; Eng. trans., Aquinas, *The Summa Theologica of St. Thomas Aquinas*, vol. 4, trans. Fathers of the English Dominican Province (Notre Dame, IN: Ave Maria Press, 1948), 2348—translation modified ("sacramenta . . . sunt quaedam *sensibilia* signa *invisibilium* rerum, quibus homo sanctificatur"). See also q.60, a.4, reply.

4. *Contra gentes*, IV, c.56; Eng. trans., Thomas Aquinas, *Summa contra gentiles*, trans. C. J. O'Neil (Notre Dame, IN: University of Notre Dame Press, 1975) bk. 4, ch. 56 ("virtus divina *invisibiliter* [operatur] sub *visibilibus signis*").

5. According to Duns Scotus (*Ordinatio*, I, d.3, p.1, q.3, n. 139, *O.o.*, ed. C. Balic, 3:87); Suarez (*Disputationes metaphysicae*, XXXVIII, s.2, n.8, *O.o.*, ed. C. Berton, 26:503); and Descartes (*Principia philosophiae* I, §52: "non potest substantia primum animadverti ex hoc solo, quod sit res existens, quia hoc solum nos non afficit") [Eng. trans., *Principles of Philosophy* in *The Philosophical Writings of Descartes*, trans. John Cottingham, Robert Stoothoff, and Dugald Murdoch (Cambridge: Cambridge University Press, 1985), 1:210]; see our analysis in *Questions cartésiennes II:* (Paris: Presses Universitaires de France, 1996), c.III §3, 99.

6. In this sense, the process explained by the Thomistic theory of the Eucharist (real accidents of sensible substances are replaced by the body and blood of Christ) does not differ formally from Cartesian eucharistic physics (numerical identity of the space is initially attributed principally to the physical body, then transferred to the body from Christ). See J.-R. Armogathe, *Theologia cartesiana: L'explication physique de l'Eucharistie chez Descartes et dom Desgabets* (The Hague: Martinus Nijhoff, 1977).

7. *Discours de la méthode*, AT VI, p. 76, 16–22; Eng. trans., René Descartes, *Discourse on the Method*, in *The Philosophical Writings of Descartes*, 1:150.

8. *Summa theologiae*, IIIa, q.62, a.5, reply; Eng. trans., 2353 ("Principalis autem causa efficiens gratiae est ipse Deus, ad quam comparatur humanitas Christi sicut instrumentum conjunctum").

9. Augustine, *De civitate dei* X, 5 (loc. cit.). Thomas Aquinas, *Summa theologiae*, IIIa, q.60, a.1, reply; Eng. trans., 2339.

10. *Summa theologiae*, IIIa, q.60, a.6, reply.

11. *Summa theologiae*, IIIa, q.60, a.3, reply.

12. Immanuel Kant, *Critique of Pure Reason*, A109.

13. *Ideen zu einer reinen Phänomenologie und phänomenologischen Philosophie. Erstes Buch. Allgemeine Einführung in die reine Phänomenologie*, ed. Karl Schuhman (The Hague: Martinus Nijhoff, 1976) [Hua. III] §10,25; Eng. trans., Edmund Husserl, *Ideas Pertaining to a Pure Phenomenology and a Phenomenological Philosophy: First Book, General Introduction to a Pure Phenomenology*, trans. Fred Kersten (The Hague: Martinus Nijhoff, 1983), 20.

14. *Sein und Zeit*, §7, respectively "das Sich-an-ihm-selbst-zeigende" (31), and "Das was sich zeigt, so wie es sich von ihm selbst her zeigt, von ihm selbst

her sehen lassen" (34); Eng. trans., Martin Heidegger, *Being and Time*, trans. John Macquarrie and Edward Robinson (New York: Harper & Row, 1962), 54, 58.

15. *Prolegomena zur Geschichte des Zeitsbegriffs* (Frankfurt: Klostermann, 1979) §32, 423; Eng. trans., Martin Heidegger, *History of the Concept of Time: Prolegomena*, trans. Theodore Kisiel (Bloomington: Indiana University Press, 1985), 307.

16. *Die Idee der Phänomenologie. Fünf Vorlesungen*, ed. Walter Biemel (The Hague: Martinus Nijhoff, 1973) [Hua. II] §3, 14; Eng. trans., Edmund Husserl, *The Idea of Phenomenology*, trans. Lee Hardy (Dordrecht: Kluwer, 1999), 69.

17. Ibid.,11; Eng. trans., 67.

18. It is what we have attempted to establish in *Being Given: Toward a Phenomenology of Givenness*, trans. Jeffrey L. Kosky (Stanford: Stanford University Press, 2002); in particular, see bk. I, §6.

19. We put ourselves here under the authority of Hans Urs von Balthasar, in particular *Herrlichkeit: Eine theologische Ästhetik*, vol. 1, *Schau der Gestalt* (Einsiedeln: Johannes Verlag, 1961), "The objective form"; Eng. trans., *The Glory of the Lord: A Theological Aesthetics*, vol. 1, *Seeing the Form* (San Francisco: Ignatius/Crossroad, 1982).

20. *Summa theologiae*, IIIa, q.62, a.1, *ad 1m*; Eng. trans. 2350—translation modified ["causa instrumentalis, si sit manifesta, potest dici signum effectus occulti"].

21. *Summa theologiae*, IIIa, respectively q.64, a.1, *reply*; and a.2, *repl*; Eng. trans., 2360– 2361—translation modified ("solus Deus opereratur interiorem effectum sacramenti" and "virtus sacramenti sit a solo Deo").

22. For the concept of saturated phenomenon and its relation, without conflation, to the phenomenon of revelation, see Marion, *Being Given*, bk. IV, §23–24.

The Human in Question: Augustinian Dimensions in Jean-Luc Marion
Jeffrey L. Kosky

1. Jean-Louis Chrétien, *The Unforgettable and the Unhoped For* (New York: Fordham University Press, 2002), 122. Hereafter cited as UU.

2. Jean-Luc Marion, *Being Given* (Stanford: Stanford University Press, 2002), 307. Hereafter cited as BG.

3. As I was writing this essay, I learned that Marion's most recent seminar at the University of Chicago was devoted to Augustine. Whether any eventual outcomes of his scholarly activity will confirm or disconfirm my thesis I cannot predict. What seems certain, however, is that Marion's work will make my insights a mere preliminary to a confrontation with Marion's work.

4. On Dionysius, see Bernard McGinn: "Although Dionysius considers the role of the intelligent human subject . . . there is a sense in which his presentation is far more cosmological and 'objective' . . . There is little theological anthropology as such in his surviving writings" (*The Foundations of Mysticism* [New

York: Crossroad, 1992]; 161). Concerning Augustine, Charles Taylor contrasts the Augustinian preference for consideration of the human being with Aquinas's predilection for arguments based on external reality. "The latter [the Thomistic *viae*] argue to God from the existence of created reality (or what the proofs show to be created reality). They pass, as it were, through the realm of objects. The Augustinian proof moves through the subject" (*Sources of the Self: The Making of the Modern Identity* [Cambridge: Harvard University Press, 1989], 141).

5. Revised and published as, respectively, Jean-Luc Marion, "*Mihi magna quaestio factus sum:* The Privilege of Unknowing," *Journal of Religion* 85, no. 1 (January 2005); and Marion, *Counter-Experiences: Reading Jean-Luc Marion* (Notre Dame University Press, 2007). Hereafter cited as, respectively, PU and BS.

6. Hans Urs von Balthasar, *The Glory of the Lord*, vol. 2 (San Francisco: Ignatius Press), 96.

7. Feuerbach's atheistic humanism as well as the Heideggerian formulation of Descartes's cogito as *cogito me cogitare* prove definitive of the human for the author of *God without Being*.

8. Mark C. Taylor, *Erring: A Postmodern A/theology* (Chicago: University of Chicago Press, 1984), 35. Taylor credits Augustine with "the discovery of the subject" (43).

9. Ibid., 44.

10. Ibid., 43.

11. Marion rehearsed this argument with regard to Descartes, in "Does the *Cogito* Affect Itself? Generosity and Phenomenology: Remarks on Michel Henry's Interpretation of the Cartesian *Cogito*," in *Cartesian Questions* (Chicago: University of Chicago Press, 1999). It was Henry who noted that objective thought (representational knowledge) could never, even in Descartes, let me appear to myself. Perhaps the first to make this argument against Descartes was Giambattista Vico in the *Ancient Wisdom of the Italians* (1708): "The rule and criterion of truth is to have made it. Hence the clear and distinct idea of the mind not only cannot be the criterion of other truths, but it cannot be the criterion of that of the mind itself; for while the mind apprehends itself, it does not make itself, and because it does not make itself it is ignorant of the form or mode by which it apprehends itself." More should be done to explore the significance of Vico's claim.

12. Martin Heidegger, *Being and Time* (San Francisco: Harper & Row, 1962), 68. Recent scholarship suggests that Heidegger's position may have been incubated during a period of time when he was reading and lecturing on Augustine. An indication of this is provided by Heidegger's citing Augustine's "*ego certe laboro hic et laboro in meipso: factus sum mihi terra difficultatis*" in *Being and Time* shortly after offering his own determination of the human as question. One should certainly consider this in light of the lectures on Augustine reprinted in *The Phenomenology of the Religious Life* (Bloomington: Indiana University Press, 2004).

13. Martin Heidegger, *An Introduction to Metaphysics* (New Haven: Yale University Press, 1959), 140.

14. These include Augustine's experience of being unable to order the prayer and perception which constitute him most intimately (Conf. X, 33, 50), Augustine's experience of dreams (probably of a sexual nature) in which he finds himself different from and even at odds with himself and his own will (Conf. X, 30, 41), and finally Augustine's discovery that his memory includes forgetting such that "my memory [Marion writes], my very inner being, escapes me and that 'factus sum mihi terra difficultatis' " (6, Conf. X, 16, 25).

15. *Responsal* renders the French *répons*. According to the *Oxford English Dictionary*, *responsal* refers to a liturgical response, but it also has meanings that extend beyond the liturgical. While *responsory* might also be a fair rendering of the French, this term has an exclusively ecclesiastical significance and therefore seems to me overly narrow.

16. Chrétien cites the first sentence of this Augustinian text in his own account of the path of his thinking (UU, 119). Oddly, Marion does not cite this specific phrase.

17. Von Balthasar, *The Glory of the Lord*, 2:105, which continues: "Neither derivation from the parental soul nor individual creation by God, neither the insertion of the precreated soul into the body nor a pre-natal fall from the original unity, none of these satisfied the searching mind."

18. There are two Taylors. So I would think to say Charles in order to distinguish it from Mark Taylor, *Sources of the Self: The Making of the Modern Identity*, 135.

19. Ibid., 135–36.

20. The notion of the immemorial, so important to Chrétien, would operate here. Unlike Plato, Augustine's refusal to offer a theory for the soul's origin in God means that he sees the human in relation to an immemorial, not just a forgotten, past. Marion, too, will invoke the notion of the immemorial in *Being Given* when elaborating his notion of a constitutive delay.

21. As an aside, I should add that this essentially forgotten or immemorial past is precisely what gives the human the possibility of a future still outstanding: "Beauty so ancient and so new." Indeed, only a beauty so ancient as to be remembered as immemorial can give the possibility of encountering a beauty so new that I cannot find it in my memory and so would not recognize when I see it.

22. This incomprehensibility, Marion claims, needs protection from any definition of the human—here, by name, the humanist, which like every definition "imposes on the human being a finite essence, following from which it always becomes possible to delimit what deserves to remain human from what no longer does" (PU, 14). The failure to protect human incomprehensibility is the greatest weakness of humanism, greater even than its taking man as the measure of all that is; for this latter problem rests on humanism's own supposition that it comprehends the human.

23. PU, 16–17, citing Gregory of Nyssa, "On the Making of Man," in *Gregory of Nyssa: Dogmatic Treatises, etc.*, vol. 5 of *Nicene and Post-Nicene Fathers of the Christian Church*, ed. Philip Schaff and Henry Wace (Grand Rapids, MI: Eerdmans, 1965); 396–97 (trans. modified). Marion could also have turned to the mystical theologian John Scotus Eriugena, who translated Nyssa's work into Latin. For Eriugena, Bernard McGinn claims, "like its divine source, [humanity] does not know *what* it is. . . . Humanity does not know God, but God does not know God either (in the sense of knowing or defining a *what*); and humanity does not know itself, nor does God know humanity insofar as it is one with the divine mind" (*The Growth of Mysticism* [New York: Crossroads, 1996], 105).

24. See also: "far from leading to the denial of finitude, the ordeal of the saturated phenomenon confirms it" (BS, 400). These texts should defend Marion against critics who suggest that his return to things themselves or the appearance of the phenomenon such as it gives itself denies human finitude.

25. The noncorrespondence of call and response is crucial to Jean-Louis Chrétien. See especially *The Call and the Response* (New York: Fordham University Press, 2004), where he contrasts it with the correspondence of call and response in Heideggerian thought of the call of Being, prophetic utterance of the word of God, and Platonic notions of beauty as a response to the call. For Chrétien, noncorrespondence of call and response introduces an originary alteration in which the human emerges, in contrast to its submergence in the forms of a call that corresponds. He suggests that this is the crucial contribution of Christianity, especially Dionysian thought, in its modification of Neo-Platonic thought.

26. "Far from being able to constitute the phenomenon, the I experiences itself as constituted by it. To the constituting subject there succeeds the constituted witness" (BG, 216).

The Poor Phenomenon: Marion and the Problem of Givenness
Anthony J. Steinbock

1. Jean-Luc Marion, *Étant donné: essai d'une phénoménologie de la donation* (Paris: PUF, 1997), 314–29; hereafter, *Étant donné*. English translation by Jeffrey L. Kosky, *Being Given: Toward a Phenomenology of Givenness* (Stanford: Stanford University Press, 2002), 225–37; hereafter, *Being Given*.

2. Cf. *Étant donné*, 309–10; *Being Given*, 221–22.

3. *Étant donné*, 316; *Being Given*, 227 (my emphasis).

4. See *Étant donné*, 318–25; *Being Given*, 228–33.

5. *Étant donné*, 326–28; *Being Given*, 235–36.

6. *Étant donné*, 367–71, 390–91; *Being Given*, 267, 283.

7. *Étant donné*, 366; *Being Given*, 266. And *Étant donné*, 371; *Being Given*, 269 ("I receive *my self* from the call that gives me to myself before giving me anything whatsoever").

8. *Étant donné*, 310; *Being Given*, 222 (my emphasis).

9. *Étant donné*, 310; *Being Given*, 222, translation modified.

10. *Étant donné*, 311–12; *Being Given*, 223.

11. *Étant donné*, 313–14; *Being Given*, 224–25.

12. See Jean-Luc Marion, *Réduction et donation: recherches sur Husserl, Heidegger et la phénoménologie* (Paris: Presses Universitaires de France, 1989). English translation as *Reduction and Givenness: Investigations of Husserl, Heidegger, and Phenomenology*, trans. Thomas A. Carlson (Evanston, IL: Northwestern University Press, 1998).

13. Jean-Luc Marion, *De surcroît: études sur les phénomènes saturés* (Paris: Presses Universitaires de France, 2001). English translation as *In Excess: Studies of Saturated Phenomena*, trans. Robyn Horner and Vincent Berraud (New York: Fordham University Press, 2002).

14. For example, *Étant donné*, 354; *Being Given*, 256: "its [the subject's] mode of apparition remains essentially determined by that of *objectness*. In effect, by being reduced to an 'I think,' the 'subject' is focused on the object, whose presenter and representer it alone becomes by virtue of the essence of representation—to the point that, when it wants to represent itself directly to itself, it has no other possibility but to assume one more time (and one time too many) *the poorest phenomenality—that of the object*" (my emphasis).

And *Étant donné*, 362; *Being Given*, 262–63: "The likely difference between the concepts that Descartes used and those that the contemporary sciences prefer . . . is less important than what they share: the *intuitively poor givenness* realized by the formula, and the quantity and coordinates of the piece of wax, which enable it to be defined but in no way seen. The concept of the wax does not yet show it; its intelligibility does not always phenomenalize it" (my emphasis).

Also *Étant donné*, 419–20; *Being Given*, 305: "But to claim that what is firmly willed should first be conceived in evidence, in short, to claim to know what one wants, one first has to admit that one sees without wanting and before wanting. Now, we know that we *see without wanting only the poorest phenomena*, indeed those that are barely constituted. As soon as a phenomenon is enriched [*sic*] with intuition, therefore as soon as its degree of givenness grows [*sic*], it is necessary that we constitute it and bear it for it to be seen, therefore wanted—truly wanted, not denied or evaded. In order to see, one must first want to see" (my emphasis).

15. See Edmund Husserl, *Analyses Concerning Passive and Active Synthesis: Lectures on Transcendental Logic*, trans. Anthony J. Steinbock (Dordrecht: Kluwer, 2001), esp. Part 2; hereafter, *Analyses*.

16. *Étant donné*, 315; *Being Given*, 226.

17. Husserl, *Analyses*, 39.

18. Husserl writes that perspectival givenness is so intrinsic to the givenness of a spatial object that even God or a superhuman intellect could not overcome this kind of inadequate givenness. Cf. *Analyses*, 56.

19. Cf. Husserl, *Analyses*, 43; and Division 3, Part 2.

20. *Étant donné*, 315; *Being Given*, 226.

21. Yet there is an obvious ambiguity here concerning eidetic objects and regarding them as "poor" phenomena. On one hand, what could be richer than

the givenness of the essence? Eidetic insight or categorial intuition is a givenness. It is not abstract, since for Husserl it is only given through a simple, perceptual, concrete intuition. For Husserl, the categorial is founded in the simple, the concrete. So as a givenness, it is an intuition, and there is a surplus of the categorial over the simple. On the other hand, in order for the categorial itself to be saturated in Marion's sense, the categorial would have to be founded in the simple such that a simple intuition would (be able to?) overthrow the categorial. I think this is the case with Husserl's notion of the optimal in the phenomenology of normality and abnormality, but this does not make it revelation in the strict sense. This only means it is not a saturated phenomenon. See my "Saturated Intentionality," in *The Body: Classic and Contemporary Readings*, ed. Donn Welton (London: Blackwell, 1999), 178–99.

22. Santa Teresa de Jesus, *Obras Completas*, ed. Efren de La Madre de Dios, OCD, and Otger Steggink, OCARM (Madrid: Biblioteca de Autores Cristianos, 1997), 690; hereafter, *Obras*. English translation by Kieran Kavanaugh, OCD, and Otilio Rodriguez, OCD, as *The Collected Works of St. Teresa of Avila* (Washington, DC: ICS Publications, 1985), vol. 3, "Foundations," Section 5.8; hereafter, *Collected Works*.

23. *Étant donné*, 314; *Being Given*, 225.

24. *Étant donné*, 419–20; *Being Given*, 304–5.

25. Cf. *Étant donné*, 425; *Being Given*, 309; *Étant donné*, 426; *Being Given*, 310. "The given comes, on its own, upon the gifted, whose structural secondariness attests an absolute finitude."

26. *Étant donné*, 425; *Being Given*, 309.

27. *Étant donné*, 426; *Being Given*, 310 (my emphasis).

28. See Jacques Derrida, *L'écriture et la différence* (Paris: Seuil, 1967), 62; hereafter, *L'écriture*.

29. Derrida, *L'écriture*, note on 86: "Il s'agit mois d'un *point* que d'une originarité temporelle en général."

30. *Étant donné*, 425–26; *Being Given*, 310.

31. *Étant donné*, 420–21, 424; *Being Given*, 305–6, 308.

32. Saint Teresa writes, for example, "I fear that it [the soul] will never attain true poverty of spirit, which means being at rest in labors and dryness and not seeking consolation or comfort in prayer—for earthly consolation has already been abandoned—but seeking consolation in trials for love of Him who always lived in the midst of them." *Obras*, 124; *Collected Works* (1976), vol. 1, sec. 22.11.

Michel Henry's Theory of Disclosive Moods
Jeffrey Hanson

1. The consistency in his interpretation over the years is partly explained by his ongoing conversation with Kierkegaard. It is Kierkegaard's analysis of despair that Henry appropriates in his crucial discussion at the end of *The Essence of Manifestation* and Kierkegaard's work on anxiety that he explicitly engages in

Incarnation: A Philosophy of the Flesh. I extensively treat Henry and Kierkegaard on despair in "Michel Henry's Problematic Reading of *The Sickness unto Death,*" *Journal of the British Society for Phenomenology* 38, no. 3 (October 2007): 248–60. In that piece I raise objections to Henry's usage of Kierkegaard, something I do not do here. I also do not discuss the material from *Incarnation,* wherein Henry specifically discusses Kierkegaard's theory and connects his own understanding of anxiety with his phenomenology of the body. In *Incarnation* Henry associates the hidden essence of human action and being, the "I Can" with the incarnation into invisible flesh that is another word for the auto-affection of the Self. He dwells in particular on Kierkegaard's discussion of innocence as the primordial condition of auto-affection, entirely alien from exteriority and the realm of thought. There is also in these pages an explicit reference to the principle of the duplicity of appearance that is treated by Henry in *I Am the Truth* and discussed herein.

2. "It is in the structure of Being itself, in the internal structure of immanence, as pure possibilities willed and prescribed by it, that the fundamental affective tonalities of existence are perceived by Kierkegaard and defined by him in *Sickness unto Death*"; Michel Henry, *The Essence of Manifestation,* trans. Girard Etzkorn (The Hague: Martinus Nijhoff, 1973), 676 [850–51]. Hereafter EM. Page numbers in the original French edition of 1963 are provided in square brackets.

3. "The internal structure of immanence, namely of affectivity itself, has been understood as the essence of non-freedom" (EM, 655 [823]).

4. Herein lies a point of agreement between Henry and Heidegger. "What we call a 'feeling' is neither a transitory epiphenomenon of our thinking and willing behavior nor simply an impulse that provokes such behavior nor merely a present condition we have to put up with somehow or other." Martin Heidegger, "What Is Metaphysics?" in *Basic Writings,* ed. David Farrell Krell, 2nd ed. (San Francisco: HarperCollins, 1993), 100.

5. Suffering and joy recur in *I Am the Truth* and will be discussed again herein, but it is worth noting here that the connection of this theme to the Beatitudes, and the theological valence that such an association provides, is already anticipated in *The Essence of Manifestation,* where Henry writes, "Assuredly, Christianity divides the whole of reality into two worlds, into two kingdoms of the visible and the invisible, and antinomy first appears as a consequence of this division, as the simple expression of the opposition which Christianity institutes. . . . Nevertheless, antinomy designates something altogether different than the reciprocal and radical exteriority of ontological areas and determinations that respectively belong to them. *Antinomy aims not at the absence of relationship but at the relationship.* The latter, the antinomic relationship finding its strict and at the same time explicit formulation in the dogmatic content of Christianity— 'blessed are they who suffer'—is situated within one and the same ontological region, in the sphere of absolute subjectivity" (EM, 671 [844]).

6. In clarifying his position Henry cites Luther's division between the spirit and the flesh and Scheler's discussion of suffering and sacrifice as examples of the

kind of illicit transformations of suffering into joy that he means to exclude from his analysis, all of them forms of thinking in which "the passage from suffering to happiness not being able to be grasped interior to suffering itself nor proceeding from its essence, but merely 'from the serene vision of a superior order of things'" (EM, 675 [849]). The quote is from Max Scheler, *Vom Sinn des Leides*, in *Schriften zur Soziologie und Weltanschauungs Lehre. Gessamelte Werke* (Bern: Franke, 1963), 6:69.

7. References to Kierkegaard are comparatively infrequent in *The Essence of Manifestation*. Of twelve total, most are in passing, and this last reference is by far the most in depth.

8. The quote is from Martin Heidegger, *Being and Time,* trans. John Macquarrie and Edward Robinson (New York: Harper & Row, 1962), 278, n. vi. Hereafter BT.

9. The quote is from Søren Kierkegaard, *The Sickness Unto Death*, trans. Walter Lowrie (Princeton: Princeton University Press, 1941), 27.

10. That unfreedom is a trait belonging to the essence is a point developed at length earlier in the first part of this chapter on the internal structure of immanence. "What is discovered by any understanding which draws near to the essential is that the internal structure of Being resides in its original passivity with regard to itself and as such is the essence of non-freedom" (EM, 297 [369]).

11. One of the others is closely related to the one I have already treated. It reads: "S. Kierkegaard in his *Concept of Dread* already noted that psychology cannot account for the qualitative leap because the latter takes place in an ontological dimension radically different from the one wherein psychology moves about. The impotence of psychology, and of knowledge in general, has not only been asserted by Kierkegaard . . . but contrary to what has been repeated in the wake of certain statements made by Heidegger his thesis is also accompanied by an implicit definition of positive ontology of subjectivity, an ontology which in the philosophy of existence plays the role of an essential foundation and which consequently prevents it from degenerating into literature and word-games or, as we will see, into the emptiness and confusion of a certain 'irrationalism'" (EM, 413 [519], n. 10). In his commentary on the internal structure of immanence Henry accuses Kierkegaard of having corrupted the nature of passivity by claiming it never appears without some measure of activity. "*Thus, ontological passivity which constitutes the internal structure of Being as structure of the original relationship of Being to itself is confused with passivity which is but a mode of freedom and of the power of assuming an attitude.* It is confused with this passivity about which Kierkegaard could say that 'It must always be such that there is in it enough activity for it to maintain its passivity'" (EM, 298 [370–71]). The translation Etzkorn uses is Walter Lowrie's second 1957 edition for Princeton University Press. The distinction that Henry is trying to make is between a fundamental, essential passivity that characterizes the immanence of auto-affection and passivity as a merely empirical posture, the opposite of activity. When one consults the page in *The Concept of Anxiety* to which Henry refers to support his accusation, the material there seems hardly apposite to the issue he is discussing. The

final note is a reference to Kierkegaard's remarks on sensibility in ancient Greece and is not directly relevant to the substance of his theory of anxiety (EM, 110 [136], n. 12).

12. Freud's theory of anxiety is summarily (and arguably uncharitably) dismissed by Henry in *The Essence of Manifestation*, but Freud, like Kierkegaard, seems to be rehabilitated by Henry in later years, receiving considerable attention in *The Genealogy of Psychoanalysis*, while, strangely, Kierkegaard receives none. See note 22.

13. See interviews with Henry at www.mercaba.org/-Filosofia/encarnacion .htm (accessed January 23, 2006) and www.psychomedia.it/jep (accessed January 23, 2006).

14. Michel Henry, *I Am the Truth: Toward a Philosophy of Christianity*, trans. Susan Emanuel (Stanford: Stanford University Press, 2003). Hereafter IT.

15. Kierkegaard may even have suggested as much about despair. He draws a distinction between "despair of" and "despair over," which seems to acknowledge that despair, while always "of" the eternal essential, is also always "over" something occurring in the experience of life. "Despair over the earthly or over something earthly is in reality also despair of the eternal and over oneself, insofar as it is despair, for this is indeed the formula for all despair" (SUD, 60). So *all* despair is of the eternal and over the self, where the distinction between prepositions is not irrelevant, as Kierkegaard explains in his footnote to this sentence: "We despair *over* that which binds us in despair—over a misfortune, over the earthly, over a capital loss, etc.—but we despair *of* that which, rightly understood, releases us from despair: of the eternal, of salvation, of our own strength, etc. With respect to the self, we say both: to despair *over* and *of* oneself, because the self is doubly dialectical" (SUD, 60–61).

16. I leave aside the question of whether Henry reads Heidegger fairly or correctly on this score but merely recount his critique with a view to establishing how it helps the reader understand Henry's thought.

17. Heidegger's analysis of the connection between Nothing and being-in-the-world appears in "What Is Metaphysics?"

18. It is perhaps worth mentioning in passing that Henry makes a very short and oblique comment on Jean-Francois Courtine's theory of anxiety that may be motivated by the same concerns he has about Heidegger's theory. In "Material Phenomenology and Language (or, Pathos and Language)" Henry discusses his thesis that phenomenology's object is phenomenality itself and not phenomena or a method of interpreting them in light of Heidegger's pivotal discussion in §7 of *Being and Time*: "we see the phenomenological reduction which constitutes the essential core of Husserl's method disappear from Heidegger's analysis of truth. The substitutes that some attempt to discover for it, the Difference between Being and the being (as Heidegger himself says), anxiety according to Jean-Francois Courtine, are only diverse formulations of the originary event of the pure phenomenality which constitutes the unique donation of Being"; *Continental Philosophy Review* 32 (1999): 343–65, 344. Henry provides no reference to any of Courtine's texts.

19. See note 26.

20. Henry places this term prominently in the title of section III in *The Essence of Manifestation*: "The Internal Structure and the Problem of Its Phenomenological Determination: The Invisible" (EM, 279). See also Dan Zahavi, "Michel Henry and the Phenomenology of the Invisible," *Continental Philosophy Review* 32 (1999): 22–34.

21. Michel Henry, *The Genealogy of Psychoanalysis,* trans. Douglas Brick (Stanford: Stanford University Press, 1993). Hereafter GP. It is worth pointing out that Henry follows the traditional distinction between anxiety, which has no particular object, or put another way, has nothing for its object, and a particular or ontic affectivity with a determinate object. He acknowledged this distinction as it appears in Heidegger in the pages discussed above (EM, 587 [736]) as well as in the passage on Freud just quoted. Of course, Heidegger, Freud, and Henry it could be argued are all following Kierkegaard, who established this distinction between fear and anxiety in *The Concept of Anxiety,* chapter I, section 5.

22. It is somewhat curious that Henry in these pages reads Freud sympathetically and as a partner in his own project. In *The Essence of Manifestation*, he explicitly rejected Freud's account of anxiety. "Once a man is alive, he experiences feelings, and this not by reason of circumstances in which he might be placed, not by reason of his psycho-physical, characteriological or hereditary structure, not by reason of everything which apparently constitutes the particularity of his life, but upon the foundation of the essence of life in him, of this essence which makes his life singular and at the same time effective, and makes this life become reality in determined tonalities" (EM, 666–67 [838]). In a footnote to that sentence, Henry wrote, "This puts an end to the Freudian theory of affectivity which looks for the origin of our affective life and its developments in anxiety or more precisely in the conditions which produce anxiety and in the traumatism of birth" (EM, 666 [838], n. 4). However, in *The Genealogy of Psychoanalysis*, it is clear that Henry has changed his mind about Freud. There he wrote: "There is a superficial reading of Freud that owes a good deal of its success to reducing it to a sort of empirical history that illumines the destiny of man—the destiny of the adult, in this instance, based on that of the child and even the fetus. According to this reading, anxiety especially has its source in infantile anxiety and ultimately in the birth trauma, which it reproduces and repeats indefinitely. . . . But if we take a step or two back from that infantile anxiety, which returns in Freud's analyses as it does in life, we see that it does not constitute a particular anxiety, tied to specific moments of an empirical history, to childhood; instead it is the model or prototype of true anxiety, or rather its essence" (GP, 311).

23. There is also in *I Am the Truth* a brief but conspicuously strange passage that apparently relates despair to anxiety in a way that can only appear inexplicable keeping in mind everything that has been said about despair in the early part of this chapter. "Taken to its extreme, this anxiety is called despair. Anxiety and despair do not happen to 'me' as a function of the vicissitudes of a personal

history, but are born in 'me,' in the phenomenological structure of the Ipseity that makes 'me' a Self, and in the affective tonality of the 'suffer oneself' in which the essence of this Ipseity consists" (IT, 200). The characterization of anxiety is again consistent with what has already been shown, but how are we to regard despair now? As an intensification of anxiety? How despair would be phenomenologically explicated in this new sense (not developed any further than in this passage to my knowledge) is a bit of a mystery.

24. The phrase "antinomic relationship" appears in *The Essence of Manifestation* in association with the Beatitudes and the identity of suffering and joy that they proclaim (EM, 671 [844]).

25. A comparison of this passage with the dynamic of call and response as it appears in the work of other contemporary French phenomenologists like Jean-Luc Marion and Jean-Louis Chrétien would be a most rewarding study.

26. See chapters 1 and 2 of *I Am the Truth*, "Material Phenomenology and Language (or, Pathos and Language)," and "Speech and Religion: The Word of God," in *Phenomenology and the "Theological Turn": The French Debate* (New York: Fordham University Press, 2000).

27. This is one of the hardest aspects of Henry's thought to appreciate. At various times in his career Henry mentions a variety of other candidates for expressions that might offer a clue to the truth of life; in "Material Phenomenology and Language (or, Pathos and Language)" alone he references Kandinsky's paintings (362), music (363), and the philosophy of Marx (361–62). The diversity (and eccentricity) of his choices only reflects the total impotence of hermeneutics to deliver the truth of life. Indeed, an expositor not as sympathetically inclined to Kandinsky, music, or Marx might very well argue that none of these expresses the truth of life, and Henry himself would be hard-pressed to prove his objector wrong.

Can We Hear the Voice of God? Michel Henry and the *Words of Christ*
Christina M. Gschwandtner

1. Of course, Gideon needed several assurances: the appearance of an angel, a burned supper, the sign of the fleece (twice with the demand of opposite results), and the dreams of his enemies. Similarly, Moses did his very best to argue the burning bush out of the commission to deliver the people, despite all assurances of the divine presence for his task.

2. Isaiah 6:8. The other stories refer to Exodus 3, Genesis 22, Judges 6, and Luke 1.

3. Michel Henry, *Paroles du Christ* (Paris: Seuil, 2002). Henceforth cited as PC. In *I Am the Truth*, Henry gives a brief preview of the argument developed much more thoroughly in *Paroles du Christ*. Whenever possible I have taken quotations from the English translation of the earlier work (*I Am the Truth*) and provide only page references to the French work (*Paroles du Christ*). "Paroles du Christ" means "Words of Christ." An English translation of this work is forthcoming.

4. Michel Henry, *I Am the Truth: Toward a Philosophy of Christianity*, trans. Susan Emanuel (Stanford: Stanford University Press, 2003), 216. Henceforth cited as IT.

5. Michel Henry, *Incarnation: Une philosophie de la chair* (Paris: Seuil, 2000).

6. Henry does spend some time in the beginning of *I Am the Truth* arguing that historical and scientific categories of "truth" (in terms of verification or proof) are useless in regard to the Scriptures but that these texts must be read as the word of God. IT, 5–8.

7. See also IT, 217 and 229.

8. IT, 217.

9. With the exception of the Eucharist example, the following paragraphs are a summary of *I Am the Truth*, 215–33; and *Paroles du Christ*, 127–55.

10. "Lying is not one possibility of language alongside another with which it might be contrasted—speaking the truth, for example. This possibility is rooted in language and is as inherent in it as its very essence. Language, as long as there is nothing else but language, can only be lying. . . . To the powerlessness of language is added all the vices belonging to powerlessness in general: lying, hypocrisy, the shrouding of truth, bad faith, the overthrowing of values, the falsification of reality in all its forms—including the most extreme form, that is, the reduction of this reality to language and ultimately, in this supreme confusing, their identification with each other. Language has become the universal evil" (IT, 8–9).

11. He does contend, however, that Scripture points to the place where our condition of divine sonship is realized and therefore "by saying 'You are Sons,' the worldly word of Scripture turns away from itself and indicates the site where another word speaks. It achieves the displacement that leads outside its own word to this other site where the Word of Life speaks" (IT, 230; see also 232–33). Yet it is clearly not Scripture itself but this other Word that is Henry's primary concern. It is not a written text but an immediate phenomenological experience. Joan of Arc's voices, then, are probably a much better example of what Henry is talking about than any of the stories from Scripture. (He does actually refer to her briefly in a question [PC, 132].)

12. PC, 91.

13. "Unlike the world's word, which turns away from itself and speaks of something other than itself—of something else that in this speech finds itself thrown outside itself, thrown away, deported, stripped of its own reality, emptied of its substance, reduced to an image, to an exterior appearance, to a content without content, both empty and opaque—Life's speech reveals Life and gives Life. Life's Word is life's self-giving, its self-revelation in the enjoyment of itself. The Logos of Life, the Word of Life, the Word of God is precisely absolute phenomenological Life grasped in the hyper-powerful process of its self-generation as self-revelation" (IT, 220–21).

14. "I hear forever the sound of my birth, which is the sound of Life, the unbreakable silence in which the Word of Life does not stop speaking my own

life to me, in which my own life, if I hear that word speaking within it, does not stop speaking the Word of God to me" (IT, 226).

15. The word is its embrace . . . it holds the person to whom its speaks by giving him life" (IT, 226).

16. PC, 118 and 134. See also IT, 226.

17. IT, 20, 23.

18. PC, 155.

19. IT, 225; emphasis mine. See also his more extensive rejection of hermeneutics as a valid access to biblical texts in the introduction to *I Am the Truth* (IT, 1–11).

20. See, for example: PC, 147.

21. PC, 149.

22. In that sense, then, Janicaud is right in perceiving a "theological turn" in Henry's work. Henry clearly maintains that Christianity is "true" and that its Truth, in fact, is the only one giving direct access to fundamental human experience. He justifies his use of religious texts and imagery by arguing that these give access to new domains of experience unknown by traditional philosophy and in so doing enlighten or possibly even invalidate philosophy: "We are in the presence of a question which we have qualified as decisive, although paradoxically it is never posed by philosophy. If such a question must take on the importance that we present, it is necessary to make this observation: the taking into consideration of certain fundamental religious themes permits us to discover an immense domain, unknown by the thought that is called rational. Far from opposing itself to a truly free reflection, Christianity would place traditional philosophy and its canonical corpus before their limits, if not to say before their blindness" (PC, 87).

23. Henry has often been accused of pantheism. Strictly speaking, that is not true, since he does not equate God and nature. Rather, he assimilates the divine and the human (especially in regard to emotion and affectivity) so closely that they are in danger of becoming indistinguishable.

24. Kearney criticizes, for example, the extreme indeterminateness of deconstruction: "How could we ever recognize a God stripped of every specific horizon of memory and anticipation? How could we give content to a faith devoid of stories and covenants, promises, alliances, and good works, or fully trust a God devoid of all names (Yahweh, Elohim, Jesus, Allah)? . . . If *tout autre* is indeed *tout autre*, what is to prevent us saying yes to a malevolent agent as much as to a transcendent God who comes to save and liberate? Is there really no way for deconstruction to discriminate between true and false prophets, between holy and unholy spirits? Surely it is important to tell the difference, even if it's only more or less; and even if we can never know for certain, or see for sure, or have any definite set of criteria? Blindness is all very well for luminary painters and writers, for Homer and Rembrandt, but don't most of the rest of us need just a little moral insight, just a few ethical handrails as we grope through the dark night of postmodern spectrality and simulacritude towards the 'absolute other,'

before we say 'yes,' 'come,' 'thy will be done'? Is there really no difference, in short, between a living God and a dead one, between Elijah and his 'phantom,' between messiahs and monsters?" Richard Kearney, *The God Who May Be: A Hermeneutics of Religion* (Bloomington: Indiana University Press, 2001), 76.

25. IT, 220.

Radical Phenomenology Reveals a Measure of Faith and a Need for a Levinasian Other in Henry's Life
Ronald L. Mercer Jr.

1. Jean-Yves Lacoste, "The Work and Complement of Appearing," in *Religious Experience and the End of Metaphysics*, ed. Jeffrey Bloechl (Bloomington: Indiana University Press, 2003), 68.

2. Bernard Prusak, "Translator's Introduction," in Dominique Janicaud et al., *Phenomenology and the "Theological Turn"* (New York: Fordham University Press, 2000), 5. Hereafter, I will refer to this edited collection as PTT.

3. Dominique Janicaud, "Contours of the Turn," in PTT, 27.

4. John Paul II, *Fides et Ratio: On the Relationship between Faith and Reason*, §83, at http://www.vatican.va/edocs/ENG0216/_PG.HTM.

5. Janicaud, "Contours of the Turn," PTT, 28.

6. Adding a Levinasian corrective on my part does not imply that Levinas found Henry to be lacking in his scholarship. Jean-Yves Lacoste reports that during the seminars he attended with Levinas in the mid-1970s, Levinas would magnanimously praise Michel Henry's phenomenology. At this particular time, Levinas would have been familiar with Henry's *Essence of Manifestation* and *Phenomenology of the Body*. Of course, Henry's *I Am the Truth: Toward a Philosophy of Christianity* appeared in French in 1996. Therefore, let the speculation begin.

7. Prusak makes abundantly clear that Janicaud focuses his reading of Husserl in the early texts of "Philosophy as Rigorous Science" and *Ideas I*. See PTT, 7.

8. For an excellent introduction to the ways in which Fink helped move Husserl's phenomenology in the final period of Husserl's life, approximately from 1928 to 1938, see Ronald Bruzina, "Translator's Introduction," in *Sixth Cartesian Meditation: The Idea of a Transcendental Theory of Method; with Textual Notations by Edmund Husserl* (Bloomington: Indiana University Press, 1995).

9. Edmund Husserl, *On the Phenomenology of the Consciousness of Internal Time (1893–1917)*, trans. John Barnett Brough (London: Kluwer, 1991), §36.

10. Michel Henry, "Speech and Religion: The Word of God," PTT, 222. Henry's discussion of being a Son is also throughout *I Am the Truth*.

11. Henry, *I Am the Truth*, 59.

12. Throughout this essay, I will be using the term "life" with and without Henry's capitalization. Whenever life is directly associated with Henry's analysis or with God, expect the capital letter, and when life is discussed in broader reference to phenomenology, particularly Husserl's life-world, I will leave it generically uncapitalized. However, in these instances, we should realize that Henry would not fail to give these a divine mark.

13. Henry, *I Am the Truth*, 70.

14. Henry, *I Am the Truth* and "Speech and Religion," 23 and 222, respectively.

15. Henry, *I Am the Truth*, 52.

16. Ronald Bruzina, *Edmund Husserl and Eugen Fink: Beginnings and Ends in Phenomenology 1928–1938* (New Haven: Yale University Press, 2004), 320.

17. Henry, *I Am the Truth*, 135.

18. Ibid., 104–5.

19. Henry, "Speech and Religion," 223.

20. *The New Brown-Driver-Briggs-Gesenius Hebrew and English Lexicon* (Peabody, MA: Hendrickson, 1979), 217–19.

21. Eugen Fink Manuscripts, Aus Mappe Z-IV (1928), 36a.

22. Eugen Fink Manuscripts, Z-VII XIV/4a.

23. Henry, "Speech and Religion," 227.

24. Henry, *I Am the Truth*, 153ff.

25. Ibid., 168.

26. Henry, *I Am the Truth*, 181.

27. Ibid., 170.

28. Emmanuel Levinas, "Philosophy and Awakening," in *Entre Nous*, trans. Michael B. Smith and Barbara Harshav (New York: Columbia University Press, 1998), 88–89.

29. Emmanuel Levinas, "The Temptation of Temptation," in *Nine Talmudic Readings*, trans. Annette Aronowicz (Bloomington: Indiana University Press, 1990), 33.

30. Emmanuel Levinas, "Hermeneutics and Beyond," in *Entre Nous*, 73.

31. Jacques Derrida, *The Work of Mourning* (Chicago: University of Chicago Press, 2001), 202.

32. Emmanuel Levinas, "The Awakening of the I," in *Is It Righteous to Be? Interviews with Emmanuel Levinas*, ed. Jill Robbins (Stanford: Stanford University Press, 2001), 182.

33. Emmanuel Levinas, "For a Jewish Humanism," in *Difficult Freedom*, trans. Sean Hand (Baltimore: Johns Hopkins University Press, 1990), 274–75.

The Truth of Life: Michel Henry on Marx
Clayton Crockett

1. See Michel Henry, *The Essence of Manifestation*, trans. Girard Etzkorn (The Hague: Nijhoff, 1973); and *Philosophy and Phenomenology of the Body*, trans. Girard Etzkorn (The Hague: Nijhoff, 1975). Henry also published three novels.

2. See Natalie Depraz, "The Return of Phenomenology in Recent French Moral Philosophy," in John J. Drummond and Lester Embree, eds., *Phenomenological Approaches to Moral Philosophy: A Handbook* (Dordrecht: Kluwer, 2002), 521.

3. See Michel Henry, *I Am the Truth: Toward a Philosophy of Christianity*, trans. Susan Emanuel (Stanford: Stanford University Press, 2003), 274: "They

will make extraordinary machines that will do everything men and women do so as to make them believe that they are just machines themselves."

4. Mark Wenzinger, "Michel Henry and the 'Trial of the Text,'" in Andrzej Wiercinski, ed., *Between Description and Interpretation: The Hermeneutic Turn in Phenomenology* (Toronto: Hermeneutic Press, 2005), 141.

5. Jean-Luc Marion, *Reduction and Givenness: Investigations of Husserl, Heidegger and Phenomenology*, trans. Thomas A. Carlson (Evanston, IL: Northwestern University Press, 1998), xi.

6. Henry, *I Am the Truth*, 30.

7. "The Emergence of the Unconscious in Western Thought: A Conversation with Sergio Benvenuto," at www.psychomedia.it/jep/number12–13/henry.htm (accessed 12/15/05).

8. Henry, *The Essence of Manifestation*, 462.

9. Ibid., 41.

10. Henry, *I Am the Truth*, 27.

11. Michel Henry, *Marx: A Philosophy of Human Reality*, trans. Kathleen McLaughlin (Bloomington: Indiana University Press, 1983), 8.

12. Ibid., 14. Henry privileges the early Marx of the 1844 Paris Manuscripts, which was the subject of an intense debate in French Marxism in the 1960s. The so-called Young Marx was read as a humanist, over against the later Marx of *Capital* and *The German Ideology*. As Lucio Colleti explains, "Marx's early works, virtually abandoned by Marxists, were to become a happy hunting-ground for Existentialist and Catholic thinkers, especially in France after the Second World War" ("Introduction," *Marx's Early Writings* [New York: Penguin, 1974], 17). The Marxists defended the later Marx, and Althusser put forward the notion of an "epistemological break" around 1845 to separate the two and discount the early Marx (see Louis Althusser, *For Marx* [London: Verso, 2005], 32–33). Althusser's reading of Marx is the implicit and sometimes explicit target of Henry's reading. Henry does not accept the notion of a break, and he reads the early Marx into the later Marx.

13. Ibid., 15.

14. Ibid., 48.

15. Ibid., 51.

16. Ibid., 90.

17. Ibid., 93.

18. Ibid., 102.

19. Ibid., 201.

20. Ibid., 224.

21. Ibid., 139.

22. Ibid., 137.

23. Ibid., 143.

24. Ibid., 153.

25. Ibid., 155.

26. Ibid., 157.

27. Ibid., 157.

28. Ibid., 158.

29. See Joseph Maréchal, *A Maréchal Reader*, ed. and trans. Joseph Donceel (New York: Herder and Herder, 1970). See also Karl Rahner, *Spirit in the World*, trans. William Dych (New York: Herder and Herder, 1969). One could also trace Henry's thought back a little further, to Maurice Blondel's influential philosophy of *Action*. See Maurice Blondel, *Action: Essay on a Critique of Life and a Science of Practice (1893)*, trans. Olivia Blanchette (South Bend, IN: University of Notre Dame Press, 2004).

30. Henry, *I Am the Truth*, 244.

31. Ibid., 98. See also Henry's reading of Meister Eckhart in *The Essence of Manifestation*, where "the knowledge of God upon which the phenomenological, i.e., the effective, meaning of union is founded is nevertheless the fact of God himself such that the auto-revelation of the absolute, as it takes place in unity, determines in its unity and with it, and consequently as being phenomenologically identical to it, the very essence of the soul" (329). Henry affirms with Eckhart that "man is theognostic" (329). This unity of God with the soul or transcendental ego, that I am calling quasi-gnostic, is affirmed in both *The Essence of Manifestation* and *I Am the Truth*.

32. Ibid., 98.

33. Ibid., 7.

34. *Marx*, 230.

35. Antonio Negri, *Marx Beyond Marx: Lessons on the Grundrisse*, trans. Harry Cleaver, Michael Ryan, and Maurizio Viano (New York: Autonomedia, 1991), 18.

36. Ibid., 70.

37. See ibid., 104.

38. For a further appreciation of the philosophical and political significance of Negri, with some important theological implications, see Antonio Negri, *Time for Revolution*, trans. Matteo Mandarini (London: Continuum, 2003).

39. John Milbank, "Materialism and Transcendence," in *Theology and the Political: The New Debate*, ed. Creston Davis, John Milbank, and Slavoj Žižek (Durham, NC: Duke University Press, 2005), 393–426, 394.

40. Ibid., 425.

41. For an excellent discussion of the theoretical stakes of religion and politics, see Hent de Vries, *Religion and Violence: Philosophical Perspectives from Kant to Derrida* (Baltimore: Johns Hopkins University Press, 2002), esp. 87–122. According to de Vries, "Kant presents religion as the 'middle ground' on which power and reason meet, penetrate, and permeate each other, then keep each other in balance," avoiding "two formalist extremes—absolute sovereignty and pure critique—neither of which can account for the commonality as well as the dissensus, that marks modern and ancient states." This "liberal" reading of religion "manifests an ontological pluralism that is the essence of the political" (87). Derrida will also come to emphasize a "rhythm of alternation" that consists of a

pragmatic balance of pluralistic alternatives in order to avoid "the worst" (117–18). This negotiation is missing from Milbank, Henry, and Marx, for different reasons and in different ways.

42. Antonio Negri, *The Savage Anomaly: The Power of Spinoza's Metaphysics and Politics*, trans. Michael Hardt (Minneapolis: University of Minnesota Press, 1991), 62–63.

43. Ibid., 140.

44. Jacques Derrida, *The Gift of Death*, trans. David Wills (Chicago: University of Chicago Press, 1995), 108.

45. Ibid., 108.

The Call of Grace: Henri de Lubac, Jean-Louis Chrétien, and the Theological Conditions of Christian Radical Phenomenology
Joshua Davis

1. The phrase "radical phenomenology" is utilized by Michel Henry, and I have adopted it here in order to underscore my contention that this phenomenology does not represent a "new" analysis so much as a more fundamental, and thereby more revolutionary, form of phenomenology. For a discussion of Henry's use of the term, see Ruud Welten, "God Is Life: On Michel Henry's Arch-Christianity," in *God in France: Eight Contemporary French Thinkers on God*, ed. Peter Jonkers and Ruud Welten (Leuven: Peeters, 2005), 119–42.

2. These four thinkers are taken as expressing the paradigmatic forms of what will be referred to throughout this essay specifically as "Christian radical phenomenology." Although there are marked differences between their positions, the arguments that will be advanced can be generally applied to all four thinkers in different ways. Levinas, as a Jewish thinker, is excluded, because I acknowledge that I am in no position to assess his relationship to his tradition or religion. Ricoeur is excluded because he does not emphasize the questions of epistemology and ontology that are the subject of my critique. Finally, Henry is excluded, principally because of the ambiguity of his relationship to the Christian tradition. Nonetheless, it is quite clear that his work stands firmly in the Blondel-Bergsonian strand of phenomenology highlighted here, following Dupont (see n. 4 below). These points of clarification should further reveal that any reference to "theology" in this essay refers specifically and solely to the discourse of the Christian tradition.

3. Christian Yves Dupont, "Receptions of Phenomenology in French Philosophy and Religious Thought, 1889–1939," Ph.D. dissertation, University of Notre Dame, 1997. Dupont notes that the "first impetus" to the phenomenological turn in French thought was provided by Bergson's "insights into lived duration and Maurice Blondel's genetic description of action" (i). He claims these ideas developed from within what he dubs the "spiritualist" current that influenced "French philosophy at the end of the nineteenth century" (ibid.). Dupont understands the term "spiritualist" to refer to those "philosophies centered upon the interior life of the individual subject understood as spontaneous, active, and

creative" (ibid., 38). This essay is, in many ways, an attempt to provide the theological reflection that Dupont anticipates for his work (see ibid., 7 and 470).

4. Dupont notes that the religious appropriation of Blondel and Bergson as a way of addressing the theological issues of nature and grace is intimately linked to the mediating role of Le Roy, Héring, Rabeau, Maréchal, and Rousselot (see Dupont, *Receptions of Phenomenology*, 250–450, 457–70).

5. See James K. A. Smith, *Speech and Theology: Language and the Logic of Incarnation* (New York: Routledge, 2002), 8. Smith's note suggests that this connection is Janicaud's own, citing "The Theological Turn of French Phenomenology," in Dominique Janicaud et al., *Phenomenology and the "Theological Turn": The French Debate* (New York: Fordham, 2000), 51–52, hereafter PTT; the French-language version is Dominique Janicaud, *Le tournant théologique de la phénoménomogie française* (Paris: Éditions de l'éclat, 1991), 40 (henceforth citations from the French version are in brackets). But Janicaud's own wording is not *la nouvelle théologie*, but *le néothomisme* (neo-Thomism). This appears to be a bit of confusion, for both Janicaud and Smith, over what is designated by "neo-Thomism." (For clarification on this matter, see Gerald A. McCool's magisterial *Nineteenth-Century Scholasticism: The Search for a Unitary Method* [New York: Fordham University Press, 1999]; and its companion, *From Unity to Pluralism: The Internal Evolution of Thomism* [New York: Fordham University Press, 2002].) Nonetheless, agreeing with Smith's assessment, I have attributed the association to Smith himself rather than Janicaud. On the matter of the neoscholastic reaction to Lubac, see Reginald Garrigou-Lagrange, "La nouvelle théologie où va-t-elle?" *Angelicum* 23 (1946): 126–45.

6. PTT, 35–49 [25–38]. Janicaud interprets the turn as stemming from Levinas' appropriation of Sartre and Merleau-Ponty's misreading of Husserl (see PTT, 16–34 [7–24]).

7. See Jeffrey Kosky, "Translator's Preface: The Phenomenology of Religion," PTT, 112–14. For the influence of Blondel, see Dupont, *Receptions of Phenomenology*, 470.

8. See Dupont, *Receptions of Phenomenology*, 457–62.

9. See ibid., 105–6.

10. Ibid., citing Blondel's explicit claim in *Letter on Apologetics and History of Dogma*, trans. Alexander Dru and Illtyd Trethowan (Grand Rapids, MI: Eerdmans, 1994), 171 [54]. He also notes the significance of *Le Problème de la philosophie catholique* (Paris: Bloud et Gay, 1932). Husserl's assessment of phenomenology and religion is well known. For Heidegger's thoughts on this point, compare his assessment in "Phenomenology and Theology," in *The Piety of Thinking*, trans. James G. Hart and John C. Maraldo (Bloomington: Indiana University Press, 1976) to Blondel's *Letter on Apologetics*, 150–68.

11. PTT, 46–49 [34–37].

12. See Kosky's discussion of these points, "Translator's Preface," 114–19. On the insistence that this work is strictly phenomenological, see Peter Jonkers, "God in France: Heidegger's Legacy," in Jonkers and Welten, *God in France*, 7ff.

13. PTT, 99–103 [85–91].

14. We find an example of just this type of argument developed in James K. A. Smith, *Speech and Theology*, 153–59, where the *idea* of incarnation is judged necessary to the structure of language and manifestation, and the *actual* incarnation is apparently the great boon to this structure.

15. PTT, 51 [40].

16. On this point, I am greatly indebted to Nathan R. Kerr's unpublished essay, "From Description to Doxology: The Dogmatic Bases of Christian Vision," which develops this point specifically in conversation with Levinas and Philip Blond. See also Smith, *Speech and Theology*, 166–68, which argues for the necessity of revealability over revelation for revelation. Although he insists that the structure of revealability must be understood as a passive capacity, Smith misunderstands the nature of the priority of revelation as it pertains to the creature's natural *relation* to God, especially insofar as the creature is nothing but this relation (see *Summa Theologia* 1.13.7).

17. The limits of this essay do not permit this point to be argued in full. It will suffice to say that this is not to be equated with Levinas and Marion's objection that the privileging of immanence over transcendence renders the horizon of the finite ego the condition for the phenomenon's appearance; rather, this point is an attempt to account for Blondel's observation that "immanence" and "transcendence" are only immanently meaningful (see Blondel, *Letter on Apologetics*, 150–68). As the remainder of the essay will show, by drawing on Blondel, it is not analysis of the structures of consciousness and perception that can avoid this, but rather emphasis on the dynamic openness of human action and judgment.

18. See note 53. I am here only thinking of phenomenologies that investigate the conditions under which phenomena appear (e.g., Marion and Chrétien). In this regard, "necessity" implies that transcendence is a constitutive aspect of manifestation.

19. My use of the term "judgment" here is closer to Newman than Kant. See John Henry Newman, *Fifteen Sermons Preached Before the University of Oxford Between A.D. 1826 and 1843* (Notre Dame: University of Notre Dame Press, 1997), 176–221. My thoughts on this notion have also been shaped by Bernard Lonergan. See especially Bernard Lonergan, *Insight: A Study of Human Understanding*, ed. Frederick E. Crowe and Robert M. Doran (Toronto: University of Toronto Press), 296–303.

20. This quotation is taken from Terrence Malick's film *The Thin Red Line*. It is not insignificant that Terrence Malick is the English translator of Heidegger's *The Essence of Reasons* (Evanston, IL: Northwestern University Press, 1969) and is reported to be a devout Christian (see Michael Beschloss, "True Believer," in *Reader's Digest* 160, no. 962 [2002]: 80).

21. Chrétien has also associated these claims with prayer, but we have focused on election because it will be the subject of the discussion that follows (see "The Wounded Word: Phenomenology of Prayer," PTT, 147–75).

22. Ibid., 70.

23. Blondel's influence on Lubac is clear, but often unrecognized. He edited the correspondence between Blondel and Teilhard de Chardin in *Pierre Teilhard de Chardin/Maurice Blondel: Correspondence*, trans. William Whitman (New York: Herder and Herder, 1967), composing extensive notes and commentaries on those letters; he reflects on Blondel's influence in his collection of essays, *Theological Fragments*, trans. Rebecca Howell Balinski (San Francisco: Ignatius Press, 1989); and, he regularly mentions him throughout his texts as decisive for his thesis (see, for example, *The Mystery of the Supernatural*, trans. Rosemary Sheed [New York: Crossroad Herder, 1998], 187–88). As Dupont shows, Blondel's influence was always implicit in the work of Maréchal and Rousselot, both of whom Lubac relied on heavily in formulating the thesis of *Surnaturel* and *The Mystery of the Supernatural* (see Dupont, *Receptions of Phenomenology*, 125); also Henri de Lubac, *Surnaturel* (Paris: Aubier, 1946). Lubac himself mentions this influence several times in his journals. See Henri de Lubac, *At the Service of the Church: Henri de Lubac Reflects on the Circumstances That Occasioned His Writings*, trans. Anne Elizabeth Englund (San Francisco: Ignatius Press, 1989), 18–21, 35, 64–65; Henri de Lubac, "Maurice Blondel," in *Theological Fragments* (San Francisco: Ignatius Press, 1989), 377–404; *Théologies d'occasion* (Paris: Desclée, 1984). Bruno Forte's essay "Nature and Grace in Henri de Lubac: From *Surnaturel* to *Le Mystère du surnaturel*," *Communio* 23 (Winter 1996): 729, notes the importance of Blondel for Lubac, citing the research of A. Russo's *Henri de Lubac: teologia e dogma nella storia. L'influsso di Blondel* (Rome: Studium, 1990) for his claims.

24. Although the argument cannot be developed in full here, the concerns driving my analysis of both Lubac and radical phenomenology pertain to its adherence to the paradigm of the early, more Neoplatonic Augustine to the neglect of the logic of his later position on grace. This paradigm can be seen to shift within the body of his *To Simplician*, where Augustine moves to a stronger sense of the divine initiative in the act of faith (this is the interpretation of J. Patout Burns, *The Development of Augustine's Doctrine of Operative Grace* [Paris: Études augustiniennes, 1980], whom I follow on this point). This is important to note because it highlights the unfolding of a particular logic of election that ineluctably leads to what theology names "predestination," and works against Chrétien's interpretation of that idea, revealing a formally Pelagian thrust of his thinking.

25. This difference between creating and the inscription of the end is one that Lubac does not make until *The Mystery of the Supernatural*. It appears to have been the result of his reflections upon the discussions that ensued following the publication of *Surnaturel*, culminating in the issuance of *Humani Generis*. On the significance of *Humani Generis* for Lubac's thesis, see Guy Mansini, "Henri de Lubac, the Natural Desire to See God, and Pure Nature," in *Gregorianium* 83, no. 1 (2002): 87–93. After *Humani Generis*, Lubac no longer argued in such a way as to suggest that an intellectual creature, simply by virtue of being intellectual, must have a supernatural end. But, Mansini notes, along with Knasas, that

the more nuanced position of *Mystery* appears to be not that there could not have been an intellectual creature without a supernatural end, but that it was only possible to conceive of an intellectual creature without such an end as a transcendentalized abstraction (see Mansini, "Henri de Lubac," 94, n. 15; reference is to J. F. X. Knasas, "The Liberationist Critique of Maritain's New Christendom," *The Thomist* 52 [1988]: 254, n. 19). A different interpretation of this shift is given by John Milbank, *The Suspended Middle: Henri de Lubac and the Debate Concerning the Supernatural* (Grand Rapids, MI: Eerdmans, 2005).

26. Lubac, *Surnaturel*, 490–91.

27. Jean-Louis Chrétien, *The Call and the Response*, trans. Anne A. Davenport (New York: Fordham University Press, 2004), 5–32. Page numbers will henceforth be cited parenthetically.

28. Whether Chrétien is accurate in his reading of Heidegger on this point is open to dispute. For a discussion of the significance of the categories of disproportion and correspondence for not only Chrétien's work here but for the general argument concerning the "theological turn"; see Anne Davenport's "Translator's Preface" in *The Call and the Response*, vii–xxix.

29. Martin Heidegger, "Language," in *Poetry, Language, Thought*, trans. Albert Hofstadter (New York: Harper and Row, 1971), 199. Cited in Chrétien, *The Call and the Response*, 8.

30. Paul Claudel, *The Eye Listens*, trans. Elsie Pell (New York: Philosophical Library, 1950), quoted from Chrétien, *The Call and the Response*, 9.

31. Pseudo-Dionysius, *De divinis nominibus* (Eng. trans. *The Divine Names*, in Pseudo-Dionysius, *The Complete Works*, trans. Colin Luibheid and Paul Rorem [New York: Paulist, 1987]), 701 C, quoted from Chrétien, *The Call and the Response*, 15.

32. It should be noted that this precedence is of a logical, not a temporal, order in much the same way as Levinas's distinction between the Saying and the Said.

33. See Smith, *Speech and Theology*, 168. The context of Smith's claim relates specifically to analogical speech about the divine, but the point as it applies here to Chrétien is the same regarding the call-response structure of language itself.

34. As Davenport notes, xxvii: "We have already answered the call by our very presence, and the infinite saturation of the creative love consists in the fact that we were never able *not* to answer it." This should be coupled with Lubac's statement in *Surnaturel* that we are required to will God as our end because "we cannot not will it" [*nous l'exigeons parce que nous ne pouvons pas ne pas le vouloir*] (*Surnaturel*, 490).

35. This does not (necessarily) mean that the category of election must refer to an extrinsic divine will to be intelligible; or, even that it be given from beyond being; although, it could refer to both. To say that election is "independently related" to manifestation is simply to say that it conditions appearance in such a way as to not be deducible *from* appearance. Whether this conditioning is a priori or a posteriori to appearance is wholly undecidable solely on the basis of appearance, and does not affect the validity of the claim. Derrida's recognition of this

is precisely his reason for hesitating with regard to the priority of revealability and revelation (see note 38).

36. This would not be to make the priority of the call subject to intentionality; it does, however, imply that the priority of the call is only known as prior to a will averring its status as such, a will in subjection to the call.

37. This statement is in agreement with Derrida's assessment of Marion's analysis of "givenness." See "On the Gift," in *God, the Gift, and Postmodernism*, ed. John D. Caputo and Michael J. Scanlon (Bloomington and Indianapolis: Indiana University Press, 1999), 73: "I do not know if this structure [*khôra*] is really prior to what comes under the name of revealed religion or even of philosophy, or whether it is through philosophy or the revealed religions, the religions of the book, or any other experience of revelation, that retrospectively we think what I try to think. I must confess, I cannot make the choice between these two hypotheses. Translated into Heidegger's discourse, which is addressing the same difficulty, this is the distinction between *Offenbarung* and *Offenbarkeit*, revelation and revealability. Heidegger said, this is his position, that there would be no revelation or *Offenbarung* without the prior structure of *Offenbarkeit*, without the possibility of revelation and the possibility of manifestation. That is Heidegger's position. I am not sure. Perhaps it is through *Offenbarung* that *Offenbarkeit* becomes thinkable, historically. That is why I am constantly hesitating." I am indebted to Daniel Barber for drawing my attention to this quotation. This same claim can be made with regard to Marion's analysis of the *givenness* of phenomena, which follows the same logic. See the brief discussion of Marion herein.

38. See Paul Ricoeur, "Experience and Language in Religious Discourse," PTT, 127–46.

39. If this claim seems specious, one need only consider the possibility of undertaking this project without such an assumption.

40. This can be understood as a failure to adhere to the grammar of the Christian idiom that shapes the projects.

41. On the possibility of a postmodern apologetic, see J. Aaron Simmons, "Continuing to Look for *God in France:* On the Relationship Between Phenomenology and Theology," in this volume. The following suggestions are offered in agreement with Simmons's affirmation of such an enterprise, and should be read as an attempt to establish the theological delimitations of that project.

42. In connection with our observations about the centrality of judgment, intentionality, and the will, it is appropriate to point to Augustine's monumental realization in the *Confessions* that God is not present to the world, as Neo-Platonism assumes, by virtue of participation in divine Being, but rather through the intentionality of the will (see, *Confessions* 710.16–17.23). This is perhaps the most definitive theological insight for western Christianity; but, it is likewise the least assimilated, especially inasmuch as it pertains to the logic of grace. I am grateful to the work of and conversations with J. Patout Burns for this.

43. The following observations concerning the significance of both the will and operative habitual grace are wholly guided by Bernard Lonergan's thesis in

Grace and Freedom: Operative Grace in the Thought of St. Thomas Aquinas (Toronto: University of Toronto Press, 2000). My reading of this difficult material is thoroughly indebted to J. Michael Stebbins's invaluable interpretative work, *The Divine Initiative: Grace, World-Order, and Human Freedom in the Early Writings of Bernard Lonergan* (Toronto: University of Toronto Press, 1995).

44. See Pierre Rousselot, *The Intellectualism of St. Thomas*, trans. James E. O'Mahony trans. (London: Sheed and Ward, 1935); cited from Fergus Kerr, *After Aquinas: Versions of Thomism* (New York: Blackwell, 2002), 138.

45. That Lubac rejected this notion is clear from his defense of Teilhard de Chardin against the charge (see *The Religion of Teilhard de Chardin*, trans. René Hague [New York: Desclee, 1967]).

46. It is worth noting that it is precisely this moment that John Milbank rejects in Lubac's account, contending that it compromises the divine simplicity (see John Milbank, *Being Reconciled* [New York: Routledge, 2003], 224, n. 6). This charge appears to overlook Aquinas's articulation of the nature of the priority of the divine operation, especially insofar as he underscores change in the patient and not in the agent with regard to the acts of creation and supernatural elevation (see Stebbins, *The Divine Initiative*, 212–90; note, especially, the discussion of vital act, 107–10).

47. See Aquinas, *Summa Theologiae* I–II, q. 110, a.2 and a. 4.

48. See Lonergan, *Grace and Freedom*, 14–20, and Stebbins, *The Divine Initiative*, 67–78.

49. See Aquinas, *Summa Theologiae* I–II, q. 111.

50. On this, see Stebbins's reflections in *The Divine Initiative*, 280–90.

51. How this reality can be affirmed without falling into the problems associated with neoscholasticism is another question altogether, and one that cannot be decided here. It will suffice simply to note that I find Rahner's proposal much more consistent and intelligible than Lubac's.

52. My use of these categories "necessary" and "possibility" throughout this essay is wholly indebted to Blondel's discussion of the matter in the *Letter on Apologetics*, see especially 156–61.

53. Blondel, *Letter on Apologetics*, 156–61.

54. I am grateful to John D. Caputo for drawing my attention to this as a possible critique.

55. G. W. F. Hegel, *The Encyclopaedia Logic: Part I of the Encyclopaedia of Philosophical Sciences with the* Zusätze, trans. T. F. Geraets et al. (Indianapolis: Hackett, 1991), 105 (§60).

56. See Paul Guyer, "Thought and Being: Hegel's Critique of Kant's Theoretical Philosophy," in *The Cambridge Companion to Hegel*, ed. Frederick C. Beiser (Cambridge: Cambridge University Press, 1993), 203–4.

57. I am indebted to conversations with Merold Westphal for drawing my attention to this possible critique.

58. See Jean-Luc Marion, *Being Given: Phenomenology of Givenness*, trans. Jeffrey L. Kosky (Stanford: Stanford University Press, 2002), 5 and 235.

59. Ibid., 1–6.

60. Ibid., 234–47.

61. This claim is not inimical to Marion's analysis of the role of disposition in his discussion of the idol and the icon in *God Without Being: Hors-texte*, trans. Thomas A. Carlson (Chicago: University of Chicago Press, 1991), 7–24. The distinction that is drawn here pertains to the phenomenological arguments developed in *Being Given* to support this analysis; there, the argument requires demonstrating that the structure of revealability demands the excess of phenomenal givenness, and does not pivot on intentional disposition.

62. By way of example, one could point here to the apostolic witness of the event of Jesus' resurrection; but, one could equally make the claim that any act of *agape* fulfilled this condition of the gift as analyzed by Derrida.

63. For similar expression of the heuristic, rather than apologetic, nature of radical phenomenology, see Jonkers, "God in France," in *God in France*, 1–42.

64. Lubac, *The Mystery of the Supernatural*, 223.

Between Call and Voice: The Antiphonal Thought of Jean-Louis Chrétien
Joseph Ballan

1. Paul Claudel, *The Eye Listens*, trans. Elsie Pell (New York: Philosophical Library, 1950).

2. *The Call and the Response* (1992), trans. Anne A. Davenport (New York: Fordham University Press, 2004), 60. Hereafter cited in text as CR.

3. "The Film and the New Psychology," *Sense and Non-Sense* (1948), trans. Hubert L. Dreyfus and P. A. Dreyfus (Evanston, IL: Northwestern University Press, 1964), 50.

4. In CR, 15, he quotes Merleau-Ponty with approval: "the call of the sensible is nothing other than what Merleau-Ponty will try to elucidate in *The Visible and the Invisible*—call that, in his words, is 'the *logos* that pronounces itself silently in every sensible thing.'"

5. *The Ark of Speech* (1998), trans. Andrew Smith (New York: Routledge, 2003), 72. Hereafter cited in text as AS.

6. Such a synesthesia would not have to be, of necessity, mystical. It could be a more mundane feature of our engagement of the world, though intensified by those experiences we call "aesthetic." So Martin Seel: "It is the interlacing of the senses that is decisive in all perception, be it in a hidden or an explicit manner. One sense does what it can do by virtue of its distinction from and support by the other senses. . . . But although this interaction of the senses transpires inconspicuously in many situations, it often becomes noticeable in situations of aesthetic perception in one way or another; we *sense* ourselves listening and seeing and feeling." *Aesthetics of Appearing* (2000), trans. John Farrell (Stanford: Stanford University Press, 2005), 30–31. As we shall see shortly, this account, though strictly speaking unproblematic, would likely remain, for Chrétien , unsatisfactory as a complete story about the senses. He hopes to provide an account, not only of the way we "sense ourselves," i.e., of the way the

senses relate to one another, but of the way in which the senses, by virtue of their cooperation, involve the entire body in a welcome of and response to the transcendent other.

7. See, e.g., Adriaan Peperzak, *Elements of Ethics* (Stanford: Stanford University Press, 2003), 105–8. Peperzak's salient example here is that of Levinas's exposition of the face as that which forbids me to kill. The crucial moment—and the advance beyond scholasticism—is the realization that "once our eyes are opened . . . an appeal to tradition is no longer needed; instead of believing what it says, we have seen that it is true." For another model in which hermeneutics and phenomenology are intimately intertwined, comparable to the one which remains by and large implicit in Chrétien's work, see the "evential hermeneutics" of Claude Romano in, e.g., *Il y a* (Paris: Presses Universitaires de France, 2003), 21–54; *Event and World*, trans. Shane Mackinlay (New York: Fordham University Press, 2009), 49–55.

8. Jacques Derrida, *On Touching—Jean-Luc Nancy* (2000), trans. Christine Irizarry (Stanford: Stanford University Press, 2005), 246–47.

9. CR 83–131. Brian Treanor treats this essay elsewhere in this volume.

10. "To be sensitive to touch, feel contact, and to sense, is to *consent*. The sense of touch is, first of all, like the sense of every sensation, a sense of consent; it is and has this sense: *yes, to consent*, which always, and in advance, implies transitivity (*yes to, to consent to*)." Derrida, *On Touching*, 246.

11. Jean-Louis Chrétien, *Hand to Hand: Listening to the Work of Art* (1997), trans. Stephen E. Lewis (New York: Fordham University Press, 2003), 19. Hereafter cited in text as HH.

12. Vladimir Jankélévitch, *Music and the Ineffable* (1961), trans. Carolyn Abbate (Princeton: Princeton University Press, 2003), 136–37. Because the tenor of Jankélévitch's meditations on music bears a remarkable similarity to that of Chrétien's reflections on art, we appeal, at various points throughout this essay, to this classic statement of his philosophy of music in the discussion of themes appearing in Chrétien's work.

13. Ibid., 154.

14. Plotinus, *Enneads* I.4.16. All citations taken from the Steven MacKenna translation, *The Enneads* (New York: Penguin, 1991). See HH, 30.

15. John Keats, *Selected Poems and Letters*, ed. Douglas Bush (Cambridge, MA: Riverside Press, 1959), 207–8.

16. Jean-Louis Chrétien, *L'effroi du beau* (Paris: Éditions du Cerf, 1987), 87. Hereafter cited in text as EB.

17. Keats, *Selected Poems and Letters*, 208.

18. Rainer Maria Rilke, "Archaic torso of Apollo," *The Selected Poetry of Rainer Maria Rilke*, ed. and trans. Stephen Mitchell (New York: Vintage International, 1989), 60–61.

19. For the impossible as a phenomenological structure, see John D. Caputo, "The Experience of God and the Axiology of the Impossible," *The Experience of God: A Postmodern Response,* ed. Kevin Hart and Barbara Wall (New York: Fordham University Press, 2005), 20–21.

20. I thank Edward Mooney and Jeffrey Hanson for posing this question to me.

21. On the relation of Heidegger's thought to the concept of the sublime, see Philippe Lacoue-Labarthe, "Sublime Truth," *Of the Sublime: Presence in Question*, trans. Jeffrey Librett (Albany: SUNY Press, 1993), 75–83, 92–96.

22. Although, significantly, in a discussion of the *thaumazein* in which philosophy is born and out of which it grows, Chrétien cites with approval Kant's distinction, developed in the third *Critique*, between astonishment, that is, the surprise and shock of novelty, and admiration, which, on the contrary, "remains open to the excess of what happens to it" (AS, 118).

23. Moreover, far from serving a straightforwardly theological appeal to the transcendent, the possibility for beauty to call lies in its phenomenal quality: "beauty . . . is a self-manifestation, it is that which manifests itself of its own accord, and *it is only thus that it calls*" (AS, 79; emphasis added).

24. See, e.g., Immanuel Kant, *Critique of Judgment*, trans. Werner S. Pluhar (Indianapolis: Hackett, 1987), 99.

25. Jean-Luc Nancy, "The Sublime Offering," *A Finite Thinking*, ed. Simon Sparks, trans. Jeffrey Librett (Stanford: Stanford University Press, 2003), 236.

26. William Desmond, *Art, Origins, Otherness* (Albany: SUNY Press, 2003), 83. Emphasis in original.

27. Kant, *Critique of Judgment*, 123.

28. In the history of (theological) aesthetics, Chrétien's thought of the beautiful is perhaps closest to that of Bonaventure's. Besides the frequent reference to wounds that remind us of Francis's, Chrétien shares with Bonaventure an aesthetic that could aptly be characterized as a "theology of *gloriae* [that] . . . remains . . . a theology of *excessus*," to use Hans Urs von Balthasar's description. Such a theology would give an account of the superabundance that exceeds the soul's capacity to receive it but which precisely thereby exercises a demand, an inextricable call on the individual believer to faith, humility, and spiritual poverty. See *The Glory of the Lord*, vol. 2, ed. John Riches, trans. Andrew Louth, Francis McDonagh, and Brian McNeil, CRV (San Francisco: Ignatius Press, 1984), 260–82.

29. See Jean-Louis Chrétien, *La voix nue: Phénoménologie de la promesse* (Paris: Editions de Minuit, 1990), 31–60.

30. *The Collected Works of John of the Cross*, ed. and trans. by Kieran Kavanaugh, OCD, and Otilio Rodriguez, OCD (Washington, DC: ICS Publications, 1979), 462. See also the commentary on 472–73: "[The soul] calls this music 'silent' because it is tranquil and quiet knowledge, without the sound of voices. And thus there is in it the sweetness of music and the quietude of silence . . . even though that music is silent to the senses, it is sounding solitude for the spiritual faculties."

31. "*Hiersein ist herrlich.*" See the seventh of the "Duino Elegies," *Selected Poetry of Rainer Maria Rilke*, ed. and trans. Stephen Mitchell (New York: Vintage, 1989), 188–89. AS 80.

32. *Enneads*, V.8.9. "Certainly no reproach can rightly be brought against this world save only that it is not That" (V.8.8).

33. Saint Bonaventure, *Bonaventure*, ed. and trans. Ewert Cousins (New York: Paulist Press, 1978), 69.

34. Chrétien, *La voix nue*, 144.

35. Another translation of this essay on prayer may be found in Jean-Louis Chrétien, "The Wounded Word," *Phenomenology and the "Theological Turn": The French Debate*, trans. Jeffrey Kosky and Thomas Carlson (New York: Fordham University Press, 2000), 147–75.

36. Jacques Derrida, *Memoirs of the Blind*, trans. Pascale-Anne Breault and Michael Naas (Chicago: University of Chicago Press, 1993), 126.

37. Jean-Louis Chrétien, *The Unforgettable and the Unhoped For*, trans. Jeffrey Bloechl (New York: Fordham University Press, 2002), 121.

38. Jean-Louis Chrétien, *Le regard de l'amour* (Paris: Desclée de Brouwer, 2000), 23.

39. Jankélévitch, *Music and the Ineffable*, 148.

40. Ibid., 149.

Chrétien on the Call That Wounds
Bruce Ellis Benson

1. Jean-Louis Chrétien, "The Wounded Word" (hereafter WW) in Dominique Janicaud et al., *Phenomenology and the "Theological Turn": The French Debate* (New York: Fordham University Press, 2000), 174–75, hereafter PTT.

2. Jean-Louis Chrétien, "Retrospection," in Jean-Louis Chrétien, *The Unforgettable and the Unhoped For*, trans. Jeffrey Bloechl (New York: Fordham University Press, 2002); hereafter cited as UU. 122. *Corps à corps* has been translated into English as *Hand to Hand: Listening to the Work of Art*, trans. Stephen E. Lewis (New York: Fordham University Press, 2003).

3. Jean-Louis Chrétien, *The Call and the Response*, trans. Anne A. Davenport (New York: Fordham University Press, 2004); hereafter cited as CR.

4. Jean-François Courtine asserts that the guiding question for the essays that comprise the text of *Phenomenology and Theology* can be stated as follows: "Is there, in religious experience, a specific form of phenomenality, of appearance, or epiphanic arising, that can affect phenomenology itself in its project, its aim, its fundamental concepts, indeed its methods?" (PTT, 122). In effect, Emmanuel Levinas had already given the answer to that question: "*The absolute experience is not disclosure* [dévoilement] *but revelation* [révélation]" (*Totality and Infinity: An Essay on Exteriority*, trans. Alfonso Lingis [The Hague: Martinus Nijhoff, 1979], 65–66). Revelation, of course, is what "breaks into" phenomenological intuition and so decenters the transcendental ego. As such, it is the overturning of the phenomenological "as such." Phenomenologically speaking, it would be hard to imagine more of a "wounding" experience. Not surprisingly, then, Janicaud zeroes in on this quotation (PTT 42). To trace the development of Chrétien's thought in roughly this same direction, see his *La voix nue: Phénoménologie de la promesse* (Paris: Éditions de Minuit, 1990).

5. Here Chrétien is citing the French translation of Heidegger's *Unterwegs zur Sprache* [*On the Way to Language*] (*Acheminement vers la parole*, trans. Jean Beaufret, Wolfgang Brockmeier, and François Fédier [Paris: Gallimard, 1976], 241). Interestingly enough, whereas the French *toujours déjà* would translate as "always already," Heidegger only uses *schon* (rather than *immer schon*) in this passage. However, the "*immer*" can be read as implied.

6. CR, 28.

7. CR, 1.

8. Given that the call "provokes" and thus is part of an agonic struggle, an immediate question would be whether there is or could be an agonic dimension to the Trinity. Such a question would take us too far afield to be answered adequately here. Yet at least one possible example of such an agonic aspect to their relationship would be Jesus praying on the Mount of Olives. "Father, if you are willing, remove this cup from me; yet not my will but yours be done" (Lk. 22:42). One can hardly deny that there is a struggle going on here. And yet it is heavily qualified. Jesus' request is inscribed between two phrases in which he explicitly gives up any rights to assert his own will. What would our encounters with the other look like were we to inscribe our requests between deference to the other?

9. CR, 1.

10. Rudolf Bernet, "The Other in Myself," in *Tradition and Renewal: The Centennial of Louvain's Institute of Philosophy* (Leuven: Leuven University Press, 1992), 1:85.

11. WW, 156.

12. John Milbank, *Theology and Social Theory: Beyond Secular Reason* (Oxford: Blackwell, 1990), 427.

13. Ibid., 429. Milbank does go on to say the following: "To say (with Deleuze) that dissonance and atonality are here 'held back' or 'not arrived at,' would be a mistake of the same order as claiming that nihilism is evidently true in its disclosure of the impossibility of truth. Instead, one should say, it is always possible to place dissonance back in Baroque 'suspense'; at every turn of a phrase, new, unexpected harmony may still arrive. Between the nihilistic promotion of dissonance, of differences that clash or only accord through conflict, and the Baroque risk of a harmony stretched to the limits—the openness to musical grace—there remains an undecidability." Open discourses do not *simply* have a harmony "stretched to its limits." They also have dissonances that may resist harmonization—or at least harmonization in the here and now. While "new, unexpected harmony may still arrive," there must be the openness and even the promotion of creativity that creates dissonance. Without such openness to such dissonance, we would not have the late Beethoven quartets or Stravinsky's *Rite of Spring*. Harmony may *arrive*, but that arrival may well have to do with a change in *us* as listeners, and perhaps a radical revision of what counts as "harmony" (as in the case of Peter's vision).

14. David Cunningham rightly points out that "polyphony" and "harmony" are *not* synonymous, even though they are often taken to be such. Given that

difference, he thinks the notion of polyphony is sufficient, since "polyphony could theoretically be either 'harmonious' or 'dissonant.'" Yet it is precisely because I want to emphasize the existence of (and *need for*) dissonance and difference that I think we need the notion of heterophony. See David S. Cunningham, *These Three Are One: The Practice of Trinitarian Theology* (Malden, MA: Blackwell, 1998), 128.

15. See my "Improvising Texts, Improvising Communities: Jazz, Heteronomy, and *Ekklêsia*," in *Resonant Witness*, ed. Jeremy S. Begbie and Steven Guthrie (Grand Rapids, MI: Eerdmans, forthcoming).

16. CR, 24.

17. Ibid., 23.

18. Ibid.

19. Ibid., 72.

20. Ibid.

21. Ibid., 82.

22. WW, 147.

23. Ibid., 150.

24. Emmanuel Levinas, "God and Philosophy," *Basic Philosophical Writings*, ed. Adriaan T. Peperzak, Simon Critchley, and Robert Bernasconi (Bloomington: Indiana University Press, 1996), 146. Chrétien likewise speaks of the "here I am," when he says that "the gift to which one is opened without recourse, about being the only one who can say *Me voici*, here I am" (UU, 120).

25. Given that it also means "to support," it is not surprising that there is a connection with the office of "suffragan bishop," who (in the Roman Catholic and Anglican Churches) is a subordinate to the main bishop and in effect "supports" the bishop.

26. WW, 153.

27. CR, 22.

28. WW, 156.

29. Hand to hand is the English equivalent of the French "*corps à corps*" (literally, body to body), which is why the text in which Chrétien discusses Jacob's struggle has been translated as *Hand to Hand*.

30. *The Oxford English Dictionary*, 2nd ed., s.v. "bless."

31. Ernest Weekley notes, "*blêtsian*, in its etym. sense, would explain F. *blesser*, to wound, which has no Rom. cognates." See Ernest Weekley, *An Etymological Dictionary of Modern English* (New York: Dutton, 1921), s.v. "bless."

32. UU, 122.

33. CR, 16.

34. Jean-Louis Chrétien, *Hand to Hand: Listening to the Work of Art,* trans. Stephen E. Lewis (New York: Fordham University Press, 2003), 2; hereafter cited as HH.

35. Ibid., 4.

36. Ibid., 5.

37. Ibid.

38. UU, 126.

39. HH, 6.

40. UU, 9.

41. HH, 16.

42. Here it would seem Chrétien has followed the injunction of Georges Bataille, "to say everything to a point that makes people tremble." See Michel Surya, *Georges Bataille* (London: Verso, 2002), 479.

43. UU, 15.

Embodied Ears: Being in the World and Hearing the Other

Brian Treanor

1. Plato, *The Republic*, trans. Allan Bloom (New York: Basic Books, 1968), 188 (508c).

2. Plato, *Meno*, in *Five Dialogues*, trans. G. M. A. Grube (Indianapolis: Hackett), 70 (81d).

3. Emmanuel Levinas, *Totality and Infinity*, trans. Alphonso Lingis (Pittsburgh: Duquesne University Press), 95.

4. Levinas, *Totality and Infinity*, 62.

5. Jean-Louis Chrétien, *The Call and the Response*, trans. Anne A. Davenport (New York: Fordham University Press, 2004).

6. Martin Heidegger, *Being and Time*, trans. John Macquarrie and Edward Robinson (San Francisco: HarperCollins, 1962), 58.

7. Chrétien, *The Call and the Response*, 84.

8. Ibid., 85.

9. Ibid., 115. Chrétien attributes this latter point to none other than Levinas (*De l'existence à l'existant* [Paris: Vrin, 1947], 119–20).

10. Ibid., 98.

11. Ibid., 97.

12. The reference to hunger stems from Levinas's characterization: "In enjoyment [*jouissance*] I am absolutely for myself. Egoist without reference to the Other, I am alone without solitude, innocently egoist and alone. Not against the Others, not 'as for me . . .'—but entirely deaf to the Other, outside of all communication and all refusal to communicate—without ears, like a hungry stomach" (Levinas, *Totality and Infinity*, 134).

13. Chrétien, *The Call and the Response*, 86.

14. Ibid., 107. Citing Thomas Aquinas, *In duodecim libros metaphysicorum Aristotelis expositio* (Torino: Marietti, 1964), L. I, lectio 1, sections 8–9.

15. Levinas, *Totality and Infinity*, 39 and 62.

16. See, for example, *Modernity and Its Discontents*, ed. James L. Marsh, John D. Caputo, and Merold Westphal (New York: Fordham University Press, 1992), 136, 140–41. Note, however, that in this context, "contamination" expresses the postmodern, positive possibility of introducing an element of ambiguity that will loosen up ossified systems. Nevertheless, this leaves us with new problems, notably the difficulty of encouraging an account that allows things to get "messy"

while trying to insure that things do not degenerate into a mere mess. As Caputo point out in *The Prayers and Tears*: "the problem for a quasi-transcendental philosophy [like deconstruction] is how to keep things from running into each other and contaminating everything" (John D. Caputo, *The Prayers and Tears of Jacques Derrida: Religion Without Religion* [Bloomington and Indianapolis: Indiana University Press, 1997], 13).

17. For example: "Truth (uncoveredness) is something that must always first be wrested from entities. Entities get snatched out of their hiddenness. The factical uncoveredness of anything is always, as it were, a kind of *robbery*" (Heidegger, *Being and Time*, 265).

18. For example, Levinas, *Totality and Infinity*, 42.

19. Of course, it would be false to say that philosophers favoring the oral/aural metaphor, such as Levinas and Derrida, completely ignore our embodiment (which is one of the concerns I hope a tactile metaphor might highlight)—far from it. Nevertheless, the discussion of touch in such philosophies is neglected and tends to focus on the negative possibilities associated with contact and grasping.

20. This is not to imply that these three points summarize the whole of the postmodern critique of the visual metaphor of knowledge, but to point out three central critiques that do not apply to the tactile metaphor as easily as one might suppose.

21. Chrétien, *The Call and the Response*, 95.

22. Ibid., 116. Emphases mine.

23. Ibid., 129.

24. Ibid.

25. Ibid. See Saint Bonaventure, *The Journey of the Mind to God*, trans. Philotheus Boehner (Indianapolis: Hackett, 1990), 24.

26. *The Dark Night of the Soul* is an incomplete work, and the later stanzas of the work are without commentary, including the intriguing "The breeze blew from the turret As I parted his locks; With his gentle hand he wounded my neck And caused all my senses to be suspended."

27. See Richard Kearney, *The God Who May Be* (Bloomington: Indiana University Press, 2001), 59, and, more generally, 53–79. Kearney also points out the carnal aspects of several biblical encounters with Christ's (ibid., 49). Indeed, the very notion of an incarnation implies that there is something significant about embodiment and, therefore, touch.

28. Levinas, *Totality and Infinity*, 195.

29. Chrétien, *The Call and the Response*, 88. "The theoretical mistake of those who hold touch to be immediate rests on its own phenomenological occultation" (ibid.).

30. Ibid., 83.

31. Ibid., 84. See also Maurice Merleau-Ponty, *The Visible and the Invisible*, trans. Alphonso Lingis (Chicago: Northwestern University Press, 1969).

32. Ibid., 118. See also Maurice Pradines, *Philosophie de la sensation*, part 2, *La Sensibilité élémentaire*, vol. 2, *Les Sens de la défense* (Paris, 1934), 245.

33. Ibid., 120.

34. Ibid., 85. "Such reversibility, however, is not the same as symmetry. It does not mean that things touch me as I touch them. Only the touch of a living being, for whom touch is always in some form or other a matter of life and death, can bring about the 'near' and 'far,' since only through a living being is there an absolute here, relative to which the far and the near are deployed. Things do not touch each other but are there only for a nearby third party" (ibid.).

35. That is to say, we can see without being seen and hear without being heard (both of which are part of covert surveillance of the other), but we cannot touch without being touched. While touch may be used abusively, it cannot be used covertly. On the implications of an oblique, non-forthright approach to the Other, see Levinas, *Totality and Infinity*, 70. "Rhetoric, absent from no discourse, and which philosophical discourse seeks to overcome, resists discourse. . . . It approaches the other not to face him, but obliquely." When do we approach something obliquely? When we are stalking it. Oblique approach suggests the intent to harm—we approach in this manner when we deceive, hunt, or kill.

36. Chrétien, *The Call and the Response*, 98.

37. "We feel only the other, and if we feel ourselves this will be only on the occasion of, and by dependence on, a feeling of the other, not through a reflexivity of the flesh that would be conjectured as its original source" (ibid., 120).

38. Ibid., 99.

39. Ibid. Emphasis mine.

40. Ibid., 93. "We seek principles of the sensible body, which is to say the tangible body" (Aristotle, *De generatione et corruptione*, II, 2, 329 B 6–7).

41. Ibid., 104. "The eventual excellence of the other senses presupposes the excellence of touch, as Pradines himself recognizes: 'The higher senses are not superior to touch, there are simply *a superior form of touch*'" (ibid.).

42. Ibid., 85.

43. Ibid., 86. "Without touch, animal life is able neither to be nor to preserve in being. Consequently, touch takes a supreme and direct interest in events" (ibid., 97).

44. Ibid., 122–23.

45. "It is not sight that sees or touch that touches but the same and unique individual man who touches and sees" (ibid., 103). On abstraction, see my "Constellations: Gabriel Marcel's Philosophy of Relative Otherness," *American Catholic Philosophical Quarterly* 79, no. 2 (2005): 369–92.

The Witness of Humility
Norman Wirzba

1. We should recall here Augustine's maxim: "the punishment of every disordered mind is its own disorder" (*Confessions* I:19).

2. Jean-Louis Chrétien, *The Ark of Speech*, trans. Andrew Brown (London: Routledge, 2004), 9; hereafter AS.

3. Listening is not confined to the ears. Following Chrétien, I will assume throughout that "listening exceeds by far the sense of hearing. Everything in us

listens, because everything in the world and of the world speaks" (Jean-Louis Chrétien, *The Call and the Response*, trans. Anne A. Davenport [New York: Fordham University Press, 2004], 14; hereafter CR).

4. Speaking of a Babylonian idol, Isaiah declares: "They lift it to their shoulders, they carry it, they set it in its place, and it stands there; it cannot move from its place. If one cries out to it, it does not answer or save anyone from trouble" (46:7). An idol cannot save them because it is but the reflection/projection of the evil that has led to their destruction in the first place.

5. The story of how technology became the new sacred is worked out clearly in Bronislaw Szerszynski's *Nature, Technology and the Sacred* (Oxford: Blackwell, 2005). See also David Noble's less technical rendering in *The Religion of Technology: The Divinity of Man and the Spirit of Invention* (New York: Penguin Books, 1997).

6. Bonaventure, *The Journey of the Mind to God,* trans. Philotheus Boehner, OFM (Indianapolis: Hackett, 1956), 2.

7. Graham Ward echoes this sentiment precisely in *Christ and Culture* when he writes: "Christ, as second person of the Trinity, is the archetype of all relation. All relations, that is, participate in and aspire to their perfection in the Christological relation. Not only in him is all relation perfected, but the work and economy he is implicated in . . . the reconciliation of the world to God" (Oxford: Blackwell, 2005), 1.

8. Christopher Cullen argues that for Bonaventure "the summary of the whole of Christian perfection consists in humility" (*Bonaventure* [Oxford: Oxford University Press, 2006], 13).

9. Ibid. Cullen is right to suggest that genuine humility is tied to and grows out of an appreciation for human beings *as creatures.* What this means, and how the connection between creatureliness and humility is maintained, will be developed in this essay.

10. Bonaventure, *The Journey of the Mind to God,* 39.

11. Iris Murdoch, *The Sovereignty of Good* (London: Routledge, 1970), 103–4. Earlier in the text she elaborates by saying that humility is a "selfless respect for reality and one of the most difficult and central of all virtues" (95).

12. Norvin Richards, "Is Humility a Virtue?" *American Philosophical Quarterly* 25, no. 3 (July 1988): 253 (italics in the original). Richards uses as his example Bernard of Clairvaux, who says (in *Sermon 42 on Canticle 6*), "if you examine yourself inwardly by the light of truth and without dissimulation, and judge yourself without flattery; no doubt you will be humbled in your eyes, becoming contemptible in your own sight as a result of this true knowledge of yourself." Richards observes that, outside of an allegiance to the archaic belief in original sin, this "depressing view is not obviously correct. In fact, it is difficult to see a reason to hold it" (253). As we will see, Richards has failed to consider what it means to be a creature.

13. See Bruce V. Foltz's "Nature's Other Side: The Demise of Nature and the Phenomenology of Givenness," in *Rethinking Nature: Essays in Environmental*

Philosophy, ed. Bruce V. Foltz and Robert Frodeman (Bloomington: Indiana University Press, 2004), 330–41. This idolatrous signification is the exact opposite of Bonaventure's view, which argued that the natural world is a vestige "in which we can perceive our God" (*The Journey of the Mind to God*, 13).

14. Bernard of Clairvaux, "On the Steps of Humility and Pride," in *Bernard of Clairvaux: Selected Works*, trans. G. R. Evans (New York: Paulist Press, 1987), 103. Bernard, who is here following Augustine in his definition, reflects a common view within spiritual literature.

15. Consider here the sobering observations of Pascal (*Pensées*, trans. A. J. Krailsheimer [Harmondsworth: Penguin, 1966], 48, 95): "When I consider the brief span of my life absorbed into the eternity which comes before and after . . . the small space I occupy and which I see swallowed up in the infinite immensity of spaces of which I know nothing and which know nothing of me, I take fright and am amazed to see myself here rather than there: there is no reason for me to be here rather than there, now rather than then. Who put me here?" and "Man is only a reed, the weakest in nature, but he is a thinking reed. There is no need for the whole universe to take up arms to crush him: a vapour, a drop of water is enough to kill him."

16. It is important to underscore that a limiting factor both closes *and* opens possibilities. Rather than being simply negative, a limit is the practical condition in terms of which our living is successful and appropriate.

17. "No experience of the self can bracket the body, and thus bracket the relations of proximity to which the body binds us; the experience of the self is the experience of place as much as of time" (Jean-Yves Lacoste, *Experience and the Absolute: Disputed Questions on the Humanity of Man* [New York: Fordham University Press, 2004], 8).

18. Jacques Derrida wonders if touch is not best understood as "unrepresentable presence." See *On Touching—Jean-Luc Nancy*, trans. Christine Irizarry (Stanford: Stanford University Press, 2005), 250. Chrétien says, "Touch veils itself" (CR, 87).

19. I have developed the significance of the soil/humanity relationship in *The Paradise of God: Renewing Religion in an Ecological Age* (New York: Oxford University Press, 2003).

20. It is instructive to wonder how much Descartes's description of the self as a disembodied mind is symptomatic of this dawning ecological amnesia. It would have been inconceivable to a peasant or farmer to cast the person primarily as a thinking thing (*res cogitans*). People, rather than being the measure of themselves, are measured by the earth and how well they fit within its life. Consider here the ancient peasant maxim: "The earth shows up those of value and those who are good for nothing" (quoted by Jean Pierre Vernant in *Myth and Thought According to the Greeks* [Cambridge: Zone Books, 2006]. To be of value is to live and work in a manner that respects the earth and that contributes to the health and flourishing of the entire biological and social community. Here the quality of a life is judged in terms of our ability to move responsibly among the memberships that constitute our living.

21. For a detailed historical examination of the indispensability of "place" for world- and self-understanding, see Edward S. Casey's *The Fate of Place: A Philosophical History* (Berkeley: University of California Press, 1997).

22. Jean-Louis Chrétien, "Retrospection," in *The Unforgettable and the Unhoped For*, trans. Jeffrey Bloechl (New York: Fordham University Press, 2002), 119.

23. Derrida, *On Touching*, 246.

24. Chrétien, "Retrospection," 122.

25. It is significant that in theological traditions God creates through speaking. God's speaking, as Dietrich Bonhoeffer notes, must not be understood in a causal way, because God is transcendent and creates in freedom. This means that even as God can be said to commit to creation through love, God is not bound out of some kind of causal necessity. Creation is not, therefore, an effect but an expression of freedom and love. The difference between an effect and an expression is that the former would indicate a sharing of nature or essence between Creator and creation, as though God and creatures were on an ontological continuum, while the latter indicates God's utterly gratuitous commitment to and presence in the created work. Bonhoeffer notes that "between Creator and creature there is neither a law of motive nor a law of effect nor anything else. Between Creator and creature there is simply nothing: the void. For freedom happens in and through the void. . . . Creation comes out of this void" (*Creation and Fall: A Theological Interpretation of Genesis 1–3* [New York: Macmillan, 1959], 18).

26. Ward, *Christ and Culture*, 76. Ward is here simply echoing the sentiment of Tertullian, who argued that God lived with us as a person so that we can be taught to live like God.

27. Rowan Williams, *On Christian Theology* (Oxford: Blackwell, 2000), 69.

28. Ibid., 72.

29. Or, in Ward's formulation, "Touch is an orientation towards being incarnate and it finds its true self-understanding in love" (*Christ and Culture*, 76).

30. Oliver Davies has done an excellent job demonstrating the connection between compassion and creation. Insofar as we live compassionately, we "align our 'being' with God's 'being,' and thus, performatively . . . participate in the ecstatic ground of the Holy Trinity itself" (*A Theology of Compassion: Metaphysics of Difference and the Renewal of Tradition* [Grand Rapids, MI: Eerdmans, 2001], 252). And again more recently in *The Creativity of God: World, Eucharist, Reason* (Cambridge: Cambridge University Press, 2004), Davies writes: "Compassion *is* the divine creativity. It is the outflowing of the inner Trinitarian life in the formation of the world. Human compassion is a sacrament or sign of the joyful, life-giving creativity of God" (164).

31. "Every voice, hearing without cease, bears many voices within itself because there is no first voice. . . . Between my voice as it speaks and my voice as I hear it vibrates the whole thickness of the world whose meaning my voice attempts to say, meaning that has gripped it and swallowed it up, as it were, from time immemorial" (CR, 1).

32. That Aristotelian metaphysics would come to be governed by a substance ontology stressing the identification of things being this rather than that, as things being what they are in separation from other things, suggests that Aristotle did not heed his own profound insight. For an illuminating discussion of how the Cappadocian church fathers struggled to correct this substance ontology in the process of developing a Trinitarian account of God, see John D. Zizioulas's *Being as Communion: Studies in Personhood and the Church* (Crestwood, NY: St. Vladimir's Seminary Press, 1997).

33. Ward, *Christ and Culture*, 145.

34. Davies, *A Theology of Compassion*, 8.

35. More precisely, creation is the scene in terms of which our speaking of an Economic Trinity becomes possible. Who God is in Godself (the Immanent Trinity) exceeds our comprehension. As Aquinas says in *Summa Theologiae* I.13.8, "God is not known to us in His nature, but is made known to us from His operations."

36. We need to remember that our speaking of God's Trinitarian life continually leads us to conceptual breaking points. Put simply, the Trinity is beyond space-time representation. This means our speaking must be understood to be analogical, as participating in a reality that exceeds our comprehension.

37. David S. Cunningham, *These Three Are One: The Practice of Trinitarian Theology* (Oxford: Blackwell, 1998), 169.

38. "We cannot say *yes* except in unison, and the speech that expresses the unity of the world can itself be nothing if not unifying" (AS, 147).

39. Bonaventure, *The Journey of the Mind to God*, 24. For a wonderful short description of the spiritual transformation of our senses in the light of gardening work—one of the most ancient practices of humility—see Vigen Guroian's *The Fragrance of God* (Grand Rapids, MI: Eerdmans, 2006).

Contributors

Joseph Ballan is a doctoral candidate at the University of Chicago Divinity School.

Bruce Ellis Benson is Professor of Philosophy at Wheaton College (IL).

Jeffrey Bloechl is Associate Professor of Philosophy at Boston College.

Clayton Crockett is Associate Professor of Religion at the University of Central Arkansas.

Joshua Davis is a doctoral candidate in religion at Vanderbilt University.

Christina M. Gschwandtner is Associate Professor of Philosophy at the University of Scranton.

Jeffrey Hanson is Adjunct Assistant Professor of Philosophy at Boston College.

Kevin Hart is the Edwin B. Kyle Professor of Christian Studies in the Department of Religious Studies at the University of Virginia.

Jeffrey L. Kosky is Associate Professor of Religion at Washington and Lee University.

Jean-Yves Lacoste is a fellow of the College of Blandings. He has also taught at the universities of Cambridge and Chicago.

Jean-Luc Marion is Professor of Philosophy at the University of Paris—IV (Sorbonne). He is also Professor of the Philosophy of Religions and Theology in the Divinity School, as well as Professor in the Department of Philosophy and on the Committee on Social Thought at the University of Chicago.

Ronald L. Mercer Jr. is Assistant Professor of Philosophy at Chapman Seminary of Oakland City University.

J. Aaron Simmons is Visiting Assistant Professor at Hendrix College.

Anthony J. Steinbock is Professor of Philosophy at Southern Illinois University.

Brian Treanor is Associate Professor of Philosophy at Loyola Marymount University.

Norman Wirzba is Research Professor of Theology, Ecology, and Rural Life at Duke University Divinity School.

Index

polyphony, 212
poor phenomenon, 120, 122–31
praxis, 171–72, 173, 174, 175
prayer, 208, 214–16
preexistence of the soul, 111–12
present, 38
pride, 130
principle of all principles, 17, 43, 47
protention, 160
Pseudo-Dionysius, 104

Rahner, Karl, 34–37
reality, 42–43, 47, 50–51, 52
reason, 27
recollection, 106
reduction, 42–44, 48, 51, 52, 54–55, 59,
    60, 68, 75, 161; spontaneous,
    46–47, 58–59; transcendental, 71
Reduction and Givenness, 124
reference, 156
referent, 94
relation, being in, 244–46
religious experience, 63–64, 65–66
religious hope, 39
religion (religious tradition), 22; particular,
    26; relationship with politics,
    256*n*50
resistance, 116
response, 108–9, 115, 128–29, 154–55,
    187, 188–89, 213
revelation, 99–100, 121–22, 141–42, 184,
    193, 294*n*4; divine, 36, 39, 40
Rilke, Rainer Maria, 85
Roman Catholicism, 36

sacrament, the, 89–95, 98–102
salvation, 152–53, 164
saturated phenomenon, 3, 100, 120–22,
    124, 125–27, 128
scientific knowledge, 107, 127
Scripture, 150
Sein und Zeit. See *Being and Time*
self, the, 138–39, 141, 144–46, 214
self-knowledge, 107, 109
semiotics, 94
senses, 196–98, 226
sensory perception, 45, 46
September Song, 69, 72–86

Shoah, the, 69–70, 80–81, 84
Sickness Unto Death, The, 135–36
sign, 94
silence, 198–200, 203–4, 205
Smith, James K. A., 182, 189
Socrates, 240
son of God. *See* child of God
species, 170–72
speech (speaking), 57–58, 62, 204–5,
    209–10, 243; event of, 54–55, 66
Spinoza, Baruch, 176
Stevens, Wallace, 69
subject, 105, 107–8, 109–12, 215
sublime, 202–3
substance metaphysics, 92–93
suffering, 137, 144–46, 156, 214–15, 250
supernatural, 194
supernatural transcendental, 35

Taylor, Charles, 111
Taylor, Mark C., 106
technology, 127
theological materialism, 175
theological turn, 69, 181–82
theology, 34, 37, 61, 167, 173, 175;
    definitions of sacraments, 92–95;
    relationship to phenomenology,
    17–18, 22–28, 29, 183–85, 190
theory, 172, 173, 174
Thomas, Dylan, 77–78
Todesfuge, 80–81
touch, 224–32, 241, 244, 247
transcendence (transcendent), 17, 58,
    142–43, 145, 158–60, 164, 166,
    175, 184, 194
transcendental neo-Thomism, 172
transcendental subject, 96, 173
translation, 213–14
Trinity, 210, 248, 295*n*8, 303*n*36
truth, 83, 118–19; of Christianity,
    151–52, 162; of the world, 151–52

visual metaphor, 222, 227
voice, 205–6, 214
voice of God, 148, 152, 153, 157
Vom Wesen der Wahrheit. See *On the Essence
    of Truth*
de Vries, Hent, 20

Perspectives in
Continental Philosophy Series
John D. Caputo, series editor

Dominique Janicaud, *Phenomenology "Wide Open": After the French Debate.* Translated by Charles N. Cabral.

Ian Leask and Eoin Cassidy, eds., *Givenness and God: Questions of Jean-Luc Marion.*

Jacques Derrida, *Sovereignties in Question: The Poetics of Paul Celan.* Edited by Thomas Dutoit and Outi Pasanen.

William Desmond, *Is There a Sabbath for Thought? Between Religion and Philosophy.*

Bruce Ellis Benson and Norman Wirzba, eds., *The Phenomoenology of Prayer.*

S. Clark Buckner and Matthew Statler, eds., *Styles of Piety: Practicing Philosophy after the Death of God.*

Kevin Hart and Barbara Wall, eds., *The Experience of God: A Postmodern Response.*

John Panteleimon Manoussakis, *After God: Richard Kearney and the Religious Turn in Continental Philosophy.*

John Martis, *Philippe Lacoue-Labarthe: Representation and the Loss of the Subject.*

Jean-Luc Nancy, *The Ground of the Image.*

Edith Wyschogrod, *Crossover Queries: Dwelling with Negatives, Embodying Philosophy's Others.*

Gerald Bruns, *On the Anarchy of Poetry and Philosophy: A Guide for the Unruly.*

Brian Treanor, *Aspects of Alterity: Levinas, Marcel, and the Contemporary Debate.*

Simon Morgan Wortham, *Counter-Institutions: Jacques Derrida and the Question of the University.*

Leonard Lawlor, *The Implications of Immanence: Toward a New Concept of Life.*

Clayton Crockett, *Interstices of the Sublime: Theology and Psychoanalytic Theory.*

Bettina Bergo, Joseph Cohen, and Raphael Zagury-Orly, eds., *Judeities: Questions for Jacques Derrida.* Translated by Bettina Bergo and Michael B. Smith.

Jean-Luc Marion, *On the Ego and on God: Further Cartesian Questions.* Translated by Christina M. Gschwandtner.

Jean-Luc Nancy, *Philosophical Chronicles.* Translated by Franson Manjali.

Jean-Luc Nancy, *Dis-Enclosure: The Deconstruction of Christianity.* Translated by Bettina Bergo, Gabriel Malenfant, and Michael B. Smith.

Andrea Hurst, *Derrida Vis-à-vis Lacan: Interweaving Deconstruction and Psychoanalysis.*

Jean-Luc Nancy, *Noli me tangere: On the Raising of the Body.* Translated by Sarah Clift, Pascale-Anne Brault, and Michael Naas.

Jacques Derrida, *The Animal That Therefore I Am.* Edited by Marie-Louise Mallet, translated by David Wills.

Jean-Luc Marion, *The Visible and the Revealed.* Translated by Christina M. Gschwandtner and others.

Michel Henry, *Material Phenomenology.* Translated by Scott Davidson.

Jean-Luc Nancy, *Corpus.* Translated by Richard A. Rand.

Joshua Kates, *Fielding Derrida.*

Michael Naas, *Derrida From Now On.*

Shannon Sullivan and Dennis J. Schmidt, eds., *Difficulties of Ethical Life.*

Catherine Malabou, *What Should We Do with Our Brain?* Translated by Sebastian Rand, Introduction by Marc Jeannerod.

Claude Romano, *Event and World*. Translated by Shane Mackinlay.

Vanessa Lemm, *Nietzsche's Animal Philosophy: Culture, Politics, and the Animality of the Human Being*.

B. Keith Putt, ed., *Gazing Through a Prism Darkly: Reflections on Merold Westphal's Hermeneutical Epistemology*.

Eric Boynton and Martin Kavka, eds., *Saintly Influence: Edith Wyschogrod and the Possibilities of Philosophy of Religion*.

Kevin Hart and Michael A. Signer, eds., *The Exorbitant: Emmanuel Levinas Between Jews and Christians*.

Shane Mackinlay, *Interpreting Excess: Jean-Luc Marion, Saturated Phenomena, and Hermeneutics*.